Legal and Regulatory Aspects of Abrahamic Finance

Camille Silla Paldi
Colgate University, USA

Phillip Lieberman
United States Naval Academy, USA & Vanderbilt University, USA

Mohammad Kabir Hassan
University of New Orleans, USA

Isaac Lifshitz
Shalem College, Israel

IGI Global
Scientific Publishing
Publishing Tomorrow's Research Today

Vice President of Editorial Melissa Wagner
Director of Acquisitions Mikaela Felty
Director of Book Development Jocelynn Hessler
Production Manager Mike Brehm
Cover Design Jose Rosado

Published in the United States of America by
IGI Global Scientific Publishing
701 East Chocolate Avenue
Hershey, PA, 17033, USA
Tel: 717-533-8845 | Fax: 717-533-7115
Website: https://www.igi-global.com E-mail: cust@igi-global.com

Library of Congress Cataloging-in-Publication Data
Names: Paldi, Camille Silla, 1975- editor
Title: Legal and regulatory aspects of Abrahamic finance / [edited by] Camille Silla Paldi, Phillip Lieberman, Mohammad Kabir Hassan, Joseph Isaac Lifshitz.
Description: Hershey, PA : IGI Global Scientific Publishing, [2026] | Includes bibliographical references and index. | Summary: "This book aims to provide a blueprint for an Abrahamic finance industry as well as provide an invaluable research tool for those who will work to further research on this topic as well as those who will pioneer the Abrahamic finance industry"-- Provided by publisher.
Identifiers: LCCN 2025021317 (print) | LCCN 2025021318 (ebook) | ISBN 9798337318875 hardcover | ISBN 9798337318882 paperback | ISBN 9798337318899 ebook
Subjects: LCSH: Finance--Religious aspects--Judaism | Finance--Religious aspects--Islam | Finance--Law and legislation
Classification: LCC HG103 .L44 2026 (print) | LCC HG103 (ebook) | DDC 332--dc23/eng/20250710
LC record available at https://lccn.loc.gov/2025021317
LC ebook record available at https://lccn.loc.gov/2025021318

British Cataloguing in Publication Data
A Cataloguing in Publication record for this book is available from the British Library.

Table of Contents

Detailed Table of Contents

This chapter critically examines the failings of the global economic and financial system and advocates for integrating moral values from Abrahamic religions into economic thought and policy. It argues that neoliberal capitalism, driven by financial oligarchies, speculative returns, and debt-based consumption, undermines equity, democracy, and sustainability. The chapter critiques the rationalist "Homo economicus" model and calls for normative frameworks grounded in ethics, human dignity, and accountability to divine authority. Islamic economic principles—risk-sharing, prohibition of interest, and social responsibility—are offered as an alternative. It highlights the unsustainability of finance decoupled from the real economy and calls for integrity-focused regulatory transformation. With global development goals off-track, the chapter proposes a values-based, inclusive economic order rooted in divine ethics, emphasizing stewardship, solidarity, and shared prosperity.

This chapter examines the legal and regulatory challenges facing Islamic banking in Africa, focusing on the complex relationship between Sharia governance and conventional financial regulation. It highlights the fragmented legal systems across African countries, the lack of standardized Sharia interpretation, and weak regulatory frameworks as main challenges to the growth of the sector. The chapter used comparative case studies from Nigeria, Sudan, and Kenya, which analyzes the varying approaches to Sharia integration and supervision. It draws lessons from global Islamic finance leaders such as Malaysia, Indonesia, and the GCC to recommend a harmonized African regulatory model. The chapter proposes legal reforms, centralized Sharia advisory structures, regional cooperation, and capacity building as pathways to strengthening Islamic banking. These strategies aim to enhance compliance, financial inclusion, and sustainable development across the continent.

This chapter explores Islamic finance as a sustainable alternative to conventional sovereign borrowing, emphasizing risk-sharing and asset-backed models over usury (riba). With developing nations facing severe debt crises, Islamic finance offers solutions through instruments like sukuk (Islamic bonds) and profit-loss-sharing (PLS) arrangements, enhancing fiscal resilience and aligning with Sustainable Development Goals (SDGs). Case studies from Malaysia, Indonesia, Nigeria, and non-Muslim-majority countries demonstrate sukuk's success in infrastructure financing, lower defaults, and green investments. However, regulatory gaps, market limitations, and expertise shortages hinder adoption. The study concludes that Islamic finance can transform sovereign debt by promoting ethical, stable, and inclusive economic growth.

This chapter examines Waqf, Islamic endowment, as a powerful tool for enabling sustainable cities and communities. It looks at the history and legal basis for Waqf and its diversification and application in different Islamic societies. In this context, Waqf has many characteristics for community development across social, economic, and environmental dimensions. The chapter examines Waqf through the analysis of legal mechanisms regulating Waqf geared towards the local, and ordinary citizen experience, but also includes traditional arrangements and "new" Waqf arrangements (e.g. corporate Waqf, Waqf sukuk). The chapter includes challenges and opportunities in Waqf management today for consideration and understanding. Lack of transparency and accountability for Waqf management and local political reform, is crucial because reform in these areas may prepare the development of Waqf to better achieve the Sustainable Development Goals (SDGs) and ensure resilient cities, through the complexity and diversity of Waqf processes.

Chapter 5

Islamic law of finance and Islamic law of contract strongly emphasize the need and importance of a contract for any specific financial or non-financial activity between two or more parties. This importance is strongly highlighted by Almighty Allah and Holy Prophet (SAW). Fulfillment of the contract is a religious obligation, and only contracts that contain all *Sharia'h*-compliant conditions can be considered as Islamic contracts. There are two major types of contracts: compensatory (financial) and non-compensatory (non-financial). Similarly, under these two types, there are several types of subsidiary contracts, which are related with partnership-based trade agreements, profit sharing trade agreements, and supporting trade agreements or contracts. In addition, there are certain rules, regulations, and options for both sellers and buyers, which they have to follow. *Sharia'h* has provided detailed instructions on which conditions can be part of the Islamic contract, and vice versa. All types of valid sales are executed with the help of a contract. Therefore, in Islamic finance, all Islamic financial institutions, including Islamic banks, follow *Sharia'h*-compliant contracts for selling their products and services.

Chapter 6

Cryptographic currencies are digital means of transferring value through a network of computers that operates independently of any central authority, such as a government or a bank. These currencies enable various uses, including payment and investment. They are generated through technological processes, and their value is determined by the consensus of participants, rather than by the value of a commodity or the decree of a central body. This raises the question: What is the halachic (Jewish legal) stance on such forms of money? In this chapter, the author claims that the foundation of Jewish monetary law is mutual consent. The transfer of property must be conducted with the agreement of both parties; unauthorized transfer is considered a theft. To ensure this consent, halacha traditionally prefers tangible reality and concrete forms. For instance, halacha does not recognize a transfer of ownership to a fetus. These principles raise fundamental questions about the compatibility of halacha with the modern economy. Yet halachic authorities adjusted halachic demands to tangibility if mutual consent is achieved, mainly if a market for these abstract transactions is in existence. Since cryptographic currencies have a vital market, halacha must accept them.

This chapter examines rabbinic authority in Sasanian Persia through three instances where rabbinic authorities intervened to lower prices for the community. It argues that these interventions should not be interpreted solely through traditional legal frameworks, such as Talmud commentaries by Rashi and the Tosafot, or ethical lenses found in moral readings of Talmudic texts. Instead, they should be analyzed within the broader context of business ethics, considering the complex political and theological dimensions at play. The ethical considerations are rooted in the relationships between rabbinic, Jewish, and secular institutions. This perspective allows for a more nuanced discussion of economic issues and concessions in the post-Talmudic era, exploring the interaction between sacred and secular domains, and offering a deeper understanding of the economic implications of religious authority and secularization.

Enforcement of securities laws is increasingly an international—indeed, a global—affair. On the one hand, this globalization broadens funding streams and facilitates capital formation across borders, allowing new ideas to flourish amidst growing financial liquidity. On the other, globalization engenders a host of problems at the national and international level, from a single nation's tracking the ultimate beneficial owner of securities in order to avoid benefiting their competitors or enemies (whether state or non-state actors) to investing in commodities or concerns forbidden in one country or another. The rise of cryptocurrencies has exacerbated some of these problems. In this chapter, I will discuss international collaboration across countries whose financial regimes are explicitly guided by one or another Abrahamic legal tradition to show how mutual recognition across Abrahamic lines can lead to more effective securities law enforcement—and hence enhanced capital formation—within any individual country.

Probing the contradiction between the limited attention to finance within Catholic social teaching and the widespread involvement of the Church in credit operations, this essay explores the economic role of the Catholic Church in the period 1891–1950. Exploring institutional history and unpublished archival sources, the aim is to reconstruct the role of diocesan endowments and the Vatican Administration for the Works of Religion. The study examines asset management models, investment strategies, center-periphery dynamics, and the degree of autonomy exercised by individual dioceses. Particular attention is dedicated to the cases of Milan and Bergamo, analyzed on the basis of quantitative data and evaluated in terms of innovative practices. The paper shows how the Catholic Church functioned as an institutional investor in a "charity market", developing financial practices aligned with religious and social aims, yet lacking a coherent theoretical framework. This research opens up a new area for historiographical inquiry.

Preface

The intersection of finance, law, and religion has long shaped human societies, yet the integration of Abrahamic principles—rooted in Judaism, Christianity, and Islam—into modern financial systems offers a unique lens through which to address contemporary economic challenges. This book explores the legal and regulatory dimensions of Abrahamic finance, drawing on the ethical and moral frameworks of these traditions to propose solutions for a more equitable, sustainable, and inclusive global financial order. By examining diverse perspectives, from Islamic banking and Jewish legal traditions to Catholic financial practices, this work bridges sacred values with practical economic applications, offering insights into how faith-based principles can inform and transform modern finance.

The chapters in this volume critically analyze the interplay between religious ethics and financial systems, addressing issues such as debt, speculation, community development, and regulatory enforcement. Through case studies, historical analyses, and comparative approaches, contributors highlight the potential of Abrahamic finance to foster stability, equity, and social responsibility in an era marked by economic volatility and ethical dilemmas. This book is intended for scholars, policymakers, and practitioners seeking to understand how religious principles can guide legal and regulatory frameworks toward a more just and sustainable economic future.

CHAPTER OVERVIEW

Chapter 1 critiques the global economic system, advocating for the integration of Abrahamic moral values to promote equity, sustainability, and accountability, with a focus on Islamic economic principles like risk-sharing and social responsibility.

Chapter 2 examines the legal and regulatory challenges of Islamic banking in Africa, proposing harmonized frameworks and regional cooperation to enhance compliance and financial inclusion.

Chapter 3 explores Islamic finance as an alternative to conventional sovereign borrowing, highlighting sukuk and profit-loss-sharing models to address debt crises in developing nations.

Chapter 4 analyzes the role of Waqf in fostering sustainable communities, examining its legal structures and proposing reforms to enhance transparency and alignment with sustainable development goals.

Chapter 5 defines the Islamic law of contract, emphasizing its principles as derived from the Quran and Hadith, and its significance in governing agreements.

Chapter 6 investigates the Jewish legal (halachic) perspective on cryptocurrencies, addressing their status as decentralized digital currencies.

Chapter 7 examines rabbinic interventions in economic speculation in Sasanian Persia, analyzing their implications within the context of business ethics and religious authority.

Chapter 8 discusses securities enforcement across Abrahamic legal systems, emphasizing international collaboration to enhance capital formation and regulatory effectiveness.

Chapter 9 explores the Catholic Church's financial practices from 1891–1950, analyzing diocesan endowments and investment strategies in the absence of a coherent doctrinal framework.

This book aims to spark dialogue and inspire action toward a financial system that not only drives economic progress but also upholds the ethical imperatives of justice, stewardship, and shared prosperity. By weaving together the wisdom of Abrahamic traditions with modern financial challenges, it offers a path forward for creating a more resilient and morally grounded global economy.

Camille Paldi
Colgate University, USA

Phillip Lieberman
United States Naval Academy, USA & Vanderbilt University, USA

M. Kabir Hassan
University of New Orleans, USA

Joseph Lifshitz
Shalem College, Israel

Chapter 1
The Global Political Economy and the Abrahamic Religions:
Disciplining Human Behavior for Stable and Sustainable Global Financial Order

Muhammad Ayub
https://orcid.org/0000-0003-3788-2580
Riphah International University, Islamabad, Pakistan

ABSTRACT

This chapter critically examines the failings of the global economic and financial system and advocates for integrating moral values from Abrahamic religions into economic thought and policy. It argues that neoliberal capitalism, driven by financial oligarchies, speculative returns, and debt-based consumption, undermines equity, democracy, and sustainability. The chapter critiques the rationalist "Homo economicus" model and calls for normative frameworks grounded in ethics, human dignity, and accountability to divine authority. Islamic economic principles—risk-sharing, prohibition of interest, and social responsibility—are offered as an alternative. It highlights the unsustainability of finance decoupled from the real economy and calls for integrity-focused regulatory transformation. With global development goals off-track, the chapter proposes a values-based, inclusive economic order rooted in divine ethics, emphasizing stewardship, solidarity, and shared prosperity.

DOI: 10.4018/979-8-3373-1887-5.ch001

INTRODUCTION

The universe and its systems are based on natural balance, justice and social integration. Only the proper maintenance of this balance in terms of political economics, social fabric, and ethical norms, and earnings and use of resources can lead to a broad-based and sustainable welfare and happiness model for mankind. The creation and distribution of wealth have to be based on the economic agents' ethical, responsible, and just behavior. Such a model of behavior of economic agents can be based only on divine/ revealed knowledge and sources of instructions. Accordingly, the economic theories, processes and institutions must observe the divine protocols and value system if the objective of a stable and sustainable global financial order is to be realized.

However, these institutions and processes are practically controlled by the world's oligarchs through some unethical tools, *inter alia*, including interest and short selling for speculative gains without adding value to the real economy. This system is driving democracy's death spiral, and it is being strengthened by a socioeconomic regime that puts price signals above people's needs, undermining the capacity for democratic decision making in true perspective. International infrastructure institutions, such as the International Monetary Fund (IMF) and the World Bank, work with a similar rent-seeking philosophy. Under 1944 IMF rules, the 190-member organization does not follow the principle of "one country, one vote" (IMF, n.d.). This has led to conflicts, crises, and widening gaps between the haves and the have-nots in all countries. As such, the global economic and financial system is deeply flawed because it enshrines profit maximization without moral discipline, risk transfer, and speculative wealth generation while neglecting justice, compassion, and sustainability.

With the current unsustainable systems, economists, finance experts, business groups, and policymakers around the globe likely may come forward to adopt the ethical values and norms required for realizing the Sustainable Development Goals (SDGs) as envisioned by United Nations Development Program (UNDP). With the evolution of Islamic finance since 1970s, and the growing interest in socially responsible investments there are abundant opportunities to create financial products that benefit both Muslims and non-Muslims while promoting equity, inclusion, and social responsibility (Halil Demir, 2024)

It requires rethinking economic, financial, and business theories to dovetail in all sub-systems, the social and ethical values and norms, as ordained in the revealed sources, if efficiency with respect to equity, social justice, and humane behavior with fellow human beings across the world is to be realized.

Abrahamic values challenge the core assumptions of today's exploitative systems, presenting an alternative vision where finance serves life rather than enslaves it.

This is not just a religious ideal but a civilizational necessity. To realize this vision, scholars, policymakers, and communities must work together to reshape paradigms, institutions, laws, and incentives, grounding them in ethical principles that transcend faith traditions and secular humanist thought alike.

The global economy, business, and finance have covered more than halfway since the adoption of the SDGs in 2015. A big question facing global leaders is whether the SDGs can be realized by 2030. The reality is that inequality, hunger, poverty, and instability in the systems and the economies are showing rising trends. The compound impact of geopolitical conflicts, climate change, economic shocks, the COVID-19 pandemic, and the fast-rising debt burden of poor economies has exacerbated social and economic inequalities and slowed or reversed previous progress in reducing hunger in many jurisdictions.

The very first goal, SDG 1, pertains to eliminating hunger and extreme poverty from the world by adopting the slogan, "Leave no one behind," as the central transformative promise of the United Nations. This goal can be realized only if the current paradigm and the systems are changed as required by nature. Although two-thirds of the time set for realizing the SDGs has passed, inequality and deprivation levels are on the increase. The idea of a "luxurious life of a few with billions in hunger" is not sustainable for any area, society, or country. Nature does not allow such extreme differences to exist for a long time. The United Nations and the serious leaders of the global political economy may need to rethink the theories, schemes, tools, and processes for realizing the 2030 agenda. Otherwise, the SDGs will face the failure that their predecessor MDGs experienced.

In this chapter, I encourage economic managers and regulators of the banking and financial markets to reconsider the paradigm. I also appeal to political economy leaders worldwide who wish to realize the SDGs to adopt a moral economy and ethical finance. I discuss the failure of current economic policies that are based on *Homo economicus* assumptions because they overlook behavioral nuances. Financial markets often behave irrationally because of herding, speculation, and emotional trading, leading to the phenomena of bubbles and crashes. The emergence of alternative approaches to economics, such as an ethical and moral economy, institutional economics, behavioral economics, and neuroeconomics and, in finance and investment, value-based intermediation, ethical/responsible finance, green/sustainable finance, and the terms like CSR, ESG, responsible investing, and so on, also tend to imply the irrationality of the *Homo economicus* assumption and highlight the need for value-based normative theories of economics and finance in the global economy.

Failure of the Market Economy: The Aristocratic Capitalism

Aristocratic rentier capitalism has been the prime cause of increasing inequality and poverty in Western economies and other parts of the world. Furthermore, developing states around the world and islands, from the Caribbean to the Indian and Pacific Oceans, are facing an escalating crisis fueled by unsustainable debt burdens, exorbitant borrowing costs, and geopolitical confrontations. Climate-driven disasters are adding to the problems and forcing some countries to borrow heavily for reconstruction and adaptation. The result is a vicious cycle that forces already-poor countries to accumulate more debt even as their repayment capacity shrinks.

The IMF's structural adjustment programs in sub-Saharan Africa in the 1980s were characterized by poor economic performance. The gross domestic product in many African countries rose by less than 1% between 1979 and 1992, whereas in East Asia and the Pacific countries that managed the crisis themselves—without involving IMF, and where the state played an active role in promoting industrial and social policies as well as in poverty alleviation—registered an average growth of 5% between 1986 and 1992. It is increasingly becoming clear, therefore, that "unless the Fund can find a way to give middle-income countries a greater say, its influence will inevitably wane" (Batista & Wade, 2024, Will the IMF Survive to 100? Project Syndicate, Oct 25, 2024).

In England, during the primitive period of capital accumulation, the emergence of capitalist markets was associated with increased opacity and opportunities for concealment or dishonesty as well as potentially criminal opportunity and enrichment. In later periods, money and capital began to circulate directly and systematically through production, markets, and trade, supplemented by usury as well as by extra-legal means (Webster, 2023; Pp 217-222). The East India Company, the first "rogue company" (Cross, 2021), exemplified the criminal, deceitful, and cruel origins and legacy of colonial and merchant capitalism. The rule of law itself was primarily administered through the use and language of violence, often to protect property. The law became an instrument and ideology serving the interests of the English ruling class, while the rulers themselves adhered to the law as a means of conferring legitimacy and authority on their rule. By the 18th century, governance had no end but the preservation of property. Crime was thus an attempt to stave off starvation (Webster, 2023).

In the early 1900s, the average interest rates in the United States were low, and people shifted their money from banks to the stock market, which was in wild speculative and short-selling modes and undergoing rapid expansion. In the middle of the summer of 1929, some 300 million shares in the stock market were being carried on margin. Billions of dollars were drawn from the banks into Wall Street for brokers' loans to carry margin accounts. Furthermore, brokers and banks were dishing out money to people to buy stocks and home appliances with borrowed money. People mortgaged their homes to pour their cash into the stock market. This short selling and margin trading led to the crisis that ensued. Speculation continued despite the crisis fueled in many cases by individuals who had borrowed money to buy shares. When the stock market crashed in 1929, millions of people went into default, and thousands of businesses collapsed. There was severe economic hardship, widespread unemployment, and sudden declines in industrial production and consumer spending. Keynes (1936, P. 80) maintained in this context,

> *Speculators may do no harm as bubbles on a steady stream of enterprise. But the position is serious when enterprise becomes the bubble on a whirlpool of speculation. When the capital development of a country becomes a by-product of the activities of a casino, the job is likely to be ill-done. (Chapter 12 Part VI; P. 80)*

Causes of the Failure of Theories and Disruptions in the Global Economy

The roots of the sickness lie within the rent-seeking behavior of corporate bodies and business conglomerates who seek to maximize their financial wealth and the unjust belief that "money is entitled to grow as time passes and that a financial system's efficiency is to be measured only based on quantitative criteria such as money value " (Siddiqi, 2010, p. 44). However, the issue is not of interest only and its rate—that is, lower or higher. The issue is of an "ethical foundation versus the secularism for so-called self-interest and maximization of utility for self, irrespective of the other human beings. It resulted in "the creation of bubbles, unpredictability for the future of economies, and increased vulnerability, simultaneously increasing unequal income distribution and the gap between rich and poor" (Carlos Lopes, 2012, p. 73).

The scenario I have described is the result of irrational and self-centered policies on the part of the leadership of advanced economies, ailments of capitalism that stem from the lack of a built-in discipline system. The United States plays a particular role, mainly because the dollar is used as a reserve currency for the global economy and the rent-seeking behavior of the United States.

The ban on short selling that the Islamic finance system or any ethical system imposes is missing in capitalism, which leads to the dominance of the financial sector over the real economy. Similarly, the ban on riba/interest contributes to efficient functioning of the commodity producing sectors vis-à-vis the finance sector, social inclusion, and financial diversification by offering an advantageous model of welfare both for Muslims and people of other faiths (Cattelan, 2016).

Exploitative earnings from riba, short selling, and other unethical and immoral activities, as well as lavish consumption, such as *Israaf* (extravagance even in lawful things) and *Tabzeer* (wasteful consumption in unlawful things), must be systemically prohibited by putting in the automatic stabilizers. This requires a passion for helping others, proportionately as income increases, including colleagues, friends, neighbors, kin, the sick, the poor, the unemployed, and others, for their social inclusion and so they can live a dignified life as members of human society. Accordingly, when personal disposable incomes in a society decline during recessions, more people will become eligible for compulsory levies, such as zakat and other charities in Islamic law.

Abrahamic values, particularly Islamic finance, as being evolved over the last five decades, indicates inniovative messages as indicated by Helvacıoğlu (2022) in the table 1.

Table 1. The Innovative Messages of Islamic Finance

Sr Nos.	**Warning Messages**	**Inspiring Messages**
1	"Do not work on loan contracts!"	"Get real-life existing contracts from commercial laws!"
2	"Remove fictitious and speculative practices from the heart of financial institutions."	"Plug real-life contracts into the heart of financial institutions."

Source: Helvacıoğlu (2022)

Table 2 summarizes the tools, implications, and failures of Aristocratic capitalism.

Table 2. Aristocratic Capitalism – Tools, Implications, and Failure

Category	Aspect	Details
I. Factors / Tools of Aristocratic Capitalism	Rent-Seeking & Resource Capture	Elites profit by controlling assets and influencing policies rather than creating value.
	Speculation & Financialization	Dominance of risk creation & trading (e.g., margin trading, derivatives) over productive investment.
	Regulatory Capture	Elites influence laws (e.g., Glass-Steagall repeal) to serve financial interests.
	Political Influence	Billionaires manipulate elections and policies via lobbying and campaign financing.
	Unjust Production Distribution	Exploited by big corporations, resources hoarded by elites; poor under-served.
	Tax Avoidance & CSR Manipulation	Use of tax havens; CSR used as image strategy, not genuine altruism.
	Debt-Trap Diplomacy	IMF and lender conditions burden developing nations, creating increasing dependency.
	Legal & Extra-Legal Protection	Elites use legal systems and force to secure wealth and suppress dissent.
	Secular, Self-Interest Ideology	Focus on profit maximization without moral or collective concern.
	Extractive Institutions	Institutions favor elite interests, undermining inclusive growth.
	Market Manipulation	Overreliance on free market and "rational actors" ignoring real human behavior.
II. Implications of Aristocratic Capitalism	Widening Inequality	Top 1% amass wealth while majority face stagnating or declining wages in real terms.
	Mass Poverty & Hunger	Hundreds of millions face hunger despite food surpluses.
	Homelessness & Living Standards Decline	Housing unaffordability rises even in rich nations (e.g., 770,000 homeless in the U.S. in 2024).
	Erosion of Democracy	Elites distort elections and policies, reducing public trust in institutions.
	Financial Crises	Cycles of boom and bust crises caused by speculation and regulatory failures.
	Unethical Corporate Behavior	Exploitative labor policies, environmental harm, and unchecked profit-driven activities.
	Failed Poverty Alleviation programs	Decades of aid and charity failed due to structural injustices.
	Social Breakdown	Increased mental health issues, crime, and political polarization.

continued on following page

Table 2. Continued

Category	Aspect	Details
III. Failures of Aristocratic Capitalism	Unsustainable Wealth Concentration	Excessive inequality leads to economic stagnation, and instability.
	Failed Trickle-Down Effects	Little to no wealth redistribution; top hoards gains.
	Neglect of Collective Goods	Undermines public infrastructure, health, education, and cohesion.
	Flawed Economic Models	Reliance on "Homo Economicus" ignores emotion, ethics, and cooperation.
	Moral & Ethical Failure	Prioritizes profit over people and planet; lacks humanistic grounding.
	Structural Exploitation	Global systems designed to perpetuate inequality and dependency.
	Debt Crisis	Unsustainable personal and national debt driven by financial elites.
	Collapse of Trust	Public disillusionment with economic and political institutions.
	Social Backlash and Distrust	Growing movements against economic hardships, inequality (e.g., sit-ins, protests).

Source: Author's Own

STRENGTHENING THE BASIC TRUST FOR MEANINGFUL LIVING

Economics and finance, being part and parcel of the lives of all human beings, have historically been emphasized in all major Holy Scriptures of the monotheist religions, Judaism, Christianity, and Islam, though with slightly different paradigms. The source of all Islamic scriptures has been the same: Allah Almighty, the divine authority. "It is He Who has named you Muslims, both before and in this (Revelation); that the Messenger may be a witness for you, and ye be witnesses for mankind!" (Quran, 22:78). The objective is to strengthen the bond of trust among all in the universe under divine guidance.

The ultimate divine guidance that all need to accept has been provided in the "Religion of Abraham," as Quran (2:130) says: "And who turns away from the religion of Abraham but such as debase their souls with folly? Him We chose and rendered pure in this world: and he will be in the Hereafter in the ranks of the righteous" (translated by Abdullah Yusuf Ali). "And this was the legacy that Abraham left to his sons and so did Jacob; 'O my sons! God hath chosen the faith for you; then die not except in the faith of Islam'" (2:132). Verse 2:136 reiterates,

Say ye: "We believe in God and the revelation given to us and to Abraham, Isma`il, Isaac, Jacob and the Tribes and that given to Moses and Jesus and that given to (all) Prophets from their Lord we make no difference between one and another of them and we bow to God (in Islam).[1]

Islam and Judaism provide explicit wisdom about different aspects of day-to-day life, including economic practices (Habisch, 2023, p. 47). The Bible is not devoid of economic principles. In Christianity, usury was a sin of greed or failure of charity and a form of injustice (McRorie, 2018). Similarly, money was understood to be sterile, unlike livestock or crops, as Aristotle (1946) considered. As quoted by Paldi (2024) from different sources, "The Bible emphasizes 'stewardship, useful work, protection for the disadvantaged and the preservation of institutions such as marriage and family life' as of primary importance to economic life" (p. 35).

The prime objective is that all elements of society should receive their rights equitably and fulfill their obligations and duties responsibly. As Meeks (2014) indicated, "Neighbor love is the chief identifier of human participation in the economy of God and is the actual experience of salvation" (p. 8). While the Love of God and love of neighbor are inseparable, love of neighbor is nothing less than the love of all human beings.

The emergence of alternative approaches, such as ethical and moral economy and finance, institutional economics, behavioral economics, neuroeconomics and, within finance and investment, value-based intermediation, ethical/responsible finance, green/sustainable finance, and the terms like CSR, ESG, responsible investing, and so on, also tend to imply the irrationality of the *Homo economicus* assumption and highlight the need for value-based normative theories of economics and finance in the global economy. It is reiterated, therefore, that economics and finance have to move toward more refined models that incorporate psychological, social, and environmental factors to better reflect the irrational, cooperative, and adaptive nature of human decision making.

The reintroduction of *basic trust*, which is necessary for all ethical behavior, into the system in which global managers operate, is the common goal of the Humanistic Management Network (2005) and the Global Ethic Project. The Global Ethic Project has been attempting since 2005 to respond to the search for an ethical consensus for society while at the same time offering a basis for understanding and cooperation among religions that must keep in mind that ethics are founded on a divine source of knowledge and value systems as derived from Abrahamic religions in their pure revealed form. Any approach to ethics that is not informed by morality and faith can lose its direction and purpose and can even become harmful to human welfare (Kamali, 2018, P 13).

The situation was apparently further deteriorated with the impact of current neoliberal economic, financial, and business systems working for the maximization of corporate wealth and self-interest without regard for the impact on other human beings and the cosmos. Late environmental scientist Donella Meadows (1941–2001) remarked, "'Growth' is one of the stupidest purposes ever invented by any culture"; we have got to have an "enough," she added (Wellness, 2025). The global financial system is in danger of fragmenting, and the world's governments are imposing sanctions more than four times as often as previously, and Western-led institutions are either decaying or defunct (Roberts, 2024). To put the global political economy on a more ethical and responsible path, world leaders must rethink their policies to ensure a safe and sustainable future for all if they wish to realize the SDGs for the peaceful co-survival of humanity.

In addition to the operations of a large number of charity organizations, many programs intended to alleviate hunger and poverty and enhance public welfare by promoting micro finance have failed over the past three decades. They have not been able to create a visible dent in poverty, even in advanced economies. Since 2020, around 5 billion people worldwide have become poorer; in this same time frame, only five billionaires doubled their fortunes, at a rate of USD14 million/hour (Oxfam International, 2024). The issue at hand is the unjust distribution of production through unethical tools/means, overconsumption, wastage by the rich, and geopolitical protective measures. "The planet produces almost a kilo of grain per day per inhabitant and we have more than one billion people going hungry," remarked Carlos Lopes (2012, p. 74).

Economic policies based on *Homo economicus* assumptions generally fail because they overlook behavioral nuances. Financial markets often behave irrationally because of herding, speculation, and emotional trading, leading to the phenomena of bubbles and crashes. The mantras of self-interest and profit maximization can undermine efforts to address collective challenges, such as climate change, because it neglects the importance of collective action, cooperation, and social and ethical considerations.

Success cannot be realized unless vision and mission for the well-being of the community are put into place. The application of sound social and ethical/religious values in society is essential for the maintenance and realization of humanitarian targets under any conditions. Whether nations 'fail,' or not, depends on whether their political and economic institutions are inclusive or extractive is the central theme of the book by Acemoglu & Robinson (2013)

Cooperation, altruism, fairness, and other social norms are part of human behavior that must be consistently implemented as a part of beyond-market economic theory and practice. In all societies, even those in poor countries, people donate to charity and cooperate in public goods scenarios, even when it is not in their immediate self-interest. In Pakistan, for example, people donate around Rs 10 million/hour to a Karachi-based single social welfare hospital, INDUS, which provides the most advanced free health care facilities in the country. Many times, people are willing to sacrifice personal gains to undo the impact of calamities as well as an unfair and unjust system, thus contradicting the *Homo economicus* assumption of pure self-interest.

ISSUES IN INTEREST-BASED MONEY CREATION AND MONETARY MANAGEMENT

Money and credit creation policy and monetary management also have played havoc with the economy of the masses. Monetary economics and macroeconomics evolved only during and after the Great Depression. John Maynard Keynes's book *General Theory of Employment, Interest and Money*, which was published in 1936, described the concepts of macroeconomics and explained fluctuations in financial markets. Monetary policy required the role of a central bank in the creation of credit and the role of commercial banks' interest-based borrowing and lending in managing the growth and stability of the economy. This was the period when most of the Muslim world was under colonial rule, and their economies could not create any development in monetary policy, and hence in economics, that could be called Islamic economics or Islamic monetary policy.

Keynesian economics generally became a standard model in the developed world because of interest-based central and commercial banking. It became the basis of modern global finance. The abandonment of the Gold Standard, the interwar period (1914–1944), the Bretton woods system, and the Nixon shock (1971) in terms of suspension of Dollar convertibility to gold as US had pledged for the Bretton Woods system, increasingly led to the creation of money and credit in the fractional reserve banking system, and people with financial assets grabbed the wealth both at national and global levels at the cost of those creating goods and services for human use. The creation of U.S. dollars (paper gold) against the treasury bonds with no gold backing, in particular, created imbalances in global finance and led to the devastation of human societies in wars.

With respect to evolving finance theories, money/finance capital has not been differentiated from fixed capital. Whereas fixed capital, such as land, buildings, plants, vehicles, machinery, and so on, are entitled to any pre-agreed fixed return as the market may determine, money or financial capital cannot be assigned any fixed return in line with the prohibition of riba in all old philosophies and revealed religions. Economists provide no rationale for letting the banking system create money based on the fractional reserve system despite its negative implications for efficiency, stability, and equity in the economy. Of course, prominent economists like Joseph Stiglitz, Hyman Minsky, Steve Keen, Michael Hudson, Richard Werner and others have recognized that the world is at present in a mess, and the crisis it faces has no solution because of the privilege of the banking system to continue creating and issuing credit.

The banking system's loaning in the form of credit is allowing money to flow to the rich as much as they want, making the richer engage in high-risk activities and hence making the economy inefficient. Economists who think from the Islamic perspective have always been questioning the Sharīʿah justification of credit creation by the banks in two respects:

- why credit creation by the banking system should continue to be a source of money supply when the government has the sole authority to change money supply by its power to print money and
- why credit so created cannot be used productively without letting it become inflationary.

The same is the case in the economies of nations where the wealth is being transferred to the financial sector at the cost of the real sector: those who create goods and services for use by human beings. The whole concept of development and welfare has been corrupted: "Saving is sin and spending is virtue" (Gurumurthy, 2002). This notion goes against the natural and balanced approach of income and expenditures. While the Japanese save a lot and spend a little, Americans spend a lot - and save a little. Also, the US imports more than it exports as shown in the Box. Yet, the American economy is considered strong and trusted to get stronger due mainly to the Dollar as a reserve currency, and the global savings are mostly invested in the US, in dollars.

Table 3. USA's trade deficit

Year	US Trade Deficit (Bln.)
2019	$576.9
2020	$676.7
2021	$845.3
2022	$951.2
2023	$773.4

It is the creation of credit out of thin air and the charging of interest on it that is making rich people increase their luxurious and wasteful consumption to create the current mess. A monetary policy that avoids interest-based money creation by the banks can help the global economy—in particular, the poor countries—get rid of this mess.

The starting point for monetary policy with respect to credit creation by banks should be

- to not allow credit created to go to high-risk (gambling-type) investment or luxurious consumption-; and
- to increase aggregate consumption for economic growth by making riba-free credit available to the poor for fulfilling their consumption needs and for entrepreneurship.

In addition, monetary policy should directly or indirectly aim at encouraging increased spending for community well-being to help the poor and needy through formally organized channels. A properly developed system of *awqaf* foundations can lead to economic efficiency, stability, and social harmony along with economic growth.

ECONOMIC AND FINANCIAL THEORIES MUST BE SUBSERVIENT TO THE LAW OF NATURE

Nature is the basis of all human development and global resources. Man learns from God's creatures and how they function and survive, and then develops on it. Even artificial intelligence (AI), the latest technology-based revolution that is going to change the whole scenario of human societies in the next few years, is based on algorithms developed by human beings on the basis of neurons and the neurology of humans, wild animals, birds flying in the air, and Nektonic Sea animals freely swimming in the waters independent of waves and current action. AI evolved through portable computing, sequence computing, and the hybridization of computational intelligence, two categories of algorithms biologically inspired algorithms that lead to swarm intelligence with ant colony optimization, and particle swarm optimization algorithms, implying that ultimately nature is the source of all power and resources in the universe.

Human beings' fundamental rights must be protected irrespective of race, creed, and color. These rights include food as necessary nutrition; health; education; abode; job/business as per expertise; and the protection of life, belief, honor, and lineage. After World War II, global leaders decided to avoid human crises in the future. However, the dream of a safe and sustainable future for peace and co-survival could not be realized mainly because of some unethical acts and decisions on the part of global institutions and leaders who were supposed to think and act ethically. These resulted in the worst acts of immorality against humanity.

Economic theory underpins economic policy, and all philosophies since the days of the mercantilists and the physiocrats, from Adam Smith and David Ricardo to John Maynard Keynes, and from Karl Marx, a social theorist, to the divine philosophers, like the holy Prophet Muhammad (Peace Be Upon Him [PBUH]), all had implications for economic policies that were adopted at different times. All such theories at times seemed to be effective in making better policy choices and at other times causing major policy failures, except the divine theory given by the Creator of the Universe through His Messengers (Peace be upon all of them).

Today's mainstream economics, based on the Washington Consensus,[2] is founded on the concepts of money neutrality, rational expectations, deregulation, free trade, self-clearing of the markets, free capital markets, and general equilibrium. With the aristocratic approach of the leadership in advanced countries, it further deteriorated to the Neoliberal Washington Consensus. It has been troublesome for the majority of human beings in developed as well as developing countries and global economies.

As El Aynaoui and Dinh (2025) remarked, with the global economic landscape changing rapidly, developing countries face three major constraints: (a) the resurgence of protectionism, (b) shrinking macroeconomic policy space, and (c) profound technological disruption. Because the Neoliberal Washington Consensus does not have a suitable purpose, a new paradigm is urgently needed to guide development in the years ahead.

The power balance in the global economy has been spoiled for several reasons:

- the prevailing ideology, entirely dominated by monetarists thought, that has been imposed on the countries of the Global South and transition economies for more than 20 years, despite blatant failures and disastrous social impact;
- the power structure established by voting shares within the IMF and the World Bank, which offers no representation of the interests of the world's poorest peoples; and
- a distorted belief that wealthy countries would not be affected by crises (Carlos Lopsis, 2012).

Global debt, including public debt, increased from 100% of world's gross domestic product in 1950 to 238% of the gross domestic product in 2022. According to a May 2024 report by the Institute of International Finance (2024), global debt grew to $315 trillion by the end of the first quarter of 2024. Around two-thirds of that $315 trillion originates from mature economies, with Japan and the United States contributing the most to that debt. Within this debt, household debt, which includes mortgages, credit cards, and student debt, among others, amounted to $59.1

trillion. The debt of the emerging markets surged to an unprecedented high of over $105 trillion—$55 trillion more than a decade ago.

Because of the "financialization" of the American economy in the post-1970s period (Krippner, 2005), followed by the same trend in other Western economies, financial returns became the end to which all other needs and aspirations were subordinated. Financial globalization has placed the fate of entire societies in the hands of investors who care only about price signals and are oblivious to human needs (Pistor, 2024, Pp 14, 15). This happened because the need for disciplining human behavior and self-interest led corporate entities was ignored, rendering the whole system unethical and exploitative.

Political economists and finance managers thus need to explore how the market economy system, with its ethical tools and philosophy enshrined by the Creator of the Universe, was corrupted, creating chaos and instability in social life and national and global economies. The salvation lies in disciplining human behavior at the individual, corporate, and national levels and focusing on a behavioral, moral, circular, and responsible economy and finance.

Economic and institutional factors contributing to global economic disorder are detailed in Table 4.

Table 4. Economic and Institutional Drivers of Global Economic Instability

Factors	Disorder	Explanation / Examples
1. Theoretical Assumptions	Homo Economicus (Rational Self-Interest)	Assumes humans are always rational and self-interested, ignoring emotions, social norms, and altruism.
	Trickle-Down Economics	Wealth does not "trickle down" – the rich get richer while the poor stay poor.
	Money Neutrality & Market Efficiency	Assumes markets self-correct and ignore systemic shocks and bubbles.
2. Behavioral Realities	Bounded Rationality & Emotional/ speculative Decision-Making	Decisions driven by fear, greed, speculation (e.g., financial bubbles, irrational markets).
	Social & Cultural Influences on Decisions	Human behavior influenced by ethics, culture, peer pressure, not just personal gain.
3. Institutional Failures	Oligarchic & Rentier Capitalism	Wealth and political power concentrated among elites (e.g., USA's top 1% controlling vast wealth).
	IMF/World Bank Structural Adjustments	Imposed harmful policies on developing countries (e.g., Africa in the 1980s).
	Unjust Global Financial Systems	Interest-based systems, tax havens, speculative instruments widen inequality and instability.

continued on following page

Table 4. Continued

Factors	Disorder	Explanation / Examples
4. Ethical & Social Oversights	Neglect of Collective Welfare & Ethics	Economic policies fail to address hunger, inequality, and basic human rights (food, health, education).
	CSR & Philanthropy for Tax Avoidance or PR	Many charitable actions by corporations are not value-driven but profit-driven.
5. Structural Imbalances	Skewed Incentives & Production Structures	Incentives favor short-term profit over long-term social/environmental well-being.
	Financialization of the Economy	Economy driven by speculative finance, not real production (e.g., post-1970s USA).
	Global Debt Crisis	Unsustainable debt levels, especially in developing countries.
6. Historical Lessons Ignored	Ignored Ethical Models (e.g., Divine/Prophetic Economics)	Past successful ethical systems were ignored in favor of exploitative capitalism.
	Speculation-Induced Crises (1929, 2008)	Deregulation and speculative practices led to massive economic crashes.
7. Governance & Power Imbalance	Inequitable Power Structures in Global Institutions	Rich countries dominate IMF/World Bank decisions; poor nations lack representation.
	Neoliberal Washington Consensus	Failed to provide inclusive growth; promoted deregulation, free capital flows, austerity.
8. Policy Failures	Failure to Alleviate Poverty	Despite decades of programs, poverty and inequality persist and even worsen.
	Inadequate Regulation and Deregulation	Laws governing derivatives and short sales

Source: Author' Own

ECONOMICS AND FINANCE, AND THE MAJOR REVEALED RELIGIONS

The Quran indicates, in verse 57:25,[3] that economic resources are a basic need of all human beings. The phrase "Mizan" in the verse refers to the criterion of truth and falsehood, which may precisely indicate, like a balance, the golden mean between two extremes in matters of thought, morals, dealings, and resources. This golden mean is the basis of divine ethics for social, economic, business, and exchange, and professional protocols. Judaism and Islam in particular provide explicit wisdom about different aspects of day-to-day life, including economic practices (Habisch, 2023, p. 47). The ultimate goal, therefore, is to maintain this balance in all human activities. Islamic economics provides such a normative framework, what many describe as a "third way" that tries to embed moral responsibility into markets, unlike unrestrained capitalism.

Nasser (2023) examines the economic implications of ribā prohibitions in Judaism, Christianity, and Islam, highlighting both theological and practical commonalities. He found that the three faiths historically condemned usury as exploitative, rooted in texts like the Hebrew Bible (Exodus 22:25), Christian Gospels (Luke 6:35), and the Qur'an (2:275–279). However, there are divergent modern adaptations. He concludes that while Abrahamic traditions share ethical concerns about debt exploitation, their legal and economic applications diverge significantly in modernity. Islamic finance models promote risk-sharing but face scalability challenges in global markets.

As highlighted by Laldin and Furqani (2013), *ribā* and other prohibitions in Islamic finance are not merely technical constraints but serve as foundational principles guiding the system toward justice, ethical integrity, and alignment with the objectives of Sharīʿah (*maqā id al-Sharī ah*). They emphasize that *ribā* is not limited to interest on loans but encompasses all forms of unjust enrichment, particularly where one party gains at the expense of another without providing an equitable countervalue (*'iwā*). Additionally, they underscore the significance of prohibiting *gharar* (excessive uncertainty) and *maysir* (gambling), which reflect Islam's commitment to transparency, fairness, and shared risk. This ethical framework, they argue, should shape the design of financial contracts, institutional policies, and strategic direction, ensuring that Islamic finance advances social justice and human wellbeing, rather than merely replicating the profit-driven objectives of conventional finance.

With respect to economics and finance from an Islamic perspective, Islamic finance is based on pluralistic and dynamic Islamic law emanating from the divine and undiluted source of the Quran and its explanation by the Sunnah of the Prophet (PBUH). In an Islamic economy, interest (as a time-based value of money) does not exist, and financing is restricted to productive activities, trade, and real assets. As a result, neither individuals nor firms can earn speculative gains by merely holding money. In this regard, the economy resembles the classical model, where money remains neutral. Money does not yield a fixed return, whether through lending or so-called investments in liquid assets. Instead, the price of capital is determined in the real sector, as returns to the entrepreneurs that are determined by taking business risk and adding value to real business.

If money holders seek a productive return, they must invest it in profit-sharing ventures, where gains or losses depend on actual business outcomes. Otherwise, money lent without participation in real economic activity will generate no return. Liquid capital investments lose their privileged status of guaranteed fixed returns, distinguishing this system from conventional interest-based finance. This principle rejects Keynesian economic theory, emphasizing that financial or cash capital does not hold the preferential treatment it enjoys in interest-driven economies.

Zakat and *Ushr* (the tithe of agricultural produce), pillars of Islamic belief, are the primary vehicles for human upliftment and social development. Supplemented by *waqf* and other voluntary divine charities (*Sadaqat*), they provide the best system for shared growth, broader level welfare, and social inclusion.

Islamic finance is based on the pluralistic and dynamic Islamic law emanating from the divine and undiluted source of the Qur'an, and its explanation by the Sunnah of the Prophet (PBUH). Islamic finance aligns with a shared Abrahamic vision of ethical and socially responsible economics. What distinguishes Islamic finance is the formal, legalistic, and institutional application of these principles, ensuring that real-life business contracts are moral, just, and asset-based (Helvacıoğlu, 2022).

The most serious concern for the three religions is the issue of extreme inequality (Piketty, 2020, pp. 1–2) caused by *rentier capitalism* rather than by investment in productive, risk-based enterprise. Inequality is wasteful and does not advance societal good. Reducing inequality is positioned as a critical weapon in the battle to defeat the 'xenophobic "populism" that threatens the current global democratic political order (Piketty, 2020, p. 2). "Inequality is neither economic nor technological; it is ideological and political" Piketty (2020, p. 7) argues.

The concept of 'shareholder value' that has become deeply embedded in the institution of corporate governance is central to the inequality regime of hyper capitalism. Piketty argues that religious traditions demonstrate historical precedents for embedding ethical, communal, redistributive norms into economic life, challenging the notion that extreme inequality is a natural or inevitable outcome of economic development.

Key common business and economic ethics of the three religions are shown in Table 5:

Table 5. Shared and Unique Economic Ethics Across Abrahamic Faiths

Dimension	Islamic Finance	Christian Ethics	Jewish Finance
Justice, Honesty, Community Welfare	Strong emphasis; rooted in Qur'an and Sunnah	Core teachings of the Bible; echoed in Church teachings	Fundamental in Torah and Talmudic laws
Prohibition/Restriction of Interest (Usury)	Completely prohibited (riba)	Historically prohibited; relaxed in modern interpretations	Prohibited among Jews; allowed toward non-Jews in specific contexts
Accountability to God	Financial dealings must align with divine law (Shari'ah)	Stewardship and accountability before God	Ethical business as a divine duty

continued on following page

Table 5. Continued

Dimension	Islamic Finance	Christian Ethics	Jewish Finance
Socially Responsible Investing	Mandatory via moral screening (e.g., excludes alcohol, gambling)	Encouraged in modern social teaching (e.g., ethical funds, ESG)	Expected; includes communal responsibility (Tikkun Olam)
Anti-Exploitation of the Poor/Weak	Lending is charity; profit not allowed on loans	Charity and concern for the marginalized central to ethics	Lending without interest is a mitzvah; oppression strongly condemned

Source: Author's own

Islam strictly prohibits *ribā* (usury/interest), gambling (*maysir*), and excessive uncertainty (*gharar*) in transactions, particularly regarding the subject matter or price of an exchange. The Quran (2:278–279) unequivocally condemns *ribā*, equating engagement in it with "declaring war against God and His Messenger."

Shariah scholars and juristic bodies worldwide universally classify *ribā* as encompassing all forms of interest, mirroring the classical definition of usury. In Surah Al-Baqarah (2:274–281), the Quran draws a clear distinction between permissible economic activities, such as trade (which yields lawful profit) and charity, and prohibited *ribā*-based transactions. It explicitly forbids any surplus over the principal amount in a loan or debt, labeling such gains as *ribā*.

Ayub (2007) expands this definition further, stating:

"Ribā refers to any increment above the principal in a contractual obligation, unless justified by commensurate labor, commodity, risk, or expertise" (p. 53; see pp. 43–57 for elaboration).

This framework underscores Islam's emphasis on equity and real economic value, rejecting exploitative or speculative gains.

Riba al-Fadl refers to any excess in the exchange of fungible *Ribawi* goods, such as gold, silver, currency, wheat, barley, or dates, when both counter-values are of the same kind and measured by weight, volume, or count. This excess, whether the transaction is spot or deferred, is prohibited in Shari'ah as it leads to unjust enrichment. *Riba al-Fadl* also includes any surplus or benefit derived from deferring payment or delivery in such exchanges. In essence, it is what is commonly known as interest when applied to lending arrangements.

The Shariat Appellate Bench of the Supreme Court of Pakistan, in its judgment delivered in December1999; SLR, 2000), observed,

The Shariah has taken cognizance of both monetary exchange and barter exchange and has laid down principles to regulate both kinds of transactions and dealings. The law of Riba takes care of both kinds of economies. While Riba al Nasiah primarily seeks to eliminate interest from the monetary economy where goods buy money and money buys goods, the prohibition of Riba al-Fadl seeks elimination of interest from the barter economy where goods buy goods. (p. 267)

At the heart of the prohibition lies the principle of justice in all immediate transactions: the counter-values exchanged must be equitable. Any surplus received by one party without corresponding value from the other is considered *Riba al-Fadl.* Ibn al-'Arabi defined this as "all excess over what is justified by the counter value" (p. 254). Justice, therefore, demands that the value on both sides of the scale must be equal.

While Shari'ah acknowledges that time influences the value of goods, it does not allow this concept to justify earning returns on loans. Time-based pricing is legitimate in real trade and leasing transactions but not in loans (*Qard*) or debts (*Dayn*), where monetary gain from money alone is forbidden. Variations in commodity prices based on time and place are recognized, such as seasonal differences or geographic market disparities, and are permissible in pricing. However, claiming a fixed return purely on the passage of time in financial loans, without linkage to a real economic transaction, is prohibited.

This is evident in the rulings related to *bai' al-sarf,* the exchange of gold, silver, and currencies, where simultaneous delivery is mandated. Shari'ah prohibits predetermined returns on loans that are not connected to real economic activity. Therefore, claiming time value on money in such contexts contradicts Islamic finance principles.

Moreover, Islamic finance prohibits *short selling* and *maysir* (speculation and games of chance), as these practices undermine justice and stability. Profiting without owning the underlying asset, or without undertaking real economic risk, is deemed unethical. Short selling, in particular, has been a destabilizing factor in modern finance, contributing to recent economic crises.

This prohibition underlines a foundational Islamic economic principle: monetary gains must arise from genuine economic activity. Just as other factors of production (labor, land, capital goods) derive value from their contribution to the real economy, capital in the form of money must also reflect real value creation. Liquid capital (cash) should not generate returns unless it is tied to productive use through valid contracts such as partnerships (*musharakah, mudarabah*), sales (*bai'*), or leases (*ijarah*). It must be treated distinctly from fixed capital assets like land or machinery.

For example, while forward sales (*Salam* or *Salf*) of fungible goods are permitted under strict conditions—clarity in price, quantity, and delivery—*Salam* in currencies is forbidden. In a valid *Salam* contract, only one of the counter-values (usually the commodity) may be deferred. If both the payment (in currency) and the delivery are deferred, it becomes an exchange of debt, which Shari'ah strictly prohibits. Thus, if the price is in U.S. dollars and the commodity is denominated in Pakistani rupees, the transaction cannot qualify as *Salam* since currency exchanges (*bai' al-sarf*) require spot settlement on both sides.

Islamic finance mandates that all permissible financial transactions must be anchored in tangible assets or economic activities. Fixed returns on money—without exposure to business risk or value creation—are invalid. In contrast to conventional systems that treat money as a tradable commodity, Islam views money as a medium of exchange, not a source of autonomous profit. Any gain must arise from its productive deployment through legitimate contracts.

Consequently, Islamic commercial law demands a comprehensive ethical framework governing financial and business conduct. This includes transparency, equitable risk-sharing, full disclosure, fulfillment of contractual obligations, and avoidance of exploitative practices. Income that lacks value addition—such as rent on money, speculation, gambling, fraud, or manipulation—is not recognized as legitimate profit.

Subject to these ethical standards, forward or future markets may serve useful functions in the development of finance and investment products aligned with Islamic principles. However, they must remain closely tied to real economic activities and uphold the core values of justice, cooperation (*ta'āwun*), and mutual benefit (Ayub, 2022; Ayub et al., 2022).

Economics and Finance in Christianity

The Bible is not completely devoid of economic principles. As Beed and Beed (1996) indicated, "The Bible emphasizes 'stewardship, useful work, protection for the disadvantaged and the preservation of institutions such as marriage and family life' as of primary importance to economic life" (p. 101). The prime objective is that all elements of society should receive their rights equitably and fulfill their obligations and duties responsibly:

Through the extraction of spiritual principles of the Bible, one can find guidance in the material world. God is seen as the Creator of all things including natural resources and people must utilise resources for the benefit of God's will and protect family through various institutions such as marriage, which can be seen as a divine and economic institution. [Paldi (2024, pp. 35, 36, citing Beed and Beed (1996)]

Christian traditions also embraced forms of social justice, such as redistribution and charity, laying the groundwork for later welfare and socialist ideals. According to Piketty (2020, pp. vi, ix), Christianity's legacy is dual: reinforcing private property norms while also providing moral foundations for caring for the poor. Piketty (2020) acknowledges Christianity's role in legitimizing private property (e.g., through natural law traditions) while also providing ethical frameworks for redistributive justice (e.g., the "preferential option for the poor" in Catholic teaching).

Medieval theologians like Thomas Aquinas upheld the idea of a *"just price"* and condemned usury, reflecting concerns for economic fairness (Aquinas, *Summa Theologica*, II-II, q. 77–78, 13th century/1947). The Protestant Reformation and Catholic social teaching (e.g., Pope Leo XIII, 1891) further developed principles of social justice, including workers' rights and distributive justice (*Rerum Novarum*, 1891).

The Christian concept of man encapsulated in the Bible's text, "endowed by God with whatever is required for us to be representatives of God's will to the rest of creation," is similar to the concept of Khalifah in Islam, according to which mankind is on earth to serve God's will and that also has social, financial, and economic responsibilities and outcomes (Meeks, 2014, p. 5; Paldi, 2024). "Love thy neighbor" is a cardinal principle of Christian economic thought, which of course includes the widow, the wayfarer, the orphan, the needy, the poor, and people in general. "Neighbor's love is the chief identifier of human participation in the economy of God and is the experience of salvation" (Meeks, 2014, p. 8). Meeks adds that God's love is immediately connected with the needs of the neighbour. The neighbour may be the one in closest proximity, but according to the Gospel of Jesus, the love of neighbour is nothing less than the love of all human beings. As quoted by Paldi (2024, P. 35) from Beed & Beed, people should love God with all their hearts and minds and their neighbours as themselves. Hence, there is a connection between the spiritual and material, and between serving God and economic outcomes, which must be preserved in Christian economics, Paldi (2024, P. 36) concluded.

The normative principles of spiritual behavior as found in Christianity are intended to guide people in their material life (Beed & Beed, 1996, p. 102). Through the extraction of these principles, one can find guidance in the material world. God is seen as the Creator of all things, including natural resources, and people must utilize resources for the benefit of God's will and protect their family through social institutions, such as marriage, which can be seen as a divine and economic institution.

Timothy [New International Version (NIV), 6:17, 18] provides divine instructions for the wealthy:

> *"Command those who are rich in this present world not to be arrogant nor to put their hope in wealth, which is so uncertain, but to put their hope in God, who richly provides us with everything for our enjoyment. Command them to do good, to be rich in good deeds, and to be generous and willing to share.".*

In Deuteronomy 8:18, Moses reminds us, "But remember the Lord your God, for it is he who gives you the ability to produce wealth." A good deed is a free and voluntary act of service toward another person. Doing good deeds for others is the fruit of your salvation in Jesus Christ.

As theologian Martin Luther suggested to a cobbler, to become a good Christian, make a quality shoe and sell it at a fair price. Based on Luther's concept on vocation and Christian living, the same is true for a tailor, scribe, or reader. If he is a Christian tailor, he will say: I make these clothes because God has bidden me do so, so that I can earn a living, so that I can help and serve my neighbor.

In Christianity, usury was historically declared a form of robbery, a sin against the Seventh Commandment, which required restitution as well as excommunication. Harper and Smirl (2014, 566) elaborated: "Thus, by the twelfth century, attitudes toward usury had evolved from denunciation of taking interest on loans to the poor, through prohibition of interest on loans to all fellow Jews, of universal prohibition enforced by strict penalties". They added that the anti-usury movement continued to gain momentum during the Early Middle Ages and reached its peak perhaps in 1311, when Pope Clement V placed an absolute ban on usury and declared all secular legislation in its favor null and void in the eyes of the Catholic Church. Beginning in 1400, a pro-usury movement developed because Europe needed interest-bearing loans for commercial purposes, and the Church reconsidered its position. (Frierson, 1969). Thus, usury moved from being banned by the Church to being allowed for commercial purposes in the Capitalist system.

With respect to banking and finance, in Christianity usury was a sin of greed and a form of injustice (McRorie, 2018). Similarly, money was understood to be sterile, unlike livestock or crops, as Aristotle considered. The material incentives brought by the changing institutional environment compelled the Catholic Church's reversal of its prohibition on the charging of interest (McRorie, 2018). Thomas Aquinas (n.d.) precisely differentiated a house from money, which he said is more like wine. In his response to the question of whether it is sinful to take money, as the price for money lent, St. Aquinas explained,

> *"To take usury for money lent is unjust in itself, because this is to sell what does not exist, and this evidently leads to inequality which is contrary to justice. In order to make this evident, we must observe that there are certain things the use of which consists in their consumption: thus we consume wine when we use it for drink and we consume wheat when we use it for food. --------- In like manner he commits an injustice who lends wine or wheat, and asks for double payment, viz. one, the return of the thing in equal measure, the other, the price of the use, which is called usury. ---- On the other hand, there are things the use of which does not consist in their consumption: thus to use a house is to dwell in it, not to destroy it. --------- For this reason, a man may lawfully make a charge for the use of his house, and, besides this, revendicate the house from the person to whom he has granted its use, as happens in renting and letting a house. Now money, according to the Philosopher (Ethic. v, 5; Polit. i, 3) was invented chiefly for the purpose of exchange: and consequently the proper and principal use of money is its consumption or alienation whereby it is sunk in exchange. Hence, it is by its very nature unlawful to take payment for the use of money lent, which payment is known as usury: and just as a man is bound to restore other ill-gotten goods, so is he bound to restore the money which he has taken in usury".*

The charging of interest on loans is considered usury and as a tool of the wealthy to usurp the land and wealth of the people, which may lead to imminent slavery. Meeks himself stated that "The central biblical problem with interest is that it leads to debt and debt leads to poverty and poverty leads to slavery" (2014, p. 17). Usury is not only frowned upon in the Bible, but there is also an emphasis on forgiving debts.

Many Christian investors seek to align their financial decisions with environmental, social, and governance (ESG) principles while staying true to their faith. Among them is Dave Zellner, former chief investment officer of Wespath—the investment arm of the United Methodist Church—who managed $24 billion before retiring in February 2024 (Wespath, 2024). Zellner viewed his role as a pursuit of "the intersection between good business practice and church values" (*The Economist*, 2023). Under his leadership, Wespath financed affordable housing projects (albeit at market rates) and collaborated with secular advocacy groups, such as Climate Action 100+, to push energy companies toward decarbonization (*The Economist*, 2023).

Similarly, Robert Netzly of Inspire Investing applies biblical principles to investment strategies—though he rejects the ESG label, arguing it has been "weaponized by liberal activists to push forward their ... social-Marxist agenda" (*The Economist*, 2023). Nevertheless, he agrees with ESG proponents that nonfinancial criteria should guide investment choices.

This approach reflects a broader ethical framework: investment practices should combat injustice, protect human dignity within a balanced social order, and promote equity across all spheres of collective life.

Economics and Finance in Judaism

In Judaism, the interpretation of the Torah or the Oral Torah carries more weight than what is clearly written in the actual/original Torah because Judaism is an interpretative tradition. It is quite rational to understand that human interpretation can be problematic, while divinely revealed scriptures and injunctions are certainly the true reflection of the law of nature as created by the divine authority.

Jewish thought features a blend of universal humanitarian ethics and strong community bonds, shaping a view of justice grounded in both individual and communal duty. Halakhic tradition aligns with welfare-oriented state principles and encourages voluntary mutual aid through civil society institutions. It points to it as reinforcing a multi-layered social justice ethic that places economic fairness within both family, community, and broader political life.

> *The Torah is understood to directly forbid loans in which the recipient is liable to pay a known sum for the use of money. . . . This is known as apportioned interest or ribbit ketsutsa.. . . . Rabbinic Interest is distinct from that (interest) defined*

by the Torah, and so is considered "rabbinic interest." The levying of rabbinic interest is forbidden. (Tamari, 2014, pp. 192–193)

It may imply that the Torah prohibits usury between Jews. However, in Judaism, the interpretation of the Torah or the Oral Torah carries more weight than what is written in the actual Torah, as Judaism is an interpretative tradition (Paldi, 2024). According to Steven D. Fraade, the written Torah is the primary source of Judaism transmitted from God to Prophet Moses (PBUH) on Mt Sinai. However, there were gaps in the Torah that needed explanation. Sages interpreted the Written Torah into an Oral Torah and formulated the Mishnah Gemara (Talmud) and midrash (Fraade 2012, P 32). One Mishnah says, "Moreover Hillel used to say, "A woman may not lend a loaf of bread to her neighbour unless she determines its value in money, lest wheat should rise in price and they are found to be engaging in usury" (Mishnah Bava Metzia 5:9; Sefaria). In Islam, this can be seen as a kind of riba (usury) of excess or *riba al fadl*" (Paldi, 2024).

Human beings, in order to be true people of God, need to come to the undiluted pure sources of instructions with respect to all social and economic matters.

According to Dr. Joseph Isaac Lifshitz, an expert on Jewish philosophy and history, man is encouraged to be a strong creative and responsible person who builds his wealth so that he may take responsibility both for himself and for those around him. The Jewish concept of stewardship of man calls on men to take care of this world because it is given to them as responsible beings. Furthermore, charity is considered a moral duty as opposed to a civil/legal duty. The tradition of giving one-tenth of one's earnings to the poor was derived from the commandment to give one-tenth of one's agricultural yield to the poor in the third and sixth years of every 7-year agricultural cycle (Paldi, 2016)

Based on the above discussion, key common ethics in the three religions are shown in Table 6.

Table 6. Shared and Unique Economic Ethics Across Abrahamic Faiths

Dimension	Islamic Finance	Christian Ethics	Jewish Finance
Justice, Honesty, Community Welfare	Strong emphasis; rooted in Qur'an and Sunnah	Core teachings of the Bible; echoed in Church teachings	Fundamental in Torah and Talmudic laws
Prohibition/Restriction of Interest (Usury)	Completely prohibited (riba)	Historically prohibited; relaxed in modern interpretations	Prohibited among Jews; allowed toward non-Jews in specific contexts
Accountability to God	Financial dealings must align with divine law (Shari'ah)	Stewardship and accountability before God	Ethical business as a divine duty

continued on following page

Table 6. Continued

Dimension	Islamic Finance	Christian Ethics	Jewish Finance
Socially Responsible Investing	Mandatory via moral screening (e.g., excludes alcohol, gambling)	Encouraged in modern social teaching (e.g., ethical funds, ESG)	Expected; includes communal responsibility (Tikkun Olam)
Anti-Exploitation of the Poor/Weak	Lending is charity; profit not allowed on loans	Charity and concern for the marginalized central to ethics	Lending without interest is a mitzvah; oppression strongly condemned

Source: Author's own

While the U.S. Constitution and many other legal systems maintain a separation between religion and state, this arrangement must still guarantee that individual actions do not infringe upon the rights of others - whether persons, nations, vulnerable groups, or the environment. No individual possesses the right to recklessly endanger their life or wealth through hazardous activities or gambling, as such behaviors inevitably create negative externalities that impact society at large.

In addition to safeguarding against rights violations (such as discrimination or harm), the state must actively work to ensure the fulfillment of fundamental human needs. This includes guaranteeing access to adequate nutrition, healthcare, and education for all citizens. These provisions form the bedrock of a just and equitable society.

Table 5 presents a comparative analysis between Abrahamic value-based economic principles and the current global economic paradigm. This comparison serves as a timely reminder for world leaders to thoughtfully integrate these enduring ethical principles - both in practice and spirit - to foster sustainable development and the long-term flourishing of human societies worldwide.

Table 7. Comparing Current Economy with the Abrahamic Value-based Economy

Aspect	Market Economy	Ethical Value-based Economy
Key Focus	Self-interest, speculative gains, deregulation	Divine ethics, justice, social responsibility
Islamic View	Riba, gharar, maiser exploitations	Stewardship, Care/Spending for others (Zakat, Waqf, etc; risk-sharing, ethical trading, prohibition of (market Risk)-free unjust gains; value based exchange system
Christian View	Usury prohibited and greed condemned	Stewardship, neighbor love, care for fellow being, good deeds, quality products and services, fair pricing

continued on following page

Table 7. Continued

Aspect	Market Economy	Ethical Value-based Economy
Jewish View	Ribbit (interest) forbidden	Social Finance, Charity (Zakat, Ushr, waqf), stewardship, ethical business practices
Economic Outcome	Inequality, instability, and unsustainability	Balanced, just, sustainable development, social inclusion

Source: Author's own

MOVING TO ETHICAL ECONOMY AND FINANCE

Ethical principles emanate from unity, equilibrium, freedom, and responsibility (Naqvi, 1981). The divine teaching that all creatures have a single source of creation and that all mankind is united in submission to Him tends to imply that only divine ethics are perfect, leading to uniformity and unity in thinking. Therefore, any acceptable economic system for mankind is that which is directly revealed by the Creator of this universe, who has the sole authority to pronounce what is right and what is wrong for His creatures. Only these principles and philosophy are divinely guided and spiritual. Divine principles relating to the production, consumption, distribution, and exchange/transfer of wealth provide the best remedy for problems facing human beings. The injunctions relating to *Halal* (permissible) and *Haram* (forbidden) lead to ethical boundaries in the production and consumption of goods, businesses and professions. These principles are found in or derived from Quranic verses 4:29, 2:188, 2:275–283, 7:31, and 106:1–4.

God Almighty has granted man with free will. Divine norms guarantee personal freedom to human beings. Because of the free will granted by God, man can decide upon acts and perform them in a set sphere. It is only on the basis of this free will and choice of act that people are rendered accountable for their behavior in this worldly life:

> *The divine will, therefore, acknowledges freedom of action for the individual in a set sphere of life. The liberty is guaranteed and protected unless and until man does not misuse this liberty in damaging the personal liberty of other individuals or harming the collective interests. (Maududi, 1977, p. 62)*

Hence, the minimum requirement in terms of social, business and professional ethics is that my action must not negatively affect any other individual, institutions, society, economy, or the cosmos. The state and the regulators have to ensure this while leaving the belief system or religion for the people according to their discretion.

The all-pervading harmony that is based on equilibrium in the universe should also be reflected in human life and conduct, in both the individual and collective spheres, to usher in social justice and order. Ethical guidance necessitates the responsible use of freedom with in-built discipline so as not to disturb the equilibrium. The free functioning of the markets is emphasized, of course with some principles for discipline, in all revealed religions (Lapin, 2007; Richman, 2007; and Shamsuddeen, 2016), but there should be state vigilance and intervention, if needed, to bring about the redistribution of wealth and resource transfers among various classes and groups in the society (Ayub, 2022; Pp 291-328).

A fair equilibrium must exist among production, consumption, and distribution. Ethical consumer behavior demands moderation and restraint, prioritizing responsibility toward others over unchecked consumerism. This fosters an environment of initiative, human dignity, discipline, and efficiency, while promoting equity, justice, and fair treatment for all in society.

INTEGRATING DIVINE ETHICS INTO FINANCE: AN ABRAHAMIC PERSPECTIVE

Integrating divine ethics into finance is vital and feasible through commitment to human well-being, supported by institutional frameworks, legal recognition, and value-based education. Abrahamic teachings—Islamic, Jewish, and Christian—offer a moral compass beyond profit. Islamic banks avoid riba, gharar, and haram industries (El-Gamal, 2006; Ayub, 2021). Jewish halachic ethics restrict usury and emphasize collective responsibility (Tamari, 1991). Catholic Social Teaching prioritizes human dignity over profit (Pontifical Council, 2004). Table 8 highlights the institutional, legal, and educational frameworks needed to embed these ethics in finance.

Table 8. Institutional and Other Frameworks for Integrating Divine Ethics into Finance: Abrahamic Perspective

Sr. No	Theme	Summary Frameworks
1	Moral Crisis in Finance	Contemporary financial systems often lack ethical direction; divine principles from Abrahamic religions offer a moral foundation to address this issue.
2	Riba-free/Faith-Based Financial Models	Divine discipline-related institutions across Islam, Christianity, and Judaism provide finance models grounded in ethical norms like justice, stewardship, and social welfare
3	Ethical Oversight and Unity	Religious councils and bodies legitimize ethical standards and foster cooperation, promoting universal moral values in economic systems
4	Governance and Faith Synergy	Socially oriented and faith based programs (e.g., CSR, ESG, SRI, microfinance), enhancing financial inclusion and ethical investment.

continued on following page

Table 8. Continued

Sr. No	Theme	Summary Frameworks
5	Legal Accommodation	Divine ethics could be integrated through national laws or dual legal systems, with international institutions offering platforms for broader ethical adoption.
6	Education, orientation and Trainings	Integrating value systems based on Abrahamic economic and finance principles in academic and professional education ensures the formation of morally competent financial leaders.
	Shared Religious Ethics	Abrahamic traditions converge on key principles: prohibition of usury, ethical wealth stewardship, fairness in trade, and care for the poor.
	Barriers and Possibilities	While secular resistance and interpretive differences pose challenges, rising interest in ethical finance and fintech innovation presents major opportunities.
	Vision for the Future	A faith-aligned financial system is achievable through institutional, legal, and educational efforts, aiming for justice and holistic well-being

Source: Author's own.

A just balance in production, consumption, and distribution is essential. Ethical consumer behavior demands moderation and restraint, avoiding insatiable consumption. This fosters an environment of initiative, human dignity, discipline, efficiency, equity, justice, and fairness for all in society. The bases of balance and behavioral discipline are shown in Table 9.

Table: 9. Market Economy vs Beyond-Market Norms in Abrahamic Religions' Core Comparison

Aspect	Market Economy	Beyond-Market Norms (Abrahamic Religions)
Core Principles	Price signals, profit maximization, self-interest, speculation	Justice, equity, moderation, cooperation, social responsibility
Finance Practices	Interest (riba), short-selling, speculative trading	Risk-sharing, asset-backed finance, prohibition of riba, gharar, maisir
Wealth Distribution	Concentrated wealth, inequality, rent-seeking	Redistribution (Zakat, Ushr, Tzedakah), charity, stewardship
Business Ethics	Opacity, unregulated, crisis-prone	Transparency, fair dealings, contractual fulfillment, moderation
Social Impact	Poverty, instability, social exclusion	Inclusion, shared prosperity, community well-being, dignity
Environmental Aspect	Unsustainable growth, resource exploitation	Balance (Mizan), moderation, environmental stewardship
Divine Accountability	Absent (secular, utilitarian)	Present (accountability to God, ethical conduct)

Source: Author's own

EMERGING ISLAMIC FINANCE AND ETHICAL FINANCE

In the modern financial markets, where people are increasingly calling for high levels of ethical behavior on the part of institutions, the Islamic banking movement is well placed to prosper as a "principled" alternative (Riaz et al., 2017). McRorie (2018) discussed the ethical prohibition of usury in Christianity and Islam and how the Christian understanding of usury evolved from any profit returned on a loan to merely exploitative lending. She compared the historical transformation of the prohibition of usury in Christianity and the prohibited forms of return in Islam as being ribā: "Islamic scholars accordingly affirm the importance of wealth being used for the 'real economy'—that is, for the satisfaction of concrete human needs, and for the benefit of society as a whole," she wrote (p. 110). She also discussed how Islamic finance, as it has evolved, has failed in realizing its stated objectives.

The convergence between Islamic and conventional finance practices and products is evidence of the social failure of the Islamic banking and finance industry, which is oriented toward the goals of conventional banking more than toward those of the Islamic moral economy (Asutay, 2012, p. 100; see also Asutay (2013) and McRorie (2018). This failure has been caused by the "legalistic–rational method applied by the Shari'ah scholars" that "ignores the substance (cf. Asutay, 2012, pp. 107–108). Dusuki (2010) argued that too much attention to form over substance reduces Islamic banks to "practitioners of semantics" (p. 114). According to Feisal Khan (Khan, 2010), "current Islamic banking and finance (IBF) practice conforms in almost all key respects to the conventional banking norm, and IBF practice does not resemble what its advocates say IBF is supposed to be" (p. 621).

Abrahamic religions shape ethical finance through shared principles of moral integrity, social justice, and economic fairness. They emphasize compassion, transparency, and societal welfare over profit, historically opposing usury and promoting equitable wealth distribution. Today, faith-based investment funds reflect these values globally.

In Islam, *maqasid al-shariah* (Shariah's higher purposes) guide finance, prioritizing justice, welfare, and risk-based returns. Institutions follow standards like those of AAOIFI to ensure compliance. The concept of *spiritual capitalism* integrates Abrahamic ethics into modern finance, advocating stakeholder welfare and compassionate economics.

ETHICS-BASED NEW PROTOCOL AND COMMITMENTS NEEDED FOR THE GLOBAL ECONOMY

At Bretton Woods, Keynes proposed a global currency managed by an international agency, but the U.S., as the post-WWII superpower, rejected this in favor of dollar dominance to secure seigniorage. To fund the Vietnam War and boost its economy, the U.S. over-issued dollars beyond its gold reserves, exploiting other nations that lacked the power to reclaim their gold. The World Bank and IMF were created post-WWII to promote global integration and prevent conflict, yet U.S. war policies have repeatedly destabilized the world economy. Even the UN, meant to foster peace, has been rendered ineffective by U.S. actions.

The Bretton Woods system, established in 1945 by 44 nations, was dismantled when the U.S. abandoned dollar-gold convertibility. Since then, U.S. seigniorage privileges have increasingly destabilized global finance. The failure of the Washington Consensus—exposed by the Global Financial Crisis (GFC)—validated the wisdom of South Asian nations in imposing capital controls during the 1997–98 crisis, a stance supported by economists like Paul Krugman and Joseph Stiglitz. Critics of the IMF warned that Consensus policies would trigger recessions, with Stiglitz (2002) highlighting how sharp interest rate hikes worsened crises. Today, it is widely acknowledged that IMF structural adjustment programs, forcing austerity, privatization, and deregulation, devastated social policies and poverty levels (Lopes, 2012). In Africa and Latin America, the first wave of reforms slashed public spending, imposed fees on healthcare and education, and removed trade protections, fueling unemployment, deepening poverty, and exacerbating inequality.

REFORMING GLOBAL FINANCE: A PATH TOWARD FAIRNESS AND STABILITY

The world urgently needs a new financial protocol to prevent any nation from exploiting seigniorage privileges at others' expense. Surprisingly, the U.S. threat—under President Trump—to withdraw from the IMF and World Bank (Reuters, 2025) could catalyze much-needed reform. While short-term disruptions may occur due to America's outsized influence (holding 16.5% of voting shares, per IMF and World Bank, 2024), this exit could create space for a more equitable system. Major economies—including China, Japan, Russia, the EU, Australia, New Zealand, and Middle Eastern and OIC nations—could collectively assume greater capital contributions and decision-making power. This shift would realign the IMF's structure with its original 1944 vision: an institution fostering global harmony rather than dominance. Crucially, a rebalanced IMF could introduce a new international reserve currency, displacing the dollar's hegemony in global payments. Regional reserve currencies might also emerge, creating a more decentralized and resilient monetary framework.

By redistributing power, the world can dismantle the destabilizing imbalances of today and build a fairer financial future.

Regarding Economics as a system of political economy, positive economics is under severe criticism even by many senior economists. Economics has been erroneously considered like physics to predict the economic behavior of humans and market outcomes. As Piketty (2014, 2020) demonstrates, addressing inequality demands more than studying poverty or class dynamics; it requires scrutinizing the ultra-wealthy—their sources of wealth and its societal legitimacy. Piketty concedes that concentrations of wealth (if not of income) are remarkably resilient in the face of political efforts to challenge them. The 'unearned' wealth grows at a faster rate than income earned ethically. Despite political attempts to redistribute resources, Piketty (2020) acknowledges that wealth concentrations exhibit striking resilience, underscoring systemic flaws in our economic paradigms.

Nobel laureate economist Angus Deaton, who developed foundations for micro-economics and tools for engaging in micro-founded analysis in mathematical ways, recently confessed that the realities of life have compelled him to change his mind. Despite humanity's serious challenges, economists stopped thinking about ethics and human well-being, focusing on efficiency without equity. Their recommendations become little more than a license for plunder, he lamented in the Article published in the IMF magazine in March 2024:

Our emphasis on the virtues of free, competitive markets and exogenous technical change can distract us from the importance of power in setting prices and wages, in choosing the direction of technical change, and in influencing politics to change the rules of the game. (Deaton, 2024)

The lack of proper transparency, leading to a web of secret deals and hidden financial back doors, has become the basis for offshore banking and shadow financial systems. But now even some financial giants, built on corruption, are crumbling under the weight of their unethical activities and the misdeeds of the top management. Any single instance of bankruptcy could trigger a domino effect across the world economy. The solution requires discipline-oriented systems of economy and finance.

"Economic growth must deliver inclusive prosperity. According to the International Labor Organization (ILO) 2024 World Employment Report, labor's share of income has steadily eroded, falling to 52.3% in 2022 and stagnating through 2024 - a 1.6 percentage point decline over twenty years despite rising productivity. While this shift appears numerically small, it translates to a staggering $2.4 trillion annual shortfall in worker compensation relative to 2004 levels. The crisis extends beyond wages, millions of youth remain disengaged from employment

and education. The report cautions that without proactive policies to distribute technology's gains equitably, AI advancements may exacerbate inequality and jeopardize Sustainable Development Goals (ILO, 2024, p.2).

Despite the demonstrable failures of the liberal international order since the 1990s, neoliberal ideology continues to dominate global policymaking and public discourse (Mearsheimer, 2019). By this mistaken narrative - less regulation and more '***animal spirits***' capitalism produces not only greater prosperity (for a few) but more freedom for individuals and the corporates from the discipline directed by nature. The flawed paradigm and economic model have created an unsustainable system where wealth concentrates among elites who exploit offshore mechanisms to preserve class privilege, with trillions circulating annually through tax havens. Humanity must fundamentally reform this system to achieve true stability and shared prosperity.

NORMATIVE VALUES AND BELIEF SYSTEMS IN ECONOMY, BUSINESS, AND FINANCE

There is an intricate interplay between Abrahamic economic philosophy and the functioning of business and finance rooted in the belief system and divine legal principles. Faith based on the revealed vision is the best security in all respects and has been inspiring human beings at all times. These principles enable the peaceful coexistence of human societies with the spirit of cooperative risk sharing and guide the creation of risk–reward–based investment and financial instruments that offer an ethical paradigm for economic transactions.

Ethical investment and risk-sharing models foster ethical conduct, economic justice, and financial inclusivity, leading to social inclusion. They provide Islamic economic rationality in terms of asset-backed and equity-based investments, in which the division of economic resources is regulated by a criterion of risk–reward and sharing principles and participation in trading and business activities, thus laying the foundation for an alternative model of market economy derived from the Islamic view of economic justice.

Hassan et al. (2023) examine the implications of Basel III capital and liquidity requirements for Islamic banks, which operate within the ethical framework of Sharia-compliant finance. Their analysis underscores the inherent challenges in aligning Basel III's risk-weighted asset (RWA) methodology with the profit-and-loss sharing (PLS) models fundamental to Islamic finance. In response to these structural mismatches, the authors propose targeted modifications to the Basel III framework to enhance its compatibility with the principles of ethical finance.

Ethical and Islamic financial institutions, characterized by their emphasis on social responsibility and adherence to Sharia norms, face considerable challenges under Basel III's globally standardized regulatory architecture. A particular concern lies in the adaptation of liquidity instruments to formats that comply with Sharia requirements. Although the enhanced capital adequacy and liquidity coverage standards under Basel III contribute to broader financial stability, they may simultaneously constrain the financing capacity of institutions guided by ethical principles.

Rizwan and Khan (2015) explore the operational implications of the Basel III liquidity standards—specifically the Liquidity Coverage Ratio (LCR) and Net Stable Funding Ratio (NSFR)—for Islamic banks. Their findings reveal a trade-off between achieving greater financial resilience and the potential reduction in the lending capacity of Sharia-compliant institutions.

Complementing this, Azeem, Marsap, and Özari (2015) conduct an empirical analysis using data from Islamic banks in Pakistan to evaluate the effects of Basel III capital and liquidity ratios. Their results indicate that while stronger liquidity metrics reduce the probability of financial distress, increased capital requirements can limit credit expansion and profitability. These findings collectively underscore the need to tailor the Basel III framework to the distinct operational and ethical parameters of Islamic finance—an approach increasingly advocated by standards-setting institutions such as the Islamic Financial Services Board (IFSB).

The growing influence of behavioral economics, particularly since the adoption of the SDGs, marks a significant shift in economic thought. This evolving field increasingly underpins production, distribution, and consumption patterns globally. It reflects a transition from the traditional "Economic Man" of positive economic theory to a more normative, value-based framework that incorporates ethical considerations and their implications for resource use and stakeholder impacts, including the environment.

SOME SUCCESSFUL MODELS OF ABRAHAMIC FINANCE IN PRACTICE

Islamic finance is progressing in the global economy while operating based on some successful models of Abrahamic /ethical finance. These models are particularly concentrating on sukuk issuance for infrastructure and sustainability-related projects. Abrahamic finance, particularly such expression, offers asset-backed, risk-sharing, and ethically grounded financial models that align economic activity with social justice, sustainability, and faith-based values. The following case studies highlight diverse applications across sovereign, private, and hybrid financing structures.

1. Sukuk-Based Infrastructure Projects
   a) UK Sovereign Sukuk (2014, 2021)

The United Kingdom became the first non-Muslim country to issue sovereign sukuk, employing an Ijara (lease-based) structure. These issuances supported infrastructure investment and attracted Sharia-compliant funds globally, demonstrating the viability of Islamic finance within Western legal frameworks (HM Treasury, 2021).

b) DanaInfra Sukuk – Malaysia

Malaysia's DanaInfra Nasional Berhad issued multiple sukuk to fund the Mass Rapid Transit (MRT) system, structured under Murabaha and Wakalah. Retail participation through DanaInfra Retail Sukuk promoted financial inclusion and democratized infrastructure investment (IFSB, 2015).

c) Sustainable sukuk issuances – Saudi Arabia

Saudi Arabia has emerged as the leader in sustainable sukuk issuances in the GCC area for financing its sustainable power projects. From 2015 through mid-2024, Saudi Arabian entities issued the largest cumulative amount of sustainable sukuk, representing 33% of total volumes, followed by Malaysia and UAE with 21% each. (ZAWYA, September 25, 2024).

d) Green Sukuk – Indonesia

Indonesia's government launched Green Sukuk to fund roads, schools, and climate-resilient housing using Ijara and Wakalah structures. These initiatives merged Islamic finance with environmental sustainability, resonating strongly with Abrahamic ethics of stewardship and justice (Republic of Indonesia, 2020).

2. Faith-Based Investment Funds and Institutions
   a) Amana Mutual Funds Trust – USA

Operating under Islamic principles, Amana avoids interest-based instruments, alcohol, gambling, and unethical industries. Its Sharia-compliant equity screening mirrors ethical filters used in Christian and Jewish values-based investing (Saturna Capital, 2023).

b) Triodos Bank – Netherlands

Inspired by Christian ethical values, Triodos finances only projects with social or environmental benefit—such as renewable energy and social housing. Its strict transparency and impact-oriented model exemplifies faith-aligned ethical banking (Triodos Bank, 2023).

c) JLens Network – USA

Rooted in Jewish ethical teachings, JLens promotes ESG investing with a faith lens. It engages publicly listed companies on issues such as human rights, sustainability, and ethical governance, integrating Jewish values into capital markets (JLens, 2022).

3. Public-Private Partnerships under Islamic Finance
   a) IsDB Infrastructure Projects

The Islamic Development Bank employs instruments like Sukuk, Istisna‘, and Mudarabah to finance infrastructure in developing countries. Its work in Sudan, Egypt, and Kazakhstan promotes development without recourse to interest-based debt, aligning with Islamic and broader Abrahamic principles (IsDB, 2022).

b) Bilkent Health PPP – Turkey

This healthcare mega-project was financed through Ijara sukuk, enabling private Islamic capital to support public health infrastructure in Ankara. The partnership model showcased the adaptability of Islamic finance in modern PPP frameworks (World Bank, 2018).

It may be noted that the above cases pertain to specific aspects of ethical/social finance like i) Asset-Backed, Riba-Free Instruments like sukuk or equity are widely and effectively used to finance large-scale public goods; ii) Community Involvement enabling local ownership and shared benefits; iii) Hybrid Financing Layers (equity + trade culminating into loans + businesscontracts) foster flexibility and funding efficiency, and finally Social & Environmental Outcomes are measurable and central—ranging from CO_2 reduction to expanded public transit.

Of course, achieving the SDGs at national and global levels requires fostering *behavioral entrepreneurship*—a socially driven approach emphasizing shared resources and sustainable outcomes. Developed nations must support poorer economies in breaking the cycles of debt, poverty, and unemployment. As Goldin (2025) highlights, “today’s rich countries owe much of their success to the contributions of migrant workers,” whose advanced skills, particularly in emerging technologies, can enhance peaceful and sustainable development. Opportunity-driven entrepreneurs, in particular, contribute positively to the economic, social, and environmental pillars of sustainability. Dhahri et al. (2021) find that while *opportunity entrepreneurship* supports all three dimensions, *necessity entrepreneurship* may adversely affect environmental sustainability.

REINTRODUCING BASIC TRUST AND GLOBAL ETHICS

The reintroduction of basic trust, which is necessary for ethical behavior in all respects, into the system in which global managers operate is the common goal of the Humanistic Management Network (2005) and the Global Ethic Project (Keir, 2016). The phenomenon of moral bankruptcy in global business and finance reveals a prior crisis of acceptable and humane business and social ethics, including widespread denial of the very existence and even desirability of universal values (Keir, 2016).

The Global Ethic Project, which has been searching for many years for an ethical consensus for society while at the same time offering a basis for understanding and cooperation among religions, must ensure that ethics are founded on the divine source of knowledge. Any approach to ethics that is not informed by morality and faith can lose its direction and purpose and can even become harmful to human welfare (Kamali, 2018).

The cohesion of society, along with the pursuit of global peace and justice, fundamentally depends on a shared set of ethical values and standards. These universal principles can be rediscovered in the enduring moral teachings of the world's major religions as well as in the traditions of humanistic philosophy. Swiss Catholic theologian Hans Küng (2004) underscores that, despite theological and ritual differences, the world's religions converge on a core set of ethical norms. This common moral ground forms the basis of a *global ethic*—a framework essential for fostering peaceful coexistence and meaningful cooperation among diverse cultures and belief systems. Küng argues that the sustainability of any human society is inconceivable without such a global ethical foundation.

Human beings must collectively cultivate and uphold moral values. Choosing to do what is right, even when others do not, is essential for several compelling reasons. First, we instinctively recognize that acting ethically aligns us with our highest potential, allowing us to become the best version of ourselves—individuals we can genuinely respect and take pride in. Second, ethical conduct appears to be a necessary condition for the continued survival of humanity on Earth. Third, doing the right thing fosters trust, cooperation, and mutual support, all of which are vital for personal and collective well-being (Inner Peace Fellowship, n.d.).

Human intellect, while remarkable, remains inherently limited and incapable of fully grasping or predicting the long-term consequences or broader implications of human actions, practices, or traditions. As such, the behavioral norms and customs that govern social and economic interactions cannot automatically be regarded as universal ethical standards or as inherently aligned with the well-being of all living beings and the sustainability of life. History offers compelling examples: colonialism, now widely condemned, was once embraced by much of the so-called civilized world. Similarly, slavery remained an integral component of global economic systems until the 19th century, despite earlier efforts to reform the institution. Notably, Islam initiated gradual reforms in the early 7th century, discouraging slavery and promoting measures aimed at its eventual abolition. Nevertheless, formal prohibition was only achieved many centuries later in both Western and Muslim societies.

Man-made ethical systems—inevitably shaped by human limitations and external influences—lack the universality, purity, and comprehensive wisdom necessary to serve as ideal frameworks for human conduct. Only the Creator of the Universe possesses perfect knowledge of what is truly beneficial for His creation, including humanity. A striking historical illustration lies in the figure of ʿAmr ibn Hishām, originally known among the Quraysh as *Abū al- akam* ("Father of Wisdom"). Despite his intellectual stature, history remembers him as *Abū Jahl* ("Father of Ignorance")—a symbolic reminder of the limits of human judgment when divorced from divine guidance. This underscores the argument that genuine ethical and normative frameworks must be derived from original divine sources—the revealed guidance of the Creator—rather than from fallible human reasoning alone.

The final revealed Book of God—the Qur'an—affirms that the upright and perfect path for humanity is rooted in the faith of Abraham: *"Indeed, my Lord has guided me to a straight path—a perfect way—the faith of Abraham, upright and not among those who associate others with God"* (Qur'an 6:161). The ethical framework established by this divine source emphasizes moral responsibility, promising a tenfold reward for good deeds and just recompense for wrong actions: *"Whoever comes with a good deed will be rewarded tenfold, and whoever comes with an evil deed will be repaid only with its equivalent—and none will be wronged"* (Qur'an 6:160). Central to this framework is the concept of individual accountability before the Creator: *"No one will bear the burden of another; every soul will receive only what it has earned. Then to your Lord is your return"* (Qur'an 6:164). This comprehensive and individualized system of moral responsibility must serve as the foundation for any value system aimed at ensuring sustainability, collective well-being in this life, and ultimate success in the hereafter.

A similar emphasis on faith and divine accountability is present in Christian theology. Martin Luther (1483–1546), the influential priest and theologian, famously declared: *"Faith is living, daring confidence in God's grace, so sure and certain that a man could stake his life on it a thousand times"* (Luther, 2003, p. 17). More recently, Jackie Hill Perry (2018), a contemporary Christian author and convert, echoed this sentiment, writing: *"Every single thing He has ever or will ever say is true. The simplicity of faith is this: taking God's words for it"* (p. 75).

> *"We are here today because our ancestors learned that survival depended on every person doing the right thing and having each other's back. Today our survival still depends on that, as do our inner peace and sense of well-being". "Our actions change our reality. Our intentions matter. Most people believe that their actions have consequences but don't think through the implications of that belief. But Steve did. He believed, as I do, that it is precisely by acting on our intentions and staying true to our values that we change the world." [Ed Catmull]*

These Christian perspectives resonate with the Islamic emphasis on divine guidance and personal moral responsibility, underscoring the shared ethical foundations of Abrahamic faiths.

HOW HAS THE PREVAILING PARADIGM CORRUPTED PROFESSIONAL AND BUSINESS NORMS?

The dominant global economic paradigm, fundamentally rooted in debt, personal, household, corporate, or public, has profoundly distorted professional and business ethics. Public debt, in particular, is closely tied to future taxation, aligning with the Ricardian Equivalence Theorem, postulated by David Ricardo over two centuries ago (Seater, 1993). This theorem suggests that government efforts to stimulate economic growth through debt-financed spending are ultimately ineffective, as rational economic agents anticipate future tax liabilities to repay the debt with interest. This perspective challenges the Keynesian assertion that deficit spending can sustainably boost economic performance.

In the developing world, home to approximately 80% of the global population, persistent poverty and underdevelopment reflect the failures of the current debt-driven capitalist system. This model has failed to stimulate robust growth in the real economy, i.e., the production and equitable distribution of goods and services. Instead, it has contributed to entrenched socioeconomic disparities. International financial interventions, particularly those from the IMF, often exacerbate these challenges. Rather than offering lasting solutions, IMF programs frequently increase the debt burden of recipient nations. The application of fines and surcharges reinforces dependency without ensuring repayment or safeguarding the Fund's financial stability.

The IMF's surcharge policy, which imposes additional fees on countries exceeding certain borrowing thresholds in terms of size or duration, is particularly detrimental. This approach appears counterproductive, especially if the Fund's stated mission is to provide counter-cyclical support and promote global financial stability.

In 2020, 10 countries were paying these fees to the IMF; by 2023, with the COVID-19 shock, the Ukraine war, and rising interest rates, that number had risen to 22. . . . . The IMF's basic rate increased from under 1% to close to 5%, raising the total lending rate for those paying surcharges to as much as 7.8%. . . . It is time to end the surcharges. (Stiglitz et al., 2024)

As noted by Stiglitz et al. (2024), penalizing nations such as Ukraine, ravaged by war, or Pakistan, a lower-middle-income country devastated by catastrophic floods that submerged a third of its territory, stands in stark contradiction to the IMF's professed goals. Excessively high tax rates in low-income countries are largely a consequence of the unsustainable debt burdens they carry, debts that are effectively unpayable. For these nations to reduce tax pressures and make meaningful progress toward eradicating hunger, in line with the SDGs, advanced economies must consider comprehensive debt relief or cancellation initiatives.

GEOPOLITICAL DECEPTION, ETHICAL EROSION, AND THE NEED FOR DIVINE MORAL FOUNDATIONS

Unethical geopolitical actions have significantly destabilized the global economy, leading to the tragic loss of millions of lives and the misallocation of vast financial resources—resources that could have otherwise been directed toward human development and welfare. David Ray Griffin (2006) argued that the 9/11 attacks were not merely a terrorist act, but a calculated deception designed to consolidate imperial power both domestically and internationally. He maintained that the official narrative was fraught with inconsistencies and that the subsequent "war on terror" was largely a fabricated pretext for advancing hegemonic interests. The invasions of Iraq and Afghanistan, he contended, lacked ethical justification and violated fundamental principles of trust and justice. The devastating consequences of these actions were borne disproportionately by the people of the Middle East, Afghanistan, Pakistan, and several other regions, inflicting profound human suffering.

As noted by CNN anchor Christiane Amanpour, the ongoing genocide in Gaza/Palestine echoes the atrocities of the Bosnian genocide in the 1990s—acts of killing, siege, rape, starvation, and concentration camps that persisted for four years while the global community, particularly Europe, remained passive. Despite being a twentieth-century conflict, it was waged with medieval brutality (Bellamy, 1996; *The Independent*, July 22, 1996). Even the UN Secretary-General at the time, Boutros Boutros-Ghali, was seen as siding with the aggressors. This failure to act set a dangerous precedent, enabling further crimes against humanity, as now witnessed in Gaza.

Considering such manipulation and moral relativism, the legitimacy of any injunction, law, or policy must ultimately rest upon divine revelation, a universal source of ethical guidance. One striking example is the prohibition of *riba;* the charging of interest or seeking a risk-free return on capital—which is condemned in all major religious traditions. However, its reinterpretation in the West, distinguishing between "usury" and "interest" and legitimizing the latter, laid the foundation for systemic injustice, economic instability, and moral decay. This rationalization has contributed to the widening divide between the wealthy and the poor and has exposed the fragility of the global financial system.

A similar pattern is observed in the acceptance of practices like short selling and gambling, which, although traditionally prohibited, have been normalized through a utilitarian legal framework devoid of ethical substance. Modern business law often accommodates such activities under the guise of market efficiency, sidelining deeper moral considerations. In such an environment, even criminal groups may operate under self-defined ethical codes. But the critical question remains: who holds the authority to determine right from wrong?

Only a divine and universal moral framework can offer enduring standards for what is truly just or unjust, transcending time, geography, and self-interest. Therefore, genuine business and professional ethics must be grounded in values revealed through divine sources, which alone can ensure justice, integrity, and sustainability in human affairs.

REDEFINING THE RIGHTS AS PER DIVINE INSTRUCTIONS

God is the sole Creator, the Actor par excellence, while the human being assumes the role of a performer—an agent acting under His divine will. Within this framework of divinely established agency, it is God's rule (*ukm*) that grants legitimacy to human action. In this sense, justice (*adl*) is conceptualized in the Qur'anic framework as an essential component of rights (*aqq*), emphasizing that rights are inherently linked to duties. The ethical identity of financial systems cannot be fully understood without acknowledging the sovereignty of God's will and the corresponding moral responsibility of human beings to act in accordance with divine guidance.

Poverty, often rooted as much in mindset as in material deprivation, can be addressed by transforming collective thought. A transition from an extractive, linear economic model to a circular and inclusive economy holds significant potential for social transformation. Shifting the perspectives of financial institutions, businesses, and society at large towards values of sustainability and stewardship can enhance business ethics and reinforce social responsibility. Entrepreneurs guided by a forward-looking mindset grounded in preservation and equity can contribute profoundly to societal well-being.

Islamic finance is unique in its explicit assertion of religious law in the economic sphere—an area where secularism typically dominates. As Vogel and Hayes (1998) observe, it "represents an assertion of religious law in the area of commercial life, where secularism rules almost unquestioned throughout the rest of the world" (p. 19). This framework includes well-defined principles governing property rights. Ownership in Islamic thought entails both rights and responsibilities, with the imperative not to harm others or the environment. This is encapsulated in the well-known Prophetic tradition: *"Lā arar wa lā irār"*—"There should be neither harming nor reciprocating harm." This principle serves as an evaluative criterion for the moral and legal legitimacy of actions, particularly concerning the physical and environmental domains.

Unlike capitalist models that often treat property as a commodity to be acquired and defended in competitive markets, Islamic property rights are envisioned as moral entitlements distributed in accordance with divine justice (Cattelan, 2016). They are designed to support cooperation, economic inclusion, and social welfare, rather than individual accumulation and systemic stratification.

Professor Jamel Akbar (Akbar, 2023) contends that prevailing capitalist economic and political systems are structurally incapable of fostering sustainable environments. According to him, the dominant mode of property rights leads to regulation-heavy bureaucracies, monopolies, and deepening socio-economic divides. By contrast, the Islamic model advocates for property rights based on principles of justice, equity, and transparency. These rights serve as mechanisms for empowering individuals with access to resources, enabling economic participation without state hindrance, provided their actions do not cause harm to others or the environment. This model thus promotes a form of economic activity that minimizes stratification, monopoly, poverty, and environmental degradation.

This approach offers a compelling solution to the "tragedy of the commons"—a well-documented phenomenon in behavioral economics and ecology. When individuals exploit shared resources in the absence of ethical norms or communal regulation, collective assets are depleted (Hardin, 1968). This occurs when short-term individual utility is prioritized over long-term collective sustainability. Addressing this issue requires a normative system that can guide both consumer behavior and corporate decision-making, one grounded in divine ethics and a commitment to social and environmental responsibility.

I now address the serious issue of cultural values versus the *uquq* available to all as per the divine law. Akbar (2023) suggests dividing between peoples' customs, ethnic origin, geographical conditions, etc. which are often changing as variables on the one hand, and the residents' decisions and actions stemming from their rights which is always influenced, directed and limited by *uquq* on the other. Of course, this division is quite confusing for many scholars, especially Orientalists.

Thus, hierarchy of ethical economic principles as per Abrahamic religions can be shown as per the Flow Diagram in Box 1.

Box 1. Pyramid– Hierarchy of Ethical Economic Norms of Abrahamic Religions

Divine Source of Guidance

↕

Stewardship & Individual Accountability to Almighty God

↓

Justice & Natural Balance (Mizan)

↓

Prohibition of Exploitative Practices

↓

Market and Beyond Market Norms, Fair Dealing, Social Responsibility

↓

Risk-Reward-sharing based on value addition & Asset-Backed Finance

↓

Charity & Redistribution for shared welfare (Zakat, Awqaf/ Foundations, Tzedakah)

↓

Efficiency with Equity & Social Justice, Need Fulfillment and Sustainability

Source: Author's own

Some critical social scientists—particularly in the West—distinguish between human emotions and the so-called "animal spirits" when conceptualizing rights and freedoms. In *The Road to Freedom: Economics and the Good Society*, Joseph E. Stiglitz (2024, Chapter 1) raises fundamental questions about the nature and distribution of freedom: "Whose freedom are we—should we be—thinking about? What happens when one person's freedom comes at the expense of another's? Should the freedom of corporations be allowed to impinge upon those of individuals in the ways they now do?" Stiglitz challenges the dominant neoliberal narrative that equates unregulated markets with freedom and prosperity. Instead, he argues that such markets often undermine economic opportunity for the majority while concentrating wealth in the hands of a few, both within and across nations. Reclaiming the discourse of freedom from the political right, Stiglitz advocates for a reimagined economic and social order oriented toward genuine human flourishing. *The Road to Freedom* thus presents a compelling critique of existing economic structures and offers a roadmap for achieving a more equitable and humane society through democratic and inclusive reforms.

Cattelan (2016) employs the metaphor of a scale to contrast the foundational perspectives of Western capitalism and Islamic finance on justice and economic exchange. He explains that while Western economic thought focuses primarily on the pans of the scale and the material contents they hold, Islamic finance emphasizes the central balancing pivot, representing equilibrium, justice, and moral anchoring (p. 19). Within the Islamic framework, the concept of property rights is closely tied to the notion of *haqq*, a term that encompasses "truth," "right," and "reality," thereby imbuing rights with a tangible, substantive dimension.

Accordingly, Islamic financial transactions must be rooted in tangible realities—whether the good or service being traded currently exists (as in cash or credit sales of known items) or will be produced in the future (as in forward contracts like *salam*). While parties to a contract are free to negotiate terms, the outcomes of such exchanges are constrained by the Shariah, which ensures alignment with the substantive nature of *haqq*. This framework disallows the trading of purely nominal or abstract financial values unlinked to real assets, as such practices often involve *gharar* (excessive uncertainty) or *maysir* (speculation or gambling)—elements that disrupt the equilibrium at the heart of Islamic economic justice (Cattelan, 2016, p. 19).

Cattelan concludes that the inherent pluralism and ethical grounding of Islamic finance present a valuable model for renewing global capitalism. By fostering a market culture based on cooperation, equitable resource distribution, and mutual social welfare, Islamic finance offers innovative and morally grounded alternatives to the current dominant economic paradigm.

In the realm of macroeconomics, Paul Romer, the 2018 Nobel laureate in economics, offered a stark critique of the discipline's current state. Romer (2016) argued that macroeconomic modeling has regressed significantly, stating that "we are now back to square one" (p. 20). He criticized the reliance on implausible assumptions that lead to "absurd policy conclusions," asserting that the methodologies and outcomes of much of modern macroeconomic research have deteriorated to the extent that they can no longer be considered scientific inquiry (pp. 2, 18–20). According to Romer, contemporary models have become increasingly detached from real-world economic behavior and have failed to offer meaningful insights for policy formulation or understanding macroeconomic dynamics. He called on macroeconomists to acknowledge the depth of the discipline's methodological crisis and to abandon the long-standing pursuit of the so-called sacred simultaneous equation model. Instead, he advocated for a shift toward empirical methods akin to those used in the medical sciences, approaches grounded in observable outcomes and practical relevance, which may offer a more reliable foundation for economic analysis and policy development.

A truly dependable foundation for socio-economic life lies in the ethical principles derived from Abrahamic values. The key characteristics of an economic and financial system rooted in these values are outlined in Table 10.

Table 10. Ethical Features of an Economic and Financial Order

Based on Abrahamic Principles	
Aspect	Key characteristics /Details
1. Ethical Foundations	- Based on divine guidance from Abrahamic religions - Justice, equity, moderation, and cooperation - Accountability to God for all actions at all levels
2. Financial Principles	- Ban on interest (riba), short selling, and gambling - Emphasis on asset-backed, risk-sharing finance - Real economy linkage essential
3. Wealth Distribution	- Mandatory and voluntary charity (Sadaqat, Tzedakah) - Redistribution mechanisms for poverty eradication and inclusion - No rent-seeking behavior
4. Human Behavior Norms	- Move from Homo Economicus to cooperative behavior - Emphasize altruism, community welfare, and restraint - Encourage ethical consumerism
5. Global Governance Reform	- Democratization of IMF/World Bank ("one country, one vote") - Replace US dollar hegemony with global currency - Equitable power sharing among nations
6. Environmental Responsibility	- Balance (Mizan) and stewardship of nature - Avoid overconsumption, waste (Israaf, Tabzeer) - Support sustainable, circular economies
7. Monetary Policy Reform	- End interest-based credit creation - Promote riba-free financing for poor/entrepreneurs - Prevent credit use for speculation or luxury consumption
8. Business Ethics	- Transparency, fairness, contract fulfillment - No exploitation or fraudulent practices - Responsible corporate conduct aligned with social values
9. Economic Rights & Duties	- Rights tied to duties and justice (Adl, Haqq) - Resources use must not harm others or the environment - Encourage distributive justice and legal equity
10. Global Ethics & Trust	- Reintroduce Basic Trust in global systems - Build shared ethical values rooted in divine law - Enable interfaith cooperation and inclusive economic development

Source Author's Own.

The adoption of Abrahamic values across all levels of political economy, business, finance, and society necessitates a paradigm shift toward an ethics- and values-based framework that promotes efficiency alongside equity, justice, and sustainability, as shown in Diagram 2.

HARNESSING THE EMERGING TECHNOLOGY-CUM-AI FOR ETHICAL STANDARDS

Many authors increasingly suggest embedding ethics in economic analysis, policymaking and business, and most recently, in emerging technology necessarily including the AI. The ethics have to be applied to all activities including the conduct of business transactions, distribution of income/wealth, and more generally, the care for and treatment of others as business / corporate leaders. Further, ethical and socially responsible behavior should be constantly ensured, for example, that consumers do not pay inflated prices for services rendered (Wilson, 2000). Business ethics reflect the moral principles and standards that everyone must follow in every aspect of their lives.

Figure 1. The Transition to an Ethics- and Values-Driven Framework

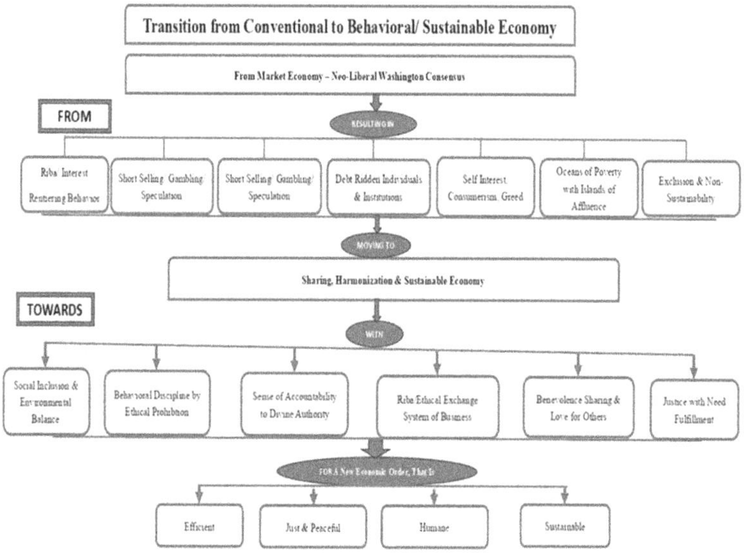

Source: Author's own

LEVERAGING EMERGING TECHNOLOGIES AND AI FOR ETHICAL GOVERNANCE

Ethical principles must guide all human endeavors, from business transactions and wealth distribution to interpersonal conduct in corporate leadership. Rodney Wilson (1997, Chapters 1–3) examines how Islamic economic thought advocates for fair pricing and condemns exploitative practices, while also exploring Christian and Jewish perspectives on economic ethics, emphasizing fairness and accountability.

Andrew Wilson (2000) underscores the necessity of embedding ethical considerations into business strategies to align with societal expectations and foster community well-being. Ethical conduct ensures, for instance, that consumers are not subjected to unjust pricing. Business ethics, as an extension of universal moral principles, must permeate every aspect of professional and personal life.

As previously discussed, all systems, including socio-economic structures, must adhere to natural laws. Artificial Intelligence (AI), as the latest technological advancement, must also operate within these foundational principles to optimize functionality and benefit humanity.

While AI and artificial general intelligence (AGI) hold transformative potential, their unchecked advancement risks exacerbating societal disparities. Daron Acemoglu (2024), Nobel laureate in economics and co-author of *Why Nations Fail*, warns:

> *"Judging by the current trajectory of the tech industry, we risk facing the worst possible outcome: AI failing to deliver transformative benefits while displacing workers, spreading misinformation, and enabling manipulation. Developers often exaggerate breakthroughs to attract investment, further distorting expectations."*

Predictive and generative AI excel at processing vast datasets to identify patterns. However, their application must prioritize augmenting human capabilities rather than mere automation. Acemoglu (2024) argues:

> *"If AI is deployed primarily for automation, it will eliminate jobs. But if it enhances workers' decision-making with better information, it will increase their value and earnings. The key lies in training individuals to collaborate effectively with AI."*

Chaudhary (2024) offers a valuable Islamic perspective on shaping the future of AI, one that prioritizes public interest over profit or progress. He emphasizes *taw īd* (divine unity) as a theological anchor, shaping a framework where AI can't assume divine attributes—it operates strictly within the human-created order. He applies core Islamic principles including *falah* (well-being), *ma la a* (public interest), *adl* (justice), *rahmah* (compassion), *ihsan* (benevolence), and *amanah* (trust/accountability), to evaluate AI's moral legitimacy. He also outlines the monotheistic teachings to identify related themes in AI and to address nuances of Islamic belief vis-à-vis the other Abrahamic traditions in consideration of AI. Chaudhary critiques what he calls '*ethics theatre*' by corporations and suggests rejecting superficial corporatized "ethics theatre", and maintaining ethical sovereignty, and engaging deeply with theology and jurisprudence to shape AI's place in faith's moral universe.

Dorobantu (2024) frames AI as suitable "test cases" for theological claims, like the nature of incarnation, divine infinity, theodicy, even demonic intelligence. He contends that Christian theology must take AI seriously as both a theological challenge and a tool. AI prompts fresh questions about personhood, salvation, and spiritual agency. It functions as a catalyst, inviting Christianity to refine its understanding of human identity, divine image-bearing, and relational existence. He suggests a middle path of curiosity and caution: embrace AI's capacity to illuminate, while resisting simplistic techno-utopianism.

Jewish theology can, in principle, accommodate relational or valued AI without undermining human dignity. AI is seen as an extension of divine–human creativity, offering a fresh lens on our own God-given role and responsibility. Kalman (2024) offers a rich, nuanced Jewish perspective on AI in terms of which Jewish law remains firmly human-centric. He argues that Judaism's ethical insights aren't just broad moral platitudes (e.g. "don't exploit the vulnerable"), but hinge on precise theological distinctions—e.g., agenthood vs. authority, creator vs. creation. It offers unique approaches to the ethics and ontology of AI—especially around moral agency and value distinctions.

Table 11. Comparative Matrix on AI and Abrahamic Religions

Aspect	Islam (Chaudhary)	Judaism (Kalman)	Christianity (Dorobantu)
Divine Relation	Taw īd: AI must not infringe divine unity	God's transcendence; AI as part of creation	Imago Dei: AI raises questions of soul, personhood
Ethical Principles	Falah, Ma la a, Adl, Rahma, Amanah	Justice, communal welfare, halakhic ethics	Stewardship, love (agape), moral testing grounds
Knowledge Role	Historical legacy of Muslim scholarship	Embrace of science in service of divine wisdom	Dialogue between human creativity and spiritual vocation
Critical Tone	Reject "ethics theatre"; affirm spiritual refusal	Ethical borderline on technology's reach	Contemplative, questioning AI's relational impact

Source: Author's own

For technology to truly serve humanity, a paradigm shift is imperative, one that realigns developments with ethical standards. Without such safeguards, AI risks undermining civilization through deepfakes, mass surveillance, and reckless automation (Citron & Chesney, 2019). Acemoglu (2024) cautions:

"If hype drives adoption, we may see rising inequality without meaningful productivity gains—a profound societal loss."

Global leaders must steer AI development toward applications that empower workers, safeguard privacy, enhance information integrity, and strengthen democratic institutions. Presently, the tech industry prioritizes replacing human roles rather than complementing them.

A Human-Centric Approach to AI

In principle, tools should address tasks where human efficiency falls short. Yet the technology sector has pursued the opposite approach, prioritizing automation over augmentation. True empowerment through AI demands parallel investments in human training and education at all levels. Only by equipping individuals with the skills to harness AI's potential—rather than being displaced by it—can we ensure ethical and equitable progress.

SUMMARY AND CONCLUSION

The concepts of humanity as stewards of God's resources and as vicegerents on Earth are central to both Islam and Christianity (Meeks, 2014, p. 5). Stewardship—rooted in the belief that all people are made in God's image—emphasizes ethical responsibility over divine resources.

Acemoglu and Robinson (2013) argue that inclusive political and economic institutions foster prosperity, while extractive institutions perpetuate poverty. Inclusive systems protect property rights, encourage innovation, and create virtuous cycles of growth and stability. In contrast, the conventional financial system—marked by exploitative practices—fuels poverty, conflict, and environmental degradation. Only divine injunctions and institutions, untainted by corruption, can establish Abrahamic finance, an ethical alternative independent of traditional banking.

Today's global system, dominated by liberal democracy, crony capitalism, and unregulated free markets, prioritizes profit over ethics, harming both society and the environment. Financial sectors increasingly monopolize wealth, leaving productive economies in distress. Exploitative innovations—such as interest-based lending, short selling, and gambling—deepen inequality and systemic fragility, eroding human welfare.

To ensure sustainable and equitable global growth, leadership must adopt a transformative, value-based approach. Below is a proposed Action Framework for systemic reform:

Suggested Action Framework by the Global Leadership Society

1. **Reform Global Institutions for Equity**
    - Democratize governance structures in the International Monetary Fund (IMF), World Bank, and United Nations (UN) to ensure fair representation (e.g., "one country, one vote").
    - Restructure the global reserve currency system to prevent any single country (via seigniorage) from disproportionately benefiting.

- Replace the Washington Consensus with a development model rooted in ethical, social, and environmental responsibility.

2. **Embed Ethical Foundations in Policy**
   - Anchor economics and finance in divine/natural ethics (justice, compassion, equity).
   - Enforce corporate accountability through regulation and culture shifts from profit-maximization to value-based missions.
3. **Rein in Exploitative Finance**
   - Prohibit interest-based money creation and speculative practices like short selling and gambling.
   - Promote riba-free, risk-sharing, asset-backed financial systems that serve real economic activity and human needs.
4. **Support Just Wealth Distribution**
   - Institutionalize redistributive mechanisms (e.g., zakat, social welfare funds, fair taxation).
   - Target poverty eradication through universal access to food, health, education, housing, and employment.
5. **Restore Human and Environmental Balance**
   - Redefine economic success beyond GDP to include well-being, dignity, and environmental harmony.
   - Enforce environmental stewardship via circular economy principles, limiting over-consumption and waste .
6. **Foster Global Ethical Consensus**
   - Reintroduce basic trust and shared ethical standards, inspired by common values in Abrahamic religions and humanistic ethics.
   - Institutionalize ethical education and training in economics, politics, and business schools globally.
7. **Redesign Monetary Policy for Inclusion**
   - Prevent credit flows toward luxury or speculative assets; direct them instead to entrepreneurship and households to become entrepreneurs.
   - Establish community-based funds (e.g., trusts, foundations, awqaf) for investment in health, education, and social infrastructure.
8. **Regulate Technology and Capital Flow**
   - Guide AI, fintech, and other technologies through ethical frameworks, ensuring that benefits are equitably distributed.
   - Place checks on capital flight, offshore havens, and tax avoidance through strong international agreements.
9. **Promote Peace and Responsible Geopolitics**
   - End wars driven by economic interest, secure human rights and international law, and promote peaceful coexistence.

- Reduce military spending in favor of development, climate resilience, and humanitarian support.

10. **Commit to Global Solidarity and SDGs**
    - Actualize the 2030 SDG agenda with ethical integrity, not just as economic targets.
    - Prioritize the principle of "Leave No One Behind" in all global and national planning.

Source: Author's own

Modern economies reward speculation (e.g., derivatives trading) over real value creation, enabling financial elites to exploit the majority (Epstein, 2005). Historically, economics diverged from moral philosophy. As Shanafelt (2021) notes, slavery's abolition stemmed from industrial capitalism's rise, not just moral appeals. Similarly, Piketty (2014) ties economic theory to cultural context, unlike today's abstract models. Anthony Annett (IMF, 2018) urges:

"Economics must return to its roots in moral philosophy, recentering policymaking on the common good."

Money, by natural law, should facilitate exchange—not serve as a commodified asset. Ethical finance must align with the real economy, banning rent-seeking and gambling. Even Islamic finance, despite its ideals, often replicates conventional systems' flaws (Paldi, 2024). Paldi advocates Abrahamic finance, integrating Jewish and Christian principles for inclusivity.

The SDGs highlight the urgency of addressing inequality and climate crises. Post-2008, value-based finance gained traction (WB-IDB, 2016), yet systemic change requires respecting nature's balance—a Qur'ānic mandate (30:41). True stability demands economies realigned with divine/natural laws. Adam Smith's vision of wealth fostering communal sympathy contrasts starkly with modern capitalism's exploitation. Without ethical frameworks, hunger and environmental collapse will persist.

This chapter calls on global leaders to adopt moral economy principles rooted in Abrahamic traditions. Pakistan, for instance, could transition to a riba-free system. Ethical policies—grounded in divine wisdom—offer a viable alternative to today's harmful paradigm.

In 2023, the Global North's wealthiest 1% extracted $30 million hourly from the Global South. By 2024, billionaire wealth grew at triple the prior rate—$5.7 billion daily (Oxfam, 2025). Without reform, trillionaires will emerge within a decade. Circular economy models are insufficient; lasting change requires a moral economy honoring divine rights (*huquq*) for all.

Banks must align financial and real assets, using forward contracts (e.g., *Salam*, *Istisnā'a*) to buffer growth. Islamic ethical finance—asset-backed and risk-sharing—

offers a model for justice and sustainability. Global institutions should promote Value-Based Intermediation (VBI) to realign finance with SDGs.

Almighty ordered and expected man to develop and beautify the earth (Quran, 11: 61), which can be accomplished by cultivating, planting, restoring and reviving it, and by avoiding disturbance in the natural system. Adam Smith (1759) linked wealth circulation to communal sympathy, yet capitalism devolved into oppression. To rectify this, economics must embrace empathy and sacrifice.

Technology's dual-edged potential demands caution. AI risks degrading ethics and science (Chomsky et al., 2023). Ethical leadership must harness innovation responsibly, safeguarding divine rights.

A robust and inclusive financial system, grounded in Abrahamic principles of economy and finance, fosters justice, equity, and fair treatment for all, promoting shared prosperity and community well-being. This ethical market economy prioritizes cooperation and compassion, ensuring support for the sick, vulnerable, and unemployed, thereby uplifting those disadvantaged by any form of inability or hardship.

REFERENCES

Acemoglu, D. (2024, November 29). The world needs a pro-human AI agenda. *Project Syndicate*. Retrieved from: https://www.project-syndicate.org/onpoint/ai-and-agi-designed-to-replace-workers-worst-of-all-possible-worlds-by-daron-acemoglu-2024-11

Acemoglu, D., & Robinson, J. A. (2013). *Why nations fail: The origins of power, prosperity, and poverty*. Profile Books. [does not have a DOI registered in Crossref or other major databases]

Akbar, J. (2023, November). *Property rights (uquq) and civilizations* [Keynote speech]. "City and Civilization Congress" Ankara, Turkey. Retrieved from https://www.researchgate.net/publication/367052857_Property_Rights_Huquq_and_Civilizations

Annett, A. (2018, March). Restoring ethics to economics: Modern economics should return to its roots. Finance & Development, 55(1). IMF, https://www.elibrary.imf.org/view/journals/022/0055/001/article-A016-en.xmlDOI: 10.5089/9781484343418.022

Aquinas, T. (n.d.). *Summa Theologica*, Secunda Secundae, Question 78, Article 1. [written in the 13th century] Christian Classics Ethereal Library; Retrieved May 11, 2025, from https://www.newadvent.org/summa/3078.htm

Aristotle. (1946). *The politics of Aristotle* (E. Barker, Trans., Book I, Ch. 10, 1258b4–8). Oxford University Press. (Original work published ca. 350 B.C.E.) https://archive.org/details/in.ernet.dli.2015.50166

Asutay, M. (2012). Conceptualising and Locating the Social Failure of Islamic Finance: Aspirations of Islamic Moral Economy vs the Realities of Islamic Finance. *Asian and African Area Studies, 11*(2), 93–113. DOI: 10.14956/asafas.11.93

Asutay, M. (2013). Islamic moral economy as the foundation of Islamic finance. In Cattelan, V. (Ed.), *Islamic Finance in Europe*. Edward Elgar., DOI: 10.4337/9781781002513.00014

Ayub, M. (2007). *Understanding Islamic finance*. John Wiley & Sons.

Ayub, M. (2021), "The Corporate Governance for Islamic Financial Institutions in Pakistan: Need for Dynamic Regulatory Policies", Azid, T., Mukhlisin, M., Akbar, N. and Tahir, M. (Ed.) *Monetary Policy, Islamic Finance, and Islamic Corporate Governance: An International Overview*, Emerald Publishing Limited, Leeds, pp. 37-60. DOI: 10.1108/978-1-80043-786-920211003

Ayub, M. (Ed.). (2022). *Economics and economic policy: Islamic perspective*. IPS.

Ayub, M., Fahim, K., & Rashid, A. (2022). Forward trading and futures markets in Islamic perspective. *Journal of Islamic Finance Accountancy*, *6*(1), 21–34. https://aaoifi.com/joifa/?lang=en

Azeem, M. M., Marsap, A., & Özari, C. (2015). Impact of Basel Accord on Banking System (Evidence from Islamic Banks of Pakistan). *Applied Finance and Accounting*, *1*(2), 1–9. DOI: 10.11114/afa.v1i2.724

Beed, C., & Beed, C. (1996). A Christian perspective on economics. *Journal of Economic Methodology, 3*(1), 91–112. https://doi.org/ C (1996). From total war to local war: it's a revolution; The Independent, 22 July; https://www.the-independent.com/voices/from-total-war-to-local-war-it-s-a-revolution-1330045.html?utm_source=chatgpt.comDOI: 10.1080/13501789600000006Bellamy

Capital, S. (2023). *Amana Mutual Funds Trust overview*. Retrieved from https://www.saturna.com/amana

Cattelan, V. (2016, January). Islamic finance as Islamic justice. *Islamic Finance Today*. https://www.scribd.com/document/818856658/Islamic-Finance-as-Islamic-Justice

Chaudhary, Y. (2024). Islam and artificial intelligence. In Singler, B., & Watts, F. (Eds.), *The Cambridge Companion to Religion and Artificial Intelligence* (pp. 109–128). Cambridge University Press., DOI: 10.1017/9781009031721.008

Chomsky, N., Roberts, I., & Watumull, J. (2023, March 8). The false promise of ChatGPT. *The New York Times*. https://www.nytimes.com/2023/03/08/opinion/noam-chomsky-chatgpt-ai.html

Citron, D. K., & Chesney, B. (2019). Deep fakes: A looming challenge for privacy, democracy, and national security. *California Law Review*, *107*(5), 1753–1819. DOI: 10.15779/Z38RV0D15J

Cross, M. S. (2021, January 27). Reincarnating the East India Company. *The Juggernaut*. https://www.thejuggernaut.com/reincarnating-east-india-company

Deaton, A. (2024, March). *Rethinking my economics. Finance & Development*. International Monetary Fund. https://www.imf.org/en/Publications/fandd/issues/2024/03/Symposium-Rethinking-Economics-Angus-Deaton

Demir, H. (2024). Story of Humanitarian Efforts from USA to the World. Executive Interview with ISFIRE; ISFIRE COVER STORY, *ISFIRE*, London; 14(6), 12–21. Retrieved from https://www.isfire.net:contentReference[oaicite:15]{index=15}

Dhahri, S., Slimani, S., & Omri, A. (2021). Behavioral entrepreneurship for achieving the sustainable development goals. *Technological Forecasting and Social Change, 165*, 120561. DOI: 10.1016/j.techfore.2020.120561

Dorobantu, M. (2024). Artificial intelligence and Christianity: Friends or foes? In Singler, B., & Watts, F. (Eds.), *The Cambridge companion to religion and artificial intelligence*. Cambridge University Press., DOI: 10.1017/9781009031721.007

Dusuki, A. W. (2010). Do equity-based Sukuk structures in Islamic capital markets manifest the objectives of Shariah? *Journal of Financial Services Marketing, 15*(3), 203–214. https://jibm.org/wp-content/uploads/2018/05/10-Asyraf-Wajdi-Dusuki1.pdf. DOI: 10.1057/fsm.2010.17

El Aynaoui, K., & Dinh, H. T. (2025, January 28). *Economic development after the Washington Consensus*. Project Syndicate. https://www.project-syndicate.org/commentary/new-development-policy-framework-to-replace-washington-consensus-by-karim-el-aynaoui-and-hinh-t-dinh-2025-01

Epstein, G. A. (Ed.). (2005). *Financialization and the World Economy*. Edward Elgar Publishing. ISBN: 978 1 84376 874 6 DOI: 10.4337/9781781008263

Fraade, S. D. (2012). Concepts of Scripture in Rabbinic Judaism: Oral Torah and Written Torah. In Sommer, B. D. (Ed.), *Jewish concepts of scripture: A comparative introduction* (pp. 31–46). New York University Press., DOI: 10.18574/nyu/9780814740620.003.0003

Frierson, J. G. (1969). Changing concepts on usury: Ancient times through the time of John Calvin. *American Business Law Journal, 7*(2), 115–130. DOI: 10.1111/j.1744-1714.1969.tb01330.x

Goldin, I. (2025, January 10). *The truth about migration. Project Syndicate*. https://www.project-syndicate.org/onpoint/migration-facts-versus-myths-by-ian-goldin-2025-01

Griffin, D. R., & Scott, P. D. (Eds.). (2006). *9/11 and American Empire: Intellectuals Speak Out* (Vol. 1). Olive Branch Press., Retrieved from https://books.google.com/books?id=Uvm66cPtb3cC

Gurumurthy, S. (2002, June 26). Neo-economics: Saving is a sin, spending is a virtue. https://gurumurthy.net/neo-economics-saving-is-sin-spending-is-virtue/

Habisch, A. (2023). The concept of economy in Christianity. In Böttigheimer, C., & Widenka, W. M. (Eds.), *The concept of economy in Judaism, Christianity, and Islam* (pp. 43–70). LSC Communications / De Gruyter., DOI: 10.1515/9783110782486-004

Hardin, G. (1968). The tragedy of the commons. *Science*, *162*(3859), 1243–1248. DOI: 10.1126/science.162.3859.1243 PMID: 5699198

Harper, K., & Smirl, L. (2014). Usury and Religion: Historical Perspectives on Jewish and Christian Views. *BMC Public Health*, *14*, 566. DOI: 10.1186/1471-2458-14-566

Hassan, K., Tarazi, A., & Echchabi, A. (2023). The Impact of Basel III on Islamic Banks: Ethical Finance and Regulatory Challenges. *Journal of Banking Regulation*, *24*(3), 345–362. DOI: 10.1057/s41261-023-00210-1

Helvacıoğlu, M. (2022). Islamic finance: What is it? In Kahf, M. (Ed.), *Towards a new theory of finance: Can Islamic finance be it?* (pp. 321–360). İstanbul Zaim University., DOI: 10.12816/0036633

Humanistic Management Network. (2005). *About us*. Retrieved from https://humanisticmanagement.network/about-us/

Inner Peace Fellowship. (n.d.). *Why we should do the right thing even when others don't*. Retrieved June 12, 2025, from https://www.innerpeacefellowship.org/do-the-right-thing

Institute of International Finance. (2024, May 7). *Global debt monitor: Navigating the new normal*. https://www.iif.com/Products/Global-Debt-Monitor

International Labour Organization. (ILO, 2024). *World employment and social outlook: September 2024 update* [Brief]. https://researchrepository.ilo.org/esploro/outputs/encyclopediaEntry/World-employment-and-social-outlook-September/995381680802676DOI: 10.54394/OPQH3749

International Monetary Fund. (2024). IMF members' quotas and voting power, Retrieved from https://www.imf.org

International Monetary Fund. (n.d.). *Articles of agreement of the International Monetary Fund*. https://www.imf.org/external/pubs/ft/aa/index.htm

Islamic Development Bank (IsDB). (2022). *Annual development effectiveness report*. https://www.isdb.org

Islamic Financial Services Board (IFSB). (2015). *Islamic financial services industry stability report*. https://www.ifsb.org

JLens. (2022). *Faith-based ESG investing framework*. https://jlensnetwork.org

Jr, B., & Wade, R. H. (2024). Will the IMF Survive to 100? Project Syndicate. https://www.project-syndicate.org/onpoint/imf-necessary-reforms-greater-influence-for-emerging-developing-economies-by-paulo-nogueira-batista-and-robert-h-wade-2024-10

Kamali, M. H. (2018). Shari'ah and the ethical tradition: Ethics and morality in Islamic thought. *Islam and Civilisational Renewal*, *9*(1), 11–32. DOI: 10.12816/0043453

Keir, J. (2016). Two hearts believing in just one mind? The Humanistic Management Network and the Global Ethic Project. *Humanistic Management Journal*, *1*(1), 139–147. https://link.springer.com/article/10.1007/s41463-016-0008-0?fromPaywallRec=true. DOI: 10.1007/s41463-016-0008-0

Keynes, J. M. (1936). *The general theory of employment, interest, and money*. Retrieved from https://www.files.ethz.ch/isn/125515/1366_KeynesTheoryofEmployment.pdf

Khan, F. (2010). How "Islamic" is Islamic banking? *Journal of Economic Behavior & Organization*, *76*(3), 805–820. DOI: 10.1016/j.jebo.2010.09.015

Krippner, G. R. (2005). The financialization of the American economy. *Socio-economic Review*, *3*(2), 173–208. DOI: 10.1093/SER/mwi008

Küng, H. (2004). *Global responsibility: In search of a new world ethic*. Imprint: Wipf and Stock. DOI: 10.1111/j.1741-2005.1991.tb03744.x

Laldin, M. A., & Furqani, H. (2013). *The foundations of Islamic finance and the Maqā id al-Sharī ah requirements*. Journal of Islamic Finance, 2(1), 31–37. IIUM Institute of Islamic Banking and Finance. DOI: https://doi.org/DOI: 10.31436/jif.v2i1.9

Lapin, D. (2007). *Jewish theology and economic theory*. Acton Institute. Retrieved from https://www.acton.org/pub/religion-liberty/volume-17-number-1/jewish-theology-and-economic-theory

Leo, X. I. I. I. (1891). Rerum Novarum [Encyclical letter on capital and labor]. Vatican. https://www.vatican.va/content/leo-xiii/en/encyclicals/documents/hf_l-xiii_enc_15051891_rerum-novarum.html

Lopes, C. (2012). Economic growth and inequality: The new post-Washington consensus. *RCCS Annual Review*, *4*(4), 69–85. DOI: 10.4000/rccsar.426

Luther, M. (2003). *Commentary on Romans* (J. T. Mueller, Trans.). Kregel Publications. (Original work published 1522). https://www.kregel.com/bible-commentaries/commentary-on-romans/

Maududi, S. A. A. (1977). *Islamic Riyasat.* Islamic Publications. https://faakhiris-lamic.wordpress.com/2015/08/04/islami-riyasat-by-syed-abul-aala-maududi/

McRorie, C. G. (2018). Religion and globalization: *Riba*, usury, and the evolution of moral finance: A comparison of two arguments. *Journal of Religion & Society*, Supplement Series 16, 109–124. https://cdr.creighton.edu/server/api/core/bit-streams/1af6d44c-7f40-4c3c-87b9-47f46596b654/content

Mearsheimer, J. J. (2019). Bound to fail: The rise and fall of the liberal international order. *International Security, 43*(4), 7–50. DOI: 10.1162/isec_a_00342

Meeks, D. M. (2014). Economics in the Christian Scriptures. In Oslington, P. (Ed.), *The Oxford handbook of Christianity and economics* (pp. 3–21). Oxford University Press., DOI: 10.1093/oxfordhb/9780199729715.013.001

Naqvi, S. N. H. (1981). *Ethics and economics: An Islamic synthesis.* The Islamic Foundation. ISBN: 0-86037-079-8 (hardback) / 0-86037-080-1 (paperback)

Oxfam. (2025, January 20). *Takers not makers.* https://www.oxfam.org.hk/en/news-and-publication/davos-2025

Oxfam International. (2024, January 15). *Wealth of five richest men doubles since 2020 as five billion people made poorer in "decade of division," says Oxfam* [Press release]. https://www.oxfam.org/en/press-releases/wealth-five-richest-men-doubles-2020-five-billion-people-made-poorer-decade-division

Paldi, C. (2016, January 8). *Financial principles found in Judaism* [Video]. YouTube. https://www.youtube.com/watch?v=2U7NzbaTeqo

Paldi, C. (2024). Abrahamic finance: The path forward? *ISFIRE*, 14(6), 34–41. Retrieved from https://www.isfire.net:contentReference[oaicite:15]{index=15}

Perry, J. H. (2018). *Gay Girl, Good God: The story of who I was, and who God has always been* (Vol. 1). B&H Publishing Group. Retrieved from https://www.bhpublishinggroup.com/products/gay-girl/

Piketty, T. (2014). *Capital in the twenty-first century.* Harvard University Press., DOI: 10.4159/9780674369542

Piketty, T. (2020). *Capital and ideology.* Belknap Press of Harvard University Press., DOI: 10.4159/9780674245075

Pistor, K. (2024, January 28). The social costs of price. *Finance & Development, 61*(1). https://www.elibrary.imf.org/view/journals/022/0061/001/article-A004-en.xml

Pope Leo, X. I. I. I. (1891). *Rerum novarum: On capital and labor*. Vatican. https://www.vatican.va/content/leo-xiii/en/encyclicals/documents/hf_l-xiii_enc_15051891_rerum-novarum.html

Republic of Indonesia, Ministry of Finance. (2020). *Green Sukuk report 2020*. https://www.djppr.kemenkeu.go.id/page/load/2790

Reuters. (2025, February 28). What happens if the US pulls out from IMF, World Bank? *Dawn*. https://www.dawn.com/news/1894790

Riaz, U., Burton, B., & Monk, E. (2017). Perceptions on the accessibility of Islamic banking in the UK—Challenges, opportunities and divergence in opinion. *Accounting Forum*, *41*(4), 353–374. DOI: 10.1016/j.accfor.2017.10.002

Richman, S. (2007). *Christianity's free-market tradition*. Mises Institute. [Page-printed not available] Retrieved from https://mises.org/mises-daily/christianitys-free-market-tradition

Rizwan, S., & Khan, N. (2015). Basel III liquidity requirement ratios and Islamic banking. *Journal of Banking Regulation*, *16*(3), 251–264. DOI: 10.1057/jbr.2014.20

Roberts, J. (2024). Worlds apart: The global financial system is in danger of fragmenting; The Economist, May 11, https://www.economist.com/special-report/2024-05-11?utm_source=chatgpt.com

Romer, P. M. (2016). The trouble with macroeconomics. *The American Economist*, *61*(1), 1–20. DOI: 10.1177/0569434516652456

Seater, J. J. (1993). Ricardian equivalence. *Journal of Economic Literature*, *31*(1), 142–190. https://www.jstor.org/stable/2728152

Shamsuddeen, M. (2016). *Islam is compatible with a free economy, argue Muslim scholars*. Institute of Economic Affairs. Retrieved from https://iea.org.uk/blog/islam-is-compatible-with-a-free-economy-argue-muslim-scholars

Shanafelt, C. D. (2021). "A world of debt": Quobna Ottobah Cugoano, *The Wealth Of Nations*, and the end of finance. *Eighteenth-Century Studies*, *55*(1), 21–43. DOI: 10.1353/ecs.2021.0106

Siddiqi, M. N. (2010). *Islamic banking and finance: What it is and what it could be*. The Islamic Foundation. [DOI not available]

Smith, A. (1759/2002). *The Theory of Moral Sentiments* (D. D. Raphael & A. L. Macfie, Eds.; Glasgow Edition, Vol. I). Indianapolis: Liberty Fund (online at Online Library of Liberty). ISBN 9780521591508

Stiglitz, J. E. (2002). *Globalization and Its Discontents*. W. W. Norton & Company. https://wwnorton.com/books/9780393324396

Stiglitz, J. E. (2024). *The road to freedom: Economics and the good society*. W. W. Norton & Company. https://wwnorton.com/books/The-Road-to-Freedom

Stiglitz, J. E., Gallagher, K. P., Guzmán, M., & Uy, M. (2024). The IMF must end its destructive surcharges. *Project Syndicate*. Retrieved from: https://www.project-syndicate.org/commentary/imf-must-end-surcharge-policy-by-joseph-e-stiglitz-et-al-2024-09

The Economist. (2023, January 26)Christians fight about how to serve God and mammon: Is ESG simply a social-Marxist agenda? Retrieved from: https://www.economist.com/finance-and-economics/2023/01/26/christians-fight-about-how-to-serve-god-and-mammon

The Economist. (2023, June 24). The trouble with sticky inflation. *The Economist*. https://www.economist.com/finance-and-economics/2023/06/24/the-trouble-with-sticky-inflation

The World Bank. (2024). Voting powers of member countries. Retrieved from https://www.worldbank.org](https://www.worldbank.org

Treasury, H. M. (2021, March 31). UK Sovereign Sukuk PLC's Offering Circular. Retrieved from https://www.gov.uk/government/publications/uk-sovereign-sukuk-plcs-offering-circular--2

Triodos Bank. (2023). *Annual impact report 2023*. https://www.triodos.com/annual-report

Vogel, E. F., & Hayes, S. L. (1998). *Islamic law and finance: Religion, risk and return*. Kluwer Law International. DOI: 10.1163/9789004634916

Webster, C. (2023). *Conclusion: 'There's One Law for the Rich and Another for the Poor'*. In *Rich Crime, Poor Crime: Inequality and the Rule of Law* (pp. 217–222). Emerald Publishing Limited. https://doi.org/DOI: 10.1108/978-1-83909-822-200230011

Wellness, W. (2025). *The Economics of Enough*. Wellness Warehouse. https://www.wellnesswarehouse.com/catalog/product/view/id/22983/terms-and-conditions?utm_source=chatgpt.com

Wespath. (2024, February 7). Wespath CIO Dave Zellner announces retirement [Press release]. https://www.wespath.org/News/Zellner-Retirement#!/page:1

Wilson, A. (2000). The new rules: Ethics, social responsibility and strategy. *Strategy and Leadership*, *28*(3), 12–16. DOI: 10.1108/10878570010348549

Wilson, R. (1997). Economics, ethics and religion: Jewish, Christian and Muslim economic thought, New York: New York University Press; ISBN 0-8147-9313-4 DOI for Chapter 1 (pp. 1–21); Palgrave Macmillan. DOI: 10.1057/9780230374720

World Bank. (2018). *Turkey public-private partnership (PPP) healthcare projects: Case study*. https://documents.worldbank.org

ZAWYA. (2024). Islamic finance. https://www.zawya.com/en/economy/islamic-economy/saudi-arabia-leads-gcc-in-sustainable-sukuk-issuances-smnx5ezs?utm_source=chatgpt.com

Zhang, S. (2024, January 15). World's richest men have added $14M to their wealth every hour since 2020. *Truthout*. https://truthout.org/articles/in-past-3-years-worlds-5-richest-men-have-doubled-their-wealth-to-870-billion/

ENDNOTES

1 The text of the verse is

2 John Williamson coined the term "Washington Consensus" in 1989. It referred to the policies adopted by Latin American policymakers in response to the macroeconomic turbulence and debt crisis of the early to mid-1980s. These policies, which were aimed at recovery from the debt crisis, were also backed by the IMF and the World Bank and other international institutions, as well as the U.S. Treasury.

3 "Indeed, We sent Our messengers with clear proofs, and with them We sent down the Scripture and the balance 'of justice' so that people may administer justice. And We sent down iron with its great might, benefits for humanity, and means for Allah to prove who 'is willing to' stand up for Him and His messengers without seeing Him" (57:25). ("Iron" in this verse refers to economic resources humans may use with their effort for their betterment.)

KEY TERMS AND DEFINITIONS

Aristocratic Capitalism: Aristocratic capitalism refers to an economic system in which wealth and power are concentrated in the hands of a privileged elite, who maintain their dominance through rent-seeking, speculative practices, and manipulation of institutional frameworks. This model of market economy has been a major driver of rising inequality and persistent poverty, both within nations and across the global economy, undermining inclusive growth and social mobility.

Basic Trust as per Abrahamic Religions: A foundational spiritual and moral covenant rooted in divine revelation that binds all human beings to God Almighty and to each other, in mutual responsibility, ethical conduct, and universal justice. The followers of monotheism are part of a divinely instituted spiritual legacy starting with Prophet Abraham (PBUH), whose faith and submission to God's will serve as the archetype for all believers (Qur'an 2:130–132). This trust entails unwavering belief in God and accountability to Him, forming the cornerstone of ethical human conduct and social contracts. Humans' stewardship involves protecting others, the environment, and future generations. As all Abrahamic scriptures underline the ethical and moral regulation of economic and social life, trust in this perspective refers to a societal mechanism for justice to all and exploitation of none, ensuring that the weak, poor, widows, and orphans are specifically safeguarded.

Divine Ethics: Divine ethics are moral principles revealed by God through sacred scriptures and prophets. They are regarded as universal and timeless, reflecting the inherent order and purpose of creation. From a normative perspective, divine ethics provide comprehensive guidance for all dimensions of economic behavior, including production, distribution, exchange, consumption, and wealth sharing, grounded in values such as honesty, fairness, compassion, and social welfare. These principles aim to ensure that economic systems serve the well-being of all, rather than narrow self-interest.

Ethical Finance: Ethical finance represents a values-driven approach to financial systems and investment practices to prioritize fairness, social justice, environmental sustainability, and long-term societal well-being. Also referred to as social finance, it advances principles of equity, inclusion, and shared responsibility, aligning financial activities with the real economy and productive enterprise. Ethical finance encompasses a broad spectrum of frameworks—including responsible finance, green and sustainable finance, ESG investing, and value-based intermediation (VBI)—all of which aim to balance financial efficiency with positive social impact, rather than pursuing profit at any cost. These models underscore the urgency of integrating value-based and normative economic theories into the design and implementation of public policy to ensure that global financial systems serve both economic and ethical imperatives.

uquq **(Human rights) as per Divine Law:** In the context of Divine Law, uqūq (human rights) are not autonomous or self-generated entitlements rooted in human desires or any social constructs. Rather, they are divinely ordained responsibilities and entitlements, derived from the Will (Hukm) of God Almighty, and tied inherently to the duties of the human being as a moral agent under divine sovereignty. These rights exist not in isolation but as balanced entitlements embedded within the framework of justice and truth, key Qur'anic values that structure ethical life, economic interaction, and environmental stewardship. Hence, the rights are rooted in divine sovereignty, and every entitlement is paired with a moral responsibility toward God, fellow humans, and the environment.

Leave no one behind: The principle of "Leave No One Behind" (LNOB) lies at the heart of the United Nations' Sustainable Development Goals (SDGs), serving as a cornerstone of their transformative agenda. SDG 1, which focuses on eradicating extreme poverty and hunger, embodies this commitment by prioritizing inclusive development that ensures all individuals, particularly the most marginalized and disadvantaged, benefit from growth and development. This principle calls for targeted and coordinated policy interventions at national and international levels to ensure that development efforts reach those most at risk of exclusion, thereby making growth inclusive, equitable, and sustainable.

Moral Economy: The term moral economy is associated with economic theories and systems that incorporate moral, ethical, and social values into decision-making processes. It refers to the normative system of the economy and challenges the notion of purely profit-driven economics by including compassion, fairness, and social justice in economic behavior. Cooperation and benevolence for the sick, weak, and unemployed in respective societies is also a feature of an ethical market economy for ensuring the welfare of those who might be disadvantaged by any type of inability or sickness. It contrasts with "positive economics," which focuses only on describing economic phenomena without value-based goals. The benefits of growth and progress, in such an economy, must be shared by all groups in the society equitably.

Real and Financial Assets Parity and Social Finance: Real and Financial Assets Parity refers to a balanced and ethical relationship between the real economy (goods, services, labor, and physical assets) and the financial economy (money, credit, and financial instruments), where financial activities and instruments are rooted in and backed by tangible productive assets. It promotes risk-sharing, economic stability, and justice, rather than risk-transfer, moral hazard, and systemic vulnerability. This parity ensures that finance serves the real sector rather than distorting or dominating it. The current debt-based system and riba (interest)-oriented financial structures have disconnected finance from the real sector, leading to inequality, fragility, and economic injustice. It requires a discipline-oriented system of economy and finance where financial mechanisms are based on real economic activities—production, trade, and services—rather than speculative or artificial financial constructs.

Responsible Human Behavior: This refers to ethical, compassionate, and socially aware actions by individuals and corporate bodies in economic roles—consumers, producers, or investors—who also consider the well-being of others, the environment, and society in their decisions. Unscrupulous human behavior in earnings, consumption, and interaction is the root cause of the symptoms of wealth concentration, poverty, hunger, and the recurring crises. It requires the passion of helping others, proportionately with increasing income.

Riba: Riba, an Arabic term often translated as interest or usury, refers to any predetermined or guaranteed gain on loans or exchanges that occurs without value creation or risk-sharing. In Islamic finance, this also includes unequal or deferred exchanges involving fungible goods that serve as money or a store of value, classified as Riba al-Fadl (excess in exchange of fungible goods)—and is categorically prohibited. Riba is deemed ethically unacceptable because it promotes income generation without any productive contribution, fostering economic exploitation, wealth concentration, and moral deterioration within financial systems. Its prohibition is not merely a religious injunction but a principle with far-reaching economic implications. Banning riba supports market efficiency, financial inclusion, and risk-sharing, contributing to a more just, equitable, and resilient economic order. To align financial systems with the principles of efficiency and fairness, the systemic elimination of riba should be embedded within automatic economic stabilizers—ensuring that financial practices promote real economic activity, social equity, and long-term sustainability.

Short-selling and speculative Exchanges: Short selling is the practice of selling assets—such as stocks or commodities—that the seller does not currently own, with the expectation of repurchasing them later at a lower price to earn a profit. This approach introduces several concerns from both ethical and legal perspectives, particularly within the framework of ethical norms. It involves uncertainty regarding the subject matter, its price, and delivery, as well as elements of maysir (gambling) and the absence of real risk-reward ownership—all of which conflict with ethical principles governing fair and just trade. Short selling also detaches financial returns from genuine economic activity. It can facilitate market manipulation, increase financial instability, and further entrench the dominance of the financial sector over the real economy. In speculative markets, financial instruments are traded with little or no connection to productive, real-world activities, driven largely by herd behavior, fear, greed, and emotional decision-making. As economist J. M. Keynes famously warned: "When the capital development of a country becomes a by-product of the activities of a casino, the job is likely to be ill-done."

Stable and Sustainable Global Financial Order: A stable and sustainable global financial architecture must be multilateral, ethically grounded, inclusive, and driven by shared values. This vision necessitates far-reaching reform of international institutions, the curtailment of rentier-based economic structures, and adherence to moral principles rooted in divine guidance, aimed at fostering equitable development and enduring global peace. Such a framework would reestablish trust-based international cooperation, promoting collaborative approaches to risk-sharing, financial systems, and governance in place of adversarial, zero-sum dynamics. Central to this paradigm is the adoption of a universal ethical code—derived from authentic divine revelation—to shape socio-economic behavior and decision-making at the global level.

Chapter 2
Legal and Regulatory Challenges of Islamic Banking in Africa:
Finding a Balance Between Sharia Governance and Regulatory Frameworks

Aishatu Usman Muhammad
Gombe State University, Nigeria

Sirajo Murtala
Gombe State University, Nigeria

Abubakar Yusuf
Gombe State University, Nigeria

ABSTRACT

This chapter examines the legal and regulatory challenges facing Islamic banking in Africa, focusing on the complex relationship between Sharia governance and conventional financial regulation. It highlights the fragmented legal systems across African countries, the lack of standardized Sharia interpretation, and weak regulatory frameworks as main challenges to the growth of the sector. The chapter used comparative case studies from Nigeria, Sudan, and Kenya, which analyzes the varying approaches to Sharia integration and supervision. It draws lessons from global Islamic finance leaders such as Malaysia, Indonesia, and the GCC to recommend a harmonized African regulatory model. The chapter proposes legal reforms,

DOI: 10.4018/979-8-3373-1887-5.ch002

centralized Sharia advisory structures, regional cooperation, and capacity building as pathways to strengthening Islamic banking. These strategies aim to enhance compliance, financial inclusion, and sustainable development across the continent.

1. INTRODUCTION

Islamic banking has experienced outstanding growth and expansion on a global scale over the past few decades. This growth is driven by the growing demand and need for financial services that are Sharia compliant, as well as the growing acceptance of Islamic finance as an alternative to traditional banking. Africa has a lot of potential for Islamic banking to grow and flourish because of its large Muslim population and diverse economic landscape (Ibrahim et al., 2024). Some countries, like Egypt, Nigeria, South Africa, and Sudan, have either put in place or are looking into ways to make Islamic banking services easier to use and more accessible. Even though awareness and interest are increasing, the growth of Islamic banking in Africa faces considerable legal and regulatory challenges that threaten its sustainability and long-term growth.

Islamic banks are required to operate in accordance with Sharia principles and standards in order to function properly. In addition, they also need to adhere to international financial and banking regulations. This dual compliance responsibility brings challenges and some complexities that are particularly obvious in countries where the legal and regulatory systems are mainly designed around conventional finance. There are quite a number of African countries that are governed by diverse or multicultural legal systems, which are characterized by the coexistence of Islamic law, civil law, common law, and customary law, often without any attempt at harmonization (Diala). Because of this, the regulatory environment for Islamic financial institutions (IFIs) becomes fractured and disorganized, which increases the risk of inconsistency, regulatory arbitrage, and confusion.

One of the major challenges in Islamic banking is balancing Sharia governance with conventional financial regulation. Sharia governance requires supervision by Sharia advisory boards and adherence to Islamic legal principles. At the same time, financial regulation must ensure consumer protection, financial stability, and regulatory integrity. Aligning these two systems is complex but also essential for the effective functioning of Islamic financial institutions. There are some instances where the regulatory frameworks do not contain the necessary measures for licensing, supervision, and dispute resolution that are specific to the Islamic banking industry. The absence of consistent Sharia interpretations and practices across different countries is another factor that further complicates the environment for Islamic banking operations in Africa.

This chapter critically examines the legal and regulatory challenges that Islamic banking institutions in Africa are facing at the moment. It investigates the ways in which the operations, credibility, and expansion of Islamic banks are impacted by the presence of dual legal systems and regulatory frameworks that are not fully developed. In addition to this, it analyses the ways in which regional differences, policy gaps, and inadequate institutional capacities hinder efforts to harmonize Islamic finance within the framework of current legal systems.

The chapter argues that for Islamic banking to thrive and expand in Africa, there is a need to build a strong regulatory structure that accepts Sharia principles without compromising regulatory objectives. It suggests an integrated regulatory strategy that incorporates international best practices, robust Sharia governance structures, and locally adapted solutions that are tailored to the many cultural and legal contexts that exist in Africa. In order to demonstrate how various regulatory approaches have influenced the growth of Islamic banking, this chapter makes use of comparative case studies from Nigeria, Sudan, and Kenya.

The chapter is organized as follows: Section 2 provides a conceptual and theoretical background to Islamic banking in Africa. Section 3 examines the legal and regulatory contexts across selected African countries. Section 4 discusses the major challenges Islamic banks face in aligning Sharia governance with existing regulatory frameworks. Section 5 presents case studies from Nigeria, Sudan, and Kenya to highlight practical experiences and lessons learned. Section 6 proposes strategic approaches to regulatory harmonization. Section 7 concludes with recommendations for policymakers, regulators, and stakeholders committed to advancing Islamic finance in Africa

2. CONCEPTUAL AND THEORETICAL BACKGROUND OF ISLAMIC BANKING IN AFRICA

2.0 Conceptual and Theoretical Background

Islamic banking is a system of banking or financial activity that operates in line with the Sharia, i.e., Islamic law (Iqbal & Mirakhor, 2011). This type of banking is also known as interest-free banking, alternative banking, participation banking, or Sharia-compliant banking. The restriction of riba (interest), gharar (excessive uncertainty), and maysir (speculation or gambling), is very important to the operation of this system. Through the use of concepts derived from the Qur'an, the Sunnah (Prophetic traditions), Ijma (scholarly consensus), and Qiyas (analogical reasoning), Islamic banking places an emphasis on ethical investing, risk sharing, asset backing, and the promotion of socio-economic fairness and justice (Sivanandan & Ahmad, 2025).

2.1 Principles of Islamic Banking

Islamic Finance has distinguishing principles that make it different from conventional banking and also require a unique regulatory and legal framework. The following fundamental concepts guide the operations of Islamic banking:

Prohibition of Interest (Riba): Riba is seen as exploitative, unfair and unjust to individuals as well as the entire financial system. Islamic banks use profit-and-loss sharing methods of financing as opposed to interest-based lending.
Risk Sharing: Financial transactions are structured in such a way that risks and rewards are shared equitably between parties. This is done through contracts such as Mudarabah (trust-based partnership) and Musharakah (joint venture).
Asset-Backed Financing: Transactions in Islamic finance must be linked to tangible assets or services. This ensures that financial activities reflect the real economic value, as seen in Murabaha (cost-plus sale), Ijara (leasing), and Istisna' (manufacturing contracts).
Prohibition of Unethical Investments: Investments in industries such as alcohol, gambling, or pork-related businesses are prohibited.
Sharia Governance: Islamic financial institutions (IFIs) must be supervised by a Sharia advisory board to ensure compliance with the Sharia.

2.2 Historical Background of Islamic Banking in Africa

Islamic finance has a long history in Africa due to the early expansion of Islam and the trans-Saharan trade routes. In many African countries, traditional Islamic financial practices, including trust-based trading and cooperative savings, have long been practiced. However, the creation of organizations like the Mit Ghamr Savings Bank in Egypt in 1963, the Arab Islamic Bank of Egypt, and the Faisal Islamic Bank of Sudan in the 1970s and 1980s marked the beginning of the formalization of the modern time Islamic banking.

The global demand for Sharia-compliant products, with support and backing from multilateral organizations like the Islamic Development Bank (IsDB), and interest from Muslim-majority and minority groups have all contributed to the rise of Islamic banking in recent decades. To support Islamic banking, countries including Nigeria, Kenya, South Africa, Morocco, Tunisia, and Ethiopia have implemented legal frameworks or licenses (Ibrahim et al., 2024). On the other hand, the progress is still not uniform across the continent.

2.3 Types of Islamic Financial Institutions in Africa

Islamic banking institutions in Africa operate under different structures, each of which reflects the respective local legal, cultural, and economic realities:

Full-Fledged Islamic Banks: These are standalone institutions operating fully according to Islamic principles. Examples include Jaiz Bank (Nigeria), Gulf African Bank (Kenya), Albarka Bank (South Africa), Banque Al Baraka D'Algerie (Algeria), Faisal Islamic Bank (Sudan) and AlBaraka Bank (Egypt).
Islamic Banking Windows: These are special departments or units within conventional banks that offer Sharia compliant products. Examples include Stanbic IBTC (Nigeria), First National Bank (South Africa) and Absa Bank (Kenya), and Kenya Commercial Bank (Kenya).
Microfinance Banks: Most Islamic microfinance institutions have emerged to offer ethical financing to small-scale entrepreneurs, utilizing models such as Qard al-Hasan (benevolent loans).
Takaful: also known as Islamic insurance, is a type of insurance that is still in its early stages in Africa, but is already being offered in countries such as Sudan and Nigeria. Takaful providers offer insurance products that are in accordance with the Sharia.

2.4 Theoretical Perspectives on Islamic Banking Regulation

Regulation of Islamic banking must take into account both maqasid al-Sharia, which refers to the objectives of Islamic law, and conventional regulatory objectives, which include the protection of consumers, the maintenance of financial stability, and the strength of the system. Regulatory frameworks for Islamic finance are based on a number of different theories which include the following:

Public Interest Theory: This theory suggests that regulation is designed to protect the public from market failures, fraud, and instability. The goal of Islamic banking regulation is to protect depositors, maintain financial stability, and ensure that all activities adhere to Sharia (Mohd Zameri et al., 2024). Sharia principles prioritize the maslahah (public interest), which promotes benefits and prevents and limits harm in society.
Private Interest (Capture) Theory: This theory argues that regulations are sometimes influenced or captured by industry participants for their benefit. In the context of Islamic banking, there is a risk that the large Islamic financial institutions could lobby regulators for favorable rulings or leniency in Sharia

compliance. Therefore, strong and independent Sharia governance frameworks must be established (Jaradat & Oudat, 2025).

Institutional Theory: The behavior of organizations is influenced by the institutional environments in which they operate, particularly the need to conform to regulations and standards. Islamic banks are regulated not only by financial authorities but also by religious bodies like Sharia supervisory boards (Alam Choudhury & Nurul Alam, 2013; Muhammad &Yusoff, 2023). In various countries such as Malaysia, Saudi Arabia, and Bahrain, have different approaches to the institutionalization of Islamic finance. These approaches reflect the local religious, legal, as well as the political situations.

Stakeholder Theory: Unlike the shareholder theory, which focuses on maximizing profits, the stakeholder theory considers the interests of all parties affected by the actions of the institution. These include customers, employees, regulators, and the entire society. Islamic principles promote a stakeholder approach, establishing it on ideas like the right to ownership, clear contract agreement, and the wider Islamic view (Iqbal & Mirakhor, 2004). In Islamic banking, accountability extends not only to the society and other stakeholders, but also to God, which further enhances the ethical dimension of regulation.

Shari'ah Governance Framework: The Shariah governance system, which is exclusive to Islamic banking, ensures that all products and services are in accordance with Sharia principles and standards. Theoretically, it is based on Islamic jurisprudence, also known as fiqh al-muamalat, and it lays emphasis on ethical behavior, justice, transparency, and the prohibition of riba (interest), gharar (extreme uncertainty), and maysir (gambling) (Wasim & Zafar, 2024).

Agency Theory: There is a principal-agent relationship between depositors (also known as investors), and the bank management (Iqbal & Mirakhor, 2004). Due to the fact that they are required to serve both financial interests and Shariah compliance standards, Islamic banks are faced with a unique dual agency challenge. However, disclosure, transparency, and Shariah audits are principles enforced by regulators to help alleviate agency problems and challenges.

Maqasid al-Sharia (Objectives of Islamic Law) Perspective: The purpose of regulation is not just to ensure that operations are carried out in an efficient manner, but also to accomplish the higher goals of the Shariah, which are the preservation of religion, life, intellect, lineage, and wealth (Chapra et al., 2008). The regulation of Islamic banking aims to strike a balance between the pursuit of financial innovation and the pursuit of ethical and social goals that are derived from Maqasid al-Sharia.

Dual Compliance Theory: Under the Dual Compliance Theory, it means that Islamic financial institutions are required to conform not just with Sharia requirements but also with national financial regulations (Shabbir, 2022).

The concept emphasizes the importance of religious and secular authorities working together to coordinate their efforts.

Legal Pluralism: Most African states have legal systems that overlap with one another, including religious law, customary law, and statutory law (Diala, 2021). This results in complex regulatory dynamics for Islamic banking. Legal pluralism theory offers a useful tool by providing a perspective through which to view the coexistence of Islamic banking with various legal systems.

2.5 Standard Setting Bodies

Creating circumstances that are beneficial to Islamic finance has also been the goal of regional collaborations. For example, the financial harmonization agenda of the African Union and partnerships between central banks can benefit Islamic finance greatly. However, the implementation process continues to be slow because of issues such as inadequate resources, political instability, and a lack of understanding among regulators and stakeholders. The integration of global standards to fit the social and legal context of Islamic finance in Africa has been influenced by international standard-setting organizations such as:

AAOIFI (Accounting and Auditing Organization for Islamic Financial Institutions): AAOIFI is responsible for developing Sharia standards and governance structures. Some African countries are members and have adopted IFSB guidelines on capital adequacy, liquidity, and risk management tailored to Islamic banks.

IFSB (Islamic Financial Services Board): The IFSB is responsible for the issuance of regulatory and supervisory standards that are specifically designed for Islamic financial institutions.

IsDB (Islamic Development Bank): The IsDB works to expand access to Islamic financial services by providing support in the form of technical assistance and capacity building.

3. LEGAL AND REGULATORY CONTEXT IN AFRICA

3.0 Legal and Regulatory Framework in Africa

The regulatory framework for Islamic banking in Africa is shaped by a complex relationship between religious principles, statutory legal systems, the actions of central banks, and international standards. Generally speaking, the regulatory framework of Africa has been developed for conventional banking, with various degrees of tolerance for Islamic financial services. This section investigates the various legal and regulatory environments that exist in African countries. It investigates the efforts that have been made to incorporate Islamic banking into national financial systems, as well as the gaps that continue to exist and the conflicts that come from multiple compliance duties.

3.1 Dual Legal Systems and Regulatory Disparity

Most African countries operate under dual or pluralistic legal systems, which combine civil or common law systems that were established during the colonial era with customary and/or Islamic legal traditions. Despite the fact that it has its roots in culture, this plurality creates challenges for the supervision of financial institutions, particularly for Islamic banking, which gets its legitimacy from the principles of Sharia.

In countries that follow civil law, such as Francophone Africa, the law governing finances is codified and centered on the state, and there is little room for religious law to participate. Because there are no legal structures that are conducive to Islamic finance, it has been difficult to implement in these systems. While in common law jurisdictions, such as Nigeria, Kenya, and Ghana, it has a significantly greater degree of flexibility when it comes to the introduction of parallel financial systems. This is especially true in cases where Islamic law is constitutionally recognized or practiced in the courts.

Regulatory uncertainty can arise as a result of the lack of legal harmonization between Sharia and state law. This can restrict the validity and legality of Sharia-compliant contracts, particularly in situations involving the resolution of disputes.

3.2 Central Bank Approaches to Islamic Banking Regulation

The role of central banks and financial regulators is essential in establishing an ideal environment for Islamic banking. Regulators in Africa used three basic approaches:

1. **Proactive Regulatory Frameworks:**

Some countries have established comprehensive legal and regulatory frameworks to license and regulate Islamic financial institutions, with examples from:

Nigeria: The Central Bank of Nigeria (CBN) has issued guidelines for non-interest financial institutions, which include capital requirements, liquidity standards, and Sharia governance frameworks. In 2011, Jaiz Bank was licensed as a full-fledged Islamic bank, and subsequent institutions have been subject to this regulatory framework.

Sudan: Sudan has a completely Islamized banking system, with Islamic finance as the main standard. The Central Bank of Sudan operates according to Islamic principles, and all banks are required to adhere to Sharia law.

Kenya: Islamic banks and windows are licensed by the Central Bank of Kenya (CBK), and tax neutrality regulations regarding Islamic finance were implemented in 2017 by the Finance Act.

2. **Context-Specific Approaches**

Certain regulators facilitate Islamic finance by issuing specific licenses or interpreting existing rules, rather than establishing a separate system. For example:

South Africa: Although there is no specific Islamic banking legislation, the South African Reserve Bank (SARB) permits Islamic windows, and tax equivalent measures have been established for Islamic finance products.

Uganda and Ethiopia: These have authorized the formation of Islamic financial services on a case-by-case basis, dependent upon the development of a comprehensive legal or statutory framework.

3. **Restrictive or Absent Regulation**

In some countries like Ghana, Cameroon, and South Sudan, Islamic banking is either unregulated or specifically excluded due to a lack of political will, religious sensitivities, or a lack of knowledge and understanding among policymakers. In these circumstances, Islamic finance is either informal or restricted to community-based arrangements lacking central supervision.

3.3 Sharia Governance Frameworks

A fundamental element of Islamic banking regulation is the Sharia governance framework, which guarantees that institutions adhere to Islamic legal principles. This includes:

i. **Internal Sharia Boards (ISBs):** Institutional entities within banks that evaluate contracts and oversee operations for Sharia compliance.
ii. **Centralized Sharia Advisory Boards:** Certain countries, such as Nigeria and Sudan, have instituted national Sharia advisory councils under the central bank or the ministry of finance to provide oversight, standardize fatwas, and issue policy directives.

Some challenges in Sharia governance in Africa include:

i. Inadequate qualified Sharia scholars possessing financial expertise.
ii. Different interpretations of Sharia across jurisdictions.
iii. The absence of national standard-setting bodies in numerous countries.
iv. Conflicts between ISBs and regulators regarding regulatory power and authority.

3.4 Conflict Resolution and Legal Compliance

The possibility of the enforcement of Islamic financial agreements constitutes an additional legal obstacle. The conventional courts may be inadequate in knowledge or jurisdiction to resolve disputes involving Islamic contracts such as Murabaha or Mudarabah. In jurisdictions where Sharia is not acknowledged in business resolution, contract interpretation may be distorted or rendered void. Some countries (e.g., Sudan, parts of Nigeria) allow Sharia-based arbitration or the incorporation of Sharia principles in contracts, hence enhancing legal certainty. Nevertheless, the majority of African states do not possess specialized commercial courts or judges proficient in Islamic finance jurisprudence.

3.5 Taxation and Accounting Standards

Islamic financial transactions often involve multiple contracts (e.g., Murabaha, which involves purchase and resale), and might attract double taxation if not specifically addressed. Few African countries have updated their tax laws to ensure neutrality for Islamic financial products. Moreover, accounting standards also create another challenge. While AAOIFI standards are used in some institutions, most countries apply the International Financial Reporting Standards (IFRS), which may not fully align with the nature of Islamic finance contracts.

However, some countries, like Kenya and Nigeria, are working to harmonize their regulatory framework with international Islamic finance standards. However, implementation is inconsistent, and capacity is limited.

4. THE INTERACTION BETWEEN SHARIA GOVERNANCE AND NATIONAL LEGAL FRAMEWORKS

4.0 Introduction

Sharia governance refers to the institutional frameworks that Islamic financial institutions (IFIs) employ to ensure adherence to the Sharia. It includes both internal mechanisms, like Sharia supervisory boards, and external regulatory frameworks that govern Sharia compliance at the national level. In the African context, this relationship is frequently complex, as Islamic finance is evolving within a predominantly secular legal framework or dual legal systems. This section examines the form of Sharia governance in African countries, the extent to which national legal frameworks integrate it, and the potential legal and regulatory challenges that may emerge.

4.1 Defining Sharia Governance

The Accounting and Auditing Organization for Islamic Financial Institutions (AAOIFI) and Islamic Financial Services Board (IFSB) provide guidance on Sharia governance frameworks, recommending both institutional and national-level Sharia oversight.

Sharia governance in Islamic finance includes the following mechanisms:

i. Ensure that all financial products and services comply with the Sharia principles.
ii. Provide continuous Sharia audit and review.
iii. Issue fatwas or rulings on financial transactions.
iv. Report to stakeholders on compliance status.

4.2 Internal Sharia Supervisory Boards (SSBs)

Most Islamic banks in Africa are mandated to establish Sharia Supervisory Boards (SSBs) that review, evaluate, and approve product structures, monitor implementation, and advise management on compliance issues.

Some challenges faced by internal SSBs in Africa:

i. Shortage of qualified scholars with dual expertise in Islamic jurisprudence and conventional finance.
ii. Lack of independence from management in some institutions.
iii. Variability in fatwas, resulting in inconsistency across institutions and jurisdictions.
iv. Lack of formal legal recognition in some countries weakens the enforcement of SSB rulings and decisions.

However, some countries, like Nigeria and Sudan, have established guidelines for the structure and function of SSBs, including qualifications, tenure, and reporting lines. However, implementation and supervision vary significantly.

4.3 Centralized Sharia Governance Structures

To ensure uniformity and mitigate conflicts of interest, some African countries have established centralized Sharia governance bodies. Such centralized frameworks enhance legal certainty and assurance, standardize compliance practices, and reduce reputational risk for the industry. However, they must operate independently, transparently, and in harmony with state law. These include countries such as:

Nigeria

The Financial Regulation Advisory Council of Experts (FRACE) under the Central Bank of Nigeria provides Sharia guidance for Islamic finance products and institutions. FRACE plays a quasi-regulatory role, reviewing products before approval and ensuring consistency across the entire sector.

Sudan

The Higher Sharia Supervisory Board (HSSB) functions within the Central Bank of Sudan and acts as the supreme authority on Sharia compliance. All banks must seek their approval before launching financial products.

Kenya and Ethiopia

There is an ongoing reform that seeks to establish national-level Sharia boards under the central bank or the Ministry of Finance.

4.4 Conflicts Between State Law and Sharia Principles

A major challenge in African countries is harmonizing Islamic legal requirements with existing banking laws. Some areas of conflict and conflicts and concern include:

Interest Prohibition (Riba): Conventional banking law is built on the acceptance of interest, while Islamic finance prohibits it outright. Therefore, licensing and reporting rules may not accommodate profit-sharing contracts like Mudarabah or Musharakah.

Asset Ownership and Taxation: Islamic finance often requires asset transfers, which may result in tax liabilities or be inconsistent with existing legal documentation standards.

Dispute Resolution: National courts may lack the capacity to adjudicate on Sharia-based contracts. In some jurisdictions, Islamic finance disputes are resolved through arbitration or special tribunals (e.g., Sharia courts in parts of northern Nigeria).

Consumer Protection and Disclosure: Regulatory guidelines may not cover the unique risks and structures of Islamic contracts, exposing consumers to misunderstandings.

4.5 Comparative Case Studies

Sudan: An Integrated Model with Full Sharia Governance

Sudan is an example of a country where Sharia governance is well integrated in the legal and regulatory framework, especially in the banking sector. In this model, all banks are required to operate in accordance with Islamic principles. This includes strict compliance with rules against interest (riba), uncertainty (gharar), and gambling (maysir), which are foundational principles in Islamic finance. The legal system in Sudan is structured in such a way that Sharia-based commercial laws govern contracts across all sectors, not just banking.

The integrated model in Sudan means that Islamic finance is the primary and dominant structure, and there is little to no reliance on conventional banking systems or legal frameworks for financial transactions. The integrated model in Sudan means that Islamic finance is the default and dominant structure, and there is little to no reliance on conventional banking systems or legal frameworks for financial transactions. However, this model may present challenges, which may limit diversity in the financial products available to customers. Additionally, it requires a highly specialized judiciary and regulatory body to oversee the system effectively.

Nigeria: A Dual Legal System with Centralized Sharia Advisory

Nigeria has a dual legal system, where both conventional and Islamic law co-exist. The legal system allows for the recognition of Sharia-compliant contracts within the wider framework of Nigerian law. Nigeria's Financial Regulation Advisory Council of Experts (FRACE) plays a central role in advising on Sharia compliance within the banking sector, providing an extra level of supervision to ensure that Islamic financial services operate according to Islamic principles.

The Nigerian dual system allows for a flexible and balanced approach to Islamic finance, offering more opportunities for legal integration while maintaining conventional legal structures. The challenge, however, is the complexity of managing two parallel systems and ensuring that both Sharia principles and conventional financial regulations are adequately enforced.

South Africa: Islamic Finance Under Conventional Regulatory Structures

South Africa offers a more flexible and practical approach to Islamic finance found in a conventional environment. There is no centralized Sharia board or Sharia-specific regulatory framework in place. Instead, Islamic banks operate under conventional legal and regulatory structures, with the addition of internal Sharia Supervisory Boards (SSBs) to ensure that financial products are compliant with Islamic principles.

The South African model allows Islamic finance to operate within the conventional legal system with a certain degree of flexibility, which may face challenges such as lack of uniformity in Sharia compliance across banks and potential conflicts between the general legal structures and specific Islamic finance principles.

Each country has adopted a unique model of incorporating Islamic finance within its legal and regulatory framework, and each model reflects a different balance between Sharia compliance, legal flexibility, and regulatory oversight. Some of the key differences and insights include:

i. **A fully integrated system in Sudan that** provides the most Sharia-compliant model, ensuring that all financial products and contracts are rooted in Islamic law. This creates strong alignment, but could limit diversity and flexibility.
ii. **The dual legal system in Nigeria that** offers a balance by incorporating Islamic finance into the broader legal system, allowing for more flexible interaction between conventional and Sharia-compliant legal principles.
iii. **The flexible approach** of South Africa that allows Islamic banks to operate under general legal structures with internal SSBs overseeing Sharia compliance. This provides significant flexibility, but can lead to inconsistencies due to the absence of a centralized Sharia regulatory authority.

5. COMPARATIVE LEGAL ANALYSIS BETWEEN AFRICA AND OTHER ISLAMIC FINANCE JURISDICTIONS

5.0 Introduction

This section provides an insight into the Islamic finance legal and regulatory framework in Africa and other prominent jurisdictions, including Malaysia, the Gulf Cooperation Council (GCC) countries, Pakistan, and Indonesia. The objective is to highlight best practices, regulatory innovations, and potential lessons for African countries seeking to strengthen their legal systems for Islamic finance. The comparison focuses on regulatory frameworks, Sharia governance models, legal recognition of Islamic contracts, dispute resolution, and integration with international standards.

5.1 Malaysia

Malaysia is often referred to as the global model for Islamic finance because to its strong legal framework, comprehensive regulatory oversight, and a well-established Sharia governance. some of the main attributes of Malaysian system include:

i. Dual Legal System: where the civil and Sharia law coexist, although Islamic banking is overseen by clear legal and regulatory frameworks.
ii. The Shariah Advisory Council (SAC) of Bank Negara Malaysia (BNM) is the sole authoritative body on Islamic finance issues. Its decisions are legally binding for courts and financial institutions.
iii. The Islamic Financial Services Act (IFSA) 2013, a specific legislation that consolidates the legal aspects of Islamic banking and requires financial firms to follow Sharia rules.

Judicial Expertise: Malaysia has developed specific courts and trained judges to handle Islamic money disputes, increasing legal certainty and enforcement.

Africa should prioritize legal acceptance and centralization of Sharia guidance to ensure consistent practice. In addition, having dedicated legislation, such as IFSA, improves clarity and reduces reliance on conventional banking laws.

5.2 Gulf Cooperation Council (GCC) Countries:

Despite their Islamic history, the GCC countries have diverse legal and regulatory approaches to Islamic banking.

The **UAE** has both Islamic and conventional banks under a dual banking framework. The Islamic finance sector is overseen by the Higher Sharia Authority (HSA), which reports to the UAE Central Bank. The Federal laws recognize Islamic financial contracts, but judicial interpretations can differ.

For **Saudi Arabia**, while the entire banking system is nominally Sharia-compliant, there is no fully fledged Islamic banking law. Legal conflicts are resolved using Sharia principles in Sharia courts, however modern financial legislation co-exists.

However, **Bahrain** is a regional leader with strong regulatory guidance from the Central Bank of Bahrain and adheres to AAOIFI standards. which has developed a legal framework to enable Islamic banking dispute resolution and contract enforcement.

Africa can benefit from institutional flexibility, even if the banking system is not fully Islamic. Additionally, the adoption of international Sharia standards (such as AAOIFI) can increase credibility and harmonization.

5.3 Pakistan:

Pakistan has stated its' intention to Islamize its banking system and has taken legal steps towards that end. The Federal Shariat Court has ruled against interest-based banking, pushing authorities to adopt Islamic models. However, the dual banking system remains in existence, but Islamic finance is growing. The State Bank of Pakistan (SBP) has issued detailed Sharia governance regulations and guidelines, and has established a Shariah Board to oversee Islamic banks.

However, there are challenges of inconsistencies in implementation, and delays in law enforcement due to political and institutional challenges. Moreover, Courts vary in capacity and interpretation of the Islamic commercial law.

For Africa to achieve full Sharia conformity, it must prioritize institutional capacity, political will, and public awareness, in addition to legal reform. In addition, a strong judicial system is required for successful implementation.

5.4. Indonesia:

Indonesia, which is the country with the highest Muslim population in the world, provides a unique example of innovation in Islamic banking within the framework of a multicultural legal and religious environment. One of the most important aspects is that the Financial Services Authority (OJK) licenses Islamic banks in addition to conventional banks, which guarantees integration.

Under the guidance of the Indonesian Council of Ulama, the National Sharia Board (DSN-MUI) is responsible for issuing fatwas on various financial products and services.

Furthermore, dispute resolution processes that are in accordance with Sharia law have been implemented, and Islamic financial products are recognized by the national law.

State-owned Islamic banks and the utilization of digital platforms for Islamic microfinance projects were established in order to improve financial inclusion has emerged.

African countries can improve transparency through institutional coordination between the Sharia boards and regulators. African countries can also leverage technology and community-based Islamic financing to expand reach and inclusion.

5.5 Implications for Africa

There are a lot of lessons to learn from the policies and implementation strategies of Malaysia, the GCC region, Pakistan and Indonesia, which can improve their operations and facilitate growth and expansion of Islamic finance across Africa. These lessons include:

i. A dedicated Islamic finance legislation like the Islamic Financial Services Act (IFSA) 2013 is fundamental in establishing a well-defined legal environment in Malaysia. This implies that a dedicated law that clearly governs Islamic finance services and products will reduce legal misconceptions in Africa. Legal clarity will also ensure that all contracts or services and products will be Sharia-compliant to both domestic and foreign investors. More so, countries like Nigeria and Kenya, that have already begun to develop Islamic finance frameworks, can take this further by codifying Islamic finance principles into national legislation.
ii. African countries should consider institutionalizing national Sharia advisory councils to avoid conflicting Sharia rulings between institutions, serve as a bridge between financial regulators and religious authorities, and also provide definitive guidance for courts, regulators, and financial institutions. The Financial Regulation Advisory Council of Experts (FRACE) in Nigeria is a good starting point, but its effectiveness depends on legal empowerment and independence.
iii. Courts in Indonesia and Malaysia have dedicated benches or trained judges for Islamic finance disputes. This ensures that Sharia-compliant contracts are adjudicated fairly and knowledgeably, preventing misinterpretations through conventional lenses. Therefore, African judicial systems must invest in training judges, magistrates, and legal practitioners in the principles, contracts, and dispute mechanisms of Islamic finance.
iv. Adopting International standards like AAOIFI and IFSB standards have become global benchmarks for Islamic finance operations, governance, and risk management. Therefore, African regulators should adopt or adapt AAOIFI and IFSB standards to local contexts. This will help in harmonizing practices across borders, improve transparency and financial reporting as well as encourage cross-border investment and regional financial integration.
v. The strong political backing and regulatory coordination in Indonesia have led to the growth of a dual financial system where Islamic finance thrives alongside conventional finance. This implies that Governments and central banks need to demonstrate clear commitment through policy statements, dedicated departments or desks for Islamic finance, and awareness campaigns to build consumer trust. This top-down support is essential for building institutional infrastructure,

driving reforms, and attracting both public and private sector investment into Islamic finance.

6. BUILDING A UNIFIED REGULATORY MODEL FOR ISLAMIC BANKING IN AFRICA

6.0 Introduction

As Islamic banking in Africa continues to grow and expand, it still faces some legal challenges, inconsistent Sharia governance, and weak implementation mechanisms. This section proposes a harmonized regulatory framework for the African setting, drawing lessons from global best practices while addressing the unique institutional realities of Africa. The framework aims to enhance regulatory clarity, promote financial inclusion, and promote investor confidence in Islamic finance.

6.1 Benefits of Harmonization

Islamic banking operates across various countries in Africa, each with its legal traditions, religious demographics, and levels of financial development. The main motivations for harmonizing Islamic finance regulation include:

i. **Legal Certainty**: A clear legal framework reduces risks associated with unclear or poor implementation of Islamic contracts.
ii. **Cross-Border Operations**: Harmonized standards facilitate regional integration and the growth of pan-African Islamic financial institutions.
iii. **Sharia Compliance Assurance**: Uniform Sharia governance standards promote consistency and reduce reputational risks.
iv. **Investor Confidence**: Investors require a reliable and sustainable regulatory environment as well as dispute resolution infrastructure.
v. **Financial Inclusion**: Regulatory clarity helps unlock the potential of Islamic finance in serving the unbanked populations.

6.2 Foundation of Harmonized Model

A harmonized Islamic banking framework in Africa should be built around the following components:

A. Legal Infrastructure Reform

i. **Dedicated Islamic Finance Legislation**: Countries should establish a specific Islamic banking act or incorporate clear provisions into existing financial laws to govern Islamic banking operations.
ii. **Recognition of Sharia Contracts**: Legal recognition of contracts like *Murabaha*, *Ijara*, *Mudarabah*, and *Musharakah* is essential for implementation.
iii. **Codification of Sharia Principles**: Embedding Sharia-compliant principles within financial regulation to avoid ambiguity.

B. Centralized Sharia Governance
i. **National Sharia Advisory Councils**: Establishment of central Sharia boards at the national level, empowered to issue binding rulings on Islamic finance practices.
ii. **Standardization of Fatwas**: Harmonizing Sharia interpretations across institutions to minimize conflicting rulings.
iii. **Mandatory Internal Sharia Boards**: All Islamic banks should maintain internal Sharia supervisory boards, with members vetted by national councils.

C. Regulatory Coordination and Oversight
i. **Dedicated Regulatory Units**: Central banks and financial authorities should establish Islamic finance directorates.
ii. **Harmonization with Global Standards**: Alignment with AAOIFI, IFSB, and Basel guidelines to ensure international compatibility.
iii. **Supervisory Capacity Building**: Training regulators and supervisors in Islamic finance principles and risks management.

D. Judicial and Dispute Resolution Mechanisms
i. **Specialized Financial Tribunals or Courts**: Setting up dedicated benches for Islamic finance disputes or integrating Islamic finance expertise into existing courts.
ii. **Alternative Dispute Resolution (ADR)**: Encouraging arbitration and mediation through Islamic finance arbitration centers.

E. Capacity Building and Awareness
i. **Professional Training**: Developing certification programs for Sharia scholars, regulators, bankers, and judges.
ii. **Public Education Campaigns**: Raising awareness about Islamic finance through outreach in local languages.
iii. **University Curriculum Integration**: Mainstreaming Islamic finance in law, economics, and business education.

6.3 The Role of Regional and Continental Institutions

Africa has several regional economic communities and institutions that can help drive harmonization:

i. **African Union (AU) and African Development Bank (AfDB)** – AU and AfDB can support the development of a model Islamic banking regulatory framework for member states. In addition to promotion of regional policy alignment and technical assistance.
ii. **The Economic and Monetary Community of Central Africa (WAEMU) and Central African Economic and Monetary Community (CEMAC)** -These monetary unions can integrate Islamic finance into their regulatory architecture, facilitating cross-border Sharia-compliant banking.
iii. **Africa Regional Technical Assistance Centers (AFRITACs and Regional Central Banks)** - The Regional Technical Assistance Centers for IMF (AFRITACs) can provide capacity building and technical support. Likewise, the regional central banks can facilitate dialogue between member countries on regulatory convergence.

6.4 Implementation Strategy: A Phased Approach

Table 1. Given the diversity in readiness across African countries, a phased approach is advisable:

Phase	Description	Activity
Assessment	Baseline assessment of legal and regulatory frameworks	Legal audits, gap analysis, stakeholder engagement
Policy design	Development of harmonized guidelines and model laws.	Drafting policy papers, consultations with Sharia scholars.
Institutional setup	Creation of central Sharia boards, regulatory bodies	Staffing, institutional development, and rulemaking
Capacity building	Training programs and technical assistance.	Workshops, curriculum development, certifications
Monitoring and evaluation	Ongoing review of progress and impact.	Compliance audits, policy revision, stakeholder feedback.

6.5 Potential Challenges and Risk Mitigation

Table 2.

Challenges	Risk	Mitigation
Legal diversity (common law, civil law, Islamic law)	Inconsistent implementation.	Inconsistent implementation.
Political resistance	Policy delays.	Engage stakeholders early, demonstrate economic value.
Lack of trained personnel	Regulatory gaps.	Partner with international Islamic finance institutions for training.
Sharia diversity	Conflicting rulings.	Promote scholarly consensus and cross-country Sharia forums.

6.6 Benefits of Harmonization

Financial Stability: harmonization will bring stronger oversight and governance, and also reduce the risks of systemic crises.
Regional Economic Integration: Facilitates intra-African investment and trade through Islamic finance.
Improved Access to Global Capital: Harmonized standards will align Africa with global Sukuk markets and investors.
Increased Financial Inclusion: Sharia-compliant options attract previously excluded populations.
Boost to SDGs: Islamic finance can support the developmental goals of Africa through ethical, and inclusive financing mechanisms.

7. CONCLUSION AND POLICY RECOMMENDATIONS

Islamic banking in Africa has a lot of opportunities as well as unique regulatory challenges. This chapter has examined the dual concept of complying with Sharia principles, while also adhering to national financial regulations, that creates a complex legal environment. African countries that have embraced Islamic finance often struggle to balance religious authenticity with financial stability, leading to inconsistencies in regulatory frameworks, insufficient Sharia governance structures, and a lack of harmonization across jurisdictions.

Several African countries have made considerable steps in the establishment of IF institutions, especially Nigeria, Sudan, Kenya, and South Africa. However, the growth of Islamic banking is slowed down due to the challenges with the legal system, limited institutional capacity, and varying degrees of political and regulatory will. These challenges are further compounded by the dominance of conventional financial systems, a shortage of qualified personnel, and the absence of robust dispute resolution mechanisms based in both Sharia and civil law.

Comparative views from more developed countries in terms of IF, such as Malaysia, Bahrain, and Pakistan, reveal that regulatory success in Islamic banking depends on establishing a sound legal foundation, integrating Sharia governance within the main financial regulatory framework, and ensuring consistent supervision by a dedicated financial expert. The different legal systems in Africa, ranging from common law and civil law to customary and Islamic law, offer both an opportunity and a challenge in this regard.

Policy Recommendations

The following policy recommendations were proposed to strengthen the legal and regulatory environment for Islamic banking in Africa:

i. **Establish Unified Legal Frameworks** - National legislatures should establish specific laws or amend existing banking legislation to recognize and support Islamic financial services. These laws should define the main Sharia-compliant instruments and clarify the legal status of Islamic banks.
ii. **Develop Centralized Sharia Advisory Councils** - Each country should create or empower a national Sharia Advisory Council that works alongside the central bank to ensure Sharia compliance and reduce different interpretations between institutions.
iii. **Enhance Regulatory Capacity** - Regulatory bodies should invest in training financial supervisors on Islamic finance principles, enabling more effective supervision and risk assessment.
iv. **Promote Cross-Border Harmonization** - Regional economic communities like ECOWAS and SADC should initiate efforts to harmonize Islamic finance regulations, enabling the growth of cross-border banking operations and Islamic capital markets.
v. **Encourage Public-Private Partnership** - Governments should work with private Islamic financial institutions, law faculties, and international organizations such as the IFSB and AAOIFI to promote innovation, capacity building, and regulatory compliance.
vi. **Enhance Consumer Protection and Awareness** - Legal frameworks should include provisions that ensure transparency in Islamic financial products, protect consumers, and promote financial literacy to promote trust in the system.

vii. **Support Dispute Resolution Mechanisms** - Establish specialized tribunals or incorporate Islamic finance expertise into existing commercial courts to handle Sharia-related banking disputes effectively.

viii. **Facilitate International Technical Assistance** - African countries can benefit from partnerships with countries that already have successful Islamic finance models through technical assistance, knowledge exchange, and regulatory support.

REFERENCES

Alam Choudhury, M., & Nurul Alam, M. (2013). Corporate governance in Islamic perspective. *International journal of Islamic and Middle Eastern finance and management, 6*(3), 180-199.

Chapra, M. U., Khan, S., & Al Shaikh-Ali, A. (2008). *The Islamic Vision of Development in the Light of Maqasid Al-Shariah (Occasional Paper).* International Institute of Islamic Thought (IIIT).

Diala, A. C. (2021). Legal Pluralism and the Future of Personal Family Laws in Africa. *International Journal of Law, Policy and the Family*, *35*(1), ebab023. DOI: 10.1093/lawfam/ebab023

Ibrahim, A. A., Hussein, J. M., & Kulmie, D. A. (2024). Islamic Banking in Africa: A Booming Market with Growing Pains. *International Journal of Religion*, *5*(9), 318–333. DOI: 10.61707/3dg7rh70

Ibrahim, A. A., Hussein, J. M., & Kulmie, D. A. (2024). Islamic Banking in Africa: A Booming Market with Growing Pains. *International Journal of Religion*, *5*(9), 318–333. DOI: 10.61707/3dg7rh70

. Iqbal, Z., & Mirakhor, A. (2004). Stakeholders model of governance in Islamic economic system.

Iqbal, Z., & Mirakhor, A. (2011). An introduction to Islamic finance [). John Wiley & Sons.]. *Theory into Practice*, *687*.

. Jaradat, H., & Oudat, M. S. (2025). Enhancing clarity and transparency in Islamic financial practices: the role of regulatory influence. *Journal of Financial Reporting and Accounting*.

Mohd Zameri, S. N., Syed Alwi, S. F., Mohammad Hatta, M. F., & Saiful Fikri, A. A. H. (2024). Maslahah and its Application in Islamic Finance. [IJIB]. *International Journal of Islamic Business*, *9*(1), 82–94.

. Muhammad, A. U., & Yusoff, M. (2023). Effect of Shari'ah Governance on Performance of Fully Fledged Islamic Banks in Africa. *KnE Social Sciences*, 754-768.

Shabbir, M. S. (2022). Regulatory and Supervisory Regime of Islamic Banking System in Nigeria: Challenges, Constraints and Way Forward. *Journal of Islamic Banking & Finance*, *39*(2).

Sivanandan, P., & Ahmad, R. (2025). Ethical Investment in Islamic Finance: The Role of ESG Toward Sustainable Growth. In *Islamic Finance and Corporate Governance: Synergies for Sustainable Growth* (pp. 43-56). Emerald Publishing Limited.

Wasim, M. H., & Zafar, M. B. (2024). Shariah governance and Islamic banks: A systematic literature review. *Journal of Islamic Accounting and Business Research*. Advance online publication. DOI: 10.1108/JIABR-11-2023-0386

KEY TERMS AND DEFINITIONS

AAOIFI (Accounting and Auditing Organization for Islamic Financial Institutions): A global organization that develops accounting, auditing, governance, and Sharia standards for the Islamic finance industry.

Gharar: Refers to excessive uncertainty or ambiguity in contractual terms or subject matter, which is not allowed in Islamic transactions.

IFSB (Islamic Financial Services Board): An international standard-setting body that issues prudential standards and guidelines for Islamic financial institutions.

Ijara: An Islamic leasing contract where the bank buys and leases out an asset, transferring ownership at the end of the lease term.

Ijma: Consensus of Islamic scholars on a legal issue, considered a secondary source of Sharia.

Islamic Development Bank (IsDB): A multilateral development institution established to foster economic development in accordance with Islamic principles across its member countries.

Islamic Finance: A financial system based on principles of Islamic law (Sharia), which prohibits interest (riba), promotes risk-sharing, and requires transactions to be backed by real assets.

Maqasid al-Sharia: The higher objectives of Islamic law, which aim to preserve religion, life, intellect, lineage, and wealth.

Maysir: Gambling or speculative behavior, which is prohibited in Islamic finance due to its unproductive and risky nature.

Mudarabah: A profit-sharing contract where one party provides capital and the other manages the investment. Profits are shared as agreed, while losses are borne by the capital provider.

Murabaha: A cost-plus sale contract where the seller discloses the cost and profit margin to the buyer.

Musharakah: A partnership structure in which all partners contribute capital and share in profits and losses proportionally.

Qard al-Hasan: An interest-free loan extended for welfare or charitable purposes, with repayment of only the principal amount.

Qiyas: Analogical reasoning used by Islamic jurists to apply established principles to new situations.

Riba: Literally translated as "increase," however, riba refers to interest or any guaranteed gain on loans, which is strictly prohibited in Islamic finance.

Sharia: Also written as Shari'ah, Shariah means Islamic law, which is derived from the Qur'an, Sunnah (Prophetic traditions), and other jurisprudential sources. It governs all aspects of Muslim life, including finance.

Sunnah: The recorded practices, sayings, and approvals of the Prophet Muhammad (peace be upon him), considered a primary source of Islamic law alongside the Qur'an.

Takaful: Islamic cooperative insurance based on mutual assistance, where members contribute to a pool to support each other in times of need.

Chapter 3
Debt Without Usury: How Islamic Finance Can Reshape Sovereign Borrowing in Developing Nations

Abdul-Hamid Abdul-Wahab
https://orcid.org/0000-0001-7219-1027
University for Development Studies, Ghana

Ibrahim Nandom Yakubu
https://orcid.org/0000-0003-4424-996X
University for Development Studies, Ghana

ABSTRACT

This chapter explores Islamic finance as a sustainable alternative to conventional sovereign borrowing, emphasizing risk-sharing and asset-backed models over usury (riba). With developing nations facing severe debt crises, Islamic finance offers solutions through instruments like sukuk (Islamic bonds) and profit-loss-sharing (PLS) arrangements, enhancing fiscal resilience and aligning with Sustainable Development Goals (SDGs). Case studies from Malaysia, Indonesia, Nigeria, and non-Muslim-majority countries demonstrate sukuk's success in infrastructure financing, lower defaults, and green investments. However, regulatory gaps, market limitations, and expertise shortages hinder adoption. The study concludes that Islamic finance can transform sovereign debt by promoting ethical, stable, and inclusive economic growth.

DOI: 10.4018/979-8-3373-1887-5.ch003

1. INTRODUCTION

1.1 Overview of Sovereign Debt Challenges in Developing Nations

Globally, developing nations are facing a sovereign debt crisis like never before, which is threatening their economic stability and development opportunities. The problem has today grown to alarmingly high levels, as the United Nations Conference on Trade and Development (UNCTAD) estimates the total debt stock of developing countries to be at $11.4 trillion at the end of 2022, a 15.7 percent increase over where it stood at the end of 2019, just as the COVID-19 pandemic began (UNCTAD, 2023). It is this exponential increase in debt service obligations that has placed countries in a debt trap, unable to service the debts they already owe while at the same time finding the need to finance their development and respond to other countries' shocks.

This cycle of debt has become more acute in the post COVID-19 context as developing countries have been unable to generate as much revenue as expected, while struggling with growing expenditures in healthcare. According to the World Bank, approximately 52% of low-income countries are evaluated as experiencing a high risk of debt distress or are currently in a state of debt distress (World Bank, 2024). This situation demonstrates not only the immediate effects of the pandemic, but long-standing structural deficiencies of mainstream forms of debt financing over several decades.

While the debt sustainability problem takes on different forms in different regions, it presents features which ultimately constitute an obstacle to sustainable economic development. Debt service obligations in Sub-Saharan Africa in 2022 stood at 11.6% of government revenues on average, depriving local governments of fiscal resources that could have been devoted to infrastructure, health, and education (African Development Bank, 2023). Debt-to-GDP ratios are spiraling upwards for small island developing states, and many are struggling to contend with public finance pressures and the increasing burden of climate change on their economies (Volz et al., 2020).

Confronted with these complex set of challenges, the standard responses to debt and debt management are clearly not sufficient. Such measures only act as temporary measures of relief without addressing structural issues, and repackaged countries become indebted again within a short period of time (World Bank, 2022). This provides evidence that a fundamental reform of sovereign borrowing regimes is needed to overcome the cycle of indebtedness as well as ensuring that sustainable financing for development is realized.

Interest-based lending tends to be procyclical rather than counter-cyclical, exacerbating economic fluctuations instead of stabilizing rough conditions. In other words, during economic contractions, in which government revenues drop and credit has to be expanded, a fixed point remains as the service of the debt, exerting further downward fiscal pressure when countries are most in need of that credit expansion (Reinhart & Rogoff, 2010; Reinhart & Rogoff, 2009). This pattern is evidenced by the 2008 global financial crises when developing countries were hit with falling commodity prices, falling export revenue, and increasing debt-service obligations (Askari et al., 2010).

Inherent moral hazard from this type of interest-based finance creates temptation for both lenders and borrowers to take on additional risk. Private sector lenders, particularly if they believe they will be bailed out, may, in the pursuit of a good profit, lend more than regular levels, or transfer risks to others (Georgiou, 2009; Admati & Hellwig, 2013). Alternatively, governments that are facing voter pressure or that have imminent needs for development may be willing to accumulate an amount of debt that is unreasonable. Democratically elected governments have incentives to focus on the electoral reward of short-term policies instead of on sound economic policy that would prevent waste or shifting of economic burdens onto future generations of taxpayers (Krugman, 1998). This distortion of borrowing incentives is exacerbated by fiscal dominance and similar issues, whereby central banks are made to feel compelled to monetize debt (Jung et al., 2025).

1.2 Emergence of Islamic Finance as an Alternative

Islamic finance has begun to emerge as a promising alternative to conventional loaning that is based on interest. Many of the systemic problems with the way in which sovereign debt financing functions can be tackled by some of the concepts and practices that it offers. Islamic finance is concerned with risk-sharing, asset-backing and ethical financial intermediation. It is a system that is governed by *Shariah* law and is based on the principles that prohibit usury (*riba*), excessive uncertainty (*gharar*) and speculative activities (*maysir*) (ISRA, 2012; El-Gamal, 2006). Such practice can create a financial structure that develops secure and long-lasting relationship among borrowers and lenders (Iqbal & Mirakhor, 2011). According to the Islamic Financial Services Board (IFSB) estimates, the total assets of the global Islamic finance industry currently stand at USD 3.88 trillion (see figure 1) as at end 2024. This represents a significant growth of 14.9% recorded in 2024 (IFSB, 2025).

Figure 1. Global Islamic Finance Total Asset Size (USD in Trillion) (2020 - 2024)

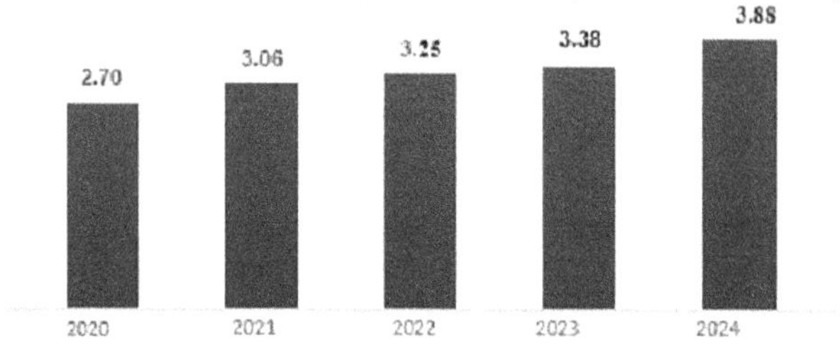

Source: IFSB (2025)

The prohibition of *riba*, or predetermined interest payments, represents perhaps the most significant departure from conventional financing mechanisms. Instead of fixed interest charges, Islamic finance employs profit-and-loss sharing arrangements, asset-backed securities, and trade-based financing structures that link returns to actual economic performance and productive activities. This fundamental shift from debt-based to equity-based financing creates more flexible and responsive financial relationships that can better accommodate the economic cycles and development needs of borrowing countries (Iqbal & Mirakhor, 2011).

Sukuk, often referred to as Islamic bonds, are financial certificates that have emerged as particularly relevant instruments for sovereign financing, representing one of the fastest-growing segments of the global Islamic finance industry (Bennett & Coyle, 2025). Unlike conventional bonds that represent debt obligations with predetermined interest payments, *sukuk* are asset-backed securities that provide investors with ownership stakes in underlying assets or projects. The favorable financing conditions and increasing demand from both governmental and corporate issuers led to a global *sukuk* issuances growth of 25.6%, reaching USD 230.40 billion, according to the Islamic Financial Services Board (IFSB, 2025). With a total issuance of around $180 billion in 2024 alone, the market is still on track to attain a total outstanding amount of $1 trillion in the coming years (Bennett & Coyle, 2025). Total outstanding sukuk surpassed USD 900 billion in 2024, as new *sukuk* issuances increased by 25.6% to USD 230.4 billion (see figure 2) (IFSB, 2025). Sovereign and quasi-sovereign *sukuk* issuances continue to dominate the sukuk market with sovereign issuers accounting for about 52.9% of total issuances (see figure 3) (IFSB, 2025).

Figure 2. Global Sukuk Issuances and Outstanding (2004-2024) (USD in Billion)

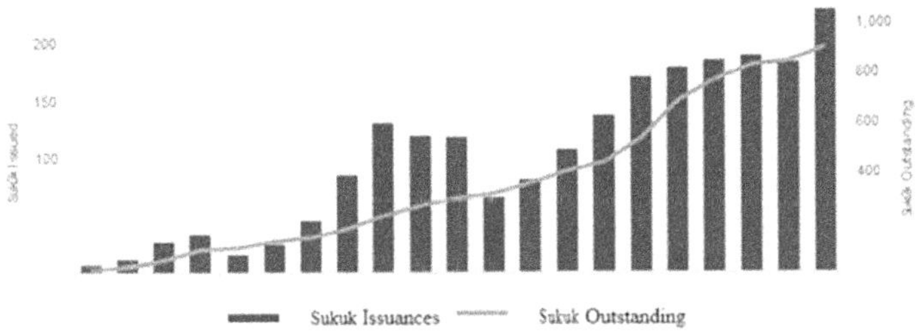

Source: IFSB (2025)

Figure 3. Sukuk issuances by Issuer Type (2024)

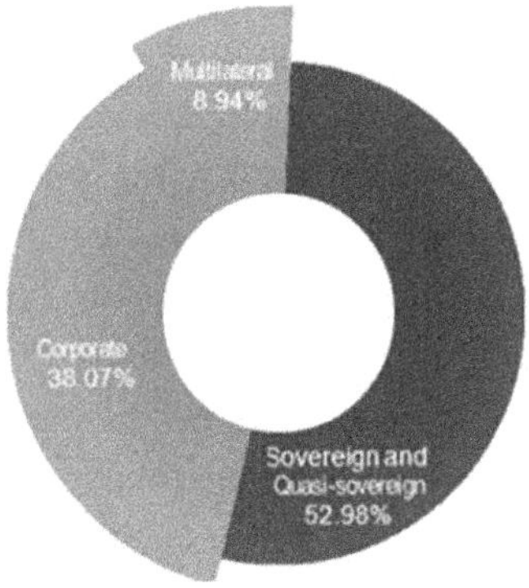

Source: IFSB (2025)

Among the other significant international deals that took place in 2024 were the $2.5 billion sustainability *sukuk* issued by the Islamic Development Bank, a $5 billion issue by Saudi Arabia, and a 30-year green *sukuk* issued by Indonesia. The remarkable breadth of this market is shown by these deals (Bennett & Coyle, 2025). Despite uneven and low growth compared to broader trends in the global sustainable bond market, the sustainability *sukuk* market continued to expand in 2024. In 2024, as shown in figure 4, the total amount of sustainability *sukuk* issuances was USD 15.3 billion, a 27.9% increase from the previous year. This accounted for 5.8% of all *sukuk* issuances worldwide (IFSB, 2025). This growth reflects increasing recognition of *sukuk's* potential to provide more stable and development-oriented financing for government projects and programs.

Figure 4. Sustainability and Green Sukuk Issuances (2017 - 2024)

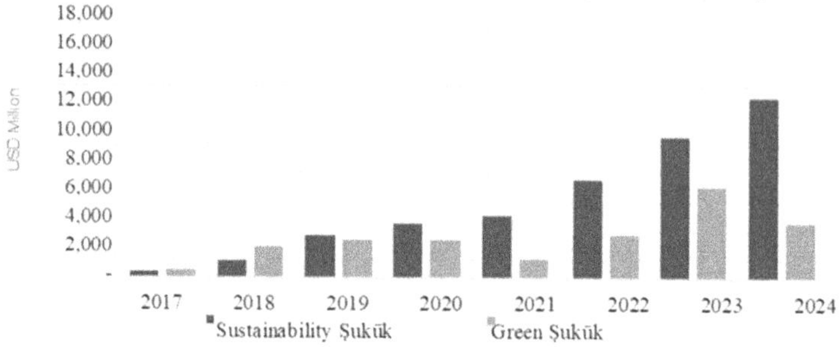

Source: IFSB (2025)

The risk-sharing principle inherent in Islamic finance creates more balanced relationships between lenders and borrowers, where both parties share in the risks and rewards of financed projects. This approach provides an incentive structure for projects to focus more on rigorous project evaluation, better risk management, and long-term sustainability factors. For sovereign borrowers, this implies that they will have partners willing to provide them with funding, partners which have direct interests in the projects and the development undertaking, and not only in the repayment of periodic commitments from the borrowing sovereign (Hassan & Dridi, 2011).

The fact that Islamic finance instruments are asset backed also means that they offer more security and transparency. This can be conducive to debt sustainability. It also connects these financing activities to a specific asset or project making accountability clearer and linking borrowers with actual investments that create revenue for servicing the the debt repayments. This direct link between financing and productive assets contrasts with traditional sovereign debt decisions, often collective funds for general government use and not specific revenue-generating endeavors (Iqbal & Mirakhor, 2011; Jobst, et al., 2008).

In addition, the ESG criteria that are gaining importance in international development finance and the sustainable development goals are inherently compatible with Islamic finance's ethical investment standards. Islamic finance is naturally compatible with sustainable development frameworks and climate finance initiatives due to its emphasis on actual economic value creation and restriction of investments in detrimental activities (Hassan et al., 2013; Mohieldin et al., 2015).

1.3 Chapter Objectives and Scope

This chapter aims to provide a comprehensive analysis of how Islamic finance principles and instruments can reshape sovereign borrowing practices in developing nations, offering viable alternatives to conventional interest-based lending that address both debt sustainability challenges and development financing needs. The primary objective is to demonstrate that Islamic finance mechanisms, particularly sukuk and other Sharia-compliant instruments, can provide more stable, equitable, and sustainable financing options for developing country governments while promoting economic growth and development outcomes.

The analysis seeks to bridge theoretical frameworks from Islamic finance and development finance with practical applications from countries that have successfully integrated Islamic finance into their sovereign borrowing strategies. By examining case studies of nations such as Malaysia, Indonesia, Nigeria, and others that have issued sovereign sukuk, the chapter illustrates how Islamic finance can provide tangible benefits in terms of reduced borrowing costs, enhanced investor diversification, and improved alignment between financing and development priorities.

A secondary objective involves identifying and analyzing the structural, regulatory, and institutional barriers that may impede the broader adoption of Islamic finance in sovereign borrowing contexts. This includes examining legal frameworks, market infrastructure requirements, regulatory harmonization needs, and capacity building priorities that developing nations must address to effectively utilize Islamic finance instruments.

The scope of analysis encompasses both theoretical and practical dimensions of Islamic sovereign finance, examining not only the principles and mechanisms involved but also the implementation challenges and policy requirements for successful adoption. The chapter analyzes various Islamic finance instruments beyond sukuk, including Islamic development finance models, public-private partnership structures compliant with Sharia principles, and innovative hybrid instruments that combine Islamic finance principles with development finance objectives.

Furthermore, the chapter explores the potential for Islamic finance to contribute to broader sustainable development goals, including climate finance, infrastructure development, and poverty reduction initiatives. This includes examining how green sukuk and other sustainable Islamic finance instruments can support environmental and social objectives while providing cost-effective financing for developing nation governments.

The geographical scope primarily focuses on developing nations with significant Muslim populations where Islamic finance has natural cultural and religious compatibility, but also examines the potential for non-Muslim majority countries to utilize Islamic finance instruments as part of diversified sovereign borrowing strategies.

Finally, the chapter contributes to the broader literature on innovative development finance by demonstrating how alternative financing mechanisms rooted in different philosophical and economic traditions can offer solutions to persistent challenges in international development finance. By providing evidence that debt without usury can promote more equitable and stable financial systems, the analysis supports the case for greater diversity and innovation in global financial architecture to better serve the development needs of emerging economies.

2. THEORETICAL FOUNDATIONS OF ISLAMIC FINANCE

Islamic finance is rooted in a comprehensive ethical and legal framework derived from *Shariah* (Islamic law), which governs economic behavior and financial transactions based on the principles of justice, risk-sharing, and social responsibility. Unlike conventional finance, which predominantly relies on interest-bearing debt instruments, Islamic finance prohibits *riba* (usury or interest) and promotes asset-backed, equity-oriented, and partnership-based financial arrangements (ISRA, 2012; El-Gamal, 2006; Ayub, 2007; Norchaevna, 2024). Table 1 below summarizes the differences between Islamic finance and conventional finance.

2.1. Prohibition of Riba and Gharar

At the heart of Islamic finance is the categorical prohibition of riba. Riba is often translated as interest or usury, widely interpreted as any predetermined and guaranteed return on a loan or investment. The Qur'an explicitly condemns riba, stating, *"Allah has permitted trade and forbidden riba"* (Qur'an 2:275). This prohibition is rooted in the belief that money itself has no intrinsic value and should not beget more money without an underlying productive activity (ISRA, 2012; Zolotova et al., 2024). The implications of this prohibition are far-reaching, shaping the structure and operation of Islamic financial institutions. This prohibition is not merely a religious decree but serves a broader economic rationale by seeking to prevent unjust enrichment, reduce debt dependency, and mitigate systemic risk (Iqbal & Mirakhor, 2011). The charging or paying of interest is seen as exploitative and unjust, as it guarantees a return for the lender regardless of the outcome of the investment (Iqbal & Mirakhor, 2017; Azmat et al., 2021).

Instead of interest-based lending, Islamic finance promotes alternative financing methods such as *Mudarabah* (profit-sharing), *Musharakah* (joint venture), and *Murabahah* (cost-plus financing) (ISRA, 2012; Hassan et al., 2013; Hanif, 2017; Samad et al., 2005). These methods emphasize fairness, transparency, and the sharing of both profits and losses between the financier and the entrepreneur (Iqbal & Mirakhor, 2017).

Additionally, Islamic finance prohibits *gharar* (excessive uncertainty or ambiguity in transactions), particularly when there is lack of information disclosure. This prohibition ensures transparency and fairness in financial dealings. This helps to avoid speculative activities akin to *maysir* (games of chance involving deception), reinforcing the importance of contracts with clearly defined terms and risk allocations (Iqbal & Mirakhor, 2011; Usmani, 2002). While the prohibition of riba is the most critical and gets the most attention, the importance of gharar and other elements such as *qimar* (gambling) and *maysir* should not be underestimated (Iqbal & Mirakhor, 2011).

2.2. Risk Sharing and Profit-Loss Partnerships

Islamic financial theory is predicated on risk-sharing mechanisms, which contrast with the risk-transfer model of conventional debt contracts. Key instruments such as *mudarabah* (profit-sharing partnerships) and *musharakah* (joint ventures) embody this philosophy. In *mudarabah*, one party provides capital while the other offers expertise; profits are shared according to a pre-agreed ratio, and losses are borne solely by the capital provider, except in cases of negligence. In *musharakah*, all partners contribute capital and share both profits and losses, aligning incentives and promoting participatory finance (Iqbal & Mirakhor, 2011; Siddiqi, 2006; Mirakhor & Krichene, 2009).

These instruments embody the concept of justice (*adl*) and mutual consent (*taradhi*), foundational to Islamic contractual ethics. They facilitate the equitable distribution of wealth and reduce the concentration of risk, which is especially important in sovereign financing contexts where excessive debt can lead to long-term dependency and vulnerability (Askari et al., 2010).

2.3. Asset-Backed and Real Economy Orientation

Islamic finance emphasizes tangibility and asset-backing, ensuring that financial transactions are tied to real economic activities. Instruments like *Ijarahh* (leasing), *murabaha* (cost-plus sale), and *sukuk* (Islamic bonds) are structured around identifiable assets and services, fostering economic value creation rather than speculative gains (Abiola-Adams et al., 2025; Iqbal & Mirakhor, 2011; Jobst et al., 2008). This emphasis aligns with macroeconomic stability goals by minimizing artificial liquidity creation and speculative bubbles.

For sovereign borrowing, this real economy orientation offers a paradigm shift: governments can raise capital through *sukuk* by monetizing existing or future infrastructure, avoiding interest-based loans while retaining productive asset utilization (AbdulKareem & Mahmud, 2019; Norchaevna, 2024). This model not only conforms to Islamic principles but also introduces fiscal discipline and transparency.

2.4. Ethical and Social Justice Framework

Islamic finance is also underpinned by a broader ethical worldview that integrates finance with social justice. It mandates that wealth be circulated rather than hoarded, and promotes financial inclusion through instruments like *qard al-hasan* (benevolent loans) and *waqf* (charitable endowments) (Iqbal & Mirakhor, 2017; Iqbal & Mirakhor, 2011; Kahf, 2004). These principles are critical for developing nations where conventional debt has often exacerbated inequality and constrained fiscal space.

Furthermore, the Islamic moral economy envisions the state not merely as a borrower but as a trustee of public resources (*amanah*), accountable to its citizens. This normative stance encourages responsible sovereign borrowing, where financial obligations are aligned with developmental goals and intergenerational equity (Iqbal & Mirakhor, 2011; Asutay, 2012).

Table 1. Islamic Finance Vs Conventional Finance

Aspect	Islamic Finance	Conventional Finance
Basis of Transactions	Prohibition of *riba* (interest), Shariah-compliant, asset-backed	Interest-based, debt-driven
Risk Allocation	Shared between parties (PLS models)	Primarily borne by borrower (fixed interest), Lender bears minimal risk
Speculation	Prohibits excessive uncertainty (*gharar*)	Allows derivatives and speculative trading
Asset-backing	Financing linked to tangible assets	Financing not necessarily asset-backed
Ethical Constraints	Avoids harmful industries (e.g., gambling, alcohol)	Profit-driven, fewer ethical restrictions
Financial Stability	Lower leverage, reduced systemic risk	Higher debt exposure, potential instability
Objective	Promote fairness, social justice, and sustainable development	Maximize profit

Source: Authors' compilation based on various sources (ISRA, 2012; Hassan et al., 2013; Iqbal & Mirakhor, 2017; Iqbal & Mirakhor, 2011; Kahf, 2004)

Despite the differences, Islamic and conventional finance can coexist and complement each other in a dual banking system (Hunjra et al., 2022). Islamic finance offers a unique and growing investment opportunity for investors seeking ethical and diversified portfolios (Svoboda, 2024). The global financial crisis exposed weaknesses within the global financial system, and Islamic finance offers a more stable and equitable financial framework (Halima et al., 2024).

3. METHODOLOGY

3.1 Research Design

This chapter is a qualitative exploration of how Islamic finance might be able to transform sovereign borrowing in the periphery through sukuk and profit-and-loss-sharing (PLS) forms of financing. For this purpose, the qualitative analysis of multiple case studies is considered as the proper methodology to better capture the scope of Islamic finance to work in sovereign debt related issues and to work towards achieving the SDGs. Such an approach helps to test the strength of both theories and empirical results and provides a wider range of perspectives across different countries.

3.2 Data Collection and Analysis

The primary method of data collection in this study included secondary sources (comprehensive desk review) comprising peer-reviewed academic articles, books, and official reports and policy documents from institutions such as the Islamic Financial Services Board (IFSB, 2025), the World Bank (2024), the United Nations Development Programme (UNDP, 2024), and national debt management offices (e.g., Ministry of Finance Malaysia, 2020; Debt Management Office Nigeria, 2017). These sources provided detailed data on sukuk issuances, market trends, and fiscal outcomes.

Case studies were purposively selected to represent a range of developing nations with significant Islamic finance adoption, alongside Muslim-minority countries. Selection criteria included the scale of sukuk issuances, diversity of applications (e.g., infrastructure, green finance), and availability of verifiable data. Specifically, the study selected case studies from Malaysia, Indonesia, Nigeria, Pakistan, and Muslim-minority nations (UK, South Africa, Hong Kong, Luxembourg, Ivory Coast, Togo) to provide a diverse sample of Islamic finance applications. Malaysia and Indonesia were chosen for their mature sukuk markets and leadership in green finance (Bennett & Coyle, 2025; UNDP, 2018). Nigeria and Pakistan represent emerging markets with growing Islamic finance adoption (Abubakar & Baba, 2020; Shahid, 2025). Muslim-minority nations were included to demonstrate cross-cultural applicability (Balibek, 2017). Each case was analyzed for its sukuk structure (e.g., ijarah, wakala), purpose (e.g., infrastructure, green projects), and outcomes (e.g., oversubscription rates, fiscal impact), ensuring alignment with the chapter's focus on debt sustainability and SDGs. Case studies were analyzed to assess the practical implementation of sukuk and PLS models, focusing on their structure, outcomes, and alignment with ethical and sustainable principles.

4. ISLAMIC FINANCIAL INSTRUMENTS FOR SOVEREIGN BORROWING

In developing countries seeking to reshape sovereign borrowing, Islamic financial instruments provide viable alternatives that diverge from traditional interest-bearing debt. Grounded in principles of *Shariah*, these instruments are characterized by asset-backing, risk-sharing, and socio-economic justice, offering a foundation for responsible public finance aligned with sustainable development goals (ISRA, 2012; Jobst, 2007; Mohieldin et al., 2015).

4.1. Sukuk: Asset-Based Sovereign Bonds

An increasing number of developing nations are leveraging Islamic finance's debt-free but asset- and risk-based structures to enhance sovereign borrowing options. Among these, *sukuk* (Islamic bonds) stand out for aligning capital-raising with tangible economic activity. *Sukuk* are not structured to represent traditional debt obligations but rather to grant ownership in actual assets or income-generating projects through Special Purpose Vehicles (SPVs) (Razak et al., 2019; Zulkhibri, 2015). *Ijarahh, Wakala, Musharakah, Murabaha*, and *Istisna* are only a few of the Islamic financial instruments that can form the basis of *sukuk*. When it comes to sovereign financing, *sukuk* structures like *Ijarahh* and *Wakala* are among the most popular options. Investment returns are distributed to investors in *Ijarahh sukuk* through the SPV's acquisition and subsequent leasing of a government-owned asset. Upon the asset's maturity, the government has the option to buy it back, thus repaying the invested funds. In other words, in a typical Ijarahh sukuk, a government or its special purpose vehicle (SPV) sells ownership of public assets, such as roads, ports, or public buildings, to investors, then leases them back. Periodic rent payments made to *sukuk*-holders mirror traditional interest, but crucially derive from real economic returns and Shariah-compliant lease structures. Sovereign Ijarahh sukuk foster investor confidence and deepen capital markets while enabling infrastructure funding within ethical bounds (ISRA, 2012; World Bank, 2019; Kammer et al., 2015). In the case of *Wakala sukuk*, an agent (SPV) manages assets for investors, which is based on the *Wakala* idea of agency. While improving transparency and ensuring *Shariah* compliance, these arrangements make it easier to finance public infrastructure including highways, ports, and public buildings (Razak et al., 2019). *Musharakah sukuk*, in contrast, are equity-style instruments in which investors and the government jointly assume ownership and share returns and risks proportional to their investment, embedding an equity participation dimension into public finance (Mohsin et al., 2020). *Sukuk* can also be in the form of hybrid *Sukuk* where the Sukuk structure blends different instruments such as *Ijarahh, Murabaha*, and

Istisna elements. This kind of Sukuk structure offers sovereigns the flexibility to tailor instruments to project-specific needs without compromising asset-backing (Razak et al., 2019). One example of a hybrid sukuk is the Government Investment Issues (GII), which mixes the *qard hassan, bay al-inah,* and *bay al-dayn* contracts. Along with the advent of Islamic banks in 1983 came GII, or Government Investment Certificates. In order to finance development initiatives that the government has begun, the Malaysian government issues the security. On the government's behalf, Bank Negara Malaysia (BNM) conducts a competitive auction to issue it (Razak et al., 2019).

4.2. Profit-and-Loss Sharing: Equitable Risk Allocation

Complementing these fixed-income instruments, Profit-and-Loss Sharing (PLS) arrangements, specifically Mudarabah and *Musharakah,* open avenues for sovereign financing grounded purely in equity. In a Mudarabah contract for instance, the sovereign acts as the capital provider (rabb-ul-mal), and teams up with a private-sector entity serving as project manager (*mudarib*). The two parties share profits according to agreed-upon ratios. The sovereign takes on financial risk as losses are primarily borne by the capital provider, unless in the event that the manager is negligent. This makes the model particularly suitable for developmental projects that rely on management capacity rather than just capital (IMF, 2017b). This model aligns sovereign resource mobilization with developmental outcomes and distributes risk ethically. The *Musharakah* form of financing is based on a partnership between the government and an investor, who both put up money and work together to run the project. Governments can progressively buy out investors' shares under the diminishing *Musharakah* version, which is ideal for infrastructure and public service projects. This helps to match ownership with the public delivery of services (IMF, 2017b; Nouman & Ullah, 2023).

4.3. Equity-Based Financing: Public-Private Collaboration

Sovereigns can avoid the traditional risks associated with borrowing money by using Islamic equity-based products to co-finance public infrastructure with private or international investors. Governments and financiers can form joint ventures called *Musharakah* partnerships to split the ownership and profits of a project. Through *Musharakah* equity stakes, sovereigns invite private-sector or international investors to co-fund and co-own public projects, promoting shared governance and shifting monetization from tax-funded debt service to value creation. Instruments like Islamic public-private partnerships and Islamic infrastructure funds further institutionalize equity financing, aligning investment returns with asset performance and contributing to economic growth (e.g., through tolls or power purchase agreements). This is especially important in industries like energy, water, and transportation where public interest and sovereign risk meet (World Bank, 2017). Moreover, diminishing *Musharakah* arrangements enable phased government acquisition, converting project capital into public assets over time (IMF, 2017). In the *Istisna-Ijarahh* model, which is common in public-private partnerships, the public sector can commission an asset (*Istisna*) and then lease it (*Ijarahh*). This allows sovereigns to use private capital to develop the asset before transferring ownership, which allows for risk-sharing and asset-backed benefits and guarantees that the public sector will use the asset once it is finished (Jobst, 2007).

4.4. Implications for Sovereign Public Finance

These Islamic financial instruments above, represent a paradigm shift in sovereign borrowing, from rigid interest obligations to flexible, asset and risk aligned financing techniques. By prioritizing performance-based returns and equitable risk distribution, they contribute to fiscal prudence, enhance transparency, and remain consistent with *Maqasid al-Shariah*, particularly justice, welfare, and moral accountability. Importantly, equity-oriented models like *Musharakah* and diminishing *Musharakah* align fiscal incentives with developmental outcomes, mitigating crowding out of public investment and fostering private sector participation. For policy-makers in developing nations, the adoption of such instruments can broaden borrowing strategies, improve debt resilience, and strengthen institutional governance, all while promoting socio-economic inclusion and long-term sustainability.

5. BENEFITS OF ISLAMIC FINANCE FOR SOVEREIGN BORROWING

Islamic finance presents a paradigm shift in sovereign borrowing by replacing interest-based debt with ethical, asset-backed, and risk-sharing models. This section explores five key advantages that position Islamic finance as a sustainable alternative for developing nations, drawing on empirical evidence and case studies from global implementations.

5.1. Enhanced Fiscal Resilience Through Risk-Sharing

Islamic finance promotes fiscal resilience through its prohibition of *riba* (usury) and emphasis on risk-sharing rather than fixed debt obligations. Unlike conventional bonds that impose rigid interest payments, *sukuk* (Islamic bonds) link returns to the performance of underlying assets, reducing repayment pressure during economic downturns (Hussain et al., 2015). Asset-backed financing ensures that borrowing is tied to productive investments, such as infrastructure or revenue-generating projects, rather than unsecured liabilities. For example, Malaysia's extensive use of *sukuk* for infrastructure development has resulted in a lower default rate compared to conventional sovereign bonds, as returns are derived from tangible assets like toll roads and utilities (Jobst et al., 2008). Additionally, during crises such as the COVID-19 pandemic, Islamic finance structures, including profit-rate adjustments in sukuk, provided fiscal flexibility, whereas conventional debt servicing exacerbated budget constraints in many developing economies (IsDB, 2020; Sa'ad et al., 2022).

5.2. Alignment with Sustainable Development Goals (SDGs)

Islamic finance is inherently aligned with ethical and sustainable investment principles, making it a natural vehicle for advancing the United Nations Sustainable Development Goals (SDGs). Green sukuk, for instance, have been instrumental in funding renewable energy, climate adaptation, and social welfare projects (Naz et al., 2025) (Figure 5). Indonesia's sovereign Green Sukuk program, which has raised over $1.25 billion, exclusively finances renewable energy projects and climate-resilient infrastructure, directly contributing to SDG 7 (Affordable and Clean Energy) and SDG 13 (Climate Action) (UNDP, 2024; UNDP, 2018; Kim, 2025; Securities Commission Malaysia & World Bank, 2019; Aldhaheri, 2025).

Figure 5. Indonesia's First Green Sukuk Proceeds and Impact

CATEGORY	IMPACT OUTCOMES	OTHER SDGS
Renewable energy	3,913,133.47 CO_2e avoided	
Energy efficiency	355,394 CO_2e Reduced	
Clean transport	1,711,615.93 CO_2e Avoided	
Total	5,776,497.49 tons of CO_2 emissions reduced	

Source: UNDP (2024)

5.3. Reduced Speculative Risk

Islamic finance's prohibition of *gharar* (excessive uncertainty) and speculative derivatives minimizes exposure to financial instability. Unlike conventional debt instruments, *sukuk* cannot be used for leveraged or speculative borrowing, reducing vulnerability to market shocks (ISRA, 2012; El-Gamal, 2006). This structural resilience was evident during the 2008 global financial crisis, when Islamic financial institutions demonstrated greater stability compared to conventional banks due to their asset-backed nature and avoidance of toxic debt instruments. By tying financing to real economic activity, Islamic finance mitigates the risks of asset bubbles and speculative trading, fostering long-term financial stability (Hassan & Dridi, 2011).

5.4. Inclusive Growth Linked to Real Economic Activity

Islamic finance channels capital into productive sectors, fostering job creation and equitable economic development. In Pakistan, the introduction of Islamic SME *sukuk* has expanded access to credit for small and medium-sized enterprises, which are often excluded from conventional financing (International Finance Corporation, 2017; Tohidi et al., 2024). Similarly, the use of *Musharakah* (partnership-based) *sukuk* for infrastructure projects has stimulated local employment and regional development. By linking financing to tangible projects, such as agriculture, manufacturing, and infrastructure, Islamic finance ensures that sovereign borrowing translates into real economic growth rather than financialization (Zain & Muhamad Sobri, 2017; Zaher & Hassan, 2002; World Bank, 2019).

5.5. Ethical Alignment: Avoiding Exploitative Lending Practices

Islamic finance's prohibition of predatory lending aligns sovereign borrowing with principles of social justice. Unlike high-interest Eurobonds, which can trap nations in cycles of debt, sukuk does not impose compounding interest, thereby preventing unsustainable debt spirals (Cakir & Raei, 2007). Returns are shared based on actual project performance rather than exploitative rates, ensuring fairness for both investors and borrowing governments (Ayub, 2022). This ethical framework not only reduces the risk of debt crises but also enhances public trust in sovereign financing mechanisms (ISRA, 2012; El-Gamal, 2006; Ayub, 2007).

6. CASE STUDIES OF ISLAMIC SOVEREIGN FINANCING

This section examines diverse national experiences where Islamic finance instruments have been used for sovereign borrowing, highlighting how sovereign sukuk issuance has offered Islamic finance-based alternatives for developing economies.

6.1. Malaysia: The Global Leader in Sovereign Sukuk

Malaysia has established itself as the world's foremost innovator in sovereign Islamic finance, with *sukuk* accounting for a greater portion of its domestic bond market. Globally, Malaysia leads the *sukuk* market, pioneering sovereign and corporate *sukuk* to fund infrastructure since the early 2000s (Bank Negara Malaysia, 2007).

Malaysia issued various types of infrastructure *sukuk*, financing projects such as the Kuala Lumpur International Airport, Maju Expressway, Pan-Borneo Highway and Klang Valley Mass Rapid Transit system, aimed at elevating the nation to high-income status (Bennett & Coyle, 2025; AbdulKareem & Mahmud, 2019; Malikov, 2017). The first global sovereign *sukuk*, issued by the Malaysian government in 2002 and raising US$600 million, set a precedent for future issuances of *sukuk* around the world (Bank Negara Malaysia, 2007; Aziz, 2014).

In 2017, the first green sukuk in the world was issued in Malaysia, when Tadau Energy Sdn Bhd, raised MYR250 million ($59 million) to finance a 50MW solar photovoltaic power plant in the country. The sukuk was issued under Malaysia's SRI sukuk framework, endorsed by the Shariah Advisory Council, and received the highest rating by the Center for International Climate and Environmental Research Oslo (CICERO). A key demonstration of the success of this project was that another issuer (Quantum Solar) followed quickly with a larger issuance amounting to MYR1 billion (Bennett & Coyle, 2025; World Bank, 2022).

The Malaysian government also led the world to issue a very innovative sukuk known as Sukuk Prihatin. As part of the government's efforts towards recovery following the Covid-19 economic devastation, the government of Malaysia issued this sukuk, raising MYR 666 million, around $150 million, for pandemic relief through a hybrid Wakala-Ijarahh structure (Ministry of Finance Malaysia, 2020; Kunhibava et al., 2024; Lee, 2022). Sovereign *sukuk* outstanding as of May 2025 amounted to about RM600 billion. In percentage terms, this is equivalent to about 48% of total government bonds recorded in May 2025 (Ghaffour, 2025).

6.2 Indonesia: Leader in Sovereign Green Sukuk

Sovereign *sukuk* has played an important role over the past decade of economic and infrastructure development in Indonesia. Through the issuance of sovereign *sukuk*, the Indonesian government not only focuses on improving the quality of infrastructure, but also provides an opportunity for citizens to participate in their country's development through ethical and responsible investment. Since sovereign sukuk was first issued in 2008, the government has shown a strong commitment to utilizing this instrument for national development (The Jakarta Post, 2024).

The Indonesian government, from 2014 to 2024, used sovereign sukuk to finance infrastructure projects worth about $14.96 billion including roads, railways, airports and seaports, as well as education and health facilities (The Jakarta Post, 2024). In March 2018, Indonesia issued the world's first sovereign green sukuk amounting to $1.25 billion to fund hydroelectric, renewable energy, and climate resilience efforts. The issuance drew diversified global capital and affirmed Indonesia's commitment to sustainable fiscal instruments and SDG-aligned financing (UNDP, 2018).

6.3 Nigeria: Nascent but Growing Islamic Public Finance

Estimates put the Islamic finance business in Nigeria at a value of about $4 billion by the end of May 2025. Islamic banking assets make up 45.2% of the Islamic finance industry, with sukuk outstanding accounting for 53.9%. Takaful and sharia-compliant funds make up the remaining portion (Fitch Ratings, 2025). The introduction of the new rules by the Securities and Exchange Commission (SEC) of Nigeria in 2013 for the issuance of Sukuk, paved way for the first Sukuk in Nigeria. The Osun State Government issued Nigeria's first sukuk in 2013 to fund educational infrastructure in the State. The issue was worth N11.4 billion naira, about US$73 million (Osun State Government, 2013; Abubakar & Baba, 2020).

The first Sovereign Sukuk (seven-year Ijarahh sukuk) was issued in 2017 worth 100 billion, about US$270 million (Debt Management Office, 2017). Proceeds were dedicated to major road infrastructure projects (Abubakar & Baba, 2020). By mid-2019, Nigeria had 200 billion in Sovereign Sukuk outstanding (Abubakar & Baba, 2020; Debt Management Office, 2013). In May 2025, the government of Nigeria issued its eighth sovereign sukuk, and the issuance was seven times oversubscribed, suggesting that demand was high. There were USD2.2 billion in outstanding sukuk in Nigeria as of mid-2025.

6.4. Pakistan: Islamic Finance in Debt Management

The Islamic finance sector in Pakistan has been growing tremendously on the back of government initiatives to convert the financial system in the country into being sharia-compliant (Fitch Ratings, 2024). The government has systematically integrated Islamic finance into its public debt management, with Sharia-compliant instruments growing from 11.5% in December 2023 to over 12.6% in December 2024 (Ministry of Finance Pakistan, 2025). Specifically, the country has recently employed Islamic finance for sovereign borrowing to tackle its debt issues in the electricity industry (Shahid, 2025).

Pakistan has recently advanced Islamic instruments in public finance to manage structural debt. In June 2025, it agreed to a PKR 1.275 trillion (approx. USD 4.5 billion) Islamic financing facility from 18 domestic banks to combat circular debt in the power sector, tied to its IMF support programme. Crucially, this facility was structured to avoid increasing public debt and advance the country's ambition to phase out interest-based banking by 2028 (Shahid, 2025).

In May 2025, the government of Pakistan also issued its first-ever sovereign domestic green Sukuk, a historic issuance signaling a focus on mobilizing Islamic capital for sustainable development. Facilitated by the Pakistan Stock Exchange (PSX), the inaugural green Sukuk auction received strong response from investors.

The target amount of PKR30 billion (US$106.48 million) was oversubscribed 5.4 times, resulting to PKR161.74 billion (US$574.05 million) in total bids (IFN, 2025). All these demonstrate how sovereign Islamic finance tools can alleviate fiscal strain while supporting broader sectoral reform.

6.5. Muslim-Minority Nations: Cross-Cultural Adoption

Despite being traditionally associated with Muslim-majority countries, Islamic finance has demonstrated significant traction in Muslim-minority nations, where governments have utilized Shariah-compliant instruments, particularly sukuk, to diversify funding and tap into the sovereign sukuk market. Initial sovereign offerings from nations with small Muslim populations, such as Luxembourg, Hong Kong Special Administrative Region (HKSAR), Ivory Coast, Togo, South Africa, and the UK, showcased the importance of the sukuk market (Balibek, 2017). The period from 2014 to 2016 witnessed the first sovereign sukuk issuances in most of these countries, where most of them followed the *Ijarah* structure (Table 2).

Table 2. First Sovereign Sukuk Issuances from Select Muslim-Minority Nations

Sovereign Issuer	Issue Date	Amount (USD Million)	Tenor	Currency	Structure
UK	Jun-2014	340	5 years	GBP	Ijarah
HKSAR	Sep-2014	1,000	5 years	USD	Ijarah
South Africa	Sep-2014	500	5.75 years	USD	Ijarah
Luxembourg	Oct-2014	254	5 years	EUR	Ijarah
Ivory Coast	Dec-2015	253.34	5 years	CFA-Franc	Ijarah
Togo	Aug-2016	251.40	10 years	CFA-Franc	Ijarah

Source: Balibek (2017)

In Junc 2014, the UK became the first non-Muslim-majority country to issue a sovereign sukuk in the West amounting to £200 million, maturing in July 2019. The five-year sukuk was structured based on Ijarah (lease-based) arrangements and backed by government-owned properties. The deal operated under existing UK property and trust law, illustrating how legal adaptation can support Islamic finance adoption. The sukuk was sold to investors based in the UK and in the major hubs for Islamic finance around the world. The issuance was oversubscribed nearly 10 times, with orders totaling around £2.3 billion. Allocations were made to a wide range of investors including sovereign wealth funds, central banks and domestic and international financial institutions (Zanev & Barchman, 2014; UK Government, 2014). By issuing its second sovereign Sukuk in 2021, with a principal amount of

£500 million and a maturity period of 5 years, the UK solidified its position as a global leader in Islamic finance within the Western world. Demand for this second offering was also high, with orders totaling more than £625 million. It was sold to a diverse group of prestigious institutional investors from all around the globe (UK Government, 2021).

In September 2014, the Republic of South Africa became the pioneer of sovereign Sukuk issuance in Africa, and among Muslim-minority nations, after issuing its debut US$500 million 5.75-year Sukuk in the international capital market. The Sukuk was based on Ijarah structure. This transaction was more than 4 times oversubscribed with an order book of US$2.2 billion (National Treasury, 2014). It has however taken about 9 years for the country to issue its second sovereign Sukuk in 2023, raising about US$1,084.99 million through a four-tranche transaction varying in tenors, volume and profit rates to be paid to Sukuk holders (DDCAP, 2023).

The issuance of US$1 billion sukuk by HKSAR for a tenor of 5 years, marks the world's first USD-denominated sukuk originated by an AAA-rated government. The Sukuk received strong demand from global investors, attracting orders exceeding US$4.7 billion. The transaction was oversubscribed 4.7 times, allowing final pricing to tighten by 7 basis points from its initial price guidance (Hong Kong Monetary Authority, 2014). The deal attracted interest from a diverse group of conventional and Islamic investors. The Sukuk was allocated to over 120 global institutional investors, with 36% of the Sukuk distributed to the Middle East, 47% to Asia, 6% to Europe and 11% to the United States (Hong Kong Monetary Authority, 2014).

In a move that follows the issuance of shariah-compliant instruments by UK, South Africa, and Hong Kong, AAA-rated Luxembourg is the first European Union member state to issue sukuk denominated in euros (Vizcaino, 2014). Aiming to position itself as a leading center for Islamic finance just like UK, Luxembourg issued a €200 million ($254 million) five-year sukuk in 2014, supported by dedicated legislation and dual listing to attract global investors (Zanev & Barchman, 2014). The issuance was distributed across 29 accounts and was oversubscribed more than 2 times. Compared to the $2.2 billion and $4.7 billion raised by South Africa and Hong Kong for their dollar-denominated issues, the orders for Luxembourg's sukuk were lower (Vizcaino, 2014).

The Republic of the Ivory Coast issued its first Sukuk in 2015 worth CFA150 billion. In dollar terms, the amount was about $253.34 million with a maturity period of 5 years. This was done to diversify infrastructure funding sources in international and regional capital markets (IFN, 2016; IFN, 2022; Mapenzauswa, 2015). Utilizing the Ijarahh structure, two government buildings located in Abidjan were chosen as the underlying assets for this transaction. The proceeds were used to finance the government's social and economic projects. The deal was arranged by the Islamic Corporation for the Development of the Private Sector (ICD), with subscription by investors from West Africa (56%), North Africa (6%) and the Middle East (38%) (IFN, 2016).

The Togolese government also issued its first *sukuk* in August 2016 for 150 billion CFA francs ($251.40 million), an effort to diversify sources of deficit funding. The 15,000,000 units of Sukuk, each with a face value of CFA10,000, were issued through the Joint Receivables Securitization Fund (FCTC). The arrangement was based on the *Ijarahh* structure. These *sukuk* yielded 6.5% and matured in 10 years. Important national economic and social development initiatives were funded by the earnings (Peyton & King, 2016; Togo First, 2025; IMF, 2017a). Table 3 below presents a summary of the above case studies, highlighting the year of first sovereign *sukuk* issuances, structure used, purpose and their key outcomes.

Table 3. Sovereign Sukuk Issuances from Select Countries

Country	**Year of First Issue**	**Structure Used**	**Purpose**	**Key Outcomes**
Malaysia	2002	Ijarahh, Musharakah	Infrastructure financing (e.g., airports, roads)	Established largest sukuk market globally
Indonesia	2008	Sukuk Negara (Ijarahh)	Infrastructure, SDG-aligned projects	Supports fiscal needs while promoting Shariah compliance
Pakistan	2004	Ijarahh	Budgetary support, infrastructure	Diversified funding, attracted Islamic investors
Nigeria	2017	Ijarahh	Road construction, infrastructure	Over 360 billion raised in multiple rounds, oversubscribed
UK	2014	Ijarahh	General government funding	£200 million sukuk; first by non-Muslim-majority country
HKSAR (Hong Kong)	2014	Ijarahh, Wakala	Infrastructure, green finance	Positioned as gateway for Islamic finance in East Asia
South Africa	2014	Ijarahh	Infrastructure funding	$500 million sukuk; successful debut in Africa
Luxembourg	2014	Ijarahh	Portfolio diversification, Islamic investor base	Enhanced Islamic finance footprint in Europe
Ivory Coast	2015	Ijarahh	Road and infrastructure projects	Financed government's social and economic projects
Togo	2016	Ijarahh	Development projects	Diversified debt strategy; growing market appetite

Source: Author's compilation based on the literature (Balibek, 2017; Bank Negara Malaysia, 2007; Aziz, 2014)

7. CHALLENGES AND BARRIERS TO ADOPTION OF ISLAMIC FINANCE IN SOVEREIGN BORROWING

The adoption of Islamic finance for sovereign borrowing has gained traction as governments seek alternative financing mechanisms that comply with *Shariah* principles. However, several challenges hinder its widespread implementation, including regulatory and legal obstacles, underdeveloped market infrastructure, and a lack of awareness and expertise (Naz et al., 2025; Ahmed, 2020). Addressing these barriers is critical for facilitating the integration of Islamic finance into sovereign debt markets.

7.1. Regulatory and Legal Frameworks

One major obstacle that sovereign sukuk and other Islamic finance instruments continue to face is the lack of supporting legal structures. Islamic financial systems prioritize asset-backing and risk-sharing, which are fundamentally different from traditional debt-based systems (ISRA, 2012; World Bank, 2019). There is a dearth of legislation that specifically addresses the creation, regulation, and taxation of Islamic instruments in many jurisdictions, especially those with developing economies. Many developing nations operate within legal frameworks designed for conventional debt, creating conflicts with Sharia-compliant structures such as sukuk and profit-sharing arrangements. Aligning Islamic contracts with existing financial standards is challenging for countries without sovereign sukuk laws or Shari'ah-compliant dispute resolution systems (Balibek, 2017; Kammer et al., 2015; Alexakis & Tsikouras, 2009). For example, sukuk require asset ownership transfers and profit-sharing mechanisms that may conflict with existing tax and securities laws (Balibek, 2017; Kammer et al., 2015; ISRA, 2012; World Bank, 2019). Some countries had to amend their financial regulations to accommodate sukuk issuances, a process that can take years due to legislative inertia (Naz et al., 2025; Razak et al., 2019). Additionally, the lack of standardization across jurisdictions complicates cross-border Islamic finance transactions. While the Islamic Financial Services Board (IFSB) and Accounting and Auditing Organization for Islamic Financial Institutions (AAOIFI) provide guidelines, national regulators often interpret Sharia compliance differently, leading to fragmentation (Smolo & Habibovic, 2012; World Bank, 2019; Balibek, 2017).

7.2. Market Infrastructure Gaps

Developing robust secondary markets for Islamic financial products remains a critical hurdle. Unlike conventional bonds, sukuk often suffer from limited liquidity due to the absence of standardized trading platforms and a shallow investor base. Limited secondary trading platforms for Shari'ah-compliant assets and underdeveloped capital markets reduce liquidity and undermine investor confidence. Different asset-screening procedures, rating/' systems, and accounting rules are necessary for Islamic financing. Institutional investors are discouraged and pricing transparency is hindered by the absence of these platforms. More so, sovereign issuers are unable to innovate or develop due to scale diseconomies and a limited product diversity (Jobst et al., 2008; Shaikh, 2014; Kusuma & Silva, 2014; Azmi & Akmal, 2024; Ulusoy & Ela, 2017).

7.3. Awareness and Expertise

A critical constraint is the shortage of technical expertise in structuring Islamic financial instruments within sovereign debt offices and regulatory agencies. Government treasuries and central banks of many countries often do not have personnel who are educated about Shariah compliant financial instruments. In some developing countries, there is less awareness about Islamic finance (Abdul-Wahab & Abdul-Razak, 2019). In other instances, there is inadequate number of Shari'ah experts with backgrounds in banking and finance. This challenge leads to reliance on expensive international advisors (Kammer et al., 2015). There are also educational gaps at the level of the investors or the rating agencies as well, which limit the demand and trust. Capacity building, in the form of technical exchanges and programs of study, is needed to broaden acceptance and understanding (Dey & Jin, 2018).

8. CONCLUSION AND POLICY RECOMMENDATIONS

8.1. Conclusion

The international sovereign debt crisis confronting the majority of developing world makes a case for new paradigms of financing that place sustainability, equity and fiscal responsibility at the forefront. Usual interest lending has maintained cycles of debt and economic instability and lack of financial flexibility. The challenges presented by these phenomena can find a relevant answer in Islamic finance that outlaws riba (usury), thrives on risk sharing and requires asset-backed transactions.

Islamic finance, via sukuk, PLS contracts and equity, connects sovereign states' debt to real economic activity in a way that lowers speculation and risky behavior, while also allowing ethical investment. Examples from Malaysia, Indonesia, Nigeria, Pakistan, and even non-Muslim majority countries like UK, and South Africa highlight that Islamic finance can contribute to a more stable economy with diverse funding options aligned with SDGs.

But existing barriers created by misalignment of regulation, lack of infrastructure in the market and lack of knowledge prevent widespread adoption. These challenges will need to be addressed through policy, legal and capacity building at a minimum to successfully deploy Islamic finance into sovereign debt considerations.

8.2. Policy Recommendations

Policymakers in developing countries must support legal and regulatory frameworks that open the space for Sharia compliant sovereign debt instruments in order to fully tap into the potential of Islamic finance in sovereign borrowing. These would include also the need for converging financial legislation to accommodate Islamic financial contracts like sukuk and musharakah, in addition to tax neutral policies to prevent double taxing of assets, in addition to adopting harmonized Shariah governance structures that comply to Shariah supervisory authorities like the Islamic Financial Services Board (IFSB) and the Accounting and Auditing Organization for Islamic Financial Institutions (AAOIFI). Improving market infrastructure is also very important. Governments can also work to create healthy secondary sukuk markets to boost liquidity, promote the issuance of sukuk in local currency to minimize foreign currency exposure, and create specific trading platforms for sukuk to capture different investor types.

Capacity building is still one of the key pillars for adoption to be sustainable. Specific training geared towards public debt managers, central banks and regulatory authorities remains necessary to enhance knowledge of structuring and risk management in Islamic finance. Nurturing a generation of new people can be achieved through collaboration between academia and financial regulators to incorporate Islamic finance into professional accreditations and university offerings. Further, governments could drive sustainable finance by issuing green and SDG sukuk; provide concessional pricing or guarantees for climate-resilient infrastructure projects; or ensure that sovereign issuances are aligned with environmental and social objectives, as a way of attracting ESG investors.

Lastly, international collaboration is critical in scaling up Islamic finance solutions. Regional economic groups like Association of Southeast Asian Nations (ASEAN) or the African Union may begin to look at cross border sukuk to finance mega infrastructure projects while multilateral institutions like the International Monetary Fund (IMF) and World Bank integrate Islamic finance into its debt sustainability frameworks and programs. This will enable developing countries to then use Islamic finance as a means for financial stability, lessening over reliance on debt and ultimately creating development focused growth.

REFERENCES

Abdul-Wahab, A., & Abdul-Razak, D. (2019). Islamic banking adoption in Ghana. *International Journal of Business, Economics and Law, 19*(2), 14-21. https://www.ijbel.com/wp-content/uploads/2019/09/BUS_66.pdf

AbdulKareem, I. A., & Mahmud, M. S. B. (2019). Infrastructure project financing through sukuk as an alternative to conventional bond financing. *Journal of management and operation research, 1*(19), 1-11.

Abiola-Adams, O., Azubuike, C., Sule, A. K., & Okon, R. (2025). Integrating asset and liability management with Islamic finance: A strategic framework for global financial institutions. *Gulf Journal of Advance Business Research, 3*(1), 128–142. Advance online publication. DOI: 10.51594/gjabr.v3i1.70

Abubakar, A. M., & Baba, I. M. (2020). *Sukuk and nation-building: A theoretical analysis of sukuk financing in Nigeria.* Ikonomika, 5(1), 76–87. https://ejournal.radenintan.ac.id/index.php/ikonomika

Admati, A., & Hellwig, M. (2013). *The bankers' new clothes: What's wrong with banking and what to do about it.* Princeton University Press. DOI: 10.1515/9780691251714

Ahmed, J. (2020). Promoting financial stability: issues and challenges in Islamic finance. *Law & Financial Stability, 193.* https://www.elibrary.imf.org/display/book/9781513523002/ch012.xml

Aldhaheri, W. (2025). Islamic Green Finance: Shariah-Compliant Pathways towards Sustainable Development Goals (SDGs). *Open Journal of Applied Sciences, 15*(5), 1294–1309. DOI: 10.4236/ojapps.2025.155090

Alexakis, C., & Tsikouras, A. (2009). Islamic finance: Regulatory framework–challenges lying ahead. *International Journal of Islamic and Middle Eastern Finance and Management,* 2(2), 90–104. DOI: 10.1108/17538390910965121

Askari, H., Iqbal, Z., & Mirakhor, A. (2010). *Globalization and Islamic finance: Convergence, prospects and challenges.* John Wiley Sons.

Asutay, M. (2012). Conceptualising and locating the social failure of Islamic finance: Aspirations of Islamic moral economy vs the realities of Islamic finance. *Asian and African area studies, 11*(2), 93-113. https://doi.org/DOI: 10.14956/asafas.11.93

Aziz, Z. A. (2014). Sukuk development and financial stability. 10th World Islamic Economic Forum. *Dubai (October)*, 1-3. https://www.bis.org/review/r141029c.htm

Azmat, S., Bhatti, A., & Hassan, M. K. (2021). Understanding "Riba" (interest): The religious and the rational. *Emerald Emerging Markets Case Studies.*, *11*(3), 1–11. Advance online publication. DOI: 10.1108/EEMCS-08-2020-0288

Azmi, K., & Akmal, K. M. (2024). Unlocking Growth Potential: How to Increase Market Depth and Liquidity in Islamic Bonds. *SSRN*, *4846112*, •••. https://www.researchgate.net/publication/380930325_Unlocking_Growth_Potential_How_to_Increase_Market_Depth_and_Liquidity_in_Islamic_Bonds

Balibek, E. (2017). *Establishing a legal framework for sovereign sukuk issuance: A public debt management perspective* (No. 116308, pp. 1-33). The World Bank. https://documents1.worldbank.org/curated/en/907001497472893193/pdf/P161573-06-14-2017-1497472889089.pdf

Bank Negara Malaysia. (2007). Development of the Financial Sector. Financial Stability and Payment Systems Report 2007. Bank Negara Malaysia. https://www.bnm.gov.my/documents/20124/856398/cp02_001_whitebox.pdf

Bennett, M., & Coyle, H. (2025). *State of the Sukuk Market and Prospects for Growth*. World Bank Group. All About Finance (Blog). https://blogs.worldbank.org/en/allaboutfinance/state-of-the-sukuk-market-and-prospects-for-growth

Cakir, S., & Raei, F. (2007). Sukuk vs. Eurobonds: is there a difference in value-at-risk? *IMF Working Paper No. 07/237*. https://papers.ssrn.com/sol3/papers.cfm?abstract_id=1087156

DDCAP. (2023). Sovereign Sukuk – South Africa ZAR20.4bn Sukuk Ijarahh. DDCAP Group. https://www.ddcap.com/sovereign-sukuk-south-africa-zar20-4bn-sukuk-Ijarahh/

Debt Management Office. (2017). *Nigeria Offers its First Sovereign Sukuk*. Central Bank of Nigeria (CBN). https://www.dmo.gov.ng/fgn-bonds/sovereign-sukuk/2095-new-advert-on-sukuk/file

Dey, D., & Jin, X. (2018). Islamic Finance in Africa: Opportunities and Challenges. *White and Case*. https://www.lexology.com/library/detail.aspx?g=a894d8a4-f5e7-45bc-9b6a-05ac657e8984

El-Gamal, M. A. (2006). *Islamic finance: Law, economics, and practice*. Cambridge University Press. ISBN-13 978-0-511-22021-0 DOI: 10.1017/CBO9780511753756

Fitch Ratings. (2024). Pakistan's Islamic Finance Prospects Positive on Government Push. Fitch Ratings. https://www.fitchratings.com/research/non-bank-financial-institutions/pakistans-islamic-finance-prospects-positive-on-government-push-30-01-2024

Fitch Ratings. (2025). Nigeria's Islamic Finance Industry to Benefit from Sovereign Sukuk; New Liquidity Tools. Fitch Ratings. https://www.fitchratings.com/research/islamic-finance/nigerias-islamic-finance-industry-to-benefit-from-sovereign-sukuk-new-liquidity-tools-03-06-2025

Georgiou, M. A. (2009). *Excessive Lending, Leverage, and Risk-Taking in the Presence of Bailout Expectations*. IMF Working Paper No. 2009/233. https://www.elibrary.imf.org/view/journals/001/2009/233/article-A001-en.xml

Ghaffour, A. R. (2025). The significance of Malaysian government bond market – resilience against global backdrop. Bank for International Settlements. The International Monetary Fund's 20th Public Debt Management Forum, Kuala Lumpur, 28 May 2025. https://www.bis.org/review/r250528p.htm

Halima, A., Betul, D., & Anitë, S. (2024). Islamic Finance as a Crisis-Resilient Framework. *Journal of Economics, Law, and Society*, *1*(2), 3. DOI: 10.70009/jels.2024.1.2.3

Hanif, M. (2017). Anatomy of Islamic Finance. *Management Accountant (Official Journal of ICMA-Pakistan) Vol, 26*, 15-21. https://papers.ssrn.com/sol3/papers.cfm?abstract_id=2921821

Hassan, M. K., Kayed, R. N., & Oseni, U. A. (2013). *Introduction to Islamic Banking and Finance: Principles and Practice*. Pearson Education Limited.

Hong Kong Monetary Authority. (2014). HKSAR Government's Inaugural Sukuk Offering. Hong Kong Monetary Authority. https://www.hkma.gov.hk/eng/news-and-media/press-releases/2014/09/20140911-3/#:~:text=The%20Sukuk%20is%20issued%20by,Exempt%20Regime)%20and%20NASDAQ%20Dubai.

Hunjra, A. I., Islam, F., Verhoeven, P., & Hassan, M. K. (2022). The impact of a dual banking system on macroeconomic efficiency. *Research in International Business and Finance*, *61*, 101647. DOI: 10.1016/j.ribaf.2022.101647

Hussain, M. M., Shahmoradi, A., & Turk, R. (2015). An overview of Islamic finance. IMF Working Paper (WP/15/120). https://www.imf.org/external/pubs/ft/wp/2015/wp15120.pdf

IFN. (2016). Ivory Coast's maiden Sukuk: A landmark deal for the West African nation. Islamic Finance News (IFN). https://www.islamicfinancenews.com/ivory-coasts-maiden-sukuk-a-landmark-deal-for-the-west-african-nation-2.html

IFN. (2022). Islamic finance in the Ivory Coast: Timid enthusiasm. Islamic Finance News (IFN). https://www.islamicfinancenews.com/islamic-finance-in-the-ivory-coast-timid-enthusiasm.html

IFN. (2025). Pakistan marks milestone in sustainable Islamic finance with debut sovereign green Sukuk. Islamic Finance News (IFN). https://www.islamicfinancenews.com/pakistan-marks-milestone-in-sustainable-islamic-finance-with-debut-sovereign-green-sukuk.html

IMF. (2017a). Togo Context and Recent Developments. IMF eLibrary. https://www.elibrary.imf.org/view/journals/002/2017/127/article-A001-en.xml?ArticleTabs=fulltext

IMF. (2017b). *Ensuring financial stability in countries with Islamic banking: Selected issues*. International Monetary Fund (IMF) Policy Paper. https://www.elibrary.imf.org/view/journals/007/2017/007/article-A001-en.xml

International Finance Corporation. (2017). Islamic Banking Opportunities Across Small and Medium Enterprises: Pakistan. International Finance Corporation. http://hdl.handle.net/10986/26098

Iqbal, Z., & Mirakhor, A. (2011). *An introduction to Islamic finance: Theory and practice* (Vol. 687). John Wiley & Sons. DOI: 10.1002/9781118390474

Iqbal, Z., & Mirakhor, A. (2017). *Ethical dimensions of Islamic finance: Theory and practice*. Springer. DOI: 10.1007/978-3-319-66390-6

IsDB. (2020). The Covid-19 Crisis and Islamic Finance Response of the Islamic Development Bank Group. Islamic Development Bank (IsDB). https://www.isdb.org/sites/default/files/media/documents/2020-10/1.%20IsDB%20Group%20Report%20on%20Covid-19%20and%20Islamic%20Finance__FINAL.pdf

ISRA. (2012). *Islamic Financial System: Principles and Operations. International Shari'ah Research Academy for Islamic Finance*. ISRA.

Jobst, A., Kunzel, P., Mills, P., & Sy, A. (2008). Islamic bond issuance: What sovereign debt managers need to know. *International Journal of Islamic and Middle Eastern Finance and Management*, *1*(4), 330–344. DOI: 10.1108/17538390810919637

Jobst, A. A. (2007). *The economics of Islamic finance and securitization* (IMF Working Paper No. 07/117). International Monetary Fund. https://www.elibrary.imf.org/view/journals/001/2007/117/article-A001-en.xml

Jung, A., Romelli, D., & Farvaque, E. (2025). Do central bank reforms lead to more monetary discipline? European Central Bank (Working Paper Series No 3049). https://www.ecb.europa.eu/pub/pdf/scpwps/ecb.wp3049~bca750cd0a.en.pdf

Kahf, M. (2004). Shariah and historical aspects of Zakah and Awqaf. *Background paper prepared for Islamic Research and Training Institute, Islamic Development Bank.*

Kammer, M. A., Norat, M. M., Pinon, M. M., Prasad, A., Towe, M. C. M., & Zeidane, M. Z. (2015). *Islamic finance: Opportunities, challenges, and policy options. International Monetary Fund (Discussion note SDN/15/05)*. International Monetary Fund., DOI: 10.5089/9781498325035.006

Kim, U. Y. (2025). The Role of Islamic Finance in Advancing the United Nations Sustainable Development Goals (SDGs): Case Studies and critical gap. Intergovernmental Research and Policy Journal. https://irpj.euclid.int/articles/the-role-of-islamic-finance-in-advancing-the-united-nations-sustainable-development-goals-sdgs-case-studies-and-critical-gaps-in-the-banking-sector-in-asean-countries/

Krugman, P. (1998). *The return of depression economics*. W. W. Norton & Company.

Kunhibava, S., Muneeza, A., Khalid, M. B., Mustapha, Z., & Sen, T. M. (2024). Social Sukuk. In *Islamic Social Finance: Law and Practice in Malaysia* (pp. 105-128). Singapore: Springer Nature Singapore. https://doi.org/DOI: 10.1007/978-981-97-1410-0_6

Kusuma, K. A., & Silva, A. C. (2014). Sukuk markets: a proposed approach for development. *World Bank Policy Research Working Paper*, (7133). https://documents1.worldbank.org/curated/en/637041468320946094/pdf/WPS7133.pdf

Lee, M. J. (2022). Islamic Finance Provides Better Solutions in Overcoming the Financial Distress Ascribable to COVID-19: Evidence from Malaysia. In *Towards a Post-Covid Global Financial System* (pp. 261-269). Emerald Publishing Limited. https://doi.org/DOI: 10.1108/978-1-80071-625-420210014

Mapenzauswa, S. (2015). Ivory Coast to issue 150 billion CFA francs worth of 5-year sukuk. Reuters. https://www.reuters.com/article/ivorycoast-sukuk-idAFJ8N12101Y20151120/

Ministry of Finance Malaysia. (2020). Sukuk Prihatin: From RM500 Million to More Than RM666 Million; Proof of Malaysians' Solidarity in Supporting Economic Recovery Efforts. Official Portal of Ministry of Finance Malaysia. https://www.mof.gov.my/portal/en/news/press-release/sukuk-prihatin-from-rm500-million-to-more-than-rm666-million-proof-of-malaysians-solidarity-in-supporting-economic-recovery-efforts

Ministry of Finance Pakistan. (2025). Semi-Annual Public Debt Bulletin (July – December 2024). Debt Management Office, Ministry of Finance – Government of Pakistan. https://www.finance.gov.pk/dpco/semi_annual_debt_bulletin_1H_28032025.pdf

Mirakhor, A., & Krichene, N. (2009). The recent crisis: Lessons for Islamic Finance. Published in: IFSB 2nd Public Lecture on Financial Policy and Stability (2009): pp. 1-92. https://mpra.ub.uni-muenchen.de/56022/

Mohieldin, M., Iqbal, Z., Rostom, A., & Fu, X. (2015). The role of Islamic finance in enhancing financial inclusion in Organization of Islamic Cooperation (OIC) countries. *Islamic Economic Studies*, *20*(2). https://ssrn.com/abstract=3158639

Mohsin, M. I. A., Khattab, I., & Alchaar, M. O. (2020). Economic and Social Impacts of Sovereign Sukuk. In *Handbook of Research on Theory and Practice of Global Islamic Finance* (pp. 732–751). IGI Global Scientific Publishing., https://www.igi-global.com/gateway/chapter/247234#pnlRecommendationForm

National Treasury. (2014). South Africa concludes debut sukuk bond. National Treasury, Republic of South Africa. https://www.treasury.gov.za/comm_media/press/2014/2014091701%20-%20Sukuk%20Statement.pdf

Naz, A., Ali, M., & Barut, A. K. (2025). Sukuk and Corporate Governance: Ethical Foundations, Economic Impact, and Global Relevance in Islamic Finance. In *Islamic Finance and Corporate Governance: Synergies for Sustainable Growth* (pp. 147-173). Emerald Publishing Limited. https://doi.org/DOI: 10.1108/978-1-83662-346-520251022

Norchaevna, N. S. (2024). Islamic Finance: Principles, Governance, Sustainability and Investment Insights. *European Journal of Management. Economics and Business*, *1*(3), 206–216. DOI: 10.59324/ejmeb.2024.1(3).17

Nouman, M., & Ullah, K. (2023). *Participatory islamic finance: Ideals, contemporary practices, and innovations*. Springer Nature., DOI: 10.1007/978-981-19-9555-2

Osun State Government. (2013, October 11). *Osun successfully completes N11.4 billion sukuk bond, Aregbesola commended for exploring new development options*. Osun State Government. https://www.osunstate.gov.ng/2013/10/osun-successfully-completes-n11-4-billion-sukuk-bond-aregbesola-commended-for-exploring-new-development-options/

Peyton, N., & King, L. (2016). Togo issues first $251 mln, 10-yr sukuk bond with 6.5 pct yield. Reuters. https://www.reuters.com/article/business/finance/togo-issues-first-251-mln-10-yr-sukuk-bond-with-65-pct-yield-idUSKCN1071OC/

Razak, S. S., Saiti, B., & Dinç, Y. (2019). The contracts, structures and pricing mechanisms of sukuk: A critical assessment. *Borsa Istanbul review, 19*, S21-S33. https://doi.org/DOI: 10.1016/j.bir.2018.10.001

Sa'ad, A. A., Muneeza, A., Haron, R., & Othman, A. H. A. (2022). ukūk structure for deficit financing during COVID-19 crisis. *Islamic Economic Studies, 30*(1), 23–41. DOI: 10.1108/IES-01-2021-0007

Samad, A., Gardner, N. D., & Cook, B. J. (2005). Islamic Banking and Finance in Theory and Practice: The Experience of Malaysia and Bahrain. *American Journal of Islam and Society*, *22*(2), 69–86. DOI: 10.35632/ajis.v22i2.458

Securities Commission Malaysia & World Bank. (2019). Islamic green finance: development, ecosystem and prospects. Securities Commission Malaysia & World Bank. https://documents1.worldbank.org/curated/en/591721554824346344/pdf/Islamic-Green-Finance-Development-Ecosystem-and-Prospects.pdf

Shahid, A. (2025). Pakistan Signs $4.5 billion Loans with Local Banks to Ease Power Sector Debt. Reuters. https://www.reuters.com/sustainability/boards-policy-regulation/pakistan-signs-45-billion-loans-with-local-banks-ease-power-sector-debt-2025-06-20/?utm_source=chatgpt.com

Shaikh, S. A. (2014). Analysis of challenges and opportunities in Islamic banking. *International Journal of Financial Services Management*, *7*(3-4), 286–300. DOI: 10.1504/IJFSM.2014.065581

Siddiqi, M. N. (2006). Islamic banking and finance in theory and practice: A survey of state of the art. *Islamic Economic Studies*, *13*(2), 1–48. https://ssrn.com/abstract=3161388

Smolo, E., & Habibovic, E. (2012). Barriers to growth of Islamic finance: Issue of standardization. *Islamic Banking and Finance: Principles, Instruments and Operations, 1st ed. Ampang: The Malaysian Current Law Journal in Malaysia, chp, 29*, 715-37. https://www.researchgate.net/profile/Edib-Smolo/publication/317063250_Barriers_to_Growth_of_Islamic_Finance_Issue_of_Standardization/links/5923e4a3a6fdcc4443fa3bca/Barriers-to-Growth-of-Islamic-Finance-Issue-of-Standardization.pdf

Svoboda, A. (2024). Investing in the Islamic World: Opportunities, Challenges, and Implications. Economics and Finance, 12(1), 13-21. https://economics-and-finance.com/archive/EF_2024_1.pdf#page=13

The Jakarta Post. (2024). Sovereign sukuk plays major role in decade of Indonesian development. *The Jakarta Post.* https://www.thejakartapost.com/business/2024/10/16/sovereign-sukuk-plays-major-role-in-decade-of-indonesian-development.html

Togo First. (2025). *Togo prepares to repay CFA12.1 billion on Islamic Sukuk loan by August 2025.* Togo First. https://www.togofirst.com/en/economic-governance/2307-16815-togo-prepares-to-repay-cfa12-1-billion-on-islamic-sukuk-loan-by-august-2025

Tohidi, M., Freydooni, M. M., & Easaei, M. (2024). Designing an innovative way for financing SMEs through Sukuk issuance. *Iranian Journal of Finance*, *8*(4), 113–135. DOI: 10.61186/ijf.2024.474814.1485

UK Government. (2014). Government issues first Islamic bond. The UK Government. https://www.gov.uk/government/news/government-issues-first-islamic-bond

UK Government. (2021). UK bolsters Islamic finance offering with second Sukuk. The UK Government. https://www.gov.uk/government/news/uk-bolsters-islamic-finance-offering-with-second-sukuk#:~:text=The%20UK%20has%20bolstered%20its,financial%20centre%20in%20the%20world

Ulusoy, A., & Ela, M. (2017). Lack of standardization in Sukuk market. *Journal of Islamic Economics, Banking and Finance, 13*(1), 147-169. https://www.researchgate.net/profile/Mehmet-Ela/publication/318787697_Lack_of_Standardization_in_Sukuk_Market/links/5a142c7eaca27240e3086299/Lack-of-Standardization-in-Sukuk-Market.pdf

UNCTAD. (2023). *Trade and development report 2023: Growth, debt and climate - Realigning the global financial architecture.* United Nations Publications. https://unctad.org/system/files/official-document/tdr2023_en.pdf

UNDP. (2018). Indonesia's green bonds & sukuk initiative. *UNDP Climate Promise.* https://climatepromise.undp.org/research-and-reports/indonesias-green-bond-sukuk-initiative

UNDP. (2024). The Potential Growth and Future Trends of Green Sukuk as a Tool for Sustainable Financing. United Nations Development Programme (UNDP). https://www.undp.org/sites/g/files/zskgke326/files/2025-05/undp-kfh-green-sukuk-tool-for-sustainable-financing.pdf

Usmani, M. T. (2002). *An introduction to Islamic finance* (Vol. 20). Kluwer Law International.

Vizcaino, B. (2014). Luxembourg's debut sukuk sees strong demand from government accounts. Reuters. https://www.reuters.com/article/markets/luxembourgs-debut-sukuk-sees-strong-demand-from-government-accounts-idUSL6N0RW0DY/

World Bank. (2017). Mobilizing Islamic Finance for Infrastructure Public-Private Partnerships. International Bank for Reconstruction and Development / The World Bank. https://ppp.worldbank.org/sites/default/files/2024-08/Mobilizing_Islamic_Finance_for_Infrastructure_PPPs_FINAL.pdf

World Bank. (2019). Reference Guide: Islamic Finance for Infrastructure PPP Projects. International Bank for Reconstruction and Development / The World Bank. https://ppp.worldbank.org/public-private-partnership/sites/ppp.worldbank.org/files/2022-02/REFERENCE_GUIDE_ISLAMIC_FINANCE_FOR_INFRASTRUCTURE_PPP_PROJECTS.pdf

World Bank. (2022). *Case study: Malaysia—Green sukuk market development.* The World Bank. https://thedocs.worldbank.org/en/doc/21c2fb7dfb189f10a0503004757b03f4-0340012022/original/Case-Study-Malaysia-Green-Sukuk-Market-Development.pdf

Zaher, T. S., & Hassan, M. K. (2002). A comparative literature survey of Islamic finance and banking. *Financial Markets, Institutions and Instruments, 10*(4), 155–199. DOI: 10.1111/1468-0416.00044

Zain, S., & Muhamad Sobri, Z. (2017). Musharakah SRI Sukuk & Development of Waqf Properties/Assets in Malaysia. *ResearchGate.* https://www.researchgate.net/publication/320540872_MUSHARAKAH_SRI_SUKUK_DEVELOPMENT_OF_WAQF_PROPERTIESASSETS_IN_MALAYSIA

Zanev, V., & Barchman, A. (2014). Luxembourg: all sukuk welcome. IFLR. https://www.iflr.com/article/2a63733ixysbvckz8y4s0/luxembourg-all-sukuk-welcome?utm_source=chatgpt.com

Zolotova, E. A., Aphudova, A. T., Klochkova, E. V., & Sidakova, D. I. (2024). *Fundamentals of Islamic Finance and Banking: Principles and Practice. EKONOMIKA I UPRAVLENIE: PROBLEMY.* RESHENIYA., DOI: 10.36871/ek.up.p.r.2024.04.05.015

Zulkhibri, M. (2015). A synthesis of theoretical and empirical research on sukuk. *Borsa Istanbul Review, 15*(4), 237–248. DOI: 10.1016/j.bir.2015.10.001

KEY TERMS AND DEFINITIONS

Adl: The Islamic principle of justice, emphasizing fairness and equity in economic transactions and contractual agreements. It underpins the risk-sharing and ethical frameworks of Islamic finance (Iqbal & Mirakhor, 2011).

Amanah: A trust or fiduciary responsibility in Islamic finance, where the state or an entity is considered a trustee of resources, accountable for their ethical and responsible management for the benefit of society. It emphasizes stewardship and accountability in sovereign borrowing (Iqbal & Mirakhor, 2011).

Asset-Backed Financing: A financing approach in Islamic finance where transactions are tied to tangible assets or real economic activities, ensuring that funds are linked to productive projects rather than speculative ventures. Examples include sukuk and Ijarahh, which enhance transparency and fiscal discipline (ISRA, 2012; Iqbal & Mirakhor, 2011).

Bay al-Dayn: A Shariah-compliant contract involving the sale of debt, often used in hybrid sukuk structures like Malaysia's Government Investment Issues (GII). It allows the transfer of receivables under specific conditions to ensure compliance with Islamic principles (Razak et al., 2019).

Bay al-Inah: A sale and buy-back agreement used in Islamic finance, where an asset is sold and then repurchased at a deferred price, often incorporated in hybrid sukuk structures like GII to facilitate financing while adhering to Shariah principles (Razak et al., 2019).

Diminishing Musharakah: A form of musharakah where one partner (e.g., the government) gradually buys out the other partner's share in a joint venture, allowing the transfer of asset ownership over time. It is ideal for infrastructure projects where public ownership is phased in (IMF, 2017; Nouman & Ullah, 2023).

Fiscal Dominance: A situation where central banks are pressured to monetize government debt, leading to distorted borrowing incentives and potential economic instability. In contrast, Islamic finance's asset-backed nature reduces such risks (Jung et al., 2025).

Gharar: Excessive uncertainty or ambiguity in financial transactions, prohibited in Islamic finance to ensure transparency and fairness. It prevents speculative contracts that lack clear terms or risk allocation (Iqbal & Mirakhor, 2011; ISRA, 2012).

Ijarahh: A Shariah-compliant leasing contract where an asset is leased to a party for periodic payments, often used in sukuk structures. In sovereign financing, governments lease assets to investors, with returns derived from lease payments (ISRA, 2012; Razak et al., 2019).

Istisna: A Shariah-compliant contract for manufacturing or constructing an asset, with payments made progressively as the project advances. Often used in combination with Ijarahh for public-private partnerships in infrastructure projects (Razak et al., 2019; Jobst, 2007).

Maqasid al-Shariah: The objectives of Islamic law, which include justice, welfare, and moral accountability. In Islamic finance, these objectives guide the structuring of financial instruments to promote social good and economic stability (ISRA, 2012).

Maysir: Speculative activities or gambling prohibited in Islamic finance, as they involve undue risk and deception, undermining fair economic transactions (Iqbal & Mirakhor (2011).

Mudarabah: A profit-sharing partnership where one party provides capital (rabb-ul-mal) and another provides expertise (mudarib). Profits are shared based on a pre-agreed ratio, while losses are borne by the capital provider unless negligence occurs (Iqbal & Mirakhor, 2011; ISRA, 2012).

Murabahah: A cost-plus financing contract where a seller discloses the cost of an asset and adds a profit margin, agreed upon by both parties. It is used in Islamic finance for asset-backed transactions (ISRA, 2012).

Musharakah: A joint venture partnership where all parties contribute capital and share profits and losses proportionally. It promotes equitable risk-sharing and is used in sovereign financing for infrastructure and development projects (Iqbal & Mirakhor, 2011; Razak et al., 2019).

Profit-and-Loss Sharing (PLS): A core principle of Islamic finance where financial returns and risks are shared between parties based on the performance of a project or investment, rather than fixed interest payments. Examples include mudarabah and musharakah (Iqbal & Mirakhor, 2011; Hassan & Dridi, 2011).

Qard al-Hasan: A benevolent, interest-free loan in Islamic finance aimed at promoting financial inclusion and social welfare. Repayment is made without additional charges, aligning with ethical principles (Iqbal & Mirakhor, 2017; Kahf, 2004).

Qimar: Gambling or speculative transactions involving deception, prohibited in Islamic finance due to their reliance on chance rather than productive activity, similar to *maysir* (Iqbal & Mirakhor, 2011).

Rabb-ul-Mal: The capital provider in a *mudarabah* contract who supplies the funds for a project while the other party (*mudarib*) provides expertise. The *rabb-ul-mal* bears financial losses unless negligence by the *mudarib* is proven (Iqbal & Mirakhor, 2011).

Riba: Usury or interest, strictly prohibited in Islamic finance as it represents unearned income detached from productive activity. Islamic finance replaces riba with risk-sharing and asset-backed mechanisms (ISRA, 2012; Iqbal & Mirakhor, 2011).

Shariah: Islamic law derived from the Qur'an and Sunnah, governing all aspects of Muslim life, including financial transactions. In Islamic finance, Shariah ensures compliance with principles such as the prohibition of *riba*, *gharar*, and *maysir* (ISRA, 2012; El-Gamal, 2006).

Special Purpose Vehicle (SPV): A legal entity created for a specific financial transaction, such as issuing sukuk, to manage assets or projects on behalf of investors, ensuring Shariah compliance and isolating financial risks (Razak et al., 2019).

Sukuk: Islamic financial certificates, often referred to as Islamic bonds, representing ownership in an underlying asset or project. Unlike conventional bonds, sukuk are asset-backed and provide returns based on project performance, not fixed interest (ISRA, 2012; Jobst et al., 2008).

Taradhi: The principle of mutual consent in Islamic contractual agreements, ensuring that all parties enter transactions willingly and with full understanding, promoting fairness and transparency (Iqbal & Mirakhor, 2011).

Wakala: An agency-based contract in Islamic finance where an agent (e.g., a special purpose vehicle) manages assets or investments on behalf of investors, often used in sukuk structures to ensure Shariah compliance (Razak et al., 2019).

Waqf: A charitable endowment in Islamic finance where assets are dedicated to social or religious purposes, promoting financial inclusion and community welfare (Iqbal & Mirakhor, 2017; Kahf, 2004).

Chapter 4

The Role of Waqf in Community Development:

Legal Structures for Sustainable Cities and Communities

Pranjal Khare
https://orcid.org/0000-0002-9937-9588
Jindal Global Law School, O.P. Jindal Global University, India

Paridhi Sharma
https://orcid.org/0009-0005-3373-0557
Jindal Global Law School, O.P. Jindal Global University, India

Md Kashif Ansari
https://orcid.org/0009-0002-3208-5646
Jindal School of Banking and Finance, O.P. Jindal Global University, India

ABSTRACT

This chapter examines Waqf, Islamic endowment, as a powerful tool for enabling sustainable cities and communities. It looks at the history and legal basis for Waqf and its diversification and application in different Islamic societies. In this context, Waqf has many characteristics for community development across social, economic, and environmental dimensions. The chapter examines Waqf through the analysis of legal mechanisms regulating Waqf geared towards the local, and ordinary citizen experience, but also includes traditional arrangements and "new" Waqf arrangements (e.g. corporate Waqf, Waqf sukuk). The chapter includes challenges and opportunities in Waqf management today for consideration and understanding.

DOI: 10.4018/979-8-3373-1887-5.ch004

Lack of transparency and accountability for Waqf management and local political reform, is crucial because reform in these areas may prepare the development of Waqf to better achieve the Sustainable Development Goals (SDGs) and ensure resilient cities, through the complexity and diversity of Waqf processes.

INTRODUCTION

In the 21st century, the world faces enormous challenges due to rapid urbanization, disparities, inequality and environmental degradation that make sustainable cities and urbanization a priority, as espoused by the United Nations (SDG 11 - Sustainable Cities & Communities). Despite various modern-day challenges, the ancient Islamic institution of Waqf, with its history and flexibility, is a largely untapped mechanism with enormous potential. Waqf involves a permanent dedication of the value of an asset such as a building, land or other resources by an individual or organization for charitable or religious purposes, where the principal remains intact, but the items derived from its benefits can be continuously spent without taking control of the principal. Waqf has its roots in the Arabic verb 'waqafa' which means to stop or halt. The spirit of Waqf is captured in the saying "habs al-asl wa tasbil al-manfaah" (detaining the principal and devoting the usufruct) which means that the asset is no longer available for sale or disposal after it has been designated as Waqf. Waqf originated in a time when Prophet Muhammad and his followers had limited resources but were able to give to charity, an essential spirit of giving centered in Islamic teachings about charity. The concept of Waqf was highlighted when Prophet Muhammad advised Umar ibn al-Khattab about dedicating the land in Khaybar (Iskandar & Sofuoglu, 2023).

This prophetic precedent ushered Waqf into an elaborate institutional form across the Islamic world, which was able to fund essential public services such as education and research through madrasas and universities, healthcare through hospitals, and extensive rehabilitation programs, as well as essential infrastructurc: bridges, roads and water systems, long before modern states assumed those roles. This temporary and there-to-reoccur nature of Waqf, as distinct from simple charity, made Waqf interesting as a powerful investment for the long haul relative to the well-being of communities broadly as Waqf Khairi (public/charitable), serving the public at large, Waqf Ahli (family/private) serving specific beneficiaries, appropriately with a reversion to charity upon no heirs, and Waqf Mushtarak serving both families and the public. Generally, a mutawalli is responsible for managing and collecting benefits and providing a distribution of benefits according to the Waqf deed, and this role varies with multiple legal constructs and standards informed by classical Islamic jurisprudence and its multiple approaches (Khan et al., 2018).

The 2030 Agenda for Sustainable Development introduced the 17 Sustainable Development Goals (SDGs) at the UN, with SDG 11: Sustainable Cities and Communities focusing on making human settlements inclusive, safe, resilient, and sustainable (Nabiyeva et al., 2023). The SDG systematically placed targets for Sustainable Cities and Human Settlements such as Target 11.1: Ensure access for all to adequate, safe and affordable housing and basic services, which is vital in addressing rapid urbanization exacerbated by the growth of informal settlements and increasing inadequacy of basic infrastructure; Target 11.2: Provide access to safe, affordable, accessible, and sustainable transport systems for all, which is urgent in a context of rising traffic congestion, air pollution, and global warming; Target 11.3: Enhance inclusive and sustainable urbanization and capacity for participatory settlement planning and management, which is important to address the issues of haphazard urban growth and lack of citizen engagement; Target 11.4: Strengthen efforts to protect and safeguard the world's cultural and natural heritage, which is key to fight the continuous development of urban areas; Target 11.5: Substantially reduce the number of deaths and the number of people affected and the economic losses directly related to disaster, with a focus on building resilience to climate events and those of geological origin (earthquakes); Target 11.6: Reduce the adverse per capita environmental impact of cities, in particular, by paying attention to air quality and waste management; Target 11.7: Provide universal access to safe, inclusive and accessible, green and public spaces, in particular for women and children, older persons and persons with disabilities. It also addresses (SDG target 11.a) by supporting positive urban-rural links by integrating urban and rural planning and supporting (SDG target 11.b) substantially increasing the number of cities that adopt and implement integrated policies and plans towards inclusion, resource efficiency, and resilience to climate change and natural disasters. Eventually also through Target 11.c, supporting least developed countries in building sustainable and resilient (both environmentally and socially) buildings utilizing local materials. Adopting targets show multi-dimensional challenges and achievements, which include rapid population growth, inadequate funding opportunities, insufficient governance, social inequalities, and climate change; in order to develop innovative financing and governance systems in lieu of these challenges (Sarac & Hassan, 2023).

While it may appear disparate at first glance, the historical institution of Waqf has an extraordinary and established relationship to contemporary sustainable development. The Waqf principles of permanence and benefit-orientation perfectly resonate with the long-term, intergenerational vision of the SDGs, and especially SDG 11. Waqf, in the past, played a major role in building and maintaining urban infrastructure - hospitals, schools, bridges, and water systems, thus acting as a key initial investment into functional, healthy vibrancy in cities, and as a model for active citizenship in urban governance. Waqf can contribute to sustainable cities and communities in many ways in the current environment, from social, economic and environmental perspectives: socially, Waqf can directly contribute to affordable housing (SDG 11.1), education (SDG 4), or access to healthcare (SDG 3) through inclusive practices; economically, in many instances it's often prime real estate, can generate a sustainable income stream to invest back into urban development programs through innovative approaches, like corporate Waqf or Waqf sukuk, thereby release of capital for development at scale or microenterprise development that can enhance local economies (SDG 8); environmentally, (Ishak et al., 2025) Waqf land can be made available for paths for green spaces (SDG 11.7) or urban farm solutions, funding renewable energy and sustainable transportation systems (SDG 11.2) while emphasizing stewardship of ecosystems for the long-term; and culturally, as custodians of historical buildings, many Awqaf serve as an important piece in capturing some aspect of heritage preservation (SDG 11.4). This accentuates Waqf as more than just charity; it is a distinctive legal and institutional framework for endowment-based development financing. It has the ability to sustainably generate resources for the public good, but being able to take full advantage of Waqf will require overcoming the challenges of legal complexity, modernizing governance, and earning the public's trust (Karimah et al., 2023).

This chapter is designed to closely investigate the role Waqf plays in sustainable development, with particular attention to its governing legal structures. It will discuss jurisprudential principles of Waqf, critically assess national regimes with respect to regulatory framework in selected jurisdictions, seek key examples and ascertain how they are contributing to sustainable urban development as a Waqf practice, produce novel legal and governance models with proposals for policy.

The methodology used will be primarily qualitative, and will incorporate doctrinal legal analysis of Islamic texts, comparative legal analysis of Waqf laws in different countries like Malaysia, Indonesia, Egypt, Turkey, India, etc. It will also include case study analysis of successful Waqf undertakings. It will involve direct consideration of the nature of the legal frameworks, and governance mechanics, associated with Waqf's contribution to SDG 11, along with illustrative examples that shed light on these aspects of Waqf, rather than comprehensively reviewing all Awqaf globally. As part of this methodology, limitations of this research will include, but are not limited to, the potential non transparency or unavailability of all Awqaf data, that Waqf law is within specific jurisdictions, that assessing the totality of socio-economic impacts is qualitative difficult, and that the emphasis on legal and governance implications of Waqf will have limited consideration on other areas such as social acceptance or interpretative ethics, as well as differences in language to understand certain historical texts. This introduction to the chapter has therefore focused on fundamental aspects of this area concerning developing the foundation of this study, including defining key terms, setting out the persuasive link between Waqf and sustainable development, and outlining the distinct scope for the research that follows.

ISLAMIC JURISPRUDENCE OF WAQF

The notion of Waqf is a deep-rooted part of the Islamic civilization, and it is not just charity; it is a complex legal and social institution which is designed to serve a continuous benefit to the community. To understand its potential in contemporary sustainable development, we need to examine its fundamental principles as enshrined in classical Islamic jurisprudence. This chapter therefore discusses the foundations of Waqf in Quran and Sunnah, the convener of the major Islamic juristic schools, the issues which comprise a Waqf, the differences in terms of Waqf, and the traditional mechanisms involved in the management and administration of Waqf (Kamaruddin et al., 2022).

Although the term 'Waqf' has not been advanced in the Quran, the divine text contains relatively strong ethical and moral bases for the spirit and action of endowments. The Quran frequently mentions charity (Sadiqah), spending in the name of Allah (Infaq fi Sabilillah) or actions of good/Hasanat. Statements along the lines of, "And whatever good you put forward for yourselves, you will find it with Allah, better and bigger in reward," and "By no means shall you attain righteousness unless you spend (freely) of that which you love," exhort believers to divest their wealth, for the benefit of others and for the sake of Allah, fostering a strong sense of social obligation and altruism that serves as a spiritual basis for charitable institutions such as Waqf. More immediately, 'Sadiqah Jariyah' (ongoing charity or perpetual charity) clearly relates back to Waqf, as the Prophet Muhammad (peace be upon him) said, "When a man dies, all his deeds come to an end except three: an ongoing charity, beneficial knowledge, or a righteous child that pray for him." The prophetic teaching sheds light on the spiritual rewards for acts of charity, the benefits of which can be beneficial even after the donors have died, clearly aligning with the principle of Waqf. The earliest and most iconic prophetic authority endorsing Waqf is the well-known Hadith of Umar ibn al-Khattab, who, when he acquired valuable land in Khaybar, sought the advice of the Prophet and was told, "If you wish, you can keep it as a property (Habis Aslaha) and give its benefits in charity." Umar did this, and dedicated it to the various beneficiaries, mandating that it could never be sold, given away, or inherited. This Hadith established the main principles of Waqf: that the principal property is protected from any reduction in its value and that its usufruct is devoted forever for charitable purposes, as well as the delegating of property providing a continuing benefit, rather than a consumable benefit. The

Quranic commands and prophetic injunctions thus provided the needed religious ardor and guidance for institutionalizing Waqf (Faruki, 2024).

The major Sunni schools of Islamic law, Hanafi, Maliki, Shafi'i, and Hanbali, are in agreement that Waqf is completely legal and immensely virtuous in Islam. Each of the four schools is in general agreement that Waqf is in effect legally dedicating an asset in perpetuity, making the asset non-transferrable, while the benefits are for a specific charitable or pious cause. Their treatment of Waqf was one of irrevocability once properly constituted, and the goal of the Waqf was to gain continual reward for the endower. However, the Hanafite, Shafiite, Malike, and Hanbalite scholars interpreted specific features differently. As it relates to the binding nature of Waqf, the Hanafi school had a comparatively complex position in which Waqf was not initially binding unless properly constituted, but it nonetheless wore the view of its two leading scholars. The Maliki, Shafi, and Hanbali schools traced a clear line to the Iqrar declaration of Waqf being binding and irrevocable upon declaration and no added steps to constitute other than an intention must also be established for proper formation. All four schools wanted the Waqf permanent, that is, the purpose must be continuous, the principal must remain intact indefinitely, and a limited-Waqf purpose would usually invalidate the Waqf. Finally, as it relates to the Waqf of movable properties (Manqulat) the Hanafi school analyzed mostly through difficult deliberately limiting Waqf to immoveable properties and based on historically the custom enlarged the Waqf with durable moveable properties, but on most occasions the Maliki, Shafiite, and Hanbali schools allowed Waqf of movable. In addition, the Malki, Shafi and Hanbali schools allowed the Waqf of movable, where the movable could curtain perpetual benefit or endogenous to larger Waqf. In regard to Waqf for oneself or for descendants (Waqf Ahli), all of the schools accepted this practice, though the Hanbali school did allow the waqif to reserve a Haq for themselves during their lifetime, as long as the ultimate goal of the Waqf was charitable, while the other schools were more cautious in this regard. For Istibdal (exchange of Waqf property), all of the schools allowed for this practice under strict conditions, mostly if the original property was either non-beneficial or exchanged it would provide greater beneficial purposes for the Waqf. In general, the Maliki school was the most permissive about Waqf, while the Hanbali and Shafi'i schools tended toward stricter stances. These differences speak to the fluid nature of ijtihad (independent legal reasoning) in Islamic law, allowing for the possibility of variation that recognized local customs and practical needs and honored fundamental principles (Abbasi, 2012).

For the Waqf to be an enforceable legal instrument under Islamic law, certain essential components must be present and properly constituted: the Waqif (Founder), the Mawquf (Endowed Property), the Mawquf Alayh (Beneficiaries), and the Sigha (Declaration). The Waqif must also affirmatively demonstrate one of the essential conditions of legal capacity (Ahliyyah) which requires the waqif to be an adult, mentally sound, and not acted upon by a duress who is able to make legal claims independently. Waqufs established by minors and persons acted upon by duress cannot establish a valid Waqf. In addition to having the legal capacity to act, the waqif must also have full ownership of the Waqf property at the time of dedication, and it must not be encumbered. This ownership provision excludes jointly owned property. So, the waqif must own the Waqf property without any other parties having interest in it, and the dedication of the Waqf must also be free and voluntary from coercion or undue influence that could compromise or contradict the waqif's genuine intentions for charitable purposes (Dallh, 2023). The Waqf property has to have value and must return benefits perpetually to others; in customary practice, Waqf has been restricted to immovable property (Usuwana), for example land and buildings, and comprises useful interests since the essence of the property remains with the Waqif, but the usufruct is dispersed in perpetuity. The Waqf of movable properties (Manqulat) was debated amongst scholars, but later scholars relied on Urf (custom) and Istihsan (the betterment of others in need) to further the inclusion of durable movable properties, such as books or tools that produced benefits into the future, and more could also add cash Waqf with the express stipulation it be invested in continuing to generate income in perpetuity. The Waqf must also be something legally owned by the Waqif at the point of dedication, and it must be clearly defined and quantifiable, so it is not ambiguous to other persons. The Waqf must also have Mawquf Alayh (beneficiary) that is clearly defined and available to be identified, though they do not have to be named separately within the public Waqf. The Waqf must also be dedicated for the purpose of Qurbah (it is something of devotion), and generally Waqf implies that the purpose is charitable, religious, educational, social, or welfare in nature. The waqif is allowed to make determinations about eligibility, as long as it does not violate Islamic law. Lastly, in understanding the Waqf as a legal institution, it is critical to understand that the Sigha is the clear and unequivocal expression, either oral or written, of the waqif's intention to create the Waqf, that was to take effect immediately upon valid expression, giving the property its Waqf status irrevocably. Once again, while a written deed (Waqfiyya) was preferred in order to avoid any ambiguity regarding Waqf property, the written deed functioned as the constitution for the Waqf to identify the property, the beneficiaries, and the conditions of management (Dar, 2020).

Customized nominally, a Waqf can be grouped into three types based on beneficiaries and use. One group is referred to as Waqf Khairi (Public or Charitable Waqf), which is a Waqf that is created purely for general charitable or pious causes or use and benefits the public at large. Historically, Waqf Khairi has financed historical Mosques, madrasas (the public schools), Bimaristans (hospitals), Hamams (public baths), bridges, roads, Sabils (water supply systems), and shelters, that benefitted the general public. The use of Waqf Khairi constructs was to serve humanity.

The other group is Waqf Ahli (Family or Private Waqf or Waqf Dhurri), defined as a Waqf constructed for the benefit of the waqif's family; ascendants; or designated individuals, in an effort to secure the financial stability of this family and protect it from poverty. Historically, this type has been a highly effective method for family estate planning, preventing wealth from being diluted and consequently allowing the wealth to flow down to chosen beneficiaries forever. There are usually provisions in place whereby when there are no more family descendants, the Waqf reverts to the general charitable purposes of Waqf Khairi to maintain ultimate charitable status. The third variant is called Waqf Mushtarak (Mixed Waqf). The mixed Waqf type can have blended characteristics of Waqf Khairi and Waqf Ahli. This structure allows the founder to designate specific shares or portions of the income of the Waqf properties for their family and allocate the rest to be used for public charitable purposes. Alternatively, the Waqf could create an income stream where the family members will be able to benefit at first, but when that stops, the Waqf reverts to public charity. Ultimately this demonstrates how the Waqf institution is flexible enough to meet diverse social and economic requirements (Sukmana, 2020).

In the classical period of Islamic law, the management and administration of Waqf properties were utterly formalized to ensure perpetual use of the Waqf properties. The primary agent was Mutawalli (Trustee/Administrator), the person responsible for the operational management of the Waqf property and for managing the flow of benefits from the Waqf. The waqif could choose the first mutawalli and also stipulate the process of succession, but if no one was appointed, or if the one appointed was unwilling, disabled or not honest, then the Islamic judge (Qadi) would be able to step in (Rasool, 2024).

As part of the mutawalli's responsibilities, they had to safeguard the property, invest the capital of the property in the Shariah compliant manner, collect revenue from the Waqf property, record all transactions, and make payment to the beneficiaries, to name a few. The mutawalli had to be trustworthy (Amin), capable (Qadir), and knowledgeable while the mutawalli was accountable for their acts and obligations to the Waqf property. If they were to act with gross negligence, they could be dismissed by the Qadi. There were layers of administrative structure whereby there would also be a nazir (supervisor). This person will also be appointed by the waqif or the Qadi, to oversee the mutawalli. The nazir would also act as checks and balances against the mutawalli's actions. The Qadi (Islamic Judge) was the ultimate judicial authority, they could intervene in disputes, interpret unclear clauses, and intervene to act if the Waqf wasn't honoring the original intent of the waqif in compliance with Islamic law. The original objective was to protect the integrity of the Waqf property in perpetuity. The Waqf deed (Waqfiyya) was the legal documents that outlined the waqif's intentions, details about the property that was donated, the names of the beneficiaries, the rules about managing the Waqf, and any other relevant clauses. Successful Waqf administration can depend on having well drafted Waqf deeds as these documents usually include details about ranging disputes that could occur. Only the Waqf deed could ensure proper functioning and dictated intentional implementation of the Waqf in perpetuity as intended by the founder (Beverley, 2011).

Financial management observed strict adherence to Islamic principles, including prohibition on Riba (interest), and typically resulted in an investment based on either Mudarabah (profit-sharing partnership) or Musharrakah (joint venture partnership) when the goal was to return an investment while also leaving the principal intact. The additional but crucial concept of Istibdal (exchange of Waqf property) was also included; while the principal of Waqf has a status of inalienability, jurists acknowledged occasions in which it would be permitted to exchange a Waqf property that was falling apart and/or not beneficial in exchange for a Waqf property that was more beneficial, as long as the change served the higher goal of Waqf and its beneficiaries and received appropriate legal oversight, sometimes needing the final approval of the Qadi. All of this and more reflects the flexibility, within very stringent conditions, in which Awqaf could respond to changing circumstances and continue to accomplish objectives for centuries. Knowing these nuanced jurisprudential considerations shows how Waqf could be resilient and adaptive and has inherent capacity as a sustainable means of community development, based upon centuries of scholarly consideration and practice (Muhmad et al., 2021).

ECONOMIC CONTRIBUTIONS OF WAQF TO SUSTAINABLE DEVELOPMENT

Waqf is a permanent form of Islamic endowment that can far exceed its intended social-welfare functions by acting as a lever for economic development and a mechanism with an intrinsic sustainability dimension. By mobilizing private sources for public goods, Waqf could provide stable, ongoing funding for projects important in creating strong and sustainable economies, especially at the urban and local level. The aim of this subchapter is to highlight the multifaceted economic advantages of Waqf including the importance of infrastructure provision, new funding modalities and Waqf's role in supporting local economies and sustainability (Ahmed, 2024).

Historically, Waqf helped to structure the economic life of Islamic cities through the provision of essential public infrastructure. This occurred long before modern municipal governments took this task over. Most Awqaf provided utilities and public goods that enabled trading efficiency, urban health, and connectedness. Endowments were commonly dedicated to the development and upkeep of pathways, bridges and roads necessary for commerce and communication, enabling people and goods to move across long distances. Similarly, water systems, such as fountains (Sabils), aqueducts and pipelines along with footpaths and irrigation canals were provided through endowments so that individuals and municipalities could access clean water for drinking, agriculture and sanitation, essential for public health and economic output. Public utilities, such as baths (Hammams) and markets (Suqs), were also considered Waqf establishments, providing staple services and markets, which served as essential components of daily life and a robust economic context of trade within the cities. This historical trend shows that Waqf can help as a sustainable financing mechanism for sustainable, non-profit generating long-term infrastructure. Waqf undoubtedly is still used to finance such projects in countries with considerable infrastructure shortfalls in both developing economies and developed economies. Waqf could offer new iterations by financing the development and maintenance of public transport infrastructure, renewable energy grids, or smart city technology, which would certainly lead to sustainable urban development and improved quality of life for their beneficiaries (Abdullah et al., 2022).

Waqf has also been associated with gentrifying affordable housing within the integrated urban realm, particularly with regard to housing and urban planning. Awqaf are already used by Waqf to finance affordable housing solutions, where Waqf financing typically involved constructing living units whose rents were free, or highly subsidized, restricted for use on a particular basis of all of the scholars, the needy or the students etc. This precedent provides an exciting opportunity for models for developing sustainable low-income housing that could remain a future investment and benefit vulnerable populations affordably for a long period. In addition, Waqf extended to land, and various amounts of urban and peri-urban land were dedicated to various public purposes. This also included land dedicated to cemeteries, public gardens, or even just land as a strategic decision for urban development to help with urban sprawl and future environmental protections to curb continued random growth. Other examples include the dedication of land for open spaces, such as parks and community gardens, which stayed attuned to the urban landscape and provided recreational opportunities while benefiting the overall environment. Waqf's land could be intended for green benefit, however, there remains opportunities for Waqf property in today's realities specifically for multi-use developments that include affordable housing, public and civic assets, and urban green space infrastructure to guide equitable urbanization. Conservative assumptions guided by perpetual endowments versus capital markets. Looking at land in the frame of market pressures, it can significantly and quickly skew social and environmental factors, as they are much clearer and relevant (Riani & Fatoni, 2022).

Moreover, Waqf's economic impact extends directly to providing people and establishing local economies; for example, historically, Awqaf capital or resources, which directly translated into economic activity for the beneficiary, such as a set of tools, seed for agriculture, and even a small store, storefront for craftsmen and traders. In the modern context, this translates well into the support of microfinance activities where Waqf funds would be established as interest-free loans (Qard Hasan) or equity investments (Mudarabah, Musharrakah), that would help entrepreneurs, small businesses and poor individuals who do not have access to conventional finances. By providing capital without exploitative interest, Waqf-based microfinance has the potential to break the cycle of poverty while ensuring that individuals obtain self-sufficiency. Moreover, Waqf can support entrepreneurship directly by subsidizing spaces for start-up businesses or vocational training centers that will arm the participant with skills they need for the job market, which in-turn would support the number of job-creating initiatives when Waqf-supported businesses grow to a point of needing people. Beyond just causing a direct capital input, an active Waqf can deploy Waqf assets, such as commercial real estate including shops and markets to generate revenue streams to fund social programs without financially crippling local businesses through overpriced rents. This also allows the community to have local places to shop, eat, learn, and play. This model shows how philanthropic capital can be used to actively support economic activity at the grass-roots level while improving the livelihoods of the community members (Fauzi et al., 2023).

Effective financial utilization and Sharia Compliance investment models are necessary to achieve the continuity and enhancement of Waqf assets. Within the classical scholarship, Istibdal was explicitly made available for Waqfs. Istibdal was a means to know whether to exchange the Waqf property with another of equal value when consumed delivery from the original property or when it was in the best interest of the Waqf. This flexibility is vital as it allows previously unemployable properties to be revitalized to more benevolent ones, such as exchanging a derelict property for a newer income-generating property with sufficient yield. Beyond Istibdal, Waqf entities are able to explore a variety of Islamic finance models. A Musharrakah contributes funds to a personal partnership with other capital. They will participate in a joint venture to complete the designated project and share the profits and risks. This model is designed for large developments, such as housing estates or commercial complexes. Next, you have Murabaha (cost-plus financing). The Waqf entity purchases an asset and re-sells either to a beneficiary or third party at a price over cost that follows Islamic principles and gives a clear profit. Murabaha is commonly used for goods or raw materials. Overtime Waqf sukuk has been created, as a new instrument that represents an ownership interest in a Waqf asset or project. Under Sharia based investment principles, these bonds allow for the securitization of Waqf properties or for raising funds for new Waqf projects from a wider pool of investors, thus mobilizing significant cash for large scale sustainable development projects, whether funding green infrastructure or large affordable housing schemes, while still retaining the Waqf's enduring charitable purpose. These investment vehicles allow Waqf real estate assets to function as positive agents of economic growth instead of static charitable contributions (Nafar, 2019).

Together as a collective force, Waqf acts as an important catalyst for local economic growth and resilience. Waqf directly assists local governments' financial burden by supporting public services like education, health care and infrastructure, freeing up valuable public resources for alternative investments. Waqf owned commercial estate provides a stable and often affordable space for businesses which ultimately assist in supporting local entrepreneurs, small and medium sized enterprises, which all communities rely upon, and inclusive growth potential. Employment opportunities created by Waqf-supported businesses or Waqf-funded projects help to improve local purchasing power and create demand (Elmahgop et al., 2025). Also, in times of economic recession or crises, Waqf endowments act as a buffer and provide much-needed social safety nets by maintaining essential services, creating value and liquidity through operational expenses and charitable outgoings to local markets, assisting resilience in the community. Also, unlike conventional financing which can be very sensitive to market whims or political change, Waqf, in that it is perceptual and functional, offers consistent and reliable finance for positive community outcomes. The fact that Waqf offers permanence is what makes it a distinctive mechanism for the achievement of sustainable productive, inclusive economies that provide resistance to external shocks while assisting self-reliance and community building from the inside (Maulina et al., 2023).

LEGAL STRUCTURES FOR SUSTAINABLE WAQF MANAGEMENT

National Legal Frameworks Governing Waqf

The effectiveness and reach of Waqf institutions in contemporary contexts are heavily shaped by the national legal frameworks they operate within. These frameworks are mostly a hybrid of historical Islamic jurisprudential arguments and contemporary legislative amendments. The relevant legal parameters govern all aspects of Waqf starting from the establishment and registration of Waqf, how Waqf is managed and used, and the reporting and oversight of Waqf. A comparative analysis of the Waqf framework across several Muslim-majority countries illustrates the differences in historical legacy, legal tradition and socio-political priorities among different jurisdictions. For example, in Malaysia and Indonesia, Waqf laws are largely situated within the broader Islamic legal arrangements and are in practice subsumed in the administration of ipso facto Waqf by the State Islamic Religious

Council (SIRC). Here, the approach to Waqf tends to be unitary and often more development-oriented, at times to the exclusion of modern forms of self-categorized Waqf (Syibly et al., 2022).

However, contrasting this, in the case of India where Muslims are a minority, Waqf is regulated by a set of specific Waqf Acts, which are still governed by a secular framework. This can spur unique issues in the legal interpretation and enforcement of Waqf Acts and generates more of a preservationist approach than a developmental approach, one example of which could be redeeming Waqf property that has an alienated interest, which is treated objectively with no regard towards nuances of what is developmentally valuable. Similarly, both Egypt and Turkey also had heavily centralized state apparatuses which formally employed significant state control over Waqf, and in many cases nationalized or centralized the management of Waqf, which created diverging pathways of Waqf management and utilization than system which privileges private (or semi-private) autonomy. These varied legal environments also determine the regulators and administrative structures that oversee Waqf; they can be managed by ministries of awqaf, Waqf boards or specialized agencies that carry out functions such as registration, management, investments, and dispute resolution; these aspects can be completely centralized under a government agency or decentralized to a local committee level (Phougat et al., 2025).

The situation is not the same in each country, though all Waqf legal frameworks share some common challenges in relation to the interpretation and enforcement of law. One common challenge is that the law setting forth Waqf and its associated legal concepts, albeit unique for each country, is insufficient to respond to modern economic challenges, asset classes such as cash Waqf or ownership in shares, or innovative investment models, and can lead to significant confusion in application. In addition, inefficiencies in government bureaucracy, inconsistencies in courts; the great number of judges to whom the rule of law is written does mean differences in interpretation, incomplete land records, amongst many others, can exacerbate such challenges in respect of Waqf management and restoration (Sano & Kassim, 2021). Furthermore, diversion of Waqf assets and other disputes regarding Waqf property are still prevalent, due in part to inefficient enforcement mechanisms and poor transparency. The relationship between Waqf law and secular law adds another layer of difficulty. In many legal systems operating based on customary law or statutory law, the perpetual, and inalienable qualities of Waqf must be reconciled with property rights, trust law, and charity law (Owais & Manaf, 2023).

Typically, the reconciliation of assets and Waqf can be interrupted by legal issues or by requirements for special court or judicial interpretations which may delay or hamper development projects or put off potential endeavors. For example, referring to a Waqf as a separate legal entity can have many vulnerabilities to a secular construct of trust affecting its consideration for tax treatment, e.g. Al-Qard, or how it will conduct its business. These issues would provide a strong case for harmonization and enhancing national Waqf legislation. Support for modernization of Waqf legislation that will address ways of covering contemporary asset types and financial instruments, clarification of centralized registration systems in order to streamline registration process that will dovetail with existing systems, capacity development of judicial bodies performing Waqf jurisprudence, and cooperation among jurisdictions to formalize and harmonize the Waqf and its related asset activities in order to share best practices going forward. Once again, the development and investment of Waqf assets will need to have a combination of legislative support, enforcement processes, and preferably in highly transparent land/asset registries as local/regional authorities will be responsible for management, compliance, etc. (Ikhyanuddin, 2022).

Governance, Accountability, and Transparency in Waqf Institutions

Proper governance, efficient accountability, and transparency are key components for the sustainable management of Waqf institutions and essential for confidence in those institutions. In the absence of effective governance, Waqf properties are susceptible to mismanagement, misappropriation, or neglect that could adversely affect the capital's potential to be put towards sustainable development. Best practices in Waqf governance generally favor a clear administrative structure with a board of trustees or management committee of people with varying backgrounds, including legal, financial and development. The roles and responsibilities of mutawalli (manager) need to be clearly defined and include fiduciary responsibilities of managing the Waqf's capital, maximizing the return, and distributing the revenue timely and appropriately according to the foundation charter and Sharia. All those engaged in Waqf management should act professionally, ethically, and have a clear conflict-of-interest policy (Mohaiyadin et al., 2022).

A well-governed Waqf is built on diligent financial management and holding the Waqf institution or committee to strict reporting standards on the Waqf assets. Having Sharia-compliant accounting norms are also important, and ideally follow the norms established by the Accounting and Auditing Organization for Islamic Financial Institutions (AAOIFI), or similar. It is important to ensure the financial operations are consistent with Islamic practices but also have clarity. Independent audits by qualified people at regular intervals are important to assess integrity and compliance. Complete financial statements such as balance sheets, income statements and cash flow reports should be developed and provided to the important stakeholders, furnishing a measure of transparency and performance in the assets and how they were used. This standard represents not only good management of Waqf funds but promotes trust with prospective donors and beneficiaries. The accountability process must encompass a broadening contribution to donors, beneficiaries and regulators (Ramli & Muhamed, 2014). This requires regular and transparent accountability reporting to the founding family, or the original endower if applicable, to show what has happened to the Waqf activities and to what extent the Waqf performed financially. Beneficiary reporting processes, which include them sharing their feedback on surveys and a pathway to share complaints and suggestions, are equally as important to see the extent to which the Waqf is achieving its social impact objectives. Periodic reviews and audits by regulators, whether that be government agencies or independent Muslim councils are equally important to ensure compliance and proper governmental processes (Hasan et al., 2020).

Challenges associated with misappropriation and corruption in Waqf management are a serious concern that requires multiple approaches to resolve. Weak matters of enforcement of laws, absence of public compensation for oversight, and weaknesses in internal controls, are common trends that shape a chain of events. Solutions include strengthening legal structures with firm penalties for misused Waqf assets, creating independent investigative agencies, and having whistle-blower protections in place. Encouraging strong internal controls, segregation of duties, and open procurement processes in Waqf agencies can have a far-reaching deterrent effect on potential fraud opportunities. The long-term goal is to create an environment of integrity that is sensed throughout the Waqf administrative layer. Technology can provide diverse opportunities to increase transparency and accountability in the Waqf. Digital platforms that act as central registries for Waqf information can make publicly available comprehensive information about Waqf assets and deeds management to discourage criminal fraud and provide better monitoring. Blockchain technology can be used to record Waqf transactions permanently and transparently; to indicate ownership; to bolster confidence and transparency; prevent unapproved changes; and allow all parties direct access to a record that cannot be changed. There are many digital tools that can also provide financial reporting, beneficiary management, and real time reporting for Waqf projects to minimize administrative work and costs and allow real time access to funders and stakeholders. With the right technology, Waqf management can become less static and less prone to fraud, with a greater focus on accountability and trust which can improve the effect of Waqf on sustainable development (Ramli et al., 2015).

Innovative Legal Structures and Models for Modern Waqf

As Waqf continues to evolve in order to address new challenges in development, new legal structures and creative models are being adopted to inject new efficiency, scale and dynamism into Waqf. These innovations aim to implement the best essence of Waqf into the new financial, corporate, and philanthropic realities of current society. One key model is the development of Corporate Waqf and Waqf-Based Enterprises. These models involve creating commercial enterprises where Waqf is established by endowing shares, or the profits of an enterprise or some type of Waqf from the enterprise itself. With Waqf as a commercial entity, Waqf can directly participate in large commercial activities, achieve sustainable commercial returns and direct those returns to charitable or development purposes. These new structures also provide the mechanism for professional asset management of Waqf and proactive participation in the economy beyond traditional land or building Waqf (Hadi et al., 2025).

Another significant innovation consists of Waqf Foundations and Hybrid Legal Structures. These innovations apply some civil law or common law structures (non-profit foundations or trusts), to hold and manage Waqf assets resulting in improved legal clarity, regulatory recognition and flexibility in modern operating contexts. These hybrid combinations have been successful in combining the eternal and charitable aspect of Waqf with strong governance and effective management practices found in modern philanthropic foundations (Wan-Ismail et al., 2025). This combination also allows for better investment strategies and larger programmatic reach. Additionally, the Micro-Waqf and Crowdfunding for Waqf Projects concepts include Waqf democratization. Micro-Waqf allows individuals to give small amounts, so that Waqf becomes something that exists for all. Digital crowdfunding sites can then be used to collect those individual micro contributions toward a specific Waqf project, essentially enabling technology to provide collective action resources to a specific development, such as, a community center, supporting a social enterprise, or a new local green space. This not only enlarges the pool of donors, it also accelerates when a project will have funding (Rahmalan & Abu-Hussin, 2021).

In addition, Waqf Sukuk and other Islamic Financial Instruments for Development represent some of the most sophisticated methods of mobilizing large scale capital for development through Islamic financing tools. Waqf Sukuk, are Sharia-compliant bonds created to represent ownership in some underlying Waqf assets or to a specific project and allow Waqf institutions to raise large amounts of money from individual or institutional investors, while complying with Islamic finance (Ari & Koc, 2021). These instruments can facilitate financing large-scale infrastructure projects, affordable housing initiatives, or similar sustainable development investments. Other Islamic finance instruments, such as Mudarabah (profit-sharing partnership) and Musharrakah (joint venture partnership), are also increasingly being adapted for Waqf investments, allowing for risk-sharing and ethical financing for a range of development initiatives. Finally, Public-Private Partnerships (PPPs) constitute an exciting partnership model for Waqf Development Projects. PPPs bring together Waqf institutions, governments, private and philanthropic parties to use their strengths; Waqf can provide land or capital, the private sector can lead on the project in terms of expertise and efficiency, and the government can offer the regulatory framework and provide infrastructure. By pooling resources and sharing risks that are too great for all parties to tackle as individuals, PPPs can deliver larger, more complex sustainable development projects, including urban regeneration, public utility upgrades, or affordable housing on a large scale. Overall, this increases the scale and scope of Waqf towards enhancing the well-being of communities and catalyzing economic growth. Hence, these legal innovations and frameworks will be beneficial to further adapt Waqf to the contemporary demands of development, increase its relevance in society, and encourage it to reach its fullest potential to promote sustainable cities and communities (Manaf et al., 2025).

CONCLUSION AND WAY FORWARD

The previous sub-chapters have shown that Waqf, as a traditional Islamic institution, has a deep and broad capacity to make a significant contribution to sustainable development, specifically in the context of creating resilience and inclusive cities and communities, as outlined in SDG 11. Waqf is grounded in Quranic understanding of the ongoing nature of charity (Sadiqah Jariyah) and supported through Prophetic practice. It's essential principle of perpetual dedication to the usufruct of an asset or property for charity or pious action aligns perfectly with the vision of sustainability that extends beyond immediate needs, to long-term, intergenerational sustainability. Waqf, has provided development finance for the essential public services and infrastructure, including madrasas, hospitals, bridges, roads, and water systems, well ahead of modern nation-states and surveyed as encapsulating enormous potential for investing in community well-being.

In economic terms, Waqf provides the diversity of resources and potential support for sustainable financing toward critical infrastructure development or addressing gaps in development where there may not be sufficient traditional finance. Historically, within water systems, roads, and public facilities, Waqf could then support contemporary public transport, renewable energy, and smart city infrastructure aimed at improving the urban quality of life. Furthermore, Waqf has played in the area of housing and urban planning for affordable housing, strategic land management, and forever, the introduction of the important elements of green open space, ultimately contributing to diversified, equitable, and sustainable urbanization.

Beyond useful infrastructure, Waqf economically empowers those in poverty through its microfinance initiatives, whereby interest-free loans or equity investments are made to small businesses and entrepreneurs that break the cycles of poverty and create jobs. Income flows from the use of Waqf properties can be reinvested into urban development programs and local economies.

In order to perpetuate and expand the value of Waqf assets, innovative forms of investment remain necessary. The historical understanding of Istibdal allows unproductive assets to be reactivated, however ongoing possibilities in Islamic finance, such as Musharrakah and Murabaha, with Waqf Sukuk being the most viable, can also be employed to generate substantial capital to fund larger sustainable development projects such as green infrastructure or affordable housing. Such options create dynamic roles for Waqf as an active and financially productive entity rather than just a passive philanthropic holding. Ultimately, Waqf is an important source of local economic growth and resilience, both through the alleviation of local government fiscal pressure, by providing stable places of business, increasing local capacity for purchases, and by acting as a buffer during economic downturns to develop greater levels of self-sufficiency that engages with and empowers communities from within.

Nonetheless, harnessing the full potential of Waqf will rely on resolving important challenges in its legal infrastructures and governance. The national legal mechanisms that govern Waqf are very different and represent varying historical and political contexts, whether centralized state control in Egypt and Turkey, integrated into broader Islamic legal administration in Malaysia and Indonesia, or operated under acts in a secular system, as in India. As previously mentioned, the different frameworks suffer from old laws, day-to-day bureaucracy, ambiguities and variations of interpretation that are used for effective administration and, in some cases, diversion of Waqf assets. The interface of Waqf law with secular legal structures, especially issues pertaining to property, trusts, and charity law can create complexity that may delay development activities or deter prospective endowers. At the same time, ensuring appropriate governance, accountability and transparency are essential components for Waqf institutions.

Therefore, a clear way forward is adopting a collective approach to reform and harmonize national Waqf legislation. This would include, among others, updating and reforming laws to incorporate new types of assets and financial facility types, efficient central registration systems, developing judicial capacity to adjudicate Waqf issues and promoting collaboration across jurisdictions to share practices. Applying best practices like clear board structures, delineating roles of mutawalli accompanied with obligations of a fiduciary nature, Sharia-related practices in financial management and independent audit considerations (i.e. AAOIFI), and open and transparent reporting to all stakeholders, which include donors, beneficiaries, and regulators, are imperative. Combatting misappropriation shows that we need firmer enforcement of legal rights, independent investigation bodies, and an integrity-driven culture, including solid internal control systems and clearer processes.

Importantly, the introduction of technology represents an opportunity for a meaningful future. Digital registries for linking Waqf assets, creating permanent audit trails of transactions and events through blockchain, and modern software for financial management and reporting, as well as monitoring and evaluation of projects in real time, can enhance transparency, efficiency and accountability, reduce the risk of fraud, and assist in improving public confidence. New and innovative legal forms and arrangements, like Corporate Waqf and Waqf-Based Companies, can professionalize the management of assets and provide ways for more direct participation in the economy. Waqf Foundations, and other Hybrid Legal Entities, can accommodate Waqf's perpetuity with contemporary governance capabilities. Micro-Waqf and crowdfunding provide new ways to democratize participation and more effective means to activate projects quickly.

Lastly, developing Public-Private Partnerships (PPPs) will be important to combine the land and capital of Waqf, along with government support, with private sector resources and experience to develop larger, multi-faceted sustainable development projects. Through innovative approaches to legal issues, better governance, and innovation and technology, Waqf can take full advantage of its potential as a sustainable force for community well-being and economic opportunity in the 21st century.

REFERENCES

Abbasi, M. Z. (2012). The Classical Islamic Law of Waqf: A Concise Introduction. *Arab Law Quarterly, 26*(2), 121–153. https://www.jstor.org/stable/23234650. DOI: 10.1163/157302512X629124

Abdullah, S. F. S., Muhamad, M. D., Ishak, A. H., Rani, M. A. M., Jaapar, N., Daud, M. Z., & Bhari, A. (2022). Waqf-Based Infrastructure; Lessons Learnt from Traditional Islamic Neighborhood Practices. *Journal of Pharmaceutical Negative Results, 13*(9), 5826–5832. DOI: 10.47750/pnr.2022.13.S09.702

Ahmed, R. (2024). Waqf; an instrument of poverty elimination and development. *Maktoob Media.* https://maktoobmedia.com/opinion/Waqf-instrument-of-poverty-elimination-and-development/

Ari, I., & Koc, M. (2021). Towards sustainable financing models: A proof-of-concept for a Waqf-based alternative financing model for renewable energy investments. *Borsa Istanbul Review, 21,* S46–S56. DOI: 10.1016/j.bir.2021.03.007

Beverley, E. L. (2011). Property, authority and personal law: Waqf in colonial South Asia. *South Asia Research, 31*(2), 155–182. DOI: 10.1177/026272801103100204

Dallh, M. (2023). Accumulate but distribute: Islamic emphasis on the establishment of Waqf (pious endowment). *Religion and Development,* 2(1), 21–40. DOI: 10.30965/27507955-20230014

Dar, Z. A. (2020). Islamic Concept of Waqf: Challenges and Prospects with Reference to the Jammu and Kashmir Muslim Waqf Board. *Airlangga International Journal of Islamic Economics and Finance, 3*(2), 89. DOI: 10.20473/aijief.v3i2.23880

Elmahgop, F., Alsulami, F., Mohammed, M. G. A., Abdel-Gadir, S., & Elhassan, T. (2025). The Socio-Economic Impacts of Waqf Investment Funds as a Model for Sustainable Financing in Saudi Arabia. *Sustainability (Basel), 17*(9), 3805. DOI: 10.3390/su17093805

Faruki, A. (2024). The Concept of Waqf in Islam: A Textual Study of Hanafi Jurisprudential Thoughts. *Islamonweb.* https://en.islamonweb.net/the-concept-of-Waqf-in-islam-a-textual-study-of-hanafi-jurisprudential-thoughts#:~:text=In%20Islamic%20jurisprudence%2C%20particularly%20within,benefits%20solely%20to%20charitable%20causes

Fauzi, M., Haji-Othman, Y., & Pakkanna, M. (2023). The strategy of micro Waqf banks for job creation on micro-scale enterprises in Indonesia. *International Journal of Academic Research in Business & Social Sciences, 13*(6). Advance online publication. DOI: 10.6007/IJARBSS/v13-i6/17407

Hadi, M., Rum, J., Maguni, W., & Radiamoda, A. M. (2025). Toward a holistic legal framework for effective Waqf implementation: Integrating Islamic socio-economic models. *Volksgeist: Jurnal Ilmu Hukum Dan Konstitusi*, 15–42. https://doi.org/DOI: 10.24090/volksgeist.v8i1.12590

Hasan, R., Ahmad, A. U. F., & Bt. Siraj, S. A. (2020). Building Trust in Waqf Management - Implications of Good Governance and Transparent Reporting. *The Singapore Economic Review, 67*(01), 459–475. DOI: 10.1142/S0217590820420059

Ikhyanuddin, I. (2022). Waqf Accountability Around the World: A Mini-Review. *International Journal of Islamic Business Ethics, 7*(2), 100. DOI: 10.30659/ijibe.7.2.100-107

Ishak, A. H., Amira Mohamad, S. N., Ab Manan, S. K., Yahaya, M. H., Wan Daud, W. N., & Sharif, D. (2025). The critical success factors of Waqf land development for sustainable agriculture. *Social Sciences & Humanities Open, 11*, 101244. DOI: 10.1016/j.ssaho.2024.101244

Iskandar, I., & Sofuoğlu, H. (2023). Exploring the evolution of Waqf laws and contemporary practices in Muslim countries. *Islam Realitas: Journal of Islamic and Social Studies, 9*(1), 57. DOI: 10.30983/islam_realitas.v9i1.6229

Kamaruddin, M. I. H., Hanefah, M. M., & Masruki, R. (2022). Challenges and prospects in Waqf reporting practices in Malaysia. *Journal of Financial Reporting and Accounting, 22*(3), 752–765. DOI: 10.1108/JFRA-01-2022-0018

Karimah, D. A., Pamuncak, M. B., & Mubin, M. K. (2023). The Role of Waqf in Supporting Sustainable Development Goals: Linking theory and its practices. *SUHUF, 35*(2), 31–38. DOI: 10.23917/suhuf.v35i2.23018

Khan, M. T., Khan, S., & Khan, M. H. (2018). Historical contribution of Islamic Waqf in human capital development through funding education. *Journal of Islamic and Religious Studies, 3*(2), 57–74. DOI: 10.36476/JIRS.3:2.12.2018.12

Manaf, A. W. B. A., Siong, W. H., & Razak, H. B. A. (2025). Modernizing Waqf: Navigating Legal and Digital Frontiers in the 21st Century. *Azka International Journal of Zakat & Social Science, 6*(1), 117–135. DOI: 10.51377/azjaf.vol6no1.201

Maulina, R., Dhewanto, W., & Faturohman, T. (2023). Waqf-Based entrepreneurship direct financing model: Potential and challenges. *International Journal of Emerging Issues in Islamic Studies, 3*(1), 70–91. DOI: 10.31098/ijeiis.v3i1.1398

Mohaiyadin, N. M., Aman, A., Palil, M. R., & Muhamad Said, S. (2022). Addressing Accountability and Transparency Challenges in Waqf Management Using Blockchain Technology. *Journal of Islamic Monetary Economics and Finance, 8*, 53–80. DOI: 10.21098/jimf.v8i0.1413

Muhmad, S. N., Muhamad, R., & Sulong, F. (2021). Sustainable development goals and Islamic finance: An integrated approach for Islamic financial institutions. *Indonesian Journal of Sustainability Accounting and Management, 5*(1). Advance online publication. DOI: 10.28992/ijsam.v5i1.286

Nabiyeva, G. N., Wheeler, S. M., London, J. K., & Brazil, N. (2023). Implementation of sustainable development goal 11 (sustainable cities and communities): Initial good practices data. *Sustainability (Basel), 15*(20), 14810. DOI: 10.3390/su152014810

Nafar, N. (2019). The investment of Waqf properties and infrastructure development. *Springer International Publishing, 1*, 285–308. DOI: 10.1007/978-3-030-18445-2_14

Owais, M., & Manaf, Z. I. A. (2023). Comparative Analysis of Waqf Institutions Governance in India and Singapore. *Journal of Islamic Economics and Business, 6*(2), 257–282. DOI: 10.21154/elbarka.v6i2.5321

Phougat, A., Mishra, A., & Oinam, R. (2025). Waqf Law In India: A Critical Analysis of Estate Management, Powers and Socio-Legal Impact. *International Journal of Legal Studies and Social Sciences, 3*(2), 86–102. https://ijlsss.com/wp-content/uploads/2025/04/09.-Ashima-Phougat-Arkaja-Mishra-Rameshwori-Oinam.pdf

Rahmalan, M. T., & Abu-Hussin, M. F. (2021). A Systematic Review of Contemporary and Innovative Waqf Sources: Cash and Service Waqf. *Jurnal Syariah, 29*(2), 257–284. DOI: 10.22452/js.vol29no2.5

Ramli, N. M., Mohd Salleh, N. H., & Muhamed, N. A. (2015). Discharging Accountability Through Governance: Cases from Waqf Institutions in Indonesia. *Online Journal of Research in Islamic Studies, 2*(1). https://mojem.um.edu.my/index.php/RIS/article/view/9892

Ramli, N. M., & Muhamed, N. A. (2014). Good governance framework for corporate Waqf: Towards accountability enhancement. *SSRN.* https://ssrn.com/abstract=2437260

Rasool, T. (2024). Waqf - The Muslim endowments in India: Ideological and legal intricacies. *Trusts & Trustees, 30*(5), 258–266. DOI: 10.1093/tandt/ttae012

Riani, R., & Fatoni, A. (2022). Waqf on Infrastructure: How Far has been Researched? *International Journal of Waqf*, *2*(2). Advance online publication. DOI: 10.58968/ijf.v2i2.167

Sano, M. A., & Kassim, S. (2021). Waqf governance in the Republic of Guinea: Legal framework, issues, challenges and way forward. *ISRA International Journal of Islamic Finance*, *13*(2), 194–210. DOI: 10.1108/IJIF-03-2020-0064

Sarac, M., & Hassan, M. K. (2023). *Islamic Perspective for a Sustainable Financial System*. Istanbul University Press., DOI: 10.26650/B/SS10.2020.017

Sukmana, R. (2020). Critical assessment of Islamic endowment funds (Waqf) literature: Lesson for government and future directions. *Heliyon*, *6*(10), e05074. DOI: 10.1016/j.heliyon.2020.e05074 PMID: 33088936

. Syibly, M. R., Mustaffa, N. H., Zulkifle, M. R. B., & Ndini, C. W. (2022). A comparative analysis of legal products on the development of productive Waqf in Indonesia and Malaysia. *Millah: Journal of Religious Studies*, 1003–1024. https://doi.org/DOI: 10.20885/millah.vol21.iss3.art14

Wan Ismail, W. M., Misba, N. T., & Mat Isa, N. A. (2025). Reimagining Waqf in the digital age: A framework for smart Waqf governance through emerging technologies. *International Journal of Research and Innovation in Social Science*, *9*(5), 4704–4714. DOI: 10.47772/IJRISS.2025.905000361

KEY TERMS AND DEFINITIONS

Istibdal: A jurisprudential concept that allows for the exchange of Waqf property for another property under strict conditions, particularly if the Waqf property no longer provides a benefit or if a property exchange provides a greater benefit for the Waqf and its beneficiaries.

Mutawalli: Muttawali is the appointed trustee or administrator who has the legal obligation to manage and administer the Waqf in a prudent manner in accordance with Sharia and to preserve the Waqf, generate revenue, and distribute benefits appropriately.

Sadaqah Jariyah: A concept of ongoing charity in Islam, in which a charitable act becomes the basis for the continuation of spiritual rewards after the donor's death, which is similar to the perpetual nature of Waqf.

Waqf Ahli: This is a type of Waqf that is created to benefit the founder's family, descendants, or specified individuals. It is usually a way to plan family estate and transfer wealth, often with a conditional reversion back to general charity once the family beneficiaries have passed away.

Waqf Khairi: It is a type of Waqf established entirely for public or charitable use with the overall benefits going back to the community.

Waqf Sukuk: Waqf sukuk is Sharia compliant, and it is a term used in itself, as an innovative financial instrument, like a bond that represents proportional ownership in a Waqf asset.

Waqf: A perpetual endowment in Islamic legal tradition, by which an asset's usufruct is permanently dedicated for charitable, or religious, or philanthropic purposes, while the asset itself remains inalienable.

Waqfiyya: The individual legal document or deed that creates the Waqf which states the founder's intent, the precise description of the endowed property, the named beneficiaries, and the conditions of its management and administration.

Chapter 5
Islamic Law of Contract

Sanaullah Ansari
SZABIST University, Pakistan

ABSTRACT

Islamic law of finance and Islamic law of contract strongly emphasize the need and importance of a contract for any specific financial or non-financial activity between two or more parties. This importance is strongly highlighted by Almighty Allah and Holy Prophet (SAW). Fulfillment of the contract is a religious obligation, and only contracts that contain all Sharia'h-compliant conditions can be considered as Islamic contracts. There are two major types of contracts: compensatory (financial) and non-compensatory (non-financial). Similarly, under these two types, there are several types of subsidiary contracts, which are related with partnership-based trade agreements, profit sharing trade agreements, and supporting trade agreements or contracts. In addition, there are certain rules, regulations, and options for both sellers and buyers, which they have to follow. Sharia'h has provided detailed instructions on which conditions can be part of the Islamic contract, and vice versa. All types of valid sales are executed with the help of a contract. Therefore, in Islamic finance, all Islamic financial institutions, including Islamic banks, follow Sharia'h-compliant contracts for selling their products and services.

INTRODUCTION

A contract is defined as a promise, commitment, or agreement between two or more persons or parties to perform a specific task. This contract can be written and oral, as well. It can also be defined as an agreement that is enforceable by law, recognized by law, and affects legal rights and duties of the parties. According to Islamic principles, every action or work that takes place between two or more persons or

DOI: 10.4018/979-8-3373-1887-5.ch005

parties is a contract. Its importance has been clearly defined by Almighty Allah in many verses of the Holy Qur'an and by the Holy Prophet (SAW) in various Ahadith.

Contracts in Light of the Holy Qur'an

Almighty Allah has provided comprehensive guidelines in Surah Al-Baqarah on how and when a contract is needed, as well as its overall importance in Islam. The verse says:

O believers! When you contract a loan for a fixed period of time, commit it to writing. Let the scribe maintain justice between the parties. The scribe should not refuse to write as Allah has taught them to write. They will write what the debtor dictates, bearing Allah in mind and not defrauding the debt. If the debtor is incompetent, weak, or unable to dictate, let their guardian dictate for them with justice. Call upon two of your men to witness. If two men cannot be found, then one man and two women of your choice will witness, so if one of the women forgets the other may remind her. The witnesses must not refuse when they are summoned. You must not be against writing contracts for a fixed period, whether the sum is small or great. This is more just for you in the sight of Allah, and more convenient to establish evidence and remove doubts. However, if you conduct an immediate transaction among yourselves, then there is no need for you to record it, but call upon witnesses when a deal is finalized. Let no harm come to the scribe or witnesses. If you do, then you have gravely exceeded your limits. Be mindful of Allah, for Allah is the One Who teaches you. And Allah has perfect knowledge of all things (2:282)

In Surah Bani Israel, Almighty Allah highlights the importance of fulfillment of contracts in these words, "Do not come near the wealth of the orphan unless intending to enhance it, until they attain maturity. Honor your pledges, for you will surely be accountable for them" (17:34).

Similarly, in Surah Al- An'am, Almighty Allah provides guidance for us to fulfill our contract toward Allah and to observe justice in daily activities with each other. The Holy Qur'an says:

And do not come near the wealth of the orphan—unless intending to enhance it—until they attain maturity. Give full measure and weigh with justice. We never require of any soul more than what it can afford. Whenever you speak, maintain justice even regarding a close relative. And fulfil your covenant with Allah. This is what He has commanded you, so perhaps you will be mindful. (6:152)

The Holy Qur'an also emphasizes the fulfillment of our mutual contracts, especially those in which Allah is the witness. Almighty Allah says in Surah Al-Nahl, "Honor Allah's covenant when you make a pledge, and do not break your oaths after confirming them, having made Allah your guarantor. Surely Allah knows all you do" (16:91).

Contracts in Light of Hadith

The importance of contract, or *Wa'ad*, is highlighted by the Holy Prophet (SAW) in several Hadith. According to Abdullah bin Umar (RA), the Holy Prophet (SAW) said:

> *There are four characteristics which, if found in a person, make him a pure hypocrite. And if he has one of them, he has a trait of hypocrisy until he gives it up: When he speaks, he lies; when he makes a promise, he breaks it; when he is entrusted, he betrays the trust; and when he makes a contract, he acts treacherously. (Sahih al-Bukhari, 34; Sahih Muslim, 58)*

According to this Hadith, the person who does not fulfill his promise is declared a hypocrite by the Holy Prophet (SAW). Narrated by Abu Huraira (RA), the Holy Prophet (SAW) said, "Muslims are bound by their conditions, except a condition that makes what is unlawful lawful, or makes what is lawful unlawful" (Sunan al-Tirmidhi, 1352; Abu Dawood, 3594; Ibn Majah, 2353).

The importance of a contract in business and trade is extremely important. Hazrat Abdullah bin Umar (RA) narrated that the Holy Prophet (SAW) said,

> *The buyer and the seller have the option [to cancel the deal] as long as they have not separated. If they spoke the truth and clarified [the goods], their transaction will be blessed. But if they lied or concealed, the blessing of their transaction will be erased. (Sahih al-Bukhari, 2110; Sahih Muslim, 1532)*

Similarly, in another Hadith, Abu Huraira (RA) reported that:

> *The Holy Prophet (SAW) passed by a man selling food and put his hand inside the pile, and found it wet underneath. He said, 'What is this?' The man said, 'It was hit by rain, O Messenger of Allah.' The Prophet said, 'Why didn't you put it on top so people could see it? Whoever deceives us is not one of us. (Sahih Muslim, 102)*

According to Abdullah bin Jabir (RA), the Holy Prophet (SAW) said: "The truthful and trustworthy merchant will be with the prophets, the truthful, and the martyrs on the Day of Resurrection" (Sunan al-Tirmidhi, 1209). In this Hadith, the highest level of a person, especially a trader, who makes a contract and fulfills it, is described by the Holy Prophet (SAW) as one who will be with the Prophets on the day of judgement.

In business and trade, the importance of a contract is crucial because every business transaction requires some sort of contract. In Islam, business and trade are very important because these are declared the *Sunnah* of all Prophets. Therefore,

Islam provides detailed guidelines about the importance of the Islamic contract and its application in business transactions.

Classification of Islamic Contracts

Islamic contracts can be classified into three major categories:

1. Unilateral promises (W*a'da*);
2. Bilateral promises (*Muwa'adah* or *Muahidah*); and
3. Contracts (*Aqd*).

Unilateral Promise (Wa'da)

A unilateral undertaking or promise is an offer by a person to another person in which one person promises to fulfill or execute a contract in future, which can be of buying or selling something in future. The second person is not bound to express their acceptance or rejection against this offer. Similarly, as a future sale is not allowed in Islam, no question of a future sale arises in this contract as this is unilateral promise. In this type of contract, for example, a person promises to sell his car to another person within the next two months for $20,000, which is treated as *Wa'da*. As nothing has been executed on the time of promise, the second person has the right to accept or reject this offer at any time within the next two months.

According to Imam Abu Hanifa, *Wa'da* is not enforceable by law, but there is a moral obligation on the promisor. However, some of the Hanafi jurists argue that some of the promises can be made enforceable under the doctrine of necessity. Similarly, according to Imam Malik, *Wa'da* is enforceable by law. In light of these contradictory opinions, present day scholars have established the consensus through *Ijma* that *Wa'da* is enforceable by law until and unless the promisor is not in a position to fulfill their promise. In this situation, if this act is not due to any of their negligence, they are not bound to share any loss to the promisee. As an example, if a person promises to sell an animal to other person within the next few days, but the animal dies without any negligence of the promisor, then the promisee has no right to claim any damages from the seller. However, if the animal dies due to the negligence of the seller, the buyer has the right to claim the damages from them as they were bound to sell the animal to the promisee.

Bilateral Promise (Muwa'adah or Muahidah)

Bilateral promise (*Muwa'adah or Muahidah*) is a mutual promise between seller and buyer (promisor and promisee) for selling anything on a specific date. In this promise, the acceptance and agreement of parties is mandatory. According to the majority of present-day scholars of Islamic Jurisprudence, *Muwa'adah* is not allowed in those situations where *Aqd* is not allowed, like in forward contracts. Therefore, it is not enforceable by law. This opinion is accepted and adapted by majority of present day Islamic financial institutions in the world. Similarly, it is also accepted by the Accounting and Auditing Organization for Islamic Financial Institutions (AAOI-FI). However, some scholars of the subcontinent, who follow the Hanafi school of thought, are in the view that *Muwa'adah* is enforceable by law. However, they also agree that some *Muwa'adah* transactions, including short-selling of currencies or shares is not allowed and not enforceable by law.

Contract (Aqd)

A contract (*Aqd*) is a bilateral agreement, which is executed between two or more parties. In this contract, both parties are bound to fulfill their promises and complete the transaction according to the agreed terms and conditions. Some examples of this type of contract are contracts of sale, contracts of purchase, contracts of employment, and contracts of marriage. In Islamic jurisprudence, a contract of marriage is the most important contract as it includes all aspects of a bilateral agreement, and it also contains financial and non-financial conditions.

Types of Islamic Contracts

There are two types of basic Islamic contracts, as follows:

1. Compensatory or financial contracts (*Uqood-e-Muwa'adah*); and
2. Non-compensatory or social contracts (*Uqood-e-Ghair Muwa'adah*).

Compensatory or Financial Contracts

Contracts for the commercial exchange of goods or services against an agreed compensation, price, fee, or charges. These include contracts of trades, leases, employments, partnerships, paid agencies, and services against fees.

Figure 1 shows the types of Islamic contracts.

Figure 1. Types of Islamic Contracts

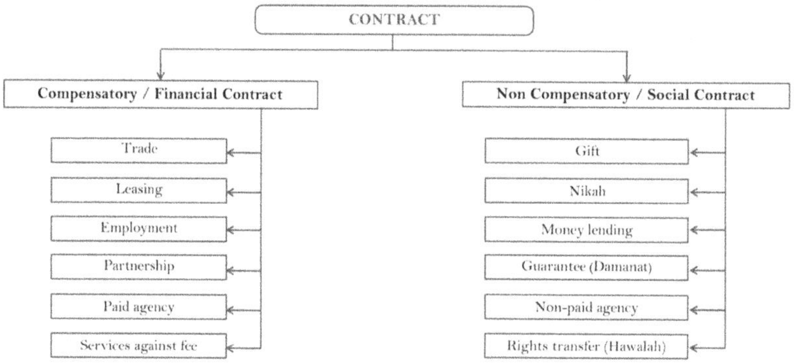

A compensatory contract is allowed in Islam with some rules and conditions.

- Permissibility as general rule: Subject-matter (services or goods) of the contract must be lawfulness, and its legality must be confined. Similarly, exchange of impermissible good or services is not allowed in compensatory contracts.
- Free mutual consent: Free mutual consent of both parties is an essential element of compensatory contracts. This free mutual consent is ensured through the law of offer and acceptance (Jalil & Rahman, 2010).
- Prohibition of interest (*Riba*): The compensatory contract should not contain any element of interest (explicit or implicit). All such contracts that involve interest are void and invalid.
- Prohibition of uncertainty (*Gharar*): The prohibition of uncertainty is very important in compensatory contracts. When this prohibition is defined, the majority of the rules are derived from the basic rule of uncertainty. Prohibition of uncertainty includes:
    - Prohibition of wagering contracts, like short sales, blank sales, etc.;
    - Prohibition of gambling (*Qimar*) and games of chance (*Maysir*);
    - Prohibition of fraud and deception (*Khilabah* and *Ghishsh*); and
    - Prohibition of complexity in structure of contract, like combining two inconsistent contracts (*Bayatan-e fi Ba'i-in*).
- Principles of entitlement to profit with risk and liability for loss: This is an important law of compensatory contracts which describes rights and responsibility of contracting parties. According to this rule, everyone has right of benefit if one bears responsibility. However, the application of this rule is different in the exchange of goods or services and joint risk contracts. Therefore,

every compensatory contract has a set of conditions, which are derived from this basic rule.

- Legality of motives behind a contract: Islamic contracts should not contradict *Sharia'h* objectives; this does not allow for twisting the transactions to develop a prohibited business structure. In light of *Sharia'h* objectives, the following types of transactions are not allowed in Islamic contracts.
    - Hiyal (Subterfuges) not Allowed
    - Bay al-Innah (Buy Back Agreement) is prohibited on pre agreed price
    - Bay bil-Wafa (Sale with promise of repurchase – redeemable sale)
    - Sale of Debt (Bai al Dain) is not permissible
- Islamic contracts should conform the rules set by *Sharia'h* for execution: All compensatory or non-compensatory contracts in Islam have a set of rules that need be complied with *Sharia'h* (Diatmoko et al., 2025). These rules explain the conditions related to parties, subject-matter, compensation, and other related issues of a particular contract.

Non-Compensatory or Social Contracts (Uqood-e-Ghair Muwa'adah)

Contracts of giving or taking goods or services without any compensation, price, fee, or charges include gifts, money lending, marriages (*Nikah*), guarantees, non-paid agencies, and rights transfers.

Basic Elements of Islamic Contracts

Islamic contracts have the following basic elements:

- Parties or persons of the contract;
- Wordings of the contract;
- Subject-matter of the contract (the thing or task intended by the contract);
- Compensation (remuneration or price for exchange); and
- Basic framework of the contract (rights and responsibilities).

These elements are illustrated in Figure 2.

Figure 2. Basic Elements of Islamic Contract

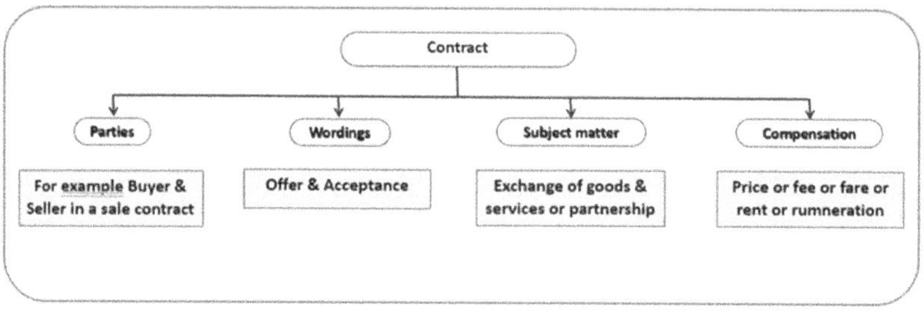

Parties or Persons of the Contract

According to Islam, all parties or persons involved in a contract must be adult and sane. Therefore, a person who is insane or a child and cannot understand the nature of a contract, cannot be the party of an Islamic contract. In addition, anyone who is a slave, cannot be the party of an Islamic contract.

Contract Wordings

The wordings, conditions, and rules must be clearly defined in an Islamic contract to avoid any misunderstanding in future. These wordings must contain an offer from one party and acceptance from the other party (*Ijab-o-Qabool*). This offer and acceptance can be oral/verbal (*Qauli*) or written. Both parties must create a sense of immediate effect, and words that give a sense of the future are not allowed; "I will buy it" does not give any sense of immediate effect. Similarly, conditional wording does not create an immediate effect; "I will accept if my father allows it" is a conditional wording that cannot be the part of an Islamic contract.

Subject-Matter

The goods or services, which are traded in an Islamic contract, must be clearly defined. The subject-matter should exist, as well as should be valuable, usable under *Sharia'h*, and capable of ownership and title and delivery and possession. Similarly, the subject-matter must be legally and Islamically allowed, and prohibited subject-matter cannot be part of an Islamic contract. The subject-matter must be legally owned by one of the parties of the Islamic contract, and it must be in existence. Most importantly, the subject-matter must be deliverable and able to be transacted and exchanged. Finally, the subject-matter must be specified in clear manner and quantified, if quantifiable. Therefore, the sale of fish that swim in the water or birds that fly in the air are not permissible in an Islamic contract because this type of sale is not specified, thus not being quantifiable.

Compensation

The remuneration or price for an exchange of goods or exchange of services should be quantified and specified. It must be decided at the time of the contract and should be accepted and binding by both parties.

Basic Framework of Islamic Contracts

In an Islamic contract, rights and responsibilities of all persons or parties must be identified and explained. Both parties should bear the responsibility and have the rights which are required by the nature of the transaction. In the case of a sale, ownership transfers after offer and acceptance, as well as the risk of ownership (Abdul Razak & Saupi, 2017). However, in the case of a rental arrangement, ownership remains with the lessor.

Conditions of Islamic Contracts

The terms and conditions of Islamic contracts must be *Sharia'h* compliant and comply with the following guidelines.

- A condition which is as per the requirements of the contract, and not against the contract, is a valid condition.
- A condition that appears to be against the contract but is in the market practice is a type of condition that is permissible, unless its voidness is proven with the clear injunctions of the Holy Qur'an and Sunnah. For example, person A buys an air conditioner with the condition that the seller will provide them with a five-year guarantee and one year of free service. As this offer does not contradict *Sharia'h,* this type of condition does not invalidate the contract.
- A condition that is against the contract and not in the practice of market but is in the favor of one of the contractors is a void condition. For example, person A says that they will sell a car with a condition that they will use it on a fixed date every month. As this condition is against *Sharia'h* rules, the whole contract will be void due to it.
- A condition which is against the contract, not in the market practice, and not in favor of any contractor is not a void condition. It is a valid condition and

fulfills the requirements of an Islamic contract, e.g., agreeing to give charity in the case of willful default by the defaulting party.

The identification of a void condition is very important in an Islamic contract because it invalidates a contract. Sometimes, a void condition does not invalidate the contract, even this condition itself becomes invalid. According to majority of Islamic jurists and scholars, a void condition invalidates a contract in full when it is a compensatory or financial contract. However, this contract becomes valid if this void condition is replaced with a valid condition or if the void condition is removed completely from the contract. Similarly, according to these Islamic jurists and scholars, a void condition does not invalidate a non-compensatory or social contract (*Uqood-e-Ghair Muwa'adah*) completely because it is not related to financial matters. However, this void condition still remains void and shall not be acted upon until replaced or removed, and the remaining contract shall remain valid. For example, if person A gives a loan to person B with a condition of a premium at the time of repayment, this condition of interest is void. However, this condition does not invalidate the contract, and all transactions done by this borrowed money shall be valid. However, the condition of interest itself is revoked. Therefore, person B is not liable for the payment of interest to person A.

Issues in Contracts (*Aqd*)

There are two major issues in Islamic contracts (*Aqd*), as follows:

1. Two contracts in one contract (*Safqatain fi Safqatin*); and
2. Agency, or *Wakalah*, contract (*Tawkeel fil Aqd*).

Two Contracts in One Contract (Safqatain fi Safqatin)

Two contracts in one contract means the accumulation or mixing of two different contracts in such a manner that execution of one becomes compulsory for the execution of another. This condition is not allowed by the Holy Prophet (SAW) in Hadith, and this type of contract becomes void. Due to this problem, sometimes, a hire purchase contract becomes void. However, if the hire purchase contract is made under the following terms and conditions, it can be valid.

According to Muhit et al. (2024), a hire purchase contract can be a valid contract if it is structured correctly, especially following the principles of leasing (*Ijarah*) and *Bai'* (sale) contracts. Therefore, the most important condition is to avoid non-Islamic elements, including interest and excessive uncertainty. Following are the rules, conditions, and situations in which a hire purchase contract can become Islamic and valid.

- Leasing: Leasing contracts are considered to be a Halal hire purchase contract. In this contract, the financier, e.g., an Islamic bank, purchases the asset, a car, and leases it to the customer for a fixed period of time at a predetermined rental amount. These rental payments are considered permissible in Islamic law as they represent the compensation for the *usufruct* (right to use) of the asset by the customer.
- Sale: After the end of leasing contract, a sale contract can be made between the financier (e.g., an Islamic bank) and the customer for transfer of ownership of the asset to the customer. The transfer process can be completed through a separate, standalone agreement, or as a promise within the leasing contract. The sale price of the asset can be agreed between the financier (e.g., an Islamic bank) and the customer at the beginning or end of a leasing contract. It can also be decided at any time during this contract.
- Avoiding interest: In hire purchase contracts, interest must be avoided. The financier (e.g., an Islamic bank) can earn profit through *Sharia'h*-compliant rental payments and also from the sale price of the asset at the end of the contract. Similarly, late payment penalties should also be structured as a donation to charity, rather than interest.
- Transparency: The hire purchase contract must be clear and transparent by indicating all terms and conditions. It must include the payment schedules, as well as any difference between the principal amount payment and rental amounts. The process of ownership transfer of the asset at the end of the contract must also be mentioned.
- Real lease: The hire purchase contract must be a real lease contract, according to the rules and regulations of Islamic law. It should not be a replica of a conventional lease.
- Avoiding uncertainty: The uncertainty should be minimized in hire purchase contract. For example, if the sale price of the asset is determined at the end of the hire purchase contract, it should be based on fair market value by avoiding uncertainty.
- Islamic hire purchase under *Shirkat-ul-Milk* (HPSM): This is a *Sharia'h*-compliant and specific type of hire purchase contract, where the bank and the customer share ownership of the asset during the contract period. The customer makes installment payments, and the bank's share is gradually reduced until the customer gains full ownership of the asset.

Tawkeel fil Aqd (Agency, or Wakalah, Contract)

In an agency, or *Wakalah*, contract, an agent (*Wakil*) is appointed on behalf of the contractor to complete the contract on behalf of the principal. Agency, or *Wakalah*, contracts are of two types.

In the first type, all the rights and obligations are passed on to the principal *(Muwakkil)* from the contractor. For example, if person A makes person B their agent to marry them with person C, then person B is not responsible for any rights, responsibilities, and benefits, as this *Nikkah* is between person A and person C. Therefore, person C can only claim their dowry *(Mehr)* and other expenses from person A directly and not from person B.

In the second type of agency, or *Wakalah*, contract, rights and obligations remains with the agent. For example, if person A appoints person B as his agent, and person B buys a car from person C for USD 50,000 on credit and does not disclose to person C that he is acting as an agent for person A, then person C can claim his money from person B only. However, if person B discloses this, then person C can claim his money from person A, as well.

Similarly, in an investment agency (*Wakalah Istithmar*) contract, one party appoints another party as its agent to carry out a trade transaction on behalf of the principal. The difference between the investment agency contract and the *Mudarabah* contract is that, in the *Mudarabah* contract, both parties share in the profit arising out of the trade transaction, whereas, in investment agency contract, the wakil is only given a fee for their services by the principal and does not share in the profit. In the classical books of *Fiqh*, it is called *Ijaratul Ashkaas*. The remuneration of the agent can be fixed, a lump sum, or on a commission basis (Nasrullah & Muthoifin, 2024).

Types of Valid Compensatory or Financial Contracts

In Islamic jurisprudence, valid compensatory or financial contracts can be divided in three categories:

1. Trading contracts;
2. Contracts of profit sharing; and
3. Supporting contracts.

Trading Contracts

Trading contracts normally deals with buying or manufacturing and selling of goods. These contracts can also be used for the buying and selling of services. Contracts related with cash sales are as follows.

- Normal cash sales: These are commonly used contracts in day to day transactions.
- *Sarf*: This contract is about the sale of foreign currency for utilization purpose only.

Similarly, the following contracts are related with sales on deferred payments.

- *Bai Murabahah*: This is a deferred payment sales which includes cost plus profit.
- *Bai Tawliyah*: In this type of contract, goods are sold at deferred payment, equal to the cost, i.e., at break-even.
- *Bai Wadhiah*: In this type of deferred payment sale contract, goods are sold less than the actual cost price due to any specific reason.
- *Bai Salam*: This is a type of sale in which goods are sold before coming into existence. Full payment is made in advance, while some remaining payment is deferred till the time of delivery of goods (Al-Zaabi, 2010).
- *Bai Istisna'a*: This contract is an order to manufacture any specific goods. Some payment is made as an advance, and the remaining amount is paid at the time of delivery of the goods.
- *Bai Bithaman Ajil*: This is also called *Bai Muajjal*. It refers to a sale in which delivery of goods is on the spot, while payment of the price is deferred to a future date. Cost is unknown to the buyer in *Bai Muajjal*.
- *Bai Istijrar*: This is a *Sharia'h*-compliant contract that involves a recurring sale agreement between buyer and seller. In this contract, a buyer purchases goods from a seller over a period of time, with payment often deferred until the end of the term or after all transactions.
- *Bai Inah*: This type of contract involves a sale on deferred payment and then buyback by the seller to provide cash to the buyer for their needs. This is a controversial contract among Islamic scholars.
- *Ijarah*: This is a leasing contract in which the lessor (owner) transfers the usufruct (right to use) of an asset to a lessee (renter) for an agreed period and rental payment. However, the ownership of the asset remains with the lessor.

Contracts of Profit Sharing

In valid compensatory or financial contracts, the following contracts are related with profit sharing.

- *Musharakah*: This contract is about the partnership between two or more persons, in which all partners invest in the business. As per *Sharia'h* rules, profit is distributed among partners as per an agreed rate, whereas loss is distributed according to the proportion of the investment by each partner.

- *Mudarabah*: This is a type of contract in which one person invests in the business, called *Rab-ul-Maal*. The other partner provides their services to run the business, called *Mudarib*. According to Sharia'h rules, profit in *Mudarabah* is distributed between partners as per an agreed rate. However, the investor (i.e., *Rab-ul-Maal*) is responsible for bearing the loss in total.
- *Muzaraah* (leasing of land for agriculture): *Muzaraah* is an Islamic contractual arrangement in which a landowner allows a farmer to cultivate land in exchange for a predetermined share of the harvest.
- *Musaqat* (watering of orchard): In this contract, the owner of fruit-bearing trees engages a person for care and maintenance of his trees. At the end, the crop is shared between both of them according to a pre-agreed ratio.

Supporting Contracts

Other than trading and profit sharing contracts, there are several supporting contracts in Islamic law to facilitate trading and mobilization of capital. Some of these are as follows.

- *Rahnu* (mortgage): This is a contract in which a valuable asset is pledged as a security against a loan, based on Islamic principles.
- *Kafalah* (guarantee): This is s contract of guarantee. In this contract, one party provides guarantee of second party to third party for any financial dealing.
- *Wakalah* (agency): In this contract, one party appoints another party as their agent to perform any specific business task.
- *Wadiah* (safe custody): This contract refers to the security of assets, provided by any party or financial institution.
- *Qardh Hasan* (benevolent loan): This is a contract of an interest-free loan.
- *Hiwalah* (transfer of debt): This contract is used to transfer the debt from one party to another party, in light of *Sharia'h* principles.
- *Tabarru'u* (donation): This contract deals with donations, gifts, or contributions toward any good cause.
- *Hibah* (gift): This contract is related with a voluntary gift or donation by one person to another during their lifetime.
- *Wakf* (endowment): This contract is to specify an asset, normally a building, for religious or spiritual activities without any interest.
- *Ibraa'* (rebate): This contract deals with the provision of a rebate (for financial benefit).

- *Muqasah* (set-off): In this contract, two parties offset their debts with each other.

Forbidden, Prohibited, and Void Contracts

All contracts which contain elements of *Gharar, Riba* and gambling are treated as forbidden, prohibited, and void contracts.

- *Bai al-Mulamasah*: It is a sale contract in which goods are sold without proper examination. As there is excessive uncertainty in this sale, it is prohibited.
- *Bai al- Munabazah*: It is a type of sale in which fresh fruits are exchanged with for dry fruits. Specially, the quantity of dry fruits is actually known, but the quantity of fresh fruits is only estimated. This is because fresh fruits are un-plucked and still on trees.
- *Bai al-Hisat*: This is sale contract in which the buyer throws a stone or pebble on different goods and then purchases those goods which are touched by their stone or pebble. This is the practical example of gambling and, therefore, prohibited in Islamic finance.
- *Bai Habl-il-Hablah*: This contract deals with the sale of unborn offspring of an animal. Due to the excessive uncertainty, this sale contract is forbidden in Islam.
- *Bai al-Malaqih*: In this sale contract, an in-process animal is sold that is in the womb of the female animal. It is also prohibited due to excessive uncertainty.
- *Bai al-Gharar*: All sale contracts which involve excessive uncertainty are prohibited in Islamic law.
- Lending and borrowing with interest: As interest is *Haram* in Islam through the Qur'an and Hadith, all lending and borrowing on interest is forbidden. Therefore, all contracts that include interest are prohibited by Islamic law.
- Betting: As betting is very close to gambling, it is prohibited in Islam.

Khiyars (Options)

Islamic law of finance and Islamic contracts give certain *Khiyars* (Options) to the buyers, which they can exercise before buying, during buying, and after buying any goods or services. These rights can be the part of any compensatory contract between a seller and a buyer (Hafid, et al., 2024; Khan, 2011).

Khiyar-e-Shart (Optional Condition)

In *Khiyar-e-Shart*, the buyer has the right to change or amend any specific condition of the contract that is not suitable for that transaction or is giving favor to one of the parties of the contract. Similarly, the buyer has the right to include any specific condition, mutually agreed upon by both parties.

Khiyar-e-Roiyyat (Option of Inspecting Goods)

This *Khiyar* (i.e., option) gives the right to the buyer that they can inspect subject-matter (goods) any time before buying, during buying, or after buying. If the buyer feels conditions are unsatisfactory, they have the right to reject the deal (Fikra, 2025).

Khiyar-e-Aib (Option of Defect)

Similarly, if the buyer finds any defect in sold goods at any time during the sale and purchase process, the buyer has the option to cancel the deal under *Khiyar-e-Aib* (option of defect). In this case, the seller is bound to repair the goods to remove the defect or replace the same goods with goods that are not defective.

Khiyar-e-Wasf (Option of Quality)

If at any time during the sale of goods process, the buyer feels that the quality of goods or services is not as per the agreed terms and conditions, they can exercise the right of *Khiyar-e-Wasf* (i.e., option of quality), under which they can terminate the sale contract.

Khiyar-e-Ghaban (Option of Price)

If the customer finds that, at any time of the sale contract, that the seller has charged a higher price as compared to the price of a similar product in the market, they have the option to claim the difference in amount given from the buyer, and the seller is bound to refund the additional amount.

Most Commonly Used Contracts in Islamic Banks

Several types of contracts are used in the modern day Islamic banking system, including:

- Partnership-based contracts: *Musharakah* and *Mudarabah*;

- Debt- or trade-based contracts: *Murabahah*, *Musawamah*, *Salam*, and *Istisna*; and
- Consumer financing contracts: leasing and *Diminishing Musharakah*.

According to Ghafar b. Ismail and Tohirin (2010), Islamic banks mostly rely on *Musharakah* and *Mudarabah*, which are partnership-based contracts. *Musharakah* is a partnership-based contract between an Islamic bank and the customer, to perform a business activity on profit-sharing basis. *Mudarabah* is a partnership-based contract between an Islamic bank and the customer, in which the Islamic bank becomes the service provider, while the customer becomes the investor.

Islamic banks use both type of contracts in the following products and services.

Asset-Side Financing

Asset-side financing relates to the following:

- short/medium/long-term financing;
- project financing;
- small and medium enterprises setup financing;
- large enterprise financing;
- import financing;
- import bills drawn under import letters of credit (LC);
- inland bills drawn under inland LC;
- bridge financing;
- LC with margin (for *Musharakah*);
- export financing (pre-shipment financing);
- working capital financing; and
- running accounts financing/short-term advances.

Liability-Side Financing

Liability-side financing relates to the following:

- for current/ saving/investment accounts (deposit giving profit based on *Musharakah*/*Mudarabah*—with predetermined ratio);
- inter-bank lending/borrowing;
- term finance certificates and certificate of investment;
- T-bills and federal investment bonds/debenture;
- securitization for large projects (based on *Musharakah*);
- certificate of investment based on *Murabahah*; and

- Islamic bank *Musharakah* bonds (based on projects requiring large amounts—profit based on return from the project).

Murabahah is a trade- or debt-based contract in which Islamic banks sale goods to customers on the basis of cost plus profit. The main condition of this contract is that the goods must be in physical form and be in constructive possession by Islamic bank. This contract is mostly used in consumer financing products.

Musawamah is a trade- or debt-based contract, wherein an Islamic bank sells goods to customers without disclosing the cost and profit amounts. It is also used in consumer financing products.

Salam contracts deal with the sale of a product before came into existence. Full payment is made in advance, and delivery of goods is deferred. Islamic banks use this contract in agriculture or commodity financing (Macsudov et al., 2024).

Istisna is one of the Islamic banking products where a buyer orders to manufacture, assemble, or construct something at an agreed upon price, to be delivered at a future date. The commodity must be known and specified, including its kind, type, quality, and quantity. The price must also be fixed in absolute and unambiguous terms and can be paid in lump sum or installments, as mutually agreed. It is used to finance manufacturing goods, constructing buildings, exporting, and paying overhead expenses, like salaries and utility bills.

Ijarah contracts deal with the sale of a commodity on cost plus rent basis. Islamic banks use this contract to finance automobiles, buildings, machinery, and equipment.

Diminishing *Musharakah* is joint contract of partnership and consumer financing. In this contract, an Islamic bank and customer enter into a partnership and buy any product. The Islamic bank is willing sell its partnership share to the customer in installments. This contract is used to finance assets, such as cars, houses, and shops.

Table 1 provides a comparison between Islamic contracts and close conventional contracts.

Table 1. Islamic Contracts vs. Close Conventional Contracts

Islamic Contracts	**Conventional Contracts**
Murabahah	No alternative
Salam	Future contracts
Istisna	Interest-based finance
Ijarah	Leasing
Musharakah	Shareholding and venture capital
Mudarabah	Venture capital

CONCLUSION

Islamic law of contracts provides comprehensive guidelines how to enter in a contract for any trade or business activity (Shebaita, 2025). It also provides a guide for the execution of social contracts, including marriage contracts. All types of financial and nonfinancial activities are possible through Islamic contracts, and, for a Muslim, it is imperative to strictly avoid conventional, interest-based contracts to grab the blessings of Almighty Allah.

Funding Statement

This research received no specific grant from any funding agency in the public, commercial, or not-for-profit sectors. Funding for this research was covered by the author of the article.

Competing Interests

The author of this publication declares that there are no competing interests.

REFERENCES

Abdul Razak, L., & Saupi, M. N. (2017). The concept and application of amān al-milkiyyah (ownership risk): Islamic law of contract perspective. *ISRA International Journal of Islamic Finance, 9*(2), 148–163. DOI: 10.1108/IJIF-06-2017-0002

Al-Zaabi, O. S. (2010). Salam contract in Islamic law: A survey. *Review of Islamic Economics, 14*(2), 91–122. https://www.iefpedia.com/english/wp-content/uploads/2011/11/rie-2010-14-2-al-zaabi-salam-contract-in-islamic-law.pdf

Diatmoko, T., Absori, A., Wardiono, K., Nashirudin, M., & Budiono, A. (2025). Islamic legal policy on ultra-micro enterprise financing and its implementation from the perspective of Maqā id al-Sharī'a. *Al-Ahkam, 35*(1), 87–116. DOI: 10.21580/ahkam.2025.35.1.25207

Fikra, A. (2025). An Islamic law perspective on online buying and selling without direct inspection of goods (Bay' al-ghaib) in e-commerce practices. *SYARIAT: Akhwal Syaksiyah, Jinayah. Siyasah and Muamala, 1*(4), 206–214. DOI: 10.35335/ha7pps79

. Ghafar, B. Ismail, A., & Tohirin, A. (2010). Islamic law and finance. *Humanomics, 26*(3), 178–199. DOI: 10.1108/08288661011074954

Hafid, A., Bahri, S., Marzuki, S. N., Muis, M., & Idayanti, R. (2024). The application of khiyar principles to e-commerce transaction: The Islamic economy perspective. *Samarah: Jurnal Hukum Keluarga Dan Hukum Islam, 8*(1), 403–420. DOI: 10.22373/sjhk.v8i1.20890

Jalil, A., & Rahman, M. K. (2010). Islamic law of contract is getting momentum. *International Journal of Business and Social Science, 1*(2), 175–192. https://ijbssnet.com/journals/Vol._1_No._2_November_2010/14.pdf

Khan, M. A. (2011). Consumer protection and the Islamic law of contract. *Islamabad Law Review, 2*(2), 20–37.

Macsudov, V. G., Amsalu, A., Souza-Junior, J., & Tattaqillah, N. (2024). Implementation of salam contracts in the Sharia principles framework: Surveys and prospects in the field. *Demak Universal Journal of Islam and Sharia, 2*(02), 111–132. DOI: 10.61455/deujis.v2i02.106

Muhit, M., & Al-Hakim, UIN, S., & Setiawan, I. (2024). Flexibility of al-ijarah contract perspective of Islamic economic law. *al-Afkar. Journal of Islamic Studies, 7*(1), 762–787. DOI: 10.31943/afkarjournal.v7i1.888

Nasrullah, N., & Muthoifin, N. (2024). Implementation of fiqh rules in economic transactions in Islamic financial institutions: A literature review study. *Demak Universal Journal of Islam and Sharia*, *2*(3), 347–360. DOI: 10.61455/deujis.v2i03.194

Shebaita, M. (2025). The general principles of law recognised by civilised nations in Islamic law. *The Liverpool Law Review*, *46*(2), 219–243. Advance online publication. DOI: 10.1007/s10991-025-09384-2

Chapter 6
Cryptocurrency:
A Halachic Perspective

Joseph Isaac Lifshitz
Shalem College, Israel

ABSTRACT

Cryptographic currencies are digital means of transferring value through a network of computers that operates independently of any central authority, such as a government or a bank. These currencies enable various uses, including payment and investment. They are generated through technological processes, and their value is determined by the consensus of participants, rather than by the value of a commodity or the decree of a central body. This raises the question: What is the halachic (Jewish legal) stance on such forms of money? In this chapter, the author claims that the foundation of Jewish monetary law is mutual consent. The transfer of property must be conducted with the agreement of both parties; unauthorized transfer is considered a theft. To ensure this consent, halacha traditionally prefers tangible reality and concrete forms. For instance, halacha does not recognize a transfer of ownership to a fetus. These principles raise fundamental questions about the compatibility of halacha with the modern economy. Yet halachic authorities adjusted halachic demands to tangibility if mutual consent is achieved, mainly if a market for these abstract transactions is in existence. Since cryptographic currencies have a vital market, halacha must accept them.

INTRODUCTION

Decentralized or cryptographic currencies are digital means of transferring value through a network of computers that operates independently of any central authority, such as a government or a bank. These currencies enable various uses, including

DOI: 10.4018/979-8-3373-1887-5.ch006

payment and investment. They are generated through technological processes, and their value is determined by the consensus of participants, rather than by the value of a commodity or the decree of a central body. This raises the question: What is the halachic (Jewish legal) stance on such forms of money?

The foundation of Jewish monetary law is mutual consent. The transfer of property must be conducted with the agreement of both parties; unauthorized transfer is considered theft. However, halacha prefers tangible reality and concrete forms. Although consent is an internal state, a contract must be formed through a formal act of acquisition (ma'aseh kinyan)—a concrete contractual gesture indicating that both parties have reached a mutual understanding, known in Talmudic terminology as "semichut da'at" (meeting of the minds). Not only must the agreement manifest itself in the physical world, but the property itself must be tangible and real. One may not legally transfer ownership of an item that does not yet exist (even though one can commit to delivering it in the future). Likewise, the contracting parties must be actual, existing people. For instance, halacha does not recognize a transfer of ownership to a fetus.

These principles raise fundamental questions about the compatibility of halacha with the modern economy. Would halacha oppose digitally formed agreements? Can a keystroke be considered a valid contractual act? Would halacha refuse to recognize trade in future goods? What is the status of corporations, which today are legal fictions? Would Jewish law deny the right of banks or corporate entities to operate? And what of abstract capital, especially in light of the fact that central banks have long since severed ties with gold reserves? How does halacha address these developments indispensable to managing a modern economy?

This paper argues that the core concern of halacha is not the concreteness of the asset or the act, but the certainty of mutual consent—*semichut da'at*. Halacha indeed requires assurance that agreements are made with full understanding and consent. This emphasis stems from a moral concern: a person must not unjustly appropriate another's property, even through legal mechanisms. While almost all contracts in halacha require a concrete act, there are notable exceptions in which mutual understanding can be sufficiently guaranteed through human experience or emotional context without a formal act. Those exceptions are based on what Shalom Albeck defines as An Objective *semichut da'at*. (Albeck, 1976, pp. 507–510)

For example, Maimonides (Rambam) rules, based on the Talmud, that when two families meet to arrange a marriage and discuss financial support for the couple, their verbal agreement is binding—even absent a formal act—because the emotional weight of the moment ensures genuine consent:

With regard to marriages, we have already explained that a special indulgence is granted when a couple is engaged, and the father of the son and father of the bride make commitments, saying: "How much will you give to your son?",

"So and so much. And how much will you give for your daughter?", "So and so much." If, afterwards, the groom consecrates the bride, the couple acquire what the parents promised by virtue of their statements alone.

Nevertheless, the transfer of property brought about by this consecration does not take effect until the time of the couple's marriage. For the intent of the promise was that the property be given to the couple when married. (Maimonides, Mishne Torah, Ownerless Property and Gifts, 6:17)

Similarly, the division of inheritance among heirs can be finalized without a formal act of acquisition if it is accompanied by a lottery or drawing, which is seen as a mutually accepted and emotionally charged process, thereby confirming mutual intent:

It is taught *in a baraita that* **Rabbi Yosei says:** *When* **brothers divide** *their father's estate between them by lottery, i.e., after dividing the property into equal shares they draw lots to determine which brother is to receive which portion,* **once the lot for one of them is drawn, they all acquire** *the remainder of the property, and they can no longer retract their decision to divide the estate in this manner. (Albeck, 1976, pp. 507–510)*

Maimonides sums it as follows:

When brothers divide an estate by lottery, once one of them receives his lot, they all acquire the remainder of the property. The rationale is that with the satisfaction that they receive from the fact that they carried out the agreement that they arranged between themselves, each one concluded the matter and transferred the appropriate share to his fellow. (Maimonides, Mishne Torah, Ownerless Property and Gifts, 6:17)

A contract must be based on meetings of the minds, on *semichut da'at*. Therefore, it should be based upon a tangible act, but when the meetings of the minds are guaranteed, tangibility is less important. This emphasis on *semichut da'at* also allows for flexibility regarding the form of the contractual act. The Talmud prescribes specific forms of acquisition for different types of property but also recognizes that commercial custom (minhag hashuq) can determine the validity of a contractual act. The talmudic example of "situmta"—a commercial gesture recognized in local markets, such as marking a barrel of wine—is accepted as a valid act of acquisition because it is understood to reflect mutual agreement, as Maimonides explains:

The following rules apply when a verbal agreement alone was concluded with regard to the sale, a price was established, and the purchaser made a mark on the article so that he will have a sign that it is his. Even though the purchaser did not pay any money at all, if either of the parties retracts after the purchaser made the mark, he is liable to receive the adjuration mi shepara. Moreover, if it is the accepted local business custom that making a mark constitutes a binding act of contract, by making that mark, the purchaser completes the transaction.

Neither can retract, and the purchaser is liable to pay the price agreed to. (Albeck, 1976, pp. 507–510)

Thus, any widely recognized commercial practice that clearly indicates consent may serve as a valid act of acquisition under halacha.

On Acquiring That Which Has Not Yet Come Into Existence

Not only must the act of acquisition be concrete, but so too must the asset being transferred. Halacha refers to this requirement as "davar she'ba la'olam"—something that has come into existence. One cannot legally transfer an object that does not yet exist, such as future agricultural yield or unborn animals:

A person cannot transfer ownership over an article that has not yet come into existence. This applies with regard to a sale, with regard to a present or with regard to the disposition of an oral will. What is implied? If a person states: "What my field will produce is sold to you," "What this tree will grow is given to you," "Give so and so the offspring that this animal bears," the recipient does not acquire anything. Similar principles apply in all analogous situations. (Albeck, 1976, pp. 507–510)

When, however, a person sells produce at the market price, although the seller was not in possession of the type of produce, the seller is obligated to purchase the amount of produce he pledged, and give it to the purchaser. If he retracts, he must receive the adjuration mi shepara. (Albeck, 1976, pp. 507–510)

Nevertheless, this rule is not absolute. If the buyer physically takes possession of the asset once it comes into existence, the transaction may be upheld post facto. This suggests that the problem is not with the asset per se, but with the concern that parties may not have full intent or mutual understanding when dealing with non-existent goods. (Albeck, 1976, pp. 507–510) Yet, this is only a concern. We should assume that the parties do have some mutual understanding. (Albeck, 1976, pp. 507–510) For this reason, it is accepted in Halacha that when there is a market for future goods, a contract on futures is valid.

Yet halacha does provide mechanisms for facilitating contracts involving future assets under certain conditions. If the asset in question is traded in a recognized market and the seller commits contractually, the agreement can be binding. This is acknowledged by later authorities, such as the Rema, who permit such transactions through personal obligation rather than formal transfer of ownership:

If one asks his friend to buy from him the value of his wine on the season that the wine will be ready to be sold, it is considered as "That Which Has Not Yet Come Into Existence". Some say that all that is true if he asks him to buy without any clarification. But if he clarifies himself specifically that he wants him to buy the wine when it exists, the acquisition is valid, even if now it does not exist yet.

But some disagree. And even though a person can not sell That Which Has Not Yet Come Into Existence, he can oblige himself. (Albeck, 1976, pp. 507–510)

Throughout time, halachic authorities became more and more agreeable regarding abstract transactions, like future goods, or non-tangible acts of acquisitions, and that when it became customary to do so, or when there was an active market for those future goods. There were two reasons for the flexibility of Halachic authorities. The first one was that they invoked the principle of "dina de'malchuta dina"—the binding nature of secular law—to justify these contractual arrangements when they reflect widely accepted commercial practices. The second was even stronger—accepting reality. Fighting against the spirit of the times would cause damage to many, and halacha has an old tradition of consideration towards the good of the market.

Rabbi Yosef Shalom Elyashiv, for example, was asked whether digital transactions involving future assets, executed without cash or written contracts and using only usernames, could be considered halachically valid. He responded affirmatively, noting that since such methods are customary in the broader marketplace, they meet the criteria of "situmta"—customary commercial practice—and are thus valid under halacha. (Albeck, 1976, pp. 507–510)

In essence, halacha's limitations regarding abstract assets and entities stem from a concern for ensuring the parties' full and genuine consent. Where this concern can be alleviated—by custom, by emotional context, or by the structure of the transaction—halacha displays significant flexibility. Understanding that tendency of Halachic authorities may help us analyze the halachic opinion towards cryptocurrency.

CRYPTOCURRENCY

Money has numerous halachic implications. This discussion focuses not on its ritual aspects but on its use in commerce. Historically, money derived its value from the precious metal it contained. Its intrinsic value was not based on any bank's or government's promise. Even then, however, money had to be "negotiable"—it had to circulate and be accepted in trade. Its virtue of circularity is what created the standard.

Historically, the monetary system was based on silver until the 1870s. Silver was traditionally considered a more common means of transfer. Since gold was rarer, it was not as commonly used. Hence the silver standard. After the 1870s, Gold became the standard of the monetary system, which was based on a fixed quantity of gold. The gold standard was largely abandoned during the Great Depression. It is interesting to note that we can find traces of that process in the halachic literature. Already in the Mishna[1] and the Talmud,[2] there is a mention of a Silver Standard, and in the 20th century there is a suggestion in halachic literature to accept the Gold

Standard in ritual obligations, because of the modern changes of the monetary system. (*Talmud Bavli, Baba Batra*, 106b)

Circularity was a sign of trust in the currency, either in the sovereign issuing it or in the material itself. As Rav Hai Gaon (Bagdad 939-1038) explained, a coin is considered money when either the king mandates its use or the people of the land agree to use it. (*Talmud Bavli, Baba Batra*, 106b)

Later authorities, such as Rabbi Moshe Sofer (the Chatam Sofer, Frankfurt and Pressburg, 1762-1839), linked the halachic status of money to the authority of the state, invoking the principle of "dina de'malchuta dina."[3] In the modern era, Rabbi Avraham Yeshayahu Karelitz (the Chazon Ish) emphasized that the value of money stems from public consensus. In his view, even paper currency and coins of various metals are essentially forms of credit. Still, when accepted as currency by the public, they acquire real halachic status. He stressed that the currency's effectiveness depends not only on the issuing authority but on the public's confidence in that authority. (Maimonides, *Mishne Torah, Neighbors*, 2:11)

Two elements thus determine the halachic status of currency: state backing and public trust. The state's authority endows currency with legal legitimacy, but this depends on the public's acceptance.

This leads to the central question: what is the halachic status of a currency that lacks state backing? This describes the reality of decentralized currencies. While such currencies may be accepted by segments of the population, they are not legally recognized in most states.

However, based on the reasoning of the Chazon Ish, if the only role of the state is to serve as a guarantor of economic trust, then a decentralized currency that achieves trust without state backing might still qualify as halachically valid. Ultimately, the key question is whether the currency circulates and is accepted in the market. In this way, cryptocurrency is comparable to trade in future goods, as previously discussed.

CONCLUSION

Halacha's general resistance to abstract transactions stems from concern that true meeting of the minds (semichut da'at) has not occurred. Legal clarity is essential, and ambiguous agreements risk fraud and misunderstanding. Nevertheless, when transactions—however abstract—are common in the market and reflect commercial norms, halacha views this as evidence of genuine agreement and treats the transaction as binding.

That is why we can see a change in halachic perspective from antiquity to our time. In antiquity, when abstract transactions were not common, meeting of the minds in such transactions was not ensured. But as the markets developed and an abstract perception of the market started taking place, rabbis became more and more keen to legitimize such transactions. They used measures like Dina Dmalchuta Dina, or the good of the market, but nonetheless, they accepted them.

The same applies to cryptographic currencies. As long as such transactions were rare and lacked broad recognition, halacha might have viewed them skeptically. However, as cryptographic currencies have become more widespread—even held by governments such as the United States, which reportedly holds over $12 billion in such assets—it becomes increasingly difficult to question their halachic validity.

REFERENCES

Albeck, S. (1976). *Dinei HaMamomnot BaTalmud* [Hebrew]. Dvir.

Avraham Yeshayau. (n.d.). *Chazon Ish*, Yoreh De'ah §272:2; Choshen Mishpat §16:26. *Choshen Mishpat, 16*, 24.

Hai Gaon. (n.d.). *Sefer HaMekach ve-haMimkar*, Sha'ar 41.

Maimonides. (n.d.). *Mishne Torah, Neighbors*, 2:11.

Maimonides. (n.d.). *Mishne Torah, Ownerless Property and Gifts*, 6:17.

Maimonides. (n.d.). *Mishne Torah, Sales*, 22:1.

Maimonides. (n.d.). *Mishne Torah, Sales*, 22:3.

Maimonides. (n.d.). *Mishne Torah, Sales*, 6:7.

Mishna. (n.d.). *Baba Mezia*, 4:1.

Rulings of the Rabbinical Court of Jerusalem. (n.d.). Monetary law ruling: "...and with this the sale is concluded." See also Feinstein, M. (n.d.). *Responsa Igrot Moshe*, Choshen Mishpat Part 1 §52.

Sofer, M. (n.d.). *Responsa Chatam Sofer*, Part 2 (Yoreh De'ah) §141; *Responsa Choshen Mishpat*, siman 200:1.

Sofer, M. (n.d.). *Responsa Chatam Sofer*, Part 2 (Yoreh De'ah) §144.

Talmud Bavli. (n.d.). *Baba Batra*, 106b.

Talmud Bavli. (n.d.). *Baba Mezia*, 44a–44b.

KEY TERMS AND DEFINITIONS

Abrahamic Finance: A financial system that is based on principles found in the Torah, Bible, and Qu'ran.

Jewish Law: A system of law based on the Written and Oral Torah.

Jewish Finance: Finance based on the principles found in the Torah (Written and Oral).

Torah: The law of God as revealed to Moses and recorded in the first Five Books of the Hebrew scriptures (the Pentateuch).

ENDNOTES

1 Baba Mezia, 4:1.

2 BT Baba Mezia, 44a-b.

3 R. Moshe Sofer, *Responsa Chatam Sofer*, Part 2 (Yoreh De'ah) §144.

Chapter 7
Economic Speculation and the Sacred in the Talmud:
Three Cases of Rabbinic Religious Intervention in Tractates Baba Batra, Pesachim, and Sukkah

Federico Dal Bo
https://orcid.org/0009-0002-1215-9708
University of Modena and Reggio Emilia, Italy

ABSTRACT

This chapter examines rabbinic authority in Sasanian Persia through three instances where rabbinic authorities intervened to lower prices for the community. It argues that these interventions should not be interpreted solely through traditional legal frameworks, such as Talmud commentaries by Rashi and the Tosafot, or ethical lenses found in moral readings of Talmudic texts. Instead, they should be analyzed within the broader context of business ethics, considering the complex political and theological dimensions at play. The ethical considerations are rooted in the relationships between rabbinic, Jewish, and secular institutions. This perspective allows for a more nuanced discussion of economic issues and concessions in the post-Talmudic era, exploring the interaction between sacred and secular domains, and offering a deeper understanding of the economic implications of religious authority and secularization.

DOI: 10.4018/979-8-3373-1887-5.ch007

INTRODUCTION

The integration of Old Iranian studies with Talmudic scholarship has opened new avenues for understanding the Talmud as a product of its time and place, rather than as an isolated religious text. This interdisciplinary approach includes philological, historical, and cultural analyses. The influence of the Sasanian imperial context on rabbinic identity and authority is well documented. (Bakhos & Shayegan, 2010) Scholars like Jason Sion Mokhtarian have explored how Persian imperial culture, including Zoroastrian religious authority and political structures, permeated the Babylonian Talmud and shaped rabbinic thought and practice. (Mokhtarian, 2015) This cultural interplay is reflected in the Talmud's portrayal of Persians, Sasanian kings, and Zoroastrian priests, revealing a dynamic interaction between Jewish and Persian societies, as also explored in Seth Schwartz's influential *Imperialism and Jewish Society* that argued that during the later stages of the Roman Empire, the Christianized government actively contributed to a renewed separation of the Jewish people by slowly excluding them from mainstream society, even as it continued to support their leadership and recognize their community structures. (Schwartz, 2004)

However, Talmudic scholarship has only recently begun to emphasize the importance of the Iranian context for interpreting the Babylonian Talmud. This approach was inaugurated by the late Yaakov Elman's pioneering research *Authority and Tradition: Toseftan Baraitot in Talmudic Babylonia* that categorized Talmudic sages based on their attitudes toward Persian culture, showing a spectrum from accommodation to resistance. This reveals the nuanced ways Jewish leaders navigated their minority status within the Sasanian milieu but also how the Talmudic sages (*amoraim*) and the Talmudic text itself were influenced by Persian culture, language, and religious ideas. Following Elman's steps, in his influential work *The Iranian Talmud: Reading the Bavli in Its Sasanian Context*, Shai Secunda provided a detailed reconstruction of late antique Iranian society and its impact on the Babylonian Talmud and analyzed the intercultural dynamics between Jews and Persian Zoroastrians, highlighting how these shaped rabbinic discourse and identity formation. In his *Babylonian Jews and Sasanian Imperialism in Late Antiquity*, Simcha Gross has recently positioned the Exilarch (*reysh galuta*) within a category of non-Iranian aristocrats operating in an ambiguous status—adopting Iranian elite characteristics while participating in imperial patronage networks. Unlike Rome's constitutionally mediated patronage and third-century bureaucratization, Sasanian governance maintained more direct aristocratic relationships, allowing the exilarch to function as a local magnate with quasi-Iranian features during the mid-fourth to early fifth centuries, precisely when the Palestinian patriarchate underwent increasing bureaucratization. Notably, rabbinic sources omit the patriarch's formal state integration, which emerges only through the *Codex Theodosianus*. However, Gross complicates this framework by acknowledging limited understanding of non-Iranian aristocrats. Rejecting recent scholarship's claim of complete Iranization upon state recognition, he argues the king maintained distinct relationships with Iranian and non-Iranian populations, governing through Iranian bureaucracy supplemented by local elites—resembling feudal mediation through regional grandees. Crucially, Gross emphasizes these arrangements' informal, improvised, and non-institutional character, lacking formal codification and easily circumvented. Minority communities operated without *Personalitätsprinzip*—possessing no official legal autonomy but relying on customary practice rather than formal rights. (Elman, 1994; Secunda, 2013; Gross, 2024)

The chapter's focus on three cases of rabbinic intervention—price control in markets, participation in ceramic speculation, and regulation of myrtle sales for the Feast of Tabernacles—illustrates the active role rabbis played in economic regulation. These interventions are linked to anti-hoarding laws found in the Babylonian Talmud, which aimed to prevent market manipulation and protect communal welfare. The analysis seeks to identify the societal groups supporting these laws and assess their broader societal impact, moving beyond simplistic ethical or legal interpretations to consider the political and economic ramifications. The literature on Talmudic business ethics is extensive. Numerous books and articles have been written examining the Talmudic business ethics philosophy and how applicable it is to the contemporary business environment that is rampant with corruption, bribery, fraud, misappropriation, misrepresentation and all other forms of unethical behavioral activities. The following are some of the authors who have devoted their time and energy to bring this unique kind of information to the world. (Friedman, 1980, 1984, 1985; Levine, 1987; Tamari, 1987, 1991, 1995; Friedman, 2000; Gellis, Giladi, & Friedman, 2002; Golinkin, 2003; Kahaner, 2003; Levine, 2005; Friedman & Klein, 2010; Friedman & Adler, 2011; Friedman, 2012; Schwartz, 2012; cf. Dal Bo, 2013, pp. 73–76, 222–234; cf. also Dal Bo, 2018) This chapter examines three instances of religious intervention in the economy as described in the Talmud. A rabbi was appointed as a price controller in a market, participated in ceramic speculation, and was involved in selling myrtle for the Feast of Tabernacles. The chapter seeks to understand the objectives of anti-hoarding laws, identify the societal groups that would support them, and assess the impact of these laws on society. By closely studying one of the earliest recorded anti-hoarding laws found in the Babylonian Talmud, which is a compilation of Jewish laws and narratives about living a good life, this chapter aims to provide insights into the prohibition of hoarding fruit and other essential commodities.

1 A First Case of Religious Intervention: Price Control in Graeco-Roman Palestine

The Talmud places significant emphasis on maintaining price stability, with market prices staying fixed and low throughout the year. According to the sages of the Talmud, the hoarding of goods with the intent to raise prices was considered a transgression, akin to usury or the manipulation of weights and measures. According to the Bible, it is considered unlawful to cause prices to rise through hoarding or any other means. The scriptural basis for price regulation can be found in the Torah's prohibition of using disparate weights and measures in trade, intended to ensure fairness in economic transactions: "you must have completely honest weights and completely honest measures... in order to endure long on the soil that the Lord is giving you" (אֶבֶן שְׁלֵמָה וָצֶדֶק יִהְיֶה־לָּךְ אֵיפָה שְׁלֵמָה וָצֶדֶק יִהְיֶה־לָּךְ לְמַעַן יַאֲרִיכוּ יָמֶיךָ עַל הָאֲדָמָה אֲשֶׁר־יְהוָה אֱלֹהֶיךָ נֹתֵן לָךְ) (Deut 25.15).

From a redactional perspective, the use of the Greek term *agoranomos* (market overseer) in a Persian context raises important questions. The *agoranomos* was an elected official similar to the Roman *aedile*, which was traditionally associated with the regulation of markets, prices, and measures. The use of this term in the Talmud reflects an original Greek-speaking environment but its introduction into the Babylonian Talmud within a Persian framework—typically through a *baraita* or a "Talmudic external source"—also suggests the imposition of Roman administrative concepts onto the governance structures of Babylonian Jewry. This raises the possibility of a superimposition between the Babylonian Exilarchate and the Palestinian Patriarchate, specifically regarding the authority and functions of these two leadership bodies. While the Jerusalem Talmud ostensibly addresses the role of the *reysh galuta* (Exilarch), it is plausible that the discussions actually refer to the Palestinian Patriarchate (396–429 c.e.), using the Exilarch as a rhetorical vehicle for anti-Patriarchal polemics. (Herman, 2012, p. 167) In his analysis, Geoffrey Herman builds on the work of Louis Jacobs to suggest that the divergent legal practices observed between Sassanid Babylonia and Roman Palestine can be attributed to the distinct economic conditions in each region. In his relatively dated article "The economic conditions of the Jews in Babylon in Talmudic times," Jacobs argues that Palestine, with its simpler economic structure, required only the regulation of measures, whereas the more complex economic system of Babylonia necessitated the supervision of both prices and measures. (Jacobs, 1957, p. 354)

A critical question, however, is whether the office of *agoranomos* actually existed in Babylonia. More recently in his long monograph *A Prince without a Kingdom*, Geoffrey Herman contends that this office did not exist in Sassanid Persia. As such, the references to the *agoranomos* in the Talmud should not be understood as historical accounts of Persian Jewish governance, but rather as political-theological constructs. In particular, Herman observes that the office of *agoranomos*—responsible for overseeing measures and prices—was an institution found exclusively within the Roman Empire. Herman indicates that it might have been placed under the authority of the Palestinian Patriarchate instead of being a historical institution in the governance of Babylonian Jewry. Moreover, Herman emphasizes that the other mentions of *agoranomoi* in the Babylonian Talmud, as well as the associated discourses, are derived from Palestinian sources, both Tannaitic and Amoraic. This supports the argument that these references are more reflective of Palestinian polemics than of Babylonian historical reality. (Herman, 2012, p. 170) Consequently, the employment of the term *agoranomos* in the Babylonian Talmud, particularly in relation to the Exilarchate, appears to be a redactional construct. It does not reflect the actual existence of this institution in Sassanid Persia but rather suggests a theological and polemical agenda, rather aligning with the administrative practices of the Babylonian Exilarchate with Roman and Palestinian models, reflecting the political dynamics and economic conditions of the time.

Daniel Sperber has shown that institutions such as the *logistes* and *agoranomos* embody a unified stance, aligned with the third-century Palmyrene expression *rav shuq* (Vog. 15), also equaling the Greek term *agoranomesanta*, later transformed into the later rabbinic concept of *ba'al ha-shuq*, ("market master") (NumRab 20:18), also corresponding to the Arabic notion of *zahib al-suq* (Geniza fragment TS 10 J). (Sperber, 1977, n. 17, pp. 231, 238) The term *agoranomos* (in its various spellings) is the earliest and most original of these terms. On the other hand, the utilization of *logistes* can be traced back to 4th-century Roman Palestine. (Cohen, 2013)

The roles of the *agoranomos* included monitoring weights and measures, controlling prices, checking the quality of market goods, ensuring sufficient supplies, and controlling imports. The figure is classically introduced in Rabbinic literature by the Tosefta:

דבלב תודמה לע אלא ,םירעשה לע ןינוממ ויה אלו ,םלשוריב היה ןימנארגיא

There was [sic!] igranamin [sic!] in Jerusalem, and they [sic!] were not appointed [to control] prices, but only measures (tBM 6:14).

The figure of the *igranamin*, presented here erroneously in the plural form, is clearly a deformation of the figure of the *agoranomos* in ancient Greece or as an *aedile* in Roman times, and similar to the institution of the *muchtasib* in Islamic times. (Herman, 2012, p. 168) However, the employment of the Greek term suggests the presence of an influence from the environment of the Land of Israel and reflects the historical figure of a market supervisor after the period of inflation that occurred in the 3rd century, before the reign of Diocletian, who implemented economic reforms that included the establishment of fixed prices. (Lauffer, 1971) This institution was likely implemented in Roman Palestine, and the *agoranomos* were tasked with overseeing prices. (Herman, 2012, p. 169; Kushnir-Stein & Holland, 2008; tAZ 7:6; tBQ 6:19; tBM 6:14; Sifra, Qodashim, 3, 8, 19b; Sifrei Deut. 294; y. Demai 2:1 [22c]; y. AZ 4:8 [44b]; Leviticus Rabba 1:8 [Margulies, 22–23]; Yalqut Shimeoni, Psalms 819 [= Yalqut Shimeoni, 763]; Pesiqta de-Rav Kahana, ʻAser taʻaser [Mandelbaum, 163]; b. AZ 58a)

It should also be noted that in Roman Palestine there were two economic title-bearers, whose links one with the other are not immediately clear; perhaps they were subordinated by a hierarchical relationship. On this Geofry Herman wrote: "as regards [...] Seleucia, [...] the title *agoranomos* does not appear on the weight, but rather a shortened version of the term *paraphylax* who was responsible for measures." (Herman, 2012, n. 40, p. 170) As discussed below, the fusion or confusion of these two roles in tractate *Baba Batra* from the Jerusalem Talmud and the homologous tractate from the Babylonian Talmud suggests a derivative and probably already "historicized" nature of this institution. For that matter, no Babylonian Hebrew source seems to associate *agoranomos* with the Persian figure of *wāzārbed*, in fact rendered in Greek as *agoranomos* in a bilingual stele. (Šāpūr I, Mid. Pers. line 35 w'c'lpt; Parth. line 28 w'šrpty; Greek line 67 agoranomou; cf. Floor, 1979, pp. 125–126) Nonetheless, the utilization of the Greek term for denoting a hypothetical Persian reality would possess a sense of antiquarianism, if not utopianism: "the prevailing assumption has been that it was the Greek term that was preserved among the Jewish Aramaic-speaking population of Babylonia. Consequently, it is presumed that the Jews were the sole group within the Sasanian Empire to maintain the use of the Greek term." (Herman, 2012, p. 171) If this assumption is valid, the utilization of a Greek term can be understood as having a historical and cultural significance and could also reflect a process of Hellenization amongst the Jewish population, that had begun under the Parthians. From this perspective, the term might be anachronistic or simply reflect the cultural needs of Babylonian Jews.

1.1 A Dispute in Tractate *Baba Batra* in the Jerusalem and the Babylonian Talmud

The first relevant source on the relationship between rabbinic and Persian authorities emerges in a passage from the Tractate *Baba Batra* from the Jerusalem Talmud that illustrates the establishment of an *agardemin* or, more properly, an *agoranomos* or "market inspector," and an administrative and penal dispute that follows. Although the market inspector is a Roman institution, the historical setting of this disputed in both the Jerusalem and the Babylonian Talmud is a Jewish regional autonomy created within the Sasanian empire, typically led by the *reysh galuta*, "the Head of the Exile," possibly a Jewish layman who acted as a sort of governor. The system was developed by the Sasanian monarchs and later adopted by the Muslim caliphs. It entailed the appointment of an official representative to serve as a mediator between the members of a significant religious minority and the central government, characterized by a significant degree of autonomy and the office was probably hereditary in nature with primary responsibilities in appointing Jewish judges and collecting taxes. (Herman, 2012, p. 84)

With respect of this relatively incongruous historical setting, the dispute involves three characters: the Exilarch, here mentioned with his Aramaic title as *reysh galuta*, "the Head of the Exile;" the 1st-generation Babylonian *amora* Rav Abba bar Aybo, who is commonly known as Abba Arikha or simply as Rav; his colleague, the 1st-generation Babylonian *amora* Rav Qarna, who is commonly mentioned simply as Qarna and traditionally believed to have compiled the *baraitot* (or "external sources") of *Seder Neziqin* (bBB 47b).

In his study, *A Prince without a Kingdom,* an accurate examination of the Jewish Exilarch in Sasanian era, Geoffrey Herman noted two important variants in this version: the one reported in *editio princeps* of the Jerusalem Talmud published in Venice in 1523 and the other in the relatively recent discovered Ms Escorial of the Jerusalem Talmud (1983). (Herman, 2012, p. 163) I follow Herman in producing the two texts synoptically:

Table 1.

yBB 5:5 15b (Venice 1523)	**yBB 5:5 15b Ms Escorial**
לע אלו אתליכמ לע יחמ הוהו סומרגנא אתולג שיר היינמ בר רמא .היבג אנרק בר לאע .אתולג שיר הישבח .אירועיש אהו .היל רמא .ןירועישל אלו תודימל ורמאש סומרגנא .היל .ןול רומא קופ .היל רמא .ןירועישלו תודימל סומרגנא .תינת רב .ןול רמאו קפנ .ןירועישל אלו תודימל ורמאש סומרגנא .היל ןישבח וניה אד השבכ הנתד שנ	אלו היירעש לע יחממ הוהו סימינורגא אתולג שיר 'תינתמ בר היבג ינרק בר לא .אתולג שיר הישבח ,אתלכמ יחממ הוה :היל 'מא ,סירעשל אלו תודמל ורמאש סימינורגא :ןול 'מא קופ :היל 'מא .ןירועישלו תודימל ורמאש סימינורגא תינת תנו 'מאו קפנ .סירעשל אלו תודימל ורמאש סימינורגא ןול 'מא .היל ןישבח יניה אד השככ ינתד שנרב ןול
The Exilarch (*reysh galuta*) appointed Rav as *angarmos* [sic!]; he intervened about measures (*mekhilata*) but not prices (*shiu'aya*). The Exilarch incarcerated him. Rav Qarna went to see him and said, the *angarmos* about whom they spoke was for measures (*middot*) but not prices (*shi'urin*). He answered, but you had stated: the *angarmos* is for both measures (*middot*) and prices. He said to him, go out and tell them, the *angarmos* [sic!] is for measures (*middot*) but not prices. He went out and said to them, a person who teaches hidden things they send to jail!	The Exilarch (*reysh galuta*) appointed Rav as *agoranomos* and he would examine the prices (*she'urayah*) but would not examine the measures (*mekhilata*). The Exilarch incarcerated him. Rav Qarna went to see him. He said to him: the *agoranomos* that they spoke of is for measures (*middot*) but not for prices (*shiu'rim*). He said to him: But behold you have taught that the *agoranomos* is for measures (*middot*) *and* for prices! He said: Go out and say to them: the *agoranomos* that they spoke of is for measures (*middot*) and not for prices. He went out and said to them: They imprison a person who teaches a basket of unripe dates (?)

The two versions of the passage under consideration both describe the Exilarch, described as *reysh galuta,* "the head of the Exile," appointing Rav as *agoranomos* and then imprisoning him for failing to abide by the legal requirements of the position as market inspector.

In the context of Roman municipal reality within a Sasanian setting, the function of the *agoranomos* as a market supervisor presents an interesting case. The Ms Escorial version accurately reports this institution as *agoranomos*, while the Venetian *editio princeps* corrupts it to *angarmos*, likely indicative of a loss of knowledge regarding the institution's true nature in the time that elapsed between the manuscript and the printed version. Additionally, the two versions also present divergent accounts of Rav's role especially regarding the distinction between prices and measures that appears in both Hebrew and Aramaic.[1] According to Ms Escorial, when appointed *agoranomos*, Rav's primary focus was on examining prices. In contrast, the Venice *editio princeps* asserts that Rav's primary focus was on measuring instruments. In both cases, his actions resulted in imprisonment by the Exilarch. A notable distinction emerges between the two versions concerning the circumstances of imprisonment. According to the Ms Escorial version, the nature of the imprisonment was Rav's prioritization of prices over measures, contravening the directives of the Exilarch, thereby suggesting that the *reysh galuta* held significant economic authority in the governance of market prices. The *editio princeps*, however, asserts that Rav examined measures *but not* prices, suggesting that the Exilarch's imprisonment of Rav was not directly justified by the transgression of some legal boundaries, but rather a form of abuse of power. Notwithstanding these discrepancies, the context of imprisonment signifies discord between rabbinic authorities and the Persian imperial institution responsible for overseeing ethnic minorities. According to Geoffrey Herman, the Ms Escorial version is regarded as superior because it depicts Rav acting based on principles that Jewish courts are not required to enforce commandments if rewards are associated with them. Coercion is typically not used in cases involving positive commandments that offer material rewards upon fulfillment as the obligation is "purely moral" in nature. (Ben-Shlomo, 1998) However, the Exilarch imprisoned him, presumably expecting Rav to assess measures according to the aforementioned Tosefta's perspective: "there were *igranamin* in Jerusalem, and they were not appointed [to control] prices, but only measures" (tBM 6:14). On the other hand, in the Venice *edition princeps*, Rav serves as *agoranomos*, but avoids examining measures, following the principle that Jewish courts neither impose nor face penalties for non-fulfillment of precepts regarding measures. However, this omission leads to disciplinary action from the Exilarch.

This episode underwent further revision in the Babylonian Talmud. However, a substantial discrepancy exists between the Jerusalem and Babylonian Talmud regarding the identities of sages, narrative sequences, rhetorical emphasis, and terminological choices they made: the Exilarch is no longer referred to as *reysh galuta*, but rather as *devey nas'yah* ("of the House of the Patriarch"); the character of Rav is eliminated and substituted with that of the 1st-generation Babylonian *amora* Shmuel of Nehardea, who is also known as Shmuel bar Abba, or Mar Shmuel; the role of Qarna undergoes significant modification, as he does instruct Rav, but is rather instructed by Shmuel; the 3rd-generation Palestinian *amora* Rabbi Yitzchaq, makes a final statement in the name of the 3rd-generation Babylonian *amora* Rami bar Chama. The passage in the Babylonian Talmud reads as follows:

ןידימעמ ןיאו ,תודמל ןימדרגא ןידימעמש דמלמ – (גי הכ םירבד) "ךל היהי (אל)" :ןנבר ונת :אנרקל לאומש היל רמא .םירעשל ןיב תודמל ןיב ןימדרגא ומיקוא האישנ יבד .םירעשל ןימדרגא ןידימעמ :והל שרד קפנ .םירעשל ןימדרגא ןידימעמ ןיאו ,תודמל ןימדרגא ןידימעמ :והל ינת קופ היל אקפנ .היניעב אנרק היל קופית .אנרק ?ךמש המ :היל רמא .םירעשל ןיב תודמל ןיב ןימדרגא ןיב ןימדרגא ןידימעמ :קחצי יבר רמא אמח רב ימר רמאד אה יכ ?רבס ןאמכ והיאו .היניעב אנרק .ןיאמרה ינפמ ,םירעשל ןיב תודמל

Our sages taught: "You shall not have" (Deut 25:13) teaches that "one appoints agardemin [sic!] to measures and does not appoint agardemin for prices" (tBB 6:14), since the house of the Nasi' appointed agardemin for both measures and prices. Shmuel said to Qarna: Go out, teach them: one appoints agardemin for measures but one does not appoint agardemin for prices. He went out, taught them: one appoints market inspectors for both measures and prices. [Shmuel] said to him: What is your name? Qarna. [Shmuel said]: Let a horn (qarna) emerge from his eye. A horn emerged from his eye. And [Qarna], in accordance with whose [opinion] did he hold? In accordance with that which Rami bar Chama says [that] Rabbi Yitzchaq says: One appoints market inspectors for both measures and prices, due to swindlers (bBB 89a).

This text is similar to the passages from the Jerusalem Talmud. It too talks about a disagreement about market regulation. In this dispute, everyone agrees that the local Jewish courthouse is responsible for choosing supervisors to make sure that the weights and measures used in business are correct. Qarna talks about the legal principles for this appointment from the point of view of "those of the Prince's house"; by doing so he goes against Shmuel's original instructions. This upsets Shmuel because Qarna's interpretation—or misunderstanding—ends with Shmuel's response, mocking Qarna with a pun on his name: "let a horn (*qarna*) emerge from his eye." This pun actually comes true, as is often the case in the *Babylonian Talmud's* manner of praising their sages. It is interesting to note again that the Greek word *agronomos* is only occasionally spelled correctly in a few manuscripts (Ms Marburg 165 and Ms Escorial), while is mostly spelled *agardemin*, which is a corruption of the original. (Herman, 2012, n. 15, p. 165)

In his study, Geoffrey Herman says that this corruption may be another reason to doubt the existence of the *agoranomos* in Babylonia during the time of the Talmud. From a linguistic perspective, the Greek term *agoranomos* changed into the Hebrew form *agardemin* in the Babylonian Talmud manuscripts and is generally perceived as an Aramaic masculine plural noun. The change in language and understanding is probably because the connection to the Roman institution was fading, and it was remembered as a remnant from the Jerusalem Talmud, but it was in fact not part of a living language. It may still have been used in this region sometime after Seleucid rule ended and the Greek cities in the Parthian Empire became less powerful. (Smith, 2018, p. 70) On the other hand, the Jerusalem Talmud depicts the imprisonment of Rav who disobeys the exilarch, a fate that does not happen to Shmuel in the Babylonian Talmud. On the contrary, the Babylonian Talmud changes the focus of the story from the role of the *agoranomos* to the conflict between Shmuel and Qarna. When we look at the Babylonian Talmud's plot weaknesses, structural inconsistencies, and other factors, we can see that it is based on the Jerusalem Talmud which suffers from no such weaknesses. (Herman, 2012, p. 114)

A list of the three versions of this episode shows important changes when moving from the Jerusalem Talmud as reported in Ms. Escorial to the Venice edition of the Jerusalem Talmud to the Babylonian Talmud:

Table 2.

Jerusalem Talmud Ms Escorial	**Jerusalem Talmud** *Editio Princeps*	**Babylonian Talmud**
Rav examines prices but not measures		
	Rav examines measures but not prices	
		Generic remark on *agoranomos* examining measures but not prices
Reysh galuta incarcerates him	*Reysh galuta* incarcerates him	
Qarna instructs him about the role of the *agoranomos* elected by the *reysh gaulta*	Qarna instructs him about the role of the *agoranomos* elected by the *reysh galuta*	
		Shmuel tells Qarna what the role of the agoranomos is who is elected by *devey nasy'ah*
		Shmuel mocks Qarna's inability to understand the role of the *agoranomos*

The Babylonian Talmud passage presents a very different story from the Jerusalem Talmud. The role of the *agoranomos*, previously identified with Rav, is now described more broadly, without giving details. Shmuel is responsible for explaining the role of the *agoranomos* to Qarna. From this point of view, the passage from the Babylonian Talmud appears to be the end of a different political and religious story about what it means to be imprisoned fairly. The Babylonian Talmud discussion also includes a general thought about the role of the *agoranomos* but implicitly raises a political issue. According to Jerusalem Talmud, the *agoranomos* was chosen by the Exilarch called *reysh galuta*, who is described in an antagonistic way in both the manuscript and printed edition of the passage. However, according to the Babylonian Talmud, the *agoranomos* was chosen by *devey nas'yah*, "the House of the Patriarch." Naming the institution, if it is indeed the same institution, with a different name may suggest a different political if not theological-political connotation. While the expression *reysh galuta* as "the Head of the Exile" clearly and primarily connotates the Exilarch as a *Sasanian* institution that controls the life of the *exiled* Jewish nation, the name *devey nas'yah* as "the House of the Patriarch" rather suggests that the Exilarch is somehow similar if not homologous to the Byzantine Patriarchate that is led by decendents of Yehudah haNasi, "Judah the Patriarch," the head of the Jewish law school in the Land of Israel. (Herman, 2012, p. 139; cf. Smith, 2018, p. 67)

This passage from the Babylonian Talmud should be considered within the context of the Tosefta that originally discusses Biblical institutions (tHor 3:3). The quotation from the Tosefta is included as a *baraita* in the *gemara* from Tractate *Horayot* (bHor 10a), extending these observations beyond their original tannaitic context. Although initially intended for examining a Biblical institution, these observations are applied to analyze contemporary institutions relevant to the rabbis. The Tosefta differentiates between two types of "princes:" "which is the *nasi*? The *nasi* of Israel and not the *nasi* of the tribes. [In a case of] the *nasi* of Israel and the *nasi* from the House of David, each brings separately" (אלו לארשי אישנ? אישנ והזיא .ומצעל איבמ הזו ומצעל איבמ הז דוד תיב אישנ 'רשי אישנ .םיטבש אישנ) (tHor 3:3, also quoted as a *baraita* in bHor 10a). As Herman argues, the existence of the Exilarch can be discussed with confidence only beginning from the mid-3rd century c.e., specifically from the second generation of *amoraim*. (Rosenfeld-Menirav, 2005, p. 155) He argues that this institution enjoyed some "regional authority" (*reshut*) and probably reflected the bureaucratic requirements of the administrative divisions in the Sasanian empire, in the same way that the Nestorian Christian minority was represented by the *Catholikos*. (Rosenfeld-Menirav, 2005, p. 155)

1.2 The Figure of Shmuel

It is evident that the Talmud addressed the issue of price stability for life-saving necessities. According to the Talmudic sages, the hoarding of goods or the implementation of other strategies aimed at manipulating prices was regarded a transgression against the Torah, akin to the practices of usury or the adulteration of weights and measures. The rationale for this perspective is articulated in Tractate *Baba Batra*, drawing upon a few specific Biblical verses that are quoted extensively:

רמוא בותכה והילע – םירעש יעיקפמו ,הפיא יניטקמו ,תיברב יולמו ,תוריפ ירצוא :ןנבר ונת:
תועלו ,לקש לידגהלו הפיא ןיטקהל ,רב החתפנו תבשהו ,רבש הריבשנו שדחה רבעי יתמ רמאל"
ינזאמ המרמ" (ה-ד ח סומע).

Our Rabbis taught: Hoarders of produce, and usurers, and those who reduce measures, and those who raise prices about them the verse states, "saying: When will the new moon be gone, that we may sell produce? And the Shabbat, that we may set forth grain? Making the measure smaller, and the shekel greater, and falsifying the balances of deceit" (Am 8:4-5) (bBB 90b).

With this midrashic baraita, the Talmud targeted individuals who engage in hoarding motivated by self-interest, leading to increased prices as a result. However, the Rabbis do not demonstrate this phenomenon through the lens of contemporary economic theory. Instead, they largely refer to a Biblical source that is infrequently quoted as the sole authoritative voice on the matter – Amos 8:4-5. The Rabbis elucidate that these prohibitions are applicable to those who procure goods from the market, for storage is permissible, in order to profit from a rise in their price. In technical terms, the Rabbis' prohibition against hoarding can be more accurately understood as a specific proscription on purchasing behavior in an essential commodity market, without conflicting with the general rule against sale profits exceeding 16% without the risk of being charged with "fraud" (*hona'ah*). (Rosenfeld, 2010, pp. 147–148)

A few lines after mentioning these general principles, Tractate *Baba Batra* also documents a separate discussion on price control that involves Shmuel once again. This passage underscores his main role in this process. Evidently, he is explicitly regarded as an authority on financial matters, particularly with regard to the acceptable profit margins that are taken into account prior to the implementation of price control. The passage delineates a clear limit beyond which economic profit is deemed illegitimate:

לא רכתשמהו ,תותשמ רתי עבטמה לע אלו ,תותשמ רתי תודמה לע ןיפיסומ ןיא :לאומש רמא
יעוקפא םושמ אמיליא ?אמעט יאמ – תותשמ רתוי תודמה לע ןיפיסומ ןיא .תותשמ רתוי רכתשי
.אל ימנ תותש ,אערת

Shmuel says: they may not increase the measures [by] more than one-sixth, and not [increase the value of] a coin [by] more than one-sixth. And one who profits may not profit by more than one-sixth. They may not increase the measures [by] more than one-sixth, what is the reason? If we say because [doing so causes market] prices to rise, [the same concern should apply to raising the prices by] one-sixth, [and therefore this should] also not [be allowed] (bBB 90a).

Shmuel's principle is explicit: the establishment of a fair profit margin for a sale price that should not exceed a sixth (17%) above the purchase price, taking into account the actual cost of the goods, expenses, and the cost of work. Additionally, Shmuel's position appears to imply that price regulation would be beneficial for the market. In the event that a vendor sells at an excessively high price, customers may opt to purchase from a competitor, potentially harming the vendor's business. Nevertheless, the process of price regulation also entails the assurance that prices do not reach excessively low levels. It is an accepted principle that a store or establishment should not be permitted to drastically reduce prices. Additionally, the figure of Shmuel and his concern for the marketplace emerge in another narrative from Tractate *Baba Batra* that follows the previous discussion on the increase of measures:

ןיבזמו ,ירפל יהשמ ,הירב לאומש .אפרח אערתב ,אפרח אערתכ ירפל והל ןיבזמ לאומשד הובא – חוורד אערת ?אמעט יאמ .ארבדמ אבאד אבט :םתמ וחלש .אפרח אערתכ – אלפא אערתב והל חוור.

Shmuel's father would sell produce during early [market] price, for the early [market] price. His son Shmuel would keep the produce and sell it during late [market] price, for the early [market] price. They sent [a message] from there: [the way] of the father is better than [the one] of the son. What is the reason? [A market] price that has been eased [remains] eased (bBB 90b).

In this regard, the implementation of price controls can be seen as a manifestation of the pervasive economic crisis that afflicted the Roman Empire during the 3rd century. This crisis exerted a profound influence on the economic infrastructure of society, both within the Roman Empire and in its external regions. (Garnsey, 1988, p.77)

2 A Second Case of Religious Intervention: Breaking Vessels for Passover?

The second case of religious intervention pertains once more to the 1st-generation Babylonian *amoraim*, Rav and Shmuel. The context is delineated by a straightforward inquiry into the Biblical injunction prohibiting the utilization of *chametz* ("leaven" or other leavening agents) during the designated period of Passover.

The discussion revolves around the ruling of the Babylonian *amora* Rav, who prescribes that used vessels must be broken before Passover, in accordance with the commandments that prohibit the mixing of leaven with other components and the cleansing of the house from leaven. However, his colleague, the Babylonian *amora* Shmuel, maintains that only the mixing of *chametz* with ingredients of the same kind is forbidden. Consequently, he permits the mixing of *chametz* with ingredients of a different kind during Passover. Thus, Rav posits the destruction of vessels utilized for *chametz*, while Shmuel sanctions their continued usage after Passover. This divergence leads to a discussion concerning economic speculation among sellers of vessels. Presumably, these sellers increased their prices around the time of Passover, since Rav, the local Jewish religious authority in the city of Sura, had ruled their destruction. Furthermore, Shmuel, who functioned as the local authority in the nearby city of Nehardea, was dutybound to respect his colleague's stringent ruling, namely, the destruction of all the vessels and the requirement to purchase new ones, despite his disagreement. The passage does not offer a rationale for the decision to counter this instance of economic speculation; however, the context strongly indicates that the aim was to uphold religious observance and promote social equity by reducing prices to safeguard the poor. However, Shmuel's more lenient ruling appears never to have been implemented. It is noteworthy that neither Jewish nor non-Jewish institutions were involved in the potential decision-making process. Instead, questions of authority and local prestige were portrayed as more significant than the welfare and social issues implicit in the manipulation of prices.

2.1 The Ruling in the Mishnah (mPes 2:2)

The requirement to break vessels or items that might be contaminated with *chametz* or derivates of it follows a long discussion on a passage from the Mishnah that rules about the treatment of leavened bread by a Jew and a non-Jew during Passover:

דל הארי אל" :רמאנש .האנהב רוסא ,לארשי לשו .האנהב רתמ ,חספה וילע רבעש ירכנ לש ץמח
ראש" (ז ג' תומש):

The chametz of a foreigner (nochri) over which Passover has passed is permitted for benefit. And [the leavened bread] of a Jew is forbidden for benefit, as it is said: "neither shall there be [chametz] seen with you" (Ex 13:7) (mPes 2.2).

This legal regulation reflects the Mishnah's characteristic parsimony in formulating legal principles. It stipulates that products containing *chametz* may be owned by non-Jews during the Passover period and are subsequently permissible for consumption, based upon the owner's non-Jewish status. However, this exceptional ruling does not apply to Jewish individuals, who are still prohibited from possessing and, by implication, consuming leavened substances during Passover. To elaborate, a Jewish individual is prohibited from consuming *chametz* that belongs to a non-Jewish proprietor during Passover, but a Jew may consume this same *chametz* after Passover ends. However, since the prohibition against *chametz* ownership during this period is specific to Jewish individuals, as outlined in Scripture: "no *chametz* shall be seen with you" (Ex 13:7). All members of the Jewish community, are prohibited from "seeing" *chametz* during Passover and thus, cannot derive benefit from any leavened products owned by themselves or by other Jewish individual.

2.2 The first economic discussion the commentaries of Rashi and the Tosafot

This discussion addresses whether the term "to benefit" (*ba-hana'ah*), as mentioned in the Mishnah (*mPes* 2:2), includes the use of vessels that could be considered ritually unsuitable for Passover. The inquiry pertains to the function or purpose that such utensils serve. Does the "benefit" that should be prohibited on principle also apply to its possible sale to a non-Jew, namely the "stranger" mentioned in the passage from the Mishnah just discussed? This also prompts a discourse on the notion of "misuse of property" (*me'ilah*), as is elaborated in the associated Talmudic tractate *Me'ilah*. The passage from the Gemara is entirely in Aramaic and involves the 3rd-generation Babylonian *amoraim* Rav Yosef bar Chiyya, simply known as Rav Yosef, his colleagues Rav Acha bar Ya'aqov and Rav Ashi—all following in the footsteps of the previous dispute between the three 2nd-century *tannaim* Rabbi Yehudah (bar Ilai), Rabbi Shimon (bar Yochai) and Rabbi Yose the Galilean. The commentary is relatively straightforward and reads as follows:

> *,םיבלכל ןליכאהל םישדקה תא ןידופ ןיא אמלע ילוכד :אנשיל אהב ףסוי ברד הימשמ אתעמש אהל*
> *ןוממל םרוגה רבד :רבסק ,לעמ רמאד ןאמ .ימד ןוממכ ןוממל םרוגה רבדב :יגלפימק אהב אכהו*
> *רב אחא בר .ימד ןוממכ ואל — ןוממל םרוגה רבד :רבסק ,לעמ אל רמאד ןאמו .ימד ןוממכ —*
> *ןועמש יברו הדוהי יברד אתגולפב אכהו ,ימד ןוממכ — ןוממל םרוגה רבד אמלע ילוכד :רמא בקעי*
> *רב אחא בר אהו .ןועמש יברכ — לעמ :רמאד ןאמו .הדוהי יברכ — לעמ אל :רמאד ןאמ :יגלפימק*
> *בקעי רב אחא בר היב רדה אלא .הייארד רואשמ הליכאד רואש ףילי הדוהי יברד רמאד אוה בקעי*
> *אכהו ,ימד ןוממכ ואל — ןוממל םרוגה רבדו ,ןידופ ןיא — אמלע ילוכד :רמא ישא בר .איההמ*
> *— לעמ אל רמאד ןאמו .יסוי יברכ — לעמ רמאד ןאמ .יגלפימק ןנברו ילילגה יסוי יברד אתגולפב*
> *.ןנברכ*
>
> *Concerning this [oral] tradition in the name of Rav Yosef [is] in the following language: The whole world agrees that one does not redeem consecrated items in order to feed them to dogs. And here, they disagree [with regard to the question of whether] something that causes a financial [loss] is [considered to be] of monetary [value] (cf. bPes 5b). The one who said [that] he misused holds [the opinion that]: a thing that causes a financial [loss] is [considered to be] like monetary [value]. And the one who said [that] he did not misuse [consecrated things] holds: a thing that causes a financial [loss] is not considered to be like monetary [value]. Rav Acha bar Ya'aqov said: the whole world agrees that a thing that causes a financial loss is [considered to be] like monetary value, and here they disagree with regard to the dispute between Rabbi Yehudah and Rabbi Shimon. The one who said that he did not misuse [consecrated things] is in accordance with Rabbi Yehudah and the one who said [that] he misused [consecrated things] is in accordance with Rabbi Shimon. But isn't it Rav Acha bar Ya'aqov who said: Rabbi Yehudah derives eating leaven from seeing leaven (cf. Ex 13:7)? Rather, Rav Acha bar Ya'aqov retracted from this [position]. Rav Ashi said: The whole world [holds] that one does not redeem [consecrated things in order to feed it to dogs] and [that] a thing that causes a financial [loss] is not [considered to be] of monetary [value]. And here, they disagree with regard to the dispute between Rabbi Yose the Galilean and the Rabbis. The one who said: he misused [consecrated things] is in accordance with Rabbi Yose the Galilean*

and the one who said: he did not misuse [consecrated things] is in accordance with the Rabbis (bPes 29b).

This passage examines a sophisticated legal and theological issue concerning the redemption of "consecrated items" (*haqdashot*) and the principle of "something that causes a financial [loss] is [considered to be] of monetary [value]" (*davar hagram le-mamon ke-mamon dami*). The passage begins with a foundational premise that asserts the generally accepted principle of the "irredeemability" of consecrated objects for the purpose of "feeding dogs." This premise may be interpreted in three different ways: literally, as a prohibition against the feeding dogs, or in an idiomatic sense, as a figurative expression of wasteful expenditure of valuable materials, or in metaphorical sense as the prohibition of the sale of goods to non-Jews. This restriction underscores the profound respect accorded to sanctified items within the framework of Jewish law, thereby prohibiting their utilization for mundane endeavors.

The passage illustrates the characteristic distinction between tannaitic legal positions and amoraic interpretative methodology regarding whether feeding consecrated property to dogs constitutes actionable "misuse" (*me'ilah*), with the *amoraim* offering competing explanations for the underlying principles that divide earlier authorities. The *tannaim* established foundational disagreements on multiple levels: Rabbi Yehudah and Rabbi Shimon disputed the interconnection between prohibitions against eating and seeing leaven (Exod 13:7), with Rabbi Yehudah deriving eating leaven from seeing leaven while Rabbi Shimon maintained a different interpretative approach; separately, Rabbi Yose the Galilean advocated for an expansive definition of consecrated property violations that encompassed even minimal indirect benefits, while the Rabbis (representing the majority tannaitic opinion) required clear, direct monetary advantage to establish actionable misuse. On the other hand, the *amoraim*, functioning as interpreters rather than legal innovators, provided three distinct frameworks to explain these tannaitic disputes: Rav Yosef located the fundamental disagreement in conflicting approaches to whether "something that causes financial loss" possesses monetary value, arguing that one position treats preventing expenditure on dog food as derivable benefit warranting a misuse ruling while the opposing view maintains that indirect financial advantage lacks sufficient materiality; Rav Acha bar Ya'aqov initially grounded the controversy in the Rabbi Yehudah-Rabbi Shimon leaven dispute, though he subsequently retracted this position when it created internal contradictions with his previously established interpretations; and Rav Ashi proposed that the dispute reflects the broader disagreement between Rabbi Yose the Galilean's expansive violation theory and the Rabbis' restrictive approach, while asserting universal agreement that consecrated items should not be redeemed for dog food and that financial loss prevention lacks true monetary value. This dynamic demonstrates the essential distinction between the *tannaim*, who established competing legal principles and practical rulings, and the *amoraim*, who sought to identify the underlying conceptual frameworks that could systematically explain and harmonize earlier authorities while engaging in the self-correcting intellectual process characteristic of Talmudic legal discourse.

At the core of this discourse lies a philosophical and legal inquiry: should potential economic benefit be considered equivalent to its actual monetary value? This conceptual framework—known as the aforementioned principle "something that causes a financial [loss] is [considered to be] of monetary [value]"—carries significant implications for Jewish jurisprudence and legal reasoning more broadly. The text presents multiple rabbinic interpretations of this principle. According to the 1st-generation Babylonian *amora* Rav Yosef, rabbinic authorities hold divergent views on whether prospective financial gain should be deemed equivalent to its current monetary value. Some authorities maintain that potential value equates to present monetary worth, while others reject this equivalence. Rav Yosef's colleagues, the 1st-generation Babylonian *amora* Rav Acha bar Ya'aqov joins the debate, suggesting universal agreement that prospective monetary benefit equals actual currency. However, the editors of the *Babylonian Talmud* reject this position, claiming that subsequently, he retracted from this position and accepted that the issue was debated between Rabbi Yehudah and Rabbi Shimon. The third perspective comes from Rav Ashi, whose nuanced interpretation proposes consensus among all parties, that consecrated objects cannot be redeemed for dog food. Furthermore, he asserts that the potential monetary value of these objects does not equate to their actual monetary worth. Rav Ashi then characterizes the debate as a disagreement between Rabbi Yose the Galilean and other rabbinic authorities.

Rashi's analysis situates the discussion within the framework of the Mishnah's debate on the potential sale of materials that have become non-kosher. He engages with the concept of *kasherut* by addressing the case of a non-Jewish individual, regarded here as a "foreigner," who is exempt from discarding vessels tainted with leaven and permitted to "benefit" from them. Accordingly, he offers a concise summary of the Talmudic discourse, articulating its central tenets as follows:

ילוכד רמולכ - ימד ןוממכ ואל ןוממל םרוגה רבדו ןידופ ןיא אמלע ילוכד רמא ישא בר ןניסרג יכה רבדד היל יביחמ אל לארשיל יזחד חספה רחאלד םושמו חספב היל ןינבזמ אל ירכנל אמלע דות ףא רמאד ילילגה יסוי יברכ הל רבסד םושמ הליעמד אמעט אכהו ימד ןוממכ ואל ןוממל םרוגה ירמאד ןנברכ לעמ אל רמאד ןאמו ולישבת תחת וקיסהלו היקרפמל יזח דכלה האנהב רתומ ונמז אוה ןוממ ואל אהימ אתשה ש"רכ ןמז רחאל ייוהשל יצמד םושמ יאו האנהב רוסא חספב ןמח:

This is the version we hold: Rav Ashi said: the whole world agrees that one does not redeem [consecrated things that have been defiled], and a thing that causes financial loss is [not considered the same] as money. That is to say, the whole world agrees that we do not sell it to a stranger during Passover, because after Passover, it would be available to an Israelite, and they would not be obligated, as a thing that causes financial loss is not considered the same as money. And here, the reason for the misuse of consecrated things (me'ilah) is because he follows the opinion of Rabbi Yose the Galilean, who says that even within its time, it is permitted for benefit. Therefore, it is fit to use it to light a fire or to cook under but according to the one who says that he did not misuse [consecrated things], it is not the opinion of the Rabbis, who say that leavened bread on Pesach is forbidden for benefit. And if it is because it could be delayed until after the time, like Rabbi Shimon, here, however, it is not considered money (Rashi, comm. on bPes 29b).

In this passage, Rashi offers a concise synopsis of the issue at hand, aligning himself with the position of the *amoraim*, who diverge from the early rulings established by Rabbi Yehudah and Rabbi Shimon. The Tosafot challenge the genealogical progression from the *tannaim* to the *amoraim* in the *gemara*. They argue that "misuse" (*me'ilah*) does not apply, as non-Jews are allowed to benefit from the burnt ashes of *chametz* (*mutar be-hana'ah*). This prompts the Tosafot to implicitly conclude that a burnt *chametz* has no intrinsic value, thereby distinguishing this case from that of vessels, which retain their value until they are broken (Tosafot on bPes 29b, *Ein Podin*).

The Tosafot proceed to elaborate further on this topic in the following longer discussion:

בר ישא רמא ילוכד אמלע - השקו ל"רי: יכיה ןניסרג? יא ןניסרג ילוכד אמלע ןידופ, םא ןכ ונברל
יאו .ומצע שדקהה ירכנל ונרכמי סוקמ לכמ ,האנהב רוסא לארשילד בג לע ףא ?לעמ אל יאמא
ןיאד בג לע ףאו ,ןידופ ןיא :'יסרגד רמול שיו ?לעמ יאמא יליגה יסוי יברל וליפא ,ןידופ ןיא :סירג
ןידופ ליכאהל םיבלכל ,םוקמ לכמ שרי קיסהל תחת תבשילו .וכדפרישית דהכא תשודקד םדמי
ןיא ןידופ ןמדרבנ ,ולא גזרו רבנ אלא שלא ליכאהלו םיבלכל ,אבל היכא ןיאד ןידופ אמדוארייתא,
(א"ע וט) תורוכבד (ק"פב) :איתנ אהד ;קיסהל 'אפי ןידופ ןיא ,ףוגה תשודק אכיאד היכא ונייהד:
אמליד .והערכה הדמעה יעבד םושמ ,ורבקי ותמ םא :יאהד יאממ :םתה רמאקו .ורבקי ,ותמ םא
?ורבקי יאמא ,ןידופ ןיאד ןידופ םישדקה ןליכאהל םיבלכל? והשתא יא אמעט םושמ ןיאד םושמ
(א"ע בכ םיחספ) ליעל ןכו .קוליח ןיא אתיירואדמ יאדו אלא .תבשילו תחת וקיסהל יואר אהו
אתיירואדמ אמלא .הקסהל וליפא יריסא[ו] הרותבש ןירוסיא לכ ,בלכל ךילשמ התא יאו :ןנישרד
ןיא קלחל האנהב .ואם תאמר לרבנן ,אמאי לא לעמ? הלא שדקה יוכל למכור לנכרי על מנת
שיסיקנו לפניו .ויש לומר דגזרינן ,שמא יאכלנו הנכרי ,וכהאי גוונא אמר במסכת ע"ז (דף טו
ע"א): אין מוכרין בהמה לנכרי על מנת לשוחטה וכו'. ומכאן מוכיח ר"י שהשהה חמץ בפסח
ודעתו לבער ,אינו עובר בשהייה ,דאי אמרת: עובר באכת ,אמאי מעל לרבי יוסי? הא מיד
כשיפדה אותו הוא שלו ,ומוהד רבי יוסי דשלך אי אתה רואה ,אלא ודאי לא עבר ,וטעמא משום
דלא יראה .הניתק לעשה ,ולכד אינו עובר כשמבער בלבוף.

Rav Ashi said that everyone agrees (bPes 29b): And Rabbi Yosef finds this difficult: How should we read the text? If we read "everyone agrees that we may redeem," then according to the Rabbis, does one not commit misuse (me'ilah)? Even though it is forbidden for an Israelite to derive benefit from it, nevertheless, the Temple treasury itself could sell it to a foreigner (nokhri). And if we read "we may not redeem," then even according to Rabbi Yose the Galilean, why would one commit misuse? One can explain that we read "we may not redeem," and even though we may not redeem it to feed to dogs, nevertheless, it is permitted to use it as fuel under one's cooking pot. As I expounded, here regarding items with monetary sanctity, we may not redeem them by rabbinic decree, and the Rabbis only prohibited feeding it to dogs, but where redemption is prohibited by Torah law, which is where there is inherent sanctity, one may not redeem it even for fuel; for it is taught in the first chapter of Bechorot (bBech 15a): "If they died, they must be buried." And it is said there: "From what [do we derive] that if they died, they must be buried?" because they require valuation and assessment. Perhaps because we may not redeem consecrated items to feed them to dogs? Now, if the reason is that we may not redeem them, why must they be buried? They should be suitable for fuel under one's cooking pot. Rather, it must be that by [a rabbinic prescription based on] Scriptural law (mi-de-oraiyyta) there is no distinction. Similarly, above (bPes 22a), we interpret "but you shall not throw it to the dog" [to mean that] all prohibitions in the Torah (she-be-Torah) are forbidden even for fuel. This demonstrates that by [a rabbinic prescription based on] Scriptural law (mi-de-oraiyyta), we do not distinguish between types of benefit. And if you say, this is according to the Rabbis, why would one not commit misuse? After all, the Temple treasury could sell it to a foreigner on condition that he burn it in his presence. One can answer that we decree [against this] lest the foreigner eat it, as is similarly said in Tractate 'Avodah Zarah (bAZ 15a): "We do not sell an animal to a foreigner on condition that he slaughter it, etc." From here, Rabbi Isaac proves that one who keeps chametz on Passover with intention (da'ato) to destroy it does not transgress [the prohibition] during that time of keeping it, for if you were to say he transgresses, why would one still commit sacrilege according to Rabbi Yose? As soon as he redeems it, it becomes his, and Rabbi Yose agrees that [the Torah says] "your own [chametz] you may not see" (Ex 13:7). Rather, it must be that he does not transgress, because "it shall not be seen" is separated from a positive commandment, and therefore one does not transgress when one eventually destroys it (Tosafot, comm. bPes 29b).

In this complex legal discussion, Tosafot examine the permissibility of redeeming consecrated items, with particular attention to the status of *chametz* during Passover. Their analysis centers on an interpretive difficulty raised by Rabbi Yosef regarding Rav Ashi's statement that "the entire world agrees" that it might be redeemed (bPes 29b). The Tosafot here argue that Rabbi Isaac problematizes Rav Ashi's assertion through a dialectical analysis of potential readings. If the statement that "the entire world agrees that we may redeem" a consecrated item is correct, a contradiction emerges: this permissibility of redemption would preclude the possibility of *me'ilah*, the "misuse" or misappropriation of sacred property. Despite prohibitions against

Jewish individuals, deriving "benefit" from such items, the Temple treasury would retain the prerogative to sell the property to "foreigners" (*nokhrim*). Conversely, the interpretation—"the entire world agrees that we may not redeem" consecrated items—presents difficulties for Rabbi Yose the Galilean's position, who says that even within its time, it is permitted for benefit. specifically regarding why one would still commit "misuse" under such circumstances.

The Tosafot resolve this hermeneutical impasse through a differentiated understanding of prohibited benefits. While the utilization of the item for the purpose of "feeding the dogs" remains strictly forbidden, its use as a cooking fuel might be permitted. This distinction is predicated on the concept of sanctity, with items possessing monetary sanctity facing rabbinically decreed redemption prohibitions specifically against "feeding to dogs," whereas items with inherent sanctity face Torah-level prohibitions (*she-be-Torah*) against any form of redemption, including for fuel purposes. The Tosafot's argument is further substantiated by a textual reference to Tractate *Bechorot*, which stipulates the mandatory burial of deceased consecrated animals (bBech 15a). The passage employs a form of *a fortiori* reasoning, positing that if these consecrated items could serve as fuel, then burial would be rendered superfluous. Consequently, a rabbinic prescription based on Scriptural law (*mi-de-oraiyyta*) appears to lack a discernible distinction between categories of prohibited benefits. As it appears, the Tosafot further delve into the absence of "misuse" (*me'ilah*) according to the Rabbis, by proposing that even engaging in transactions with foreigners that include stipulations regarding the burning of the item in one's presence. This invokes a parallel case from Tractate *'Avodah Zarah* concerning restrictions on animal sales to foreigners (bAZ 15a). In particular, Rabbi Yosef utilizes this exegesis to establish a significant legal principle: possession of *chametz* during Passover with destructive intent does not constitute transgression during the interim period of possession, even if property might pass from a Jewish to a non-Jewish individual. This conclusion is derived from the prohibition "it shall not be seen" as prescribed by Scripture (Ex 13:7) when destruction by "breaking-off" (*niteq*) is intended—thereby negating transgression when the *chametz* is eventually destroyed.

This intricate legal reasoning exemplifies the sophisticated hermeneutical methods characteristic of the Tosafot commentary, demonstrating the tradition's commitment to harmonizing contradictory positions through precise conceptual distinctions. This ambiguity gives rise to the question of whether it is permissible to break a ceramic object in order to cleanse it, or if there is an exception to this rule. This sophisticated discourse provides essential context for understanding the integrity of Pesach vessels, thereby establishing a conceptual foundation for the subsequent discussion between Rav and Shmuel.

Conversely, an examination of the provided text reveals that the Tosafot's discussion is characterized by a predominantly abstract and logical approach, as opposed to a historical or concrete political one. The Tosafot-analysis focuses on subtle conceptual distinctions regarding the redemption of consecrated items, particularly *chametz* during Passover. The argumentation progresses through a dialectical examination of potential interpretations of Rav Ashi's statement regarding universal consensus ("the entire world agrees"), without any reference to the specific historical circumstances in which such decisions were made. The fundamental distinctions in the text—such as the differentiation between objects with "monetary sanctity" and objects with "inherent sanctity," or between the prohibited use of sanctified things as "food for dogs" and their potentially permitted use as "fuel"—are founded on abstract principles and logical categorizations, rather than on practical considerations of governance or Temple administration. A particularly noteworthy aspect is the absence of any discussion about the actual role of rabbis in monetary or administrative decisions. When the text mentions the "Temple treasury" that could sell consecrated property to foreigners, the issue is treated as a theoretical principle within legal reasoning, not as a concrete institutional practice with political implications. It is a purely hermeneutical operation that reorients the question from the practical-political plane to the "logical-metaphysical" one. The discourse in its entirety remains confined to a dimension of legal abstraction, wherein apparent contradictions are resolved through refined conceptual distinctions, exhibiting no interest in concrete historical, political, or theological-political implications, as discussed above. This methodological approach discusses economics, but effectively "evacuates" the Talmudic discussion of any actual applicability, thereby transforming it into an exercise of pure logical reasoning. This inclination to abstraction has particular ramifications with respect of the religious intervention in the market, as is discussed in the next passage.

2.4 The Second Economic Discussion in Tractate *Pesachim* and the Comments of Rashi and the Tosafot

The subsequent discourse in Tractate *Pesachim* builds upon the preceding one, directing attention to religious intervention by rabbis. The Talmudic passage pertains to the subject of vessels that are no longer considered *kosher* for Passover:

הריזג, .ןנימב אלש והב דבעילו ,חספה רחא והניהשל ?יאמאו .ורבשי חספב תורידק :בר רמא והב דיבעו ,ונמז רחאל והל יהשמ לבא ,ורבשי אל :רמא לאומשו .ןנימב והב דבעימל ותא אמליד יניבז וושא :ידנכ ינבזמד והנהל לאומש רמאד ,הימעטל לאומש אדזאו .ןנימב אלש ןיב ןנימב ןיב אריבס ןועמש יברכ לאומש אהד ?והל שורדילו .ןועמש יברכ וכל אנישרד — אל יאו ,יכידנכא הוה ברד הירתא .היל.

Rav said: Pots should be broken on Passover. And why [so]? Let them spare them [until] after the period [of Passover] and use them with a different kind [of ingredient]? [Rav answers:] I fear that he will use it with the same kind [of ingredients]. Shmuel said: [pots] need not be broken [on Passover] but can be spared [until] after [Passover and] and used [then] with their own kind or with a different kind [of ingredient]. Shmuel goes according to his reason, for Samuel said to those who sell pottery: Make [the prices] of the vessels even and sell, for if not I will expound to you as Rabbi Shimeon [who allows the pots to be used during Passover]. [Why is this strange?] Shmuel (always) holds Rabbi Shimeon's (opinion)? It was in Rav's locality (bPes 30a).

The Talmudic passage features a dialectical exchange between Rav and Shmuel concerning the appropriate treatment of vessels that have previously contained *chametz* over Passover. Rav advocates for the destruction of such vessels, citing concerns regarding potential "misuse" (*me'ilah*) with their original contents. In contrast, Shmuel permits the preservation of these vessels for post-Passover utilization with either similar or different foodstuffs. This divergence in legal interpretation follows the previous discussion but here it acquires a socioeconomic, if not a political dimension through Shmuel's interaction with pottery merchants, wherein he leverages his interpretive authority to regulate commercial practices by threatening to promulgate, according to Rabbi Shimeon, that the pots may be used during Passover. In this context, Shmuel's actions bear resemblance to those of an *agoranomos*, whose job is to see that objects in the market are not over-priced, though the text does not explicitly state whether he has been formally appointed to this capacity. A juxtaposition is made between Shmuel's position and that of Rabbi Simeon, who adopts an even more lenient stance, permitting merchants to engage in exploitative pricing. The text culminates with a jurisdictional observation regarding the predominance of Rav's authority in the region under discussion, while it is implied that Shmuel held a similar position in Jewish Babylonia. As elaborated subsequently, this passage exemplifies the Talmudic integration of ritual, economic, and practical considerations within a framework of legal discourse. It demonstrates how rabbinic authorities navigated the intersection of religious ideals and material realities while exercising their interpretive power within specific sociopolitical contexts. Before proceeding with more conclusive observations about this reality, it might be useful to see how classic commentators, namely Rashi and Tosafot, expounded this text.

Although this passage does not seem related to the previous discussion, the connection is established by Rashi in his comment:

הדוהי 'רכ ,האנהב רוסא ונמז רחאל ףא ,ץמח :רמאד ,הימעטל בר - ורבשי חספב תורידק בר רמא. יקואד ,אדח :ימעט ירתמ היתווכ אתכלה תילו ;רוסא םגפל םעט ןתונ רבסקו ,והשמב היל תיאו םעט ןתונ :ל"יקד דועו .אוה תבורעתמ תוחפ יאהו .ש"רכ רתומ ונמז רחאל ,תבורעתד אתכלה אבר ילכה ינפודב םעט גפוה ,חספה ימי וילע ורבעשמ הזו ,רתומ םגפל:

Rav said: "Pots should be broken on Passover:" Rav holds, according to his opinion, that chametz is forbidden even after its time, like Rabbi Yehudah. And he holds that something with a small amount of chametz still prohibits the entire object. He also holds that giving flavor that is defect (unpleasant or foul taste) is forbidden. But the law is not like him for two reasons: First, Rav Aha holds that the law regarding mixtures after their time has passed is permitted, like Rabbi Shimon. And this is a case of less than a mixture. Second, we rule that a flavor which is foul is permitted, and since the time of Passover has passed, its flavor is no longer present in the walls of the vessel (Rashi, comm. on bPes 30a).

In his commentary, Rashi presents Rav's position that pottery vessels should be broken "during Passover" (*be-pesach*), likely because he believed they could not be properly purged of absorbed *chametz*. He then analyzes Rav's position as being based on three principles: he follows Rabbi Yehudah's view that *chametz* is forbidden even after the Passover period ends; he holds that even minute amounts of *chametz* can render an entire mixture forbidden; he believes that even when *chametz* imparts a "negative flavor" (*pegam*), it still remains prohibited, as it acts as an "ontological" agent of impurity, whose nature does not depend on "taste." In his final ruling Rashi reiterates that he disagrees with Rav for two reasons: first, Rav Aha's position is accepted, following Rabbi Shimon, that mixtures containing *chametz* after Passover are permitted; second, the established rule is that substances giving off a foul or unpleasant taste are permitted, and after Passover, any absorbed *chametz* in the vessel's walls would no longer impart a positive flavor.

In this regard the Tosafot expand on Rashi's commentary and mainly discuss the question of whether an element contained in the vessel spoils the taste of its contents. In particular, they explain why this ruling will hold water, according to what is stated in Tractate *'Avodah Zarah*:

אקפסמ ארכישב ארבכע יבג (ב"ע חס ףד) ז"ע 'סמד ארתב 'פב - ורבשי חספב תורידק בר רמא
:ל"ס יאו ,חבשמ יחובשא ארכישב 'רבכעו ,רתומ וא רוסא סגפל םעט ןתונ :בר רבסק יא .היל
,רוסא הלחתכל לבא ,ירש דבעידב .אקוד סגפל ט"נד ,ורבשי ,ריפש אכה :רמאק ה"פא ,רתומ
,לבא ןיעב אוהש ומכ ומעט םגופש יפל ,ירש םתהד ,דועו .אמוי תב וטא .אמוי תב וניאש ןנירזגד
.ילכה ינפודב ההשש תמחמ אלא ,םגופ וניא אכה

Rav said that pots used during Passover should be broken (bPes 30a): In the last chapter of Tractate 'Avodah Zarah (bAZ 68b) regarding a mouse [that has fallen] into beer, there was uncertainty whether Rav holds (qasavar) that something that imparts a spoiled flavor is forbidden or permitted. And a mouse [that has fallen] in beer actually improves it. And if he holds it is permitted, even so he correctly states here that they should be broken, because something that imparts a spoiled flavor is only permitted after the fact, but initially it is forbidden, as we make a decree about utensils that are not "daughter of his day" [= cannot be used within 24 hours] because of those who are "daughter of his day." Furthermore, it is permitted because it spoils the taste as it is in its natural state, but here it does not spoil, except due to having remained in the walls of the vessel (Tosafot, comm. on bPes 30a).

In this passage, the Tosafot offer their commentary in the manner characteristic of their approach, employing rigorous, almost abstract legal terminology. Specifically, they engage with an apparent contradiction within Rav's pronouncements regarding the permissibility of vessels, even if not entirely cleansed of *chametz*. The analysis examines the tension between Rav's explicit statement in Tractate *Pesachim*, mandating the breaking of pots used "at Passover" (*be-pesach*), and a seemingly contradictory discussion in Tractate *'Avodah Zarah* concerning substances that impart spoiled flavors – in this case a dead mouse in a cask of beer. The hermeneutical challenge at hand concerns the reconciliation of Rav's stance on those that impart "spoiled flavors" (*ta'am lifgam*). The Tosafot also observe an ambiguity in Tractate *'Avodah Zarah* regarding whether Rav considers such substances forbidden or permitted, particularly in light of the paradoxical fact that a mouse that has fallen into beer, can actually enhance rather than spoil its flavor.

The resolution offered operates along two interpretive axes. The first introduces a distinction between "initial prohibition" (*le-chatchila*) and "*ex post facto* permissibility" (*be'diavad*). Accordingly, Rav might permit consumption of food that has been affected by spoiled flavor after the fact, while simultaneously requiring the breaking of vessels as an initial precautionary measure. This interpretation invokes the principle of issuing decrees regarding vessels that "are not daughter of his day" (*eino bat yomo*), namely that have not been unused within 24 hours. In a similar manner, the second interpretive framework delineates between immediate flavor deterioration in natural states and the specific phenomenon of absorbed substances in vessel walls. According to the Tosafot, the permissibility of this practice applies when substances naturally spoil the taste in their original state, but has clear economic implications. However, in the case of Passover vessels, the deterioration results from prolonged absorption within the physical structure of the container itself.

The Tosafot appear to prioritize the examination of the internal coherence between different Talmudic passages, yet they neglect to consider the implicit political and theological inquiries that underpin any religious intervention concerning market prices. This tendency is further exemplified in the third case that will be examined subsequently.

3 A Third Case of Religious Intervention: Waving Myrtle Branches for the Festival of the Tabernacles?

The third and final instance of rabbinic intervention in market matters discussed here specifically concerns the Biblical commandment of the "four species" to be carried during the Festival of Tabernacles (Lev 23:40-43). The discussion originates in Scripture, which mandates the waving of botanical elements in connection with the construction of a tabernacle on the 15th of Tishrei, serving both as a harvest celebration and a commemoration of the Exodus narrative. On the one hand, the Mishnah provides an inconclusive deliberation regarding the precise number of plants required for this ritual fulfillment. On the other hand, this ambiguity receives further treatment in Tractate *Sukkah* from the Babylonian Talmud (bSukk 34b), where the discourse shifts to the addressing of economic speculation—specifically, the artificial inflation of myrtle prices during the festival period. As examined below, the resolution manifests through the authoritative intervention of Shmuel, who counters market manipulation by threatening to legitimize the use of "cut off" myrtles, invoking Rabbi Tarfon's earlier ruling in the Mishnah (mSukk 3:4). This legal maneuver would permit economically disadvantaged worshippers to utilize less expensive, damaged specimens, thereby undermining the profitability of the sellers' speculative practices.

Though the text does not explicitly articulate the jurisprudential reasoning behind this market intervention, the contextual implications suggest a dual motivation: preserving universal religious observance while simultaneously promoting social equity. By leveraging religious authority to counteract price manipulation, rabbinic leadership demonstrated concern for both ritual accessibility and economic justice, ensuring that financial constraints would not impede religious participation among the less affluent segments of the community. This case exemplifies the culmination of a pattern wherein religious authorities assumed regulatory functions in commercial settings, when ritual observance and economic fairness converged as matters of communal concern.

3.1 The Ruling in the Mishnah (mSuk 3:4)

The reference text for this Talmudic discussion is a relatively straightforward passage from the Mishnah involving the 3rd-generation *tannaim* Rabbi Ishmael, Rabbi Tarfon, and Rabbi Aqiva. These scholars diverge in their opinions on the permissibility of cutting myrtle branches that are aesthetically imperfect for display, particularly in circumstances where an individual is evidently impoverished and possesses only two branches:

,םימוטק םינש וליפא .דחא גורתאו ,דחא בלול ,תוברע יתשו םיסדה השלש :רמוא לאעמשי יבר דחא בלולש םשכ :רמוא אביקע יבר .םימוטק ןתשלש וליפא :רמוא ןופרט יבר .םוטק וניא דחאו .תחא הברעו דחא סדה ךכ — דחא גורתאו

Rabbi Ishmael says: [One must wave] three myrtle [branches], two willow [branches], one palm [branch] and one citron, even [if] two [of the myrtle branches] are cut off and one is not cut off. Rabbi Tarfon says: Even [if] all three are cut off.

Rabbi Aqiva says: Just as [one must wave] one palm [branch] and one citron, so [one may wave] one myrtle [branch] and one willow [branch] (mSukk 3:4).

When this Mishnaic passage is examined through the lens of economics, it reveals an implicit question concerning the allocation of resources and accessibility in religious practice. Additionally, it raises a question of inclusivity, as the varying positions of the three sages reflect different approaches to ensuring that the ritual remains accessible to all community members, irrespective of economic status. In this regard, the discourse among Rabbis Ishmael, Rabbi Tarfon, and Rabbi Aqiva can be construed as addressing a fundamental economic concern: how should religious requirements strike a balance between ritual ideals and the practical constraints of cost and availability?

Rabbi Ishmael's position necessitates the use of a greater quantity of botanical materials—namely, three myrtle branches and two willow branches—yet it permits a certain degree of imperfection, allowing for the use of two defective branches. This approach can be regarded as a compromise between strictness and practical constraints. Conversely, Rabbi Tarfon's approach is characterized by a more lenient stance, allowing for the use of three defective myrtle branches. In periods of scarcity or among economically disadvantaged communities, locating flawless specimens might be financially unfeasible or even unattainable. On the other hand, Rabbi Aqiva's minimalist approach, which requires just one of each species. Since his ruling does not allow for defective myrtles, it is questionable whether this is the most economically viable position. By reducing the required quantities, Rabbi Aqiva significantly reduces the economic burden associated with fulfilling this commandment.

3.2 The second economic discussion the commentaries of Rashi and the Tosafot

This relatively simple text is commented upon on by the Gemara, which is specifically concerned with the biblical basis for counting the leaves of the different plants for the ritual *bouquet*. The discussion elaborates on the positions of the 2nd-generation *tanna* Rabbi Eliezer ben Hyrcanus and his students, the 3rd-generation *tannaim* Rabbi Aqiva and the aforementioend Rabbi Yehudah, and also involves the contemporary *tannaim* Rabbi Ishmael, Rabbi Tarfon, and the aforementioned Babylonian *amora* Shmuel, together with the Babylonian-born Palestinian *amora* Rabbi Ammi and a not better identified 3rd-century *amora* (?) called Bira'ah:[2]

"תובע ץע ףנע". דחא — "םירמת תפכ". דחא — "רדה ץע ירפ": רמוא לאעמשי יבר ,אינת
:רמוא ןופרט יבר .םוטק וניאש דחאו ,םימוטק םינש וליפאו .םיתש — "לחנ יברע". השלש —
דחא סדה ךכ ,דחא גורתאו דחא בלולש םשכ :רמוא אביקע יבר .םימוטק ןתשלש וליפאו ,השלש
ירפ" :רמאנ יכו ,תרמא ?תחא הדוגאב ןהמע גורתא אהי לוכי :רזעילא יבר ול רמא .תחא הברעו
:רמול דומלת ?הז תא הז ןיבכעמש ןינמו !"תפכ" אלא רמאנ אל אלהו ?"םירמת תפכו רדה ץע

והלוכ ימנ יעביל — יעב ןימילש יא ?ךשפנ המ ,לאעמשי יברו .המת החיקל אהתש — "מתחקלו"
בר רמא .לאעמשי יבר וב רזח :ימא יבר רמא האריב רמא .אל ימנ דח וליפא — ןימילש יעב אל יא
ינבזמד והנהל לאומש והל רמאד ,הימעטל לאומש אדזאו .ןופרט יברכ הכלה :לאומש רמא הדוהי
(ב"ע דל הכוס 'ב) ןופרט יברכ וכל אנשירד — אל יאו ,וניבזו וושא :אסא.

It was taught: Rabbi Ishmael says: "product of hadar trees" [implies] one; "branches of palm-trees" [implies] one; "boughs of myrtles" [implies] three; "willows of the brook" [implies] two and even [if] two [of the myrtles] are cut off and one is not cut off. Rabbi Tarfon says: [three] even [if] all three are cut off. Rabbi Aqiva says: Just as [one must wave] one palm [branch] and one citron, so [does he wave] one myrtle [branch] and one willow [branch].[3] Rabbi Eliezer said to him: if one could [say that the] citron [should be bound] with them in one bundle, would you say: and so is it written: "the product of hadar trees and branches of palm-trees"? Is it not only said: "branches"? Whence [do we know] that they are a hindrance to one another? Scripture says [at the beginning of the verse]: "you shall take" [implying] that the taking is complete and Rabbi Ishmael, whichever mind he has [he is wrong], since if he demands [that the myrtle-branches] are whole, why should he not demand that they [all] be whole and if he does not demand it why should even one [have to be whole]? Bira'a said in the name of Rabbi Ammi: R. Ishmael changed his mind. Rav Yehudah said [in the name of] Shmuel: the law is as Rabbi Tarfon [maintained]. Shmuel goes according to his principle, since Samuel said to those who sold myrtle: make [the prices] even and sell, for if not I will expound to you as Rabbi Tarfon (bSukk 34b).

The related discussion between Rabbi Tarfon and Rabbi Aqiva regarding plant integrity, is a paraphrase of the mishnah just discussed, but the text includes an intervention by Rav Yehudah referring back to Shmuel, evidently harking back at Tractate *Pesachim* which is offered as a precedent. Finally, a discussion offers an explanation why Shmuel may have decided in this way.

With respect to this relatively plain reassessment of the mishnaic discussion, the parallal baraita also includes Rabbi Eliezer's challenge to Rabbi Aqiva's position through a textual analysis of the Biblical source. Rabbi Eliezer explores the internal consistency of Rabbi Ishmael's ruling regarding the requirement for intact specimens, suggesting an evolution in his thinking as reported by the *amora* Bira'a in the name of the earlier Land-of-Israel *amora* Rabbi Ammi. The conclusion mentions Samuel's authoritative ruling that follows Rabbi Tarfon's position. This legal determination appears to have had practical market implications, as Shmuel reportedly used his interpretive authority to influence the lowering of the prices of myrtle branches, suggesting that he threatened to promote Rabbi Tarfon's lenient view if vendors continued to maintain their unreasonable pricing practices. This relatively linear ruling is accepted both by Rashi and the Tosafot, with some notable differences.

While Rashi only observes that these rulings should prevent any kind of economic speculation, since "they returned and sold - sell at the same price and do not raise their price because they are requesting three myrtle branches and pay" (וושא ימלשו ןיסדה השלש םכמ םישקבמש ינפמ םהימד לע ולעת לאו הושב ורכמ - וניבזו) (Rashi, comm. on bSuk 34b). The Tosafot provide a more complex insight as they discuss the three cases of religious intervention from Tractates *Sukkah*, *Pesachim*, and *Baba Batra* together:

לאומשד חיכוהל אבש- קוידה ןמ הז לכד ,ל"יו ?ןופרט יברכ אלא ע"רכ היל אריבס אל אה ,המית ול היה ,לוזב ורכמיש ידכ ,רבס אלד ידימב והל דיחפמ יאד היל אריבס .ןופרט יברכד 'ימעטל דחמ יחיכש ןימוטק אתלתד ,ןופרט יברמ יפט ידחפמ ,'ברדא .יחדו יפט לקימד ,ע"רמ םדיחפהל (א"ע ל םיחספ) העש לכ קרפמ השק והימו .ןופרט יברכ רבסד עמשת אל םלועלו ,םיטק אלד 'ונימב אלש ןיב ונימב ןיב והב דיבעו ,חספה רחא דע והל יהשמ' :לאומש רמאד 'חספב תורידק'מ אל יאו ,וכייניבז וושא' :ידנכ ונבזמד והנהל לאומש והל רמאד- הימעטל לאומש אדזאו' :ןנירמאו אלד אידהב עמשמו .היניעב היתיל יכ חספה רחאל ץמח ירשד- רמולכ '.ןועמש יברכ וכל אנשירד אכה אמלשבד ?היל רבס אלד ידימב םדיחפהל ול המל םתהד ,ל"יו .היל רבס אלד ידימב דחפמ ,ת"או .רקוי ליבשב וענמי אלו ,היוצמ הוצמה אהתו לוזב ורכמיש ידכ םדיחפמ היהד רמימל יצמ ינשמו; (םש) העש לכ קרפב ךירפ אנווג יאה יכד היתווכ והל שורדיל ,ןופרט 'רכ הל רבס יאו אינור' יבג (םשו .ה ףד) ארתב אבב שירבו 'הוצמ רודיה' םושמ חינה אכהד ,ל"יו 'הוה ברד 'ירתא' ,אל יאו !,סייפיאד יאמב היסייפ ליז' :רמאו אברד הימקל אתאו .ויתוחור עבראמ אניבר היפקאד סייפתנש יפל ול ןד אלש המ .'רדגש המ יפל לכה' רמאד ,יסוי יברד אבילא אנוה ברכ ךל אנינייד .תוחפב ול לחמו אניבר

But does [Shmuel] not hold like Rabbi Aqiva, rather than like Rebbi Tarfon? That is to say, all this is part of the discussion (diyuq) – in that it proves that Shmuel follows his own reasoning (ta'am), that he holds like Rabbi Tarfon, because, if he would have threatened them with something that he does not hold, to induce them to sell [vessels] more cheaply, he ought to have threatened them with Rabbi Aqiva, who is even more lenient and (the Gemara) refutes this. On the contrary, the threat from Rabbi Tarfon was greater, since three cut boughs (of myrtles) are more common than one that is not cut, in which case there is no proof that he holds like Rabbi Tarfon. There is a difficulty however, from Chapter Kol Sha'ah (bPes 30a), where, in connection with vessels on Passover, Shmuel said that "they should leave them until after Passover and use them either with the same species or with other ones" (bPes 30a) and we say: Shmuel follows his own reasoning, because he said to those vessel-vendors "lower your prices, or I will rule like Rabbi Shimon who permits chametz after Passover as long as it not still intact. [This is] a clear indication that he did not threaten with something that he did not hold by. And it should be said: there, why would he need to threaten them with something that he did not hold by? Because he did it here, in order to induce them to sell more cheaply so that the commandment should be more readily available, that people should not hold back from performing it on account of the exorbitant price. If he holds like Rabbi Tarfon, why did he not rule accordingly to them, as the inquired in chapter Kol Sha'ah (bPes 30a), where it answers: "it was Rav's territory." Here, he abstained from doing so because of the beautification of the precept (hidur mitzvah). At the beginning of Tractate Baba Batra (bBB 5a-b) where [the fields of] Ravina surrounded [the fields of his gardener] Runya on all four sides, and where the latter came before Rava who ruled: "go and offer him whatever he claims! Otherwise, I will rule concerning your case like Rav Huna according to Rabbi Yosi, who said 'It all goes according to the borders he set'." This is the reason he did not rule accordingly, because Ravina was appeased and permitted him for less (Tosafot, comm. on bSukk 34b).

The Tosafot here interrogate an apparent contradiction regarding Shmuel's jurisprudential methodology across tractates. The discussion centers on whether Shmuel authentically adheres to Rabbi Tarfon's lenient position regarding the four plants or merely deploys it rhetorically to influence market behavior. In particular, the Tosafot contrast Shmuel's threat to the vendors of boughs of leafy trees in Tractate *Sukkah* with his similar intervention regarding vessels contaminated with *chametz* in Tractate *Pesachim*. The discussion shows how the fundamental tension emerges from comparing these cases: if Shmuel genuinely follows Rabbi Tarfon, why not simply rule accordingly?

The Tosafot propose a contextual distinction: In the case of boughs of the four plants, restraint stems from considerations pertaining to the "beautification of the commandment" (*hiddur mitzvah*), namely the custom of glorifying the observance of religious practices through aesthetics. Conversely, the discussion in Tractate *Pesachim* unveils the authentic jurisprudential stance of Shmuel. A parallel case study on rabbinic authority and economic leverage, ultimately resolved through accommodation rather than doctrinal imposition, is also offered by the dispute between the affluent Ravina, whose fields surround the field of his poorer gardener Runya, as discussed in Tractate *Bava Batra*.

This passage once again demonstrates the intricate relationship between legal exegesis, economic intervention, and rabbinic governance. A notable aspect of the Tosafot's methodological approach is its commitment to reconciling seemingly disparate "Talmudic units" (*sugyot*) through meticulous contextual analysis. This highlights the delicate balance maintained between abstract legal theory and its pragmatic application in rabbinic leadership. However, the potential actualization of this legal construct within the contemporary context remains unexamined. Despite its political potentiality, the passage from Tractate *Sukkah* is examined in exclusively abstract, almost "apolitical" terms. In this regard, the Tosafot demonstrate that their analytical approach transcends mere textual harmonization, reflecting a broader ethical framework and an aspiration to situate Talmudic principles within a comprehensive moral and social context. Their interpretive strategy functions as a vehicle for ethical reasoning that bridges theological abstraction and communal reality.

4 The Talmud and three Cases for (a Jewish) Business Ethics

The three instances of religious intervention by the rabbis, previously analyzed, serve as classical examples to support business ethics derived from Talmudic teachings. The authenticity of these accounts is generally accepted, and it is posited that maintaining honest and stable prices constituted an early form of business ethics that the rabbis were keen to enforce. This involved extending laws against price fraud and establishing regulations to prevent excessive speculation on essential goods.

However, the strictly legal nature of the commentary operated by the Tosafot in particular, but also the vast majority of later Talmudic commentaries preclude an appreciation of the intricate historical and political dynamics that underpin these texts, which are often integrated into Jewish ethical doctrine and employed in contemporary contexts to delineate principles of ethnic business. From this perspective, the Talmud's ethical observations are "distilled" to a more abstract level, suggesting a multifaceted relationship between religious authority and the modern capitalist market, but seem to overlook the less linear and more problematic relationship between rabbinical authority and state authority, irrespective of the latter's Jewishness. From a certain perspective, the possibility of integrating these Talmudic discussions within modern moral codes of conduct, or even within the principles of contemporary Jewish law (the so-called *Mishpat 'ivri*), depends on a historical, cultural, and political simplification of these pages. Nevertheless, as will be argued subsequently, it is precisely this intricacy that enables a more nuanced evaluation of the relationship between the Talmud and political authority. Talmudic jurisprudence establishes a fundamental requirement for transparency in commercial transactions: vendors must disclose any concealed defects in their merchandise. Accordingly, transactions that are conducted under deceptive circumstances shall be considered null and void.

During the Talmudic period in ancient Israel, essential commodities—specifically wines, oils, and flour varieties—were subject to regulations that prohibited intermediary profits. These necessities required direct producer-to-consumer sales to maintain affordability. (Herman, 2012, p. 179) Furthermore, Talmudic law imposed strict limitations on profit margins for necessities, capping them at one-sixth above cost, reflecting an ancient preoccupation with price stability that resonates with modern economic regulatory frameworks (tBM 3:26 and bBM 40a-b). This ethical framework directly contradicts contemporary business ideals that often valorize those who acquire merchandise at minimal cost, engage in strategic hoarding, and maximize selling prices. The Talmud explicitly censures practices including speculative food hoarding, measurement manipulation, charging excessive interest, and unjustified price escalation. Talmudic literature praises historical figures such as Shmuel's father, who maintained consistent pricing throughout the year by charging post-harvest rates regardless of seasonal fluctuations, thereby enhancing market stability (bBB 90b).

As explored by Hershey H. Friedman, the Talmud demonstrates concern for equitable market pricing with all possible ethical ramifications of this principle. (Friedman, 1984, 2000, 2004) For example, even in instances where verbal agreements lacked legal enforceability under ancient Talmudic jurisprudence, individuals were ethically bound to honor their commitments. Individuals who failed to uphold their commitments were regarded as "lacking in honesty," though formal sanctions were not imposed in instances where financial transactions had not yet been initiated (bBM 49a). In this regard, rabbinic authorities engaged in discourse concerning the ethical ramifications that ensue when market conditions undergo alteration subsequent to the formation of verbal agreements. However, certain commentators, including Rashi, contend that ethical violations occur exclusively when agreement retractions stem from factors unrelated to market fluctuations. On the other hand,the Tosafot contend that the termination of verbal agreements constitutes an ethical transgression, irrespective of market dynamics. Conversely, the contemporary Jewish legal consensus offers a nuanced perspective that occupies a middle ground between these two positions. While acknowledging the potential reduction in ethical responsibility resulting from changing market conditions, it also affirms the principle of honoring verbal agreements, a concept often referred to as "the way of the pious" (*midat chasidut*).

The Talmudic principles delineated in these passages encompass foundational elements of ethical commerce, including transparency, honesty, and reliability. First, the Talmud considers disclosure requirements imperative, as the prohibition against concealing product defects, which establishes an early precedent for consumer protection principles found in contemporary business ethics. Second, the concept of price regulation and ensuring fair pricing is paramount, as the limitation of markups on essential goods to one-sixth exemplifies a recognition of ethical considerations in pricing strategies, particularly for necessities. Third, the direct-to-consumer model for essentials is noteworthy, as the requirement for direct sales of necessities signifies an early intervention against market inefficiencies and artificial price inflation through intermediaries.

Yet these principles extend beyond mere commercial guidelines into a comprehensive vision of communal governance. The Talmud's condemnation of speculation and market manipulation—evidenced by ethical critiques of hoarding and the artificial creation of scarcity—reveals not just economic prudence but a political theology that subordinates market forces to communal welfare. The emphasis on verbal commitments transcends contractual ethics, establishing covenant as a foundational political concept that binds individuals to collective responsibility. By distinguishing between minimum ethical requirements and "the way of the pious," the Talmud does not merely suggest aspirational conduct, but establishes a hierarchical social order, with material consequences for community organization and resource distribution.

To interpret these teachings as merely religious prescriptions or ethical guidelines divorced from their political context encourages a potential misreading of the Talmud. Such a "reductionistic" approach strips the Talmud of its radical vision for structuring power relations and economic systems. This de-politization transforms communal obligations into individual consumer choices and converts systemic critiques of exploitation into personal ethical dilemmas. The consequences of this reductionism are significant: it neutralizes the Talmud's challenge to market supremacy, obscures its vision of economic justice as constitutive of divine covenant, and ultimately renders its wisdom compatible with the very systems of exploitation it sought to constrain. On the other hand, the political-theological dimension of these teachings demands we recognize that Talmudic business ethics aren't simply compatible with modern commercial contexts—they fundamentally question the moral legitimacy of markets unbound from communal obligation and divine accountability.

5 Jewish Self-Government in Talmudic Times: A Theological-Political Fantasy?

The theological-political dimension is the fundamental interpretive framework through which Talmudic business ethics should be understood. This framework transcends simplistic historical or moralistic readings that have predominated in much contemporary scholarship and instead requires engagement with Leo Strauss's insights on esoteric writing and political philosophy. In his seminal work, *Persecution and the Art of Writing*, Strauss argued that philosophical texts written under conditions of persecution contain both exoteric (public) and esoteric (hidden) meanings. In this way the Talmudic economic regulations could be read as texts composed under complex conditions of political subordination. The rabbis, like the philosophers Strauss examined, developed sophisticated techniques of writing between the lines—creating teachings that satisfied external authorities while conveying more radical messages to discerning readers.

This "Straussian perspective" transforms our understanding of Talmudic business ethics. What appears as merely ethical guidance on fair pricing, consumer protection, and market regulation reveals itself as a sophisticated political theology. The challenge of evaluating Talmudic economic counsel necessitates asking whether these texts represent genuine historical practices or instead constitute a religious ideal formulated through intricate negotiations between rabbinic and secular exilic authorities. The rabbis, operating under Roman and later Persian domination, could not openly challenge imperial economic systems. Instead, they encoded their critique within seemingly apolitical ethical teachings. Their discussions of price controls and market manipulation contain a veiled critique of imperial economic exploitation. Their emphasis on communal welfare over individual profit margins represents not merely ethical guidance, but a counter-political vision—an alternative conception of economic order grounded in divine authority rather than imperial power.

Following Strauss's method, we must recognize the Talmud's "noble lie"—its presentation of radical economic ideas under the guise of religious ethics. The seemingly abstract distinction between "minimum requirements" and "the way of the pious" implies political implications about the legitimacy of the existing economic arrangements. The Talmud's economic regulations constitute what Strauss might term a "political teaching that dares not speak its name." In this respect, appreciating a theological-political nuance to these texts is fundamental to our understanding of the nexus between religious authority, economic regulation, and political power in the formative period of rabbinic Judaism. It challenges contemporary readings that depoliticize these teachings, transforming them into individual ethical maxims compatible with modern capitalism. The "Straussian perspective" reveals instead a comprehensive political vision encrypted within religious language—a vision that questioned the very foundations of imperial economic systems while appearing to offer mere ethical guidance to the faithful. Only by recovering the political-theological dimension can we grasp the full significance of these teachings as both religious instruction and political resistance. From an intellectual history perspective, the Talmudic narratives, depicting amoraic price regulation, substantiate several critical propositions. These propositions include the social prominence of rabbinic figures within Persian society, their asserted or desired juridical-administrative capacity to intervene in market mechanisms, and their putative ability to exert market influence through various forms of institutional pressure. (Herman, 2012, p. 179) However, when evaluating these narratives, particularly with regard to their historicity and the rhetorical function they serve within the broader Talmudic corpus, a critical eye is essential. The Aramaic injunction to "establish fair pricing for your vessels" is documented in Tractate *Pesachim*, which constitutes a directive within Talmudic literature (bPes 30b) and which Rashi glosses as prohibiting price escalation "more than their value," namely beyond intrinsic value (Rashi, comm. on bPes 30b). These observations in Tractate *Pesachim* highlight a parallel narrative in Tractate *Sukkah* (bSukk 34b), which exhibits similar rhetorical patterns, and which we examined above. This suggests that the primary intent was not historical documentation, but rather, the strategic use of literary construction to serve specific ideological purposes.

However, the historical assessment of the Exilarchate's economic authority remains a subject of significant contention in contemporary scholarship. While

Beer attributes substantial market oversight powers to the Exilarch, including the appointment of a market supervisor (*agoranomos*), Herman contends that "any economic power that the Exilarchs may have possessed would seem to have been quite informal and perhaps local." (Herman, 2012, p. 179; cf. Beer, 1976, pp. 123–126) This is a limitation tacitly acknowledged in the Babylonian Talmud's characterization of certain interventions as occurring only within "Rav's locality" (bPes 30b). Furthermore, Herman acknowledges that this is distinct from the realm of the direct economic interests of the Exilarchs themselves, their estates, and investments. There is ample evidence that their interests were substantial, and that the Exilarchs would have closely guarded them well. On the other hand, the disagreement between Beer and Herman complicates attempts to reconstruct the historical reality behind the Talmudic narratives. The historical validity of economic regulatory episodes described in Tractates *Baba Batra*, *Pesachim*, and *Sukkah* must be analyzed on several levels: First, because of the names of the Babylonian amoraim mentioned in them, these texts facilitate precise dating within the Talmudic corpus, thereby providing crucial information about the compositional history of the Babylonian Talmud and its engagement with economic matters. Second, from a historical perspective, they offer a means for evaluating the Exilarch's actual authority within Persian and subsequently Muslim political structures. However, their reliability remains contingent on the historical reliability of the source that reports them (the Babylonian Talmud). Thirdly, from a theological perspective or, more precisely, a theological-political perspective, these texts facilitate an assessment of the imaginative dimension inherent in these passages, that function both to substantiate the legal determinations of fair prices and to articulate the theological-political aspirations of a rabbinical elite operating "in exile."

Regardless of their historicity, these passages reflect the rabbinic fantasy of their active economic intervention in a non-Jewish political reality. Yet, they should not be disregarded as mere fiction; rather, they should be understood as potent ideological formulations through which rabbinic authorities negotiated their relationship to the ruling power in a diasporic contexts. The evolution of the Exilarchate has undergone significant scholarly reinterpretation across generations of scholarship. As Herman notes in his review of previous German scholarship, the famous *Wissenschaft des Judentums* conceptualized the Exilarchate as a Jewish autonomous space within a non-Jewish hegemony or, more particularly, as "a king without a kingdom; a leader without a people" (*ein König ohne Königreich, ein Fürst ohne Volk*). (Herman, 2012, p. 3) Historical sources regarding this institution remain ambiguous and fragmentary. Indeed, the rabbinic authorities themselves did not conceptualize the Exilarchate as a prototypical Jewish statehood. Furthermore, the distribution of references to the Exilarchate within the Talmudic corpus is uneven. It has been noted that the Exilarchate is not mentioned in some "special tractates" of the Talmud, namely Tractates *Nedarim*, *Nazir*, *Temura*, *Me'ilah*, and *Kritot*, and this clearly shows that these tractates were not studied in the Geonic academies, but rather suggests a complex pattern of reception and transmission. (Herman, 2012, p. 16, n. 81) The relationship between rabbinic elites and the Exilarchate consistently manifested complexity and tension throughout the Talmudic and post-Talmudic periods. According to Beer and Neusner, the Exilarchate wielded significant authority. Neusner (1969) theorized that nascent Babylonian rabbinic movements subordinated themselves to the more established Exilarchate, functioning effectively as "employees" while concurrently striving for institutional autonomy. This characterization of confrontational competition, although not original to Neusner, was nonetheless influential. Among Neusner's more provocative but less substantiated contributions is "his hypothesis that the Exilarch was involved in international political intrigue relating to the struggle between the Parthian and Roman empires." (Herman, 2012, p. 9)

However, despite the potential for illuminating parallels in how religious minorities negotiated political authority under Sasanian rule, scholars have frequently minimized the systematic comparison between the Jewish Exilarchate and the Christian Catholicate in the Sasanian era. As Geoffry Herman has noted, both the Jewish Exilarchate and the Christian Catholicate functioned as institutionalized religious authorities that mediated their communities' relations with the Sasanian state. Their existence reflects the empire's complex religious landscape and its strategies for managing diverse religious groups. The Exilarchate and Catholicate were pivotal in sustaining their communities' internal cohesion and negotiating their political and social rights within the Sasanian imperial order. (Herman, 2021, pp. 121–137; cf. Honarchiansaky, 2018) A comparative analysis provides a more nuanced understanding of the theological and political function of the Exilarchate as an institution mediating between religious communities and imperial authority. A multitude of episodes indicates the potential political dimensions of the Exilarch's authority, that extend beyond purely economic or religious functions. While the historical reliability of these accounts varies considerably, and many entail clear polemical or apologetic tendencies, their accumulative values is in the consistent theological-political vision of Jewish autonomy and authority, negotiated within imperial contexts.

CONCLUSIONS: FOR A THEOLOGICAL-POLITICAL APPROACH TO THE TALMUD?

Determining the historicity of the passages describing the rabbis' religious intervention in economic matters facilitates the understanding of the "economic" dimension of these texts, which extends beyond promoting specific business ethics to negotiating legal authority in exile. When read in a theological-political perspective, these passages also help in engaging the "post-Zionist" question recently examined by Shaul Magid and Menachem Loberbaum regarding "the necessity of exile." (Magid, 2018; Loberbaum, 2019) This critical intersection between economic regulation and exilic authority reflects what can be termed an "economics of exile," a distinctive modality of economic thought predicated upon the absence of sovereign territorial power and the necessity of negotiating authority within imperial frameworks not fundamentally aligned with rabbinic interests. The theological-political negotiations embedded within Talmudic business ethics represent more than mere incidental context; they serve as the essential hermeneutical key to understanding their formulation and function.

Talmudic business ethics must be understood within a broader theological-political framework, as these regulations served more than just to ensure market fairness. They acted as tools through which rabbinic authorities navigated competing power structures, including imperial and communal factions, and asserted their authority in the absence of territorial sovereignty. Economic regulation was not simply a moral concern but also a theological-political assertion, reflecting the ongoing negotiation of power between rabbinic figures, the Exilarchate, imperial officials, and marketplace participants. The Talmudic texts themselves preserve multiple voices that reveal contested claims regarding rabbinic economic authority, suggesting that this negotiation of power was never fully resolved. These regulations, particularly those on fair pricing, functioned as ethical, legal, and political claims, reflecting the complex positioning of rabbinic authority within the diaspora. The rabbinic approach to economic regulation was a "political theology of everyday life," blending theological principles with practical concerns of communal life, enabling authorities to assert their power without drawing the attention of imperial rulers. This negotiation of authority in the marketplace allowed rabbinic figures to demonstrate the relevance of their leadership while preserving Jewish identity within non-Jewish imperial contexts. Contemporary scholarship should move beyond simplistic interpretations and engage with the political and theological dimensions of Talmudic business ethics, as these regulations served as part of a broader project to sustain Jewish authority and communal cohesion in exile. Economic regulation was not simply a moral concern but also a theological-political assertion, reflecting the ongoing negotiation of power between rabbinic figures, the Exilarchate, imperial officials, and marketplace participants.

The Talmudic model of embedding theological concerns within economic practice offers valuable insights for contemporary religious communities seeking to maintain their distinctive values within pluralistic economic systems. These regulations, particularly those on fair pricing, functioned as ethical, legal, and political claims, reflecting the complex positioning of rabbinic authority within the diaspora. The rabbinic approach to economic regulation was a "political theology of everyday life," blending theological principles with practical concerns of communal life, enabling authorities to assert their power without drawing the attention of imperial rulers. On the other hand, contemporary challenges in Abrahamic finance also illuminate the ongoing relevance of the Talmudic "economics of exile," especially considering the Pro-Israel funding initiatives raised from Jewish communities outside of the State of Israel. Modern Jewish minorities in Western countries face questions regarding the extent to which religious economic principles can be maintained within secular legal frameworks. For instance, modern Jewish communities face challenges in developing investment strategies that conform to Jewish law principles while remaining economically viable within global capitalism, as Aaron Levine argued at the peak of the "yuppies economy" in the late 1980s. (Levine, 1987) On the other hand, the emergence of "impact investing" and Environmental, Social, and Governance" (ESG) criteria in contemporary finance also reflects a broader return to the integration of ethical and economic considerations that characterized ancient rabbinic discourse. ESG criteria claim for a socially responsible investment policy that implies a complex negotiation with the rabbinic right of self-defense, the need for developing a strong military, and the general recommendation to avoid investing in businesses that make armaments for the military, as suggested by Socially Responsible Investing (SRI) criteria. For instance, in light of the still on-going Hamas-Israel conflict, Pro-Israel investors have recently been encouraged to exercise heightened scrutiny when considering ESG investments. (Halkjaer, 2024; see also Leff, 2025)

Jewish communities grappling with the ethics of investment in Israel or questions of divestment from companies operating in contested territories similarly navigate the intersection of economic practice and theological commitment that characterized ancient rabbinic discourse. Similarly to the ancient past, this negotiation of authority in the marketplace allowed rabbinic figures to demonstrate the relevance of their leadership while preserving Jewish identity within non-Jewish imperial contexts. Modern religious authorities face analogous challenges in establishing the practical relevance of traditional teachings for contemporary economic life but also connecting them to the question of contemporary conflicts and the question of self-defense, foreign policy, and militarism as it also reflects a growing recognition that economic practice cannot be separated from ethical and theological commitment. The historical reconstruction of Talmudic business ethics thus provides crucial insights for understanding contemporary developments in Abrahamic finance. The rabbinic model of maintaining religious authority through economic regulation while accommodating imperial power structures may offer a template for modern religious communities seeking to preserve their distinctive values within globalized economic systems. The persistence of similar challenges across different historical periods and religious traditions suggests that the theological-political negotiations

REFERENCES

Bakhos, C., & Shayegan, R. (Eds.). (2010). *The Talmud and its Iranian Context.* Mohr Siebeck. DOI: 10.1628/978-3-16-151468-5

Beer, M. (1976). *Rashut ha-golah bi-yemei ha-mishnah ve-ha-talmud* [The Babylonian exilarchate in the Mishnaic and Talmudic era]. 2nd ed.). Bar-Ilan University Press.

Ben-Shlomo, E. (1998). The Obligation to Save Life. *Assia* 3 (2), accessible online: https://www.daat.ac.il/daat/kitveyet/assia_english/benshlomo.htm

Cohen, S. (2013). Rural Trade and Economy in Hellenistic and Roman Palestine. A Case Study from Tel Zahara. *Res Antiquae, 10*, 85–100.

Dal Bo, F. (2013). *Massekhet Keritot. Text, Translation, and Commentary.* Mohr Siebeck.

Dal Bo, F. (2018). "Economic speculation and the sacred," "Market prices," "Market intervention and the common good," and "Market intervention and the common good," in M. Satlow (Ed.), *Judaism and the Economy. A Sourcebook*, London, Routledge, 2018, 46-47, 48, 53-54, 69-70.

Elman, Y. (1994). *Authority and Tradition: Toseftan Baraitot in Talmudic Babylonia.* KTAV Hokoken.

Floor, W. (1979). Das Amt des Muhtasib im Iran—Zur Kontrolle der "öffentlichen Moral" in der iranischen Geschichte. In Greussing, K., & Grevemeyer, J. H. (Eds.), *Revolution in Iran und Afghanistan* (pp. 122–139). Syndakat.

Friedman, H. H. (1980). Talmudic business ethics: A historical perspective. *Akron Business and Economic Review, 11*, 45–49.

Friedman, H. H. (1984). Ancient marketing practices: The view from Talmudic times. *Journal of Public Policy & Marketing, 3*(1), 194–204. DOI: 10.1177/074391568400300114

Friedman, H. H. (1985). Ethical behavior in business: A hierarchical approach from the Talmud. *Journal of Business Ethics, 4*(2), 117–129. DOI: 10.1007/BF00383564

Friedman, H. H. (2000). Biblical foundations of business ethics. *Journal of Markets & Morality, 3*(1), 43–57.

Friedman, H. H. (2004). Talmudic business ethics: A historical perspective. *Business and Society Review, 10*(2), 23–47.

Friedman, H. H. (2012). The Talmud as a business guide. *MJAE, 1*(1), 38–48.

Friedman, H. H., & Adler, W. D. (2011). Moral capitalism: A biblical perspective. *American Journal of Economics and Sociology*, *70*(4), 1014–1028. DOI: 10.1111/j.1536-7150.2011.00800.x

Friedman, H. H., & Klein, Y. (2010). Respect for God's world: The biblical and rabbinic foundations of environmentalism. *International Journal of Business and Globalisation*, *4*(2), 129–200. DOI: 10.1504/IJBG.2010.030668

Garnsey, P. (1988). *Famine and food supply in the Graeco-Roman world: Responses to risk and crisis*. Cambridge University Press. DOI: 10.1017/CBO9780511583827

Gellis, H., Giladi, K., & Friedman, H. H. (2002). Biblical and Talmudic basis of accounting ethics. *The CPA Journal*, (September), 11–13.

Golinkin, D. (2003). The basic principles of Jewish business ethics. *Insight Israel*, *3*(1), 1–7.

Gross, S. (2024). *Babylonian Jews and Sasanian Imperialism in Late Antiquity*. Cambridge Press. DOI: 10.1017/9781009280549

Halkjaer Pedersen, N. (2024). The defence sector in focus: Common ESG risks. *Principles for Responsible Investment*. Accessed February 19, 2025, https://www.unpri.org/pri-blog/the-defence-sector-in-focus-common-esg-risks/12689.article

Herman, G. (2012). *A prince without a kingdom: The exilarch in the Sasanian era*. Mohr Siebeck. DOI: 10.1628/978-3-16-152138-6

Herman, G. (2021), In Search of Non-Rabbinic Judaism in Sasanian Babylonia. In G. McDowell (ed.), *Diversity and Rabbinization*, Open Book Publishers, 121-137, accessible online: https://books.openedition.org/obp/19940

Honarchiansaky, A. (2018). Connected Histories in Late Antiquity. Study of a Peace between the Roman and Sasanian Empires and Its Diverging Impacts on Christianity in Greater Armenia and Iran. Unpublished PhD Thesis, UCLA, accessible online: https://escholarship.org/uc/item/1r46d0h3

Jacobs, L. (1957). The economic conditions of the Jews in Babylon in Talmudic times compared with Palestine. *Journal of Semitic Studies*, *2*(4), 349–359. DOI: 10.1093/jss/2.4.349

Kahaner, L. (2003). *Values, prosperity and the Talmud*. Wiley.

Kushnir-Stein, A. & Holland, L. (2008). New Inscribed Lead Weights from Cesarea. In K.G. Holum – J.A. Stabler – E.G. Reinhardt. *Cesarea Report and Studies. Excavations 1995-2007 within the Old City and the Ancient Harbor*. British Archeological Reports, 209-211.

Lauffer, S. (1971). *Diokletians Preisedikt*. DeGruyter. DOI: 10.1515/9783110825398

Leff, B. (2025). Ethical Investing: Praiseworthy, or Obligatory? *Rabbinic Assembly*, published online April 1, 2025: https://www.rabbinicalassembly.org/sites/default/files/2025-04/ethical-investing-final.pdf

Levine, A. (1987). *Economics & Jewish law*. Ktav Publishing.

Levine, A. (2005). *Moral issues in the marketplace in Jewish law*. Yashar Books.

Loberbaum, M. (2019). The necessity of exile in Jewish political thought. *Jewish Studies Quarterly*, *26*(4), 382–401.

Magid, S. (2018). The necessity of exile: A post-Zionist theology. *Tikkun*, *33*(4), 30–35.

Mokhtarian, J. S. (2015). *Rabbis, Sorcerers, Kings, and Priests: The Culture of the Talmud in Ancient Iran*. University of California Press. DOI: 10.1525/california/9780520286207.001.0001

Neusner, J. (1969). Israel's politics in Sasanian Iran. *Jewish Quarterly Review (Philadelphia, Pa.)*, *60*(1), 80–90.

Rosenfeld, B. Z & Menirav, J. (2005). *Markets and Marketing in Roman Palestine*. Brill.

Rosenfeld, B. Z. (2010). *Torah Centers and Rabbinic Activity in Palestine, 70-400 CE. History and Geographic Distribution*. Brill. DOI: 10.1163/ej.9789004178380.i-322

Schwartz, M. S. (2012). A Jewish approach to business ethics. *Philosophical Studies*, *2*(10), 754–766.

Secunda, S. (2013). *The Iranian Talmud: Reading the Bavli in Its Sasanian Context*. University of Pennsylvenia Press.

Smith, Q. (2018). *The Geonim of Babylonia and the shaping of medieval Jewish culture*. Yale University Press.

Sperber, D. (1977). On the office of the Agoranomos in Roman Palestine. *ZDMG*, *127*, 227–243.

Tamari, M. (1987). *With all your possessions: Jewish ethics and economic life*. The Free Press.

Tamari, M. (1991). *In the marketplace: Jewish business ethics*. Targum.

Tamari, M. (1995). *The challenge of wealth*. Jason Aronson Inc.

KEY TERMS AND DEFINITIONS

Aedile: A Roman official analogous to the Greek *agoranomos*, traditionally tasked with the regulation of markets, prices, and measures.

Agoranomos (ἀγορανόμος): A Greek term for a "market overseer" or "market inspector," an elected official similar to the Roman *aedile*, responsible for regulating markets, prices, and measures.

Amora (plural: Amoraim): A rabbinic sage from the Babylonian or Palestinian Talmudic period (3rd to 6th centuries CE) who interpreted and elaborated upon the Mishnah.

Baraita (plural: Baraitot): A "Talmudic external source," referring to traditions or teachings external to the Mishnah but cited and discussed within the Talmud and provide additional tannaitic teachings, often serving as a basis for amoraic discussion or dispute resolution.

Catholikos: The head of the Nestorian Christian minority in the Sasanian empire, mentioned as a parallel to the Jewish Exilarchate

Chametz (ץמח): "Leaven" or other leavening agents, specifically prohibited for utilization during Passover.

Davar hagram le-mamon ke-mamon dami (**ימד ןוממכ ןוממל םרוגה רבד**)**:** A principle meaning "something that causes a financial [loss] is [considered to be] of monetary [value]".

Devey Nas'yah (**האישנ יבד**)**:** An Aramaic term meaning "of the House of the Patriarch," used in the Babylonian Talmud to refer to the institution that appointed the *agoranomos*.

Eino bat yomo (**ומוי תב וניא**)**:** Literally "not daughter of his day," referring to utensils that have not been unused within 24 hours.

Exilarchate (*reysh galuta*): The institution of the Exilarch, the head of the Jewish community in Babylonia during the Sasanian and later Muslim periods, described as a Jewish autonomous space.

Feast of Tabernacles (Sukkot): A Biblical commandment involving the waving of "four species" on the 15th of Tishrei, serving as a harvest celebration and Exodus commemoration.

Gemara (ארמג): The Aramaic discussion and elaboration on the Mishnah, forming the larger part of the Talmud.

Haqdashot (תושדקה): "Consecrated items" or "sacred property"

Hiddur mitzvah (הוצמ רודיה): The "beautification of the commandment," referring to glorifying religious practices through aesthetics or exemplary performance.

Hona'ah (האנוה): "Fraud," specifically in the context of sale profits exceeding 16%.

Kasherut (תורשכ): The concept of ritual fitness or suitability, particularly in the context of Jewish dietary laws.

Me'ilah (הליעמ): "Misuse of property" or "misappropriation of sacred property"

Midat chasidut (תודיסח תדימ): "The way of the pious," referring to the principle of honoring verbal agreements even when not legally enforceable.

Mishnah (הנשמ): A foundational compilation of Jewish oral law, redacted around the 2nd century CE, serving as the primary text upon which the Gemara elaborates.

Mishpat 'ivri (ירבע טפשמ): "Contemporary Jewish law."

Muchtasib: An institution in Islamic times similar to the *agoranomos* or Roman *aedile*.

Mutar be-hana'ah **(האנהב רתומ):** A phrase meaning "permitted for benefit."

Nasi (אישנ): A Hebrew term for "prince" or "head," specifically referring to the head of the Jewish law school in the Land of Israel, often associated with Yehudah haNasi.

Palestinian Patriarchate: A Jewish leadership body in Roman Palestine (396–429 CE), mentioned as a potential referent for discussions in the Jerusalem Talmud.

Pagam (םגפ): A "negative flavor" or "unpleasant or foul taste".

Rabbi: A Jewish religious teacher or master, often referring to the sages whose teachings are recorded in the Mishnah and Talmud.

Rashi: A prominent medieval French commentator (Rabbi Shlomo Yitzchaki, 1040–1105 CE) whose commentaries on the Talmud are foundational for its study.

Rav: A prominent 1st-generation Babylonian *amora* (Rav Abba bar Aybo), also known as Abba Arikha.

Sasanian Persia: The historical empire (c. 224–651 CE) that ruled over Babylonia, providing the political and geographical context for rabbinic authority and the Jewish Exilarchate.

Shabbat (תבש): The Jewish Sabbath, a day of rest and spiritual observance, prohibited for commercial activities.

Shmuel: A prominent 1st-generation Babylonian *amora* (Shmuel of Nehardea), central to all three case studies of rabbinic market intervention.

Sugyot (תויגוס): "Talmudic units," referring to distinct discussions or passages within the Talmud.

Talmud: A central text of Rabbinic Judaism, a compilation of Jewish laws and narratives, consisting of the Mishnah and the Gemara.

Tanna (plural: Tannaim): A rabbinic sage from the Mishnaic period (1st to 3rd centuries CE) whose teachings are recorded in the Mishnah and other Tannaitic literature.

Torah (הרות)::

The foundational sacred text of Judaism: comprising the first five books of the Hebrew Bible, containing divine commandments and narratives.

Tosafot: A collection of medieval commentaries on the Talmud (12th-14th century French and German scholars), often engaging in dialectical analysis of Rashi's commentary and the Gemara.

Wāzārbed (דֵּבְראָזָן): A Persian figure whose title was rendered in Greek as *agoranomos* in a bilingual stele.

Wissenschaft des Judentums: A 19th-century German-Jewish intellectual movement dedicated to the critical, scholarly study of Jewish history, literature, and culture.

ENDNOTES

1 Notably, in Hebrew, "prices" and "measures" are called *shu'urim* and *middot* respectively, while in Aramaic they are *shi'ura* and *mekhilata*, with a notable change in terminology for "measures."

2 This is probably not the name of an individual but rather a locality. The city of Bira'ah (or Biria or Birai) was situated just north of Zefat and can modernly be identified with the ancient settlement of Baram. In some other passages from the Talmud, *Bira'ah* appears as a place name ("of Bira") with the names Jeremiah (bEruv 25a), 'Ulla (bTaan 31a), Nathan (bKet 75a), or others. In the specific case, Ms Varican 134 offers as a variant the name "Ulla of Bira'ah" that probably is the most correct version (I owe this suggestion to Prof. Dr Tal Ilan). Cf. Rosenfeld 2010, 147-148.

3 Up to this point, the *gemara* summarizes the passage from the Mishnah I have examined previously. The actual *baraita* begins with "Rabbi Ishmael, whichever mind he has" a few lines below.

Chapter 8
Securities Enforcement Across Abrahamic Legal Systems

Phil Lieberman
https://orcid.org/0000-0001-6883-8115
Vanderbilt University, USA

ABSTRACT

Enforcement of securities laws is increasingly an international—indeed, a global—affair. On the one hand, this globalization broadens funding streams and facilitates capital formation across borders, allowing new ideas to flourish amidst growing financial liquidity. On the other, globalization engenders a host of problems at the national and international level, from a single nation's tracking the ultimate beneficial owner of securities in order to avoid benefiting their competitors or enemies (whether state or non-state actors) to investing in commodities or concerns forbidden in one country or another. The rise of cryptocurrencies has exacerbated some of these problems. In this chapter, I will discuss international collaboration across countries whose financial regimes are explicitly guided by one or another Abrahamic legal tradition to show how mutual recognition across Abrahamic lines can lead to more effective securities law enforcement—and hence enhanced capital formation—within any individual country.

INTRODUCTION

Nation-states in the Middle East have spent decades working on arrangements that might reduce political and military conflict. In this article, I will explore whether financial market integration—particularly through the mutual recognition of securities

DOI: 10.4018/979-8-3373-1887-5.ch008

laws—might bring together the markets of "Abrahamic" countries. I will contend that such recognition could not only increase incentives for these nations to develop functional political arrangements, but also create a practical pathway toward them by overcoming systemic differences between their legal and regulatory frameworks.

I will begin by comparing the financial and securities regulatory regimes shaped to varying degrees by Jewish and Islamic law. From there, I will examine mutual recognition as a tool for cross-border participation in capital markets, contrasting it with foreign treaties and other formal arrangements. While I will consider the benefits and drawbacks of mutual recognition—especially the role of relative market size in determining its effectiveness—I will also address alternative mechanisms that may achieve similar ends. These include shared transnational standards (such as those developed by AAOIFI and IOSCO, to be discussed below), regulatory competition, and private-market initiatives that can reduce transaction costs and facilitate cross-border investment without formal governmental accords. In doing so, I will assess whether these approaches, alone or in combination, might offer a back-door route to closer political and economic cooperation across the Abrahamic divide.

ABRAHAMIC FINANCE: JEWISH AND ISLAMIC LEGAL STRUCTURES

Jewish law and Islamic law differ significantly from one another where commercial law is concerned, not to mention where financial instruments come into play. Additionally, neither of these systems is a monolith; regional, scholastic and methodological differences within each of these systems mean that there is no single approach within Jewish or Islamic law to some of the most fundamental aspects of contemporary financial instruments. Further, the impress of Jewish or Islamic law on the legal systems of the Israel (in the Jewish case) or the Islamic world generally is imperfect. That is to say, even countries that aspire to a role for one of these systems in their national law do not pretend to incorporate that system without adjustment.[1] (Shetreet & Homolka, 2007; Stern, 2006) Across the Islamic world, the variety of national approaches to engaging Islamic law is highly variable: even in Saudi Arabia, where the impress of Islamic law is palpable to say the least, secular authorities supplement *sharī a* with regulations promulgated in the *shūrā* and reviewed by the Council of Ministers; on the other hand, Turkey has historically eschewed a relationship between Islamic law and the law of the state, although developments under the Erdoğan administration have betokened a shift in policy introducing Islamic law into Turkey's political and legal system.[2] (Otto, 2012; Shahed, 2020)

While Israel's July 218 Basic Law on "Israel as the Nation-State of the Jewish People" (*Medinat ha-leum shel ha- am ha-yehudi*) affirmed the Jewish "character" of the state, Israeli law has absorbed conventional Western-style financial instruments in all its elements. Indeed, Jewish law itself carved out a permission for individuals to borrow money at interest through a device known as the *heter isqa*—"a form of partnership agreement designed to circumvent the textual prohibition on interest in commercial transactions,"[3] (Klein, 1995, p. 543) and the *heter isqa* has been used extensively in private banking.[4] (Kopel, 2023) However, to the outside observer, the Israeli banking system replicates conventional Western-style loans. In his article "The Islamic and Jewish Laws of Usury: A Bridge to Commercial Growth and Peace in the Middle East," Daniel Klein argues that "The establishment of equity investment, interest-free banking services in Israel, modelled on the equity investment paradigm of Islamic banks, would demonstrate that the Israeli government was, at least in one small area, taking a step toward the letter of the religious law."[5] (Klein, 1995, p. 544) Yet the gap between Israeli law and Jewish (or, for that matter, Muslim) religious law extends well beyond the question of interest on banking deposits, however fundamental that might be to the Israeli economy.

Klein's attention to the possibilities for cross-border financial dealings is relevant here, because he imagines "The Middle East and a Future Peace: The Viability of Interest-Free Banking as a Fuel for Economic Boom".[6] (Klein, 1995, p. 547) On the other hand, the fact that yields on bank deposits in general have underperformed other money market instruments[7](Federal Reserve Bank of Kansas City, n.d.) likely means that even banking practices in Israel that might be held to toe the line on Islamic law would not be much of a financial draw.

On the other hand, Klein's argument that cross-border financial engagements could be a leading rather than lagging indicator of political accord is worthy of consideration. Indeed, as noted by Pierre-Hugues Verdier, mutual recognition or substituted compliance "is less likely to be effective where one country seeks to improve regulatory standards in the other,"[8] (Verdier, n.d., p. 56) suggesting that the intent of mutual recognition should not be for, say, Israel to find in one of its neighboring countries a more stable bargaining partner with a more robust regulatory environment, but instead an enhanced mutual demand for investment in the partner country. Where that investment follows the profit motive then it is likely that equity and/or debt investments, as opposed to banking alone, would be the engine of that mutual demand. Because cross-border securities activity ultimately relies on the movement of funds, banking and securities regulation are often two sides of the same coin; harmonizing one without attention to the other risks leaving critical channels for capital formation underdeveloped. Banking structures are obviously essential to the transfer of capital from one jurisdiction to another and therefore capital formation generally; linking securities enforcement with banking enforcement would direct those cross-jurisdictional funds into opportunities for capital formation. With this in mind, linking mutual recognition in banking regulation to mutual recognition in securities enforcement would increase the incentive for investors to take advantage of cross-jurisdictional banking and help develop securities markets in turn.

Verdier notes that multilateral mutual recognition agreements are generally effective only in the presence of robust supernational institutions that can manage substituted compliance and prevent delegation to member states. Thus, within the European Union (EU), mutual recognition may be effective as part of a broader financial market integration—whereas amidst the ASEAN countries, the absence of a robust institutional framework will demand a network of bilateral agreements rather than a single regulatory regime across ASEAN member states.[9] (Verdier, n.d., pp. 104–106) Transnational institutions in the Arab World such as the Arab League or the Gulf Cooperation Council (GCC) do engage questions of economic union, but the impress of these unions' on the regulatory regimes of their members is light compared to that of the EU. Further, Israel is a member of neither the Arab League nor the GCC, suggesting that any sort of mutual recognition regime would need to look more like the bilateral partnership between the US Securities and Exchange Commission (SEC) and Australia than that of the EU. Ironically, in seeking a partner for its own 2008 mutual recognition agreement, the US set upon Australia rather than European countries because of the EU's "complexity of its state-within-a-state framework."[10] (University of Illinois Chicago School of Law, n.d., note 113)

If the model for mutual recognition would be one of bilateral ties between Israel and individual Arab League or GCC countries, then the question arises as to *which* bilateral ties might yield the most mutual benefit. However, while bilateral ties might be useful, broader "passport" agreements that allowed capital formation across a host of cross-jurisdictional borders would be still more valuable. The costs underwriters and investment managers might bear in disclosure, registration, and marketing are lower amidst shared standards or mutual recognition—benefits that are multiplied by multilateral rather than bilateral ties. As we shall see, however, mutual recognition to date has focused on bilateral agreements.

THE US-CANADA AND US-AUSTRALIA MUTUAL RECOGNITION MODEL

The SEC's mutual recognition agreement with Australia from 2008 followed on the much earlier 1991 implementation of a multilateral jurisdictional disclosure system (MJDS) between the US and Canada[11] (U.S. Securities and Exchange Commission [SEC], n.d.-a) allowing Canadian issuers to register securities and make disclosures under the US Securities Act (1033) and Securities Exchange Act (1934). The intent of the MJDS was for Canadian issuers to extend share, debt, rights offers to American counterparties (and vice versa), as well as mergers and other corporate reorganizations that extended across borders. Scholarly analysis of the impact of the MJDS on the Canadian market identified not only greater cross-border issuances and increased market integration,[12] (Wiley, 2006) but also cost savings with a net present value as high as $2.7-3.4 billion in 2003 dollars over a ten-year period.[13] (Osgoode Hall Law School, n.d.) However, the benefits to the Canadian market extend beyond these cost savings: as Australia began on the road to mutual recognition with the United States, the Australian scholar Cally Jordan noted that "MJDS has in fact created greater pressures for harmonization of the two regulatory regimes and, on the Canadian side, prompted regulatory innovations which have attempted to keep Canadian markets in the global game."[14] (University of Melbourne, 2009) Likewise, the Australian Securities & Investments Commission saw a key role for mutual recognition in the Australian financial markets.[15] (Australian Securities and Investments Commission [ASIC], n.d., p. 17)

Of course, initiating a mutual recognition regime isn't costless, and the SEC chose regulatory partners with "*'high-quality' regulatory regimes*, and then only those that survive a reciprocal *comparability assessment* by the SEC and the foreign country." (Bateman & Beyea, 2008, p. 5)[16] The importance of choosing partners for substituted compliance agreements that maintain similar regulatory regimes pre-agreement lies in avoiding a "race to the bottom" whereby jurisdictions with more permissive regimes engage in regulatory arbitrage and end up reducing the stability and reliability of the more robust system.[17] (Bateman & Beyea, 2008, p. 5)

Thus, Israel's choice of regulatory partners is about more than proximity, just as the SEC began with Canada in 1991 but then proceeded in 2008 to partner next with Australia rather than, say, Mexico—although a 2021 request from the law firm Cleary Gottlieb Steen & Hamilton argued in favor of substituted compliance between the US Commodity Futures Trading Commission (CFTC) and a cluster of Mexican issuers concerning Mexico's Capital & Reporting Framework for non-bank swap dealers.[18] (Commodity Futures Trading Commission [CFTC], 2021) The Mexico request was part of a spate of substituted compliance determinations from the CFTC in 2021—involving Japan, Mexico, the EU, and the UK.[19] (CFTC, n.d.-a)The Mexican order was subsequently adopted as a rule in the Federal Register in 2024.[20] (Federal Register, 2024) From 2021, the SEC has published substituted compliance notices submitted to the Commission on its website; these emerge from non-US security-based swap dealers and specify the various transaction acknowledgement, reconciliation, capital, margin, and filing requirements based on the Securities Exchange Act the dealers have agreed to follow.

Despite its obvious advantages in enhancing liquidity, opening up a domestic market to foreign investors, and offering opportunities for domestic investors to avail themselves of opportunities in other countries, substituted compliance has its costs. One of these is undoubtedly the perception of "legal-cultural imperialism," the oversimplified belief of a national authority in the superiority of the familiar solution developed in its domestic system in comparison with the solution of a foreign state. This national bias obstructs an objective and neutral comparative analysis and prevents the emergence of a consistent system of deference decisions.[21] (Lehmann & Schürger, 2021, p. 11)

In bringing this to light, Matthias Lehmann & Jonas Schürger argue that individual states' economic and political interests tend to trump questions of the superiority of one or another actual legal system over the other.

MUTUAL RECOGNITION BETWEEN UNEQUAL PARTNERS

If only by virtue of their size, Australia and Canada could serve as the junior partner to the US. On the other hand, Israel's economy is smaller than that of some Arab states and larger than that of others, and the road to mutual recognition between Israel and other Middle Eastern countries would likely be perceived as a jockeying for dominance that did not plague the SEC's agreements with substantially smaller markets. Indeed, Klein's prescription for Israeli acceptance of interest-free banking that fell within the constructs of Islamic law could be implemented unilaterally by Israel and hence not be perceived as yielding politically to the desires of another particular nation's regulator. Mutual recognition would likely engender just such a perception, were, say, Jordan to recognize Israel's registration and reporting requirements in its own securities markets with an eye towards accommodating Israel's investors.

If some of the success of the United States' substituted compliance regime is due to the large size of the American capital markets relative to those in Canada or Australia, Israel and its Arab neighbors might not see the same benefits. By contrast, in markets where the participating economies are closer in size, different models can emerge. The EU, for example, operates under a form of mutual recognition that has shaped transactions between member states: goods manufactured in one country may then be legally marketed elsewhere within the Union. Of course, the European case is shaped by the existence of the EU infrastructure itself, for which European legal supremacy reduces mutual recognition into states' deference to the center. That is to say, mutual recognition under a transnational regulatory body with legal supremacy is not so much substituted compliance as federal regulation, amounting to a voluntary reduction in members' individual sovereignty.[22] (Dorf, 2008) A less-federated model of a "league" of participants, standing in between the two poles of mutual recognition seen in the relationship between the US and Canada of Australia on the one hand and that of supremacy by the EU on the other, could hold potential but has not yet been tested.

PHARMACEUTICALS: A PARALLEL WORTH CONSIDERING

It is important to consider *who* will bear the regulatory burden—or, conversely, who will benefit from a reduced burden where mutual recognition is adopted. Here, the contrast between the securities markets and, say, the pharmaceutical industry is instructive. Mutual recognition agreements (MRAs) between the US and Europe date back to 1995, at roughly the same moment that the securities industry was embarking on similar agreements. The US-EU MRA took more than 20 years to implement, and hopes that other industries would follow pharmaceuticals were dashed early on when negotiations in sectors such as road safety and cosmetics failed and international standards were not reached.[23] (Nicolaïdis & Steffenson, 2005, pp. 139–140) However, the effects of mutual recognition are different in different industries: pharmaceutical MRAs reduce regulatory burdens on corporations that might intend to jump through hurdles in another country in order to penetrate new markets for their products, whereas MRAs in the securities industry open up foreign investors to opportunities in the home country that might otherwise unavailable to them as foreign investors. That is to say, in the former case, pharmaceutical manufacturers have already developed their product and are seeking to reduce the heavy burden of replicating studies in yet another country; in the other, foreign investors who have *not* already paid the sunk cost of regulatory approval in the foreign country are simply seeking heretofore unavailable opportunities for investment. The difference between these two scenarios—in one case, avoiding a large sunk cost and opening new markets for a product; in the other, new investment opportunities—may explain why the 1998 Transatlantic Economic Partnership (TEP) was unsuccessful in bringing about mutual recognition in *any* of the service sectors identified in the TEP.[24] (Nicolaïdis & Steffenson, 2005, p. 140) This comparison matters because it highlights a structural difference between product-based industries like pharmaceuticals and capital-based industries like securities. In pharmaceuticals, MRAs can be a decisive factor in recouping high upfront research and development costs; in securities, by contrast, the primary ‘product’ is capital itself, which moves more fluidly across borders and responds differently to regulatory friction. This distinction helps explain why mutual recognition may succeed in one sector but face greater barriers in the other.

SIZE MATTERS

Mutual recognition among partner states of the same size can disproportionately increase the regulatory burden on one of the partners, as that partner becomes the preferred, lead regulator. While the decreased costs of regulatory approval would presumably encourage innovation, particularly on the margins where the costs of yet another nation's regulatory approval would otherwise be so expensive as to shut out a product from that market, mutual recognition could push innovation to the market where research and development costs were lowest and approval would be fastest and cheapest. Researchers have considered the possibility that this regulatory competition could lead to a "race to the bottom" where market participants seek the most liberal regulatory regime and the lowest-cost approvals, but despite their general disinclination towards mutual recognition, Wolfgang Kerber and Roger Van den Bergh conclude that such concerns tend to be exaggerated.[25] (Kerber & Van den Bergh, 2008, pp. 457–459) While these analyses have been used to highlight concerns about pharmaceutical regulation, they could be extended to banking and securities regulation, too. However, mutual recognition could lead to other factors attracting innovation to one or another member state, with the expectation that a product once approved could then be marketed elsewhere. Tax credits, good educational institutions providing research talent, or other characteristics of a favorable institutional infrastructure for development could result in a suboptimally high regulatory burden falling on one country where the size of its perceived market is enlarged by mutual recognition. Indeed, mutual recognition could result in free-riding by jurisdictions that wished to push regulation elsewhere by creating artificially high domestic standards. Nonetheless, since jurisdictions without an MRA would have required producers to bear the burden of product approval in *both* jurisdictions, the fact that a jurisdiction could free-ride on another jurisdiction's approval process and reduce its own domestic regulatory costs can be ignored. Rather, the MRA is akin to the removal of barriers to trade across borders—while allocating the gains to trade may present problems, it cannot be gainsaid that removing those barriers makes the pie larger overall.

However, even amidst an MRA, other barriers to trade may remain: Anabela Correia de Brito, Celine Kauffmann and Jacques Pelkmans argue that

> *MRAs therefore remove or at least reduce the costs of only one specific form of TBT (technical barriers to trade)...MRAs avoid (i) double testing, (ii) the uncertainty about a possible rejection due to slight differences in testing or verification, and the costly correction as a result of that, and (iii) the delays in terms of 'time to market'.* [26]*(de Brito, Kauffmann, & Pelkmans, 2016, p. 23)*

With this in mind, the successes of MRAs in research and development-heavy industries does not necessarily suggest that a reduced compliance burden across industries will in fact successfully integrate markets and develop all industries, but only those for whom double testing, differences in testing or verification procedures, or delays in time to market is a significant factor.

Further, the benefits of moving research and development or production facilities from one jurisdiction to another might not come into play where securities laws in specific are concerned. Mutual recognition might tie economies together by allowing industries to divide research or manufacturing across national borders, but debt and equity issuance does not travel as those research and development or production facilities might. Rather, where the securities markets are concerned, it is helpful to think of mutual recognition in its guise as substituted compliance. The opening of markets to another national jurisdiction reduces the barriers to entry of foreign capital and ensures market protections at a level acceptable to all parties, but broadening the pool of capital accessible by both markets does not necessarily lead to the increased formation of cross-border enterprises. With this in mind, the benefits of mutual recognition of securities markets may not be spread equally across potential partners.

Thus, the relative size of partners considering mutual recognition of their pharmaceuticals markets might not shape the way that mutual recognition plays out so much as the relative robustness of their individual approval regimes. Also, the effectiveness of that mutual recognition may ultimately depend on whether the approval process in one country can be translated in a manner that generally accommodates the approval process in the other; here, translation can be literal, as some terms in one country's regulatory process may not be intelligible in another country's home language, or procedural, as processes may not translate across borders either. However, mutual recognition arrangements in the securities markets seems to depend more upon the relative sizes of the markets of recognition partners. Once again, America's partners in mutual recognition agreements in the securities markets have all been with nations (or, in the case of the EU, a federal system) whose markets were significantly smaller than the US. The SEC could presumably shoulder the burden of collaborating with foreign regulators on substituted compliance, as well as the additional effort demanded of the SEC as senior partner in the agreement. However, mutual recognition in the securities markets among peers or near-peers might place excessive demand on one or another state's national regulator where market participants perceived that regulator to be the more lenient. National regulators may not want this even if it were to open up new pipelines for investment.

However, where a federal regulatory infrastructure exists, the parties to an agreement need not mention the elephant-and-mouse model for substituted compliance to be successful: in the American model, SEC enforcement at the federal level is in dialogue (and sometimes in tension) with enforcement at the state level. Likewise, the existence of a EU-wide European Securities and Markets Authority (ESMA) provides the benefits of a union-wide regulatory agency, but ESMA's supremacy over nationally competent authorities (NCAs) is soft at best: Niamh Moloney writes of the ESMA's powers that:

In theory, these powers allow ESMA to act in a hierarchically superior manner over NCAs, and so represent a significant ratcheting up of ESMA's soft supervi-

> *sory convergence powers. ESMA's approach to Articles 17 and 19, however, is best characterised by reticence – which can be associated with a range of factors including a lack of appropriate cases, textual ambiguities, litigation risk, astute ESMA positioning, and conflicts of interests relating to the location of Article 17 decision-making within the Board of Supervisors. But while a reticent approach by ESMA has attractions in terms of stable ESMA/NCA relations, and while a muscular and entrepreneurial approach could generate risks to legitimation and effectiveness were ESMA to drill too deeply into NCA autonomy, ESMA's reticence also has the potential to generate legitimation and effectiveness risks.*[27] *(Moloney, 2018, p. 280)*

Moloney outlines the Scylla and Charybdis between which EU regulators must navigate, suggesting that even attempts to generate substitute compliance in a robust federal environment are somewhat limited.

ALTERNATIVE MODELS FOR INTEGRATION

While these examples focus on formal governmental or supranational frameworks, there is a parallel track of integration that arises from nonstate actors and industry bodies, whose standards can influence market practice even without binding legal authority. At the same time, nonstate actors can contribute to mutual recognition by establishing transnational standards: the Accounting and Auditing Organization for Islamic Financial Institutions (AAOIFI), established in 1991, has set more than 100 standards defining *sharī a* compliance for "central banks and national regulatory authorities, financial institutions, accounting and auditing firms, and legal firms, from over 45 countries."[28] (Accounting and Auditing Organization for Islamic Financial Institutions [AAOIFI], n.d.-a) Although AAOIFI's standards are not binding upon their members, its influence has led some countries to adopt those standards. Yet even where those standards have not been adopted, market participants' awareness of *sharī a* compliance has a detectable effect decreasing the cost of equity capital.[29] (Karimov, Balli, Ozer Balli, & de Bruin, 2020) Generating broadly accepted standards is not the same thing as substituted compliance, but AAOIFI has secured a modicum of power to set the tone for what is and is not *sharī a*-compliant. Recent challenges to AAOIFI standards in the issuance of *ukūk* debt instruments could roil a $1 trillion market dominated by sovereign issuers, because those sovereign issuers would have to contend with the proposed revised standard.[30] (Davis, 2025; Saturna Capital, n.d.) Issuers would have to balance the increased cost of capital due to the heavier compliance burden associated with the proposed standard against the perceived reduction in demand from losing *sharī a* compliance as defined by AAOIFI if they were to ignore that revised standard.

The reach of the AAOIFI is broad; 2025 saw the St. Petersburg International Commodity Exchange discuss a self-audit for compliance with AAOIFI standards so that commodity suppliers from Iran, UAE, Malaysia and Turkey could join the exchange.[31] (Realnoe Vremya, n.d.-a)Through this compliance, this exchange intends to create a common platform for trade across Brazil, China, Ethiopia, India, Indonesia, Iran, the Russian Federation, South Africa, and the UAE (that is, BRICS) and the Shanghai Cooperation Organization (SCO) The president of the exchange, Igor Artemyev, noted in an interview that "We aim to establish a global financial agency within the BRICS+ framework."[32] (Realnoe Vremya, n.d.-a) However, despite its establishment of standards that shape the industry in the Middle East and beyond, AAOIFI is not a securities regulator in that its members are financial institutions rather than nation-states. Likewise, the International Organization of Securities Commissions (IOSCO) in Madrid has representation from national securities regulators from many Middle Eastern states, and IOSCO sets standards for those regulators.[33] (Marcacci, 2023) We may see AAOIFI or IOSCO's establishment of transnational standards as an alternative to substituted compliance *per se*: domestic markets fall under the purview of their local regulator, but international partners recognize the adherence to a shared standard. While shared standards do not resolve the duplicative nature of local compliance in multiple jurisdictions, maintenance of a shared standard in securities markets means that neither the investor nor the issuer needs to duplicate due diligence. This is a softer form of mutual recognition, perhaps akin to multiple jurisdictions relying on the same corpus of clinical trials data for pharmaceutical licensing. Shared standards, then, reduce the cost for market participants and can improve the market for capital formation[34](Elmghaamez, Ntim, & Yekini, 2024) —even if they do not eliminate replication on the part of national securities regulators. At the same time, some have pointed out the ability of IOSCO to facilitate mutual recognition/substituted compliance;[35] (Transatlantic Coalition on Financial Regulation, 2012) shared standards may be seen as one step in a larger process, if from the perspective of market participants perhaps the most effective in cost reduction and most helpful in terms of actual capital formation. Figuring out exactly where such a transnational body might sit could be a controversial matter, though likely easily solved by having shared offices.

The example of AAOIFI illustrates how transnational standards can emerge from institutions rather than governments. But integration can also arise more directly from market participants themselves, as seen in Klein's proposal for interest-free, equity-based banking options in Israel. Given that the members of AAOIFI are market participants—both corporate and sovereign entities—we may return, then, to Daniel Klein's suggestion that a move towards closer economic ties between

Israel and its neighbors could be driven by changes made by market participants. His argument that the introduction of interest-free, equity-based banking options could indeed encourage investment in Israel by investors from primarily Muslim countries reminds us that market participants themselves may not care about substituted compliance *per se* so much as bringing down their costs of capital. At present, there are two members of AAOIFI from Palestine—Arab Islamic Bank and Palestine Islamic Bank—but none who are based in Israel itself.[36] (AAOIFI, n.d.-b) Issuance of *sharī a*-compliant equity share classes or debt securities by Israeli corporate entitles facilitated by Israeli members of AAOIFI could allow the Israeli market to participate in a market that some have forecasted to be as large as $7.7 trillion by 2033.[37] (Allied Market Research, n.d.)

REGULATORY COMPETITION AND ITS EFFECTS

Another advantage of transnational standards rather than substituted compliance is the benefit of continued competition between national securities regulators: Roberta Romano argues using the example of regulatory competition between states in the US that "competition among securities regulators would not only protect investors, both large and small, but would also provide a superior regulatory regime."[38] (Romano, 2001) Romano describes the effects of regulatory competition using the US markets as a parable:

> *...if the SEC's disclosure regime is not cost justified, as the data suggest, a competing regulator will emerge, from among the fifty U.S. states or other nations, with a superior regime that will attract not only non-U.S. and new U.S. issuers, who have not yet incurred the start-up costs of SEC compliance, but eventually the mature issuers as well, who are competing for capital with new issues. This is the central lesson to be drawn from the evidence of responsive state behavior in the U.S. charter market.*[39] *(Romano, 2001, p. 544)*

Romano notes, adumbrating Kerber and Van den Bergh's later conclusions, that regulatory competition does not yield a race to the bottom, and that "we have not found firms opting for minimum disclosure regimes or for states whose corporation law permits the exploitation of investors".[40] (Romano, 2001, p. 544) This is, perhaps, logical, as disclosure reduces the cost of capital.[41] (Hao, 2024) Nonetheless, market participants may suffer from bundling effects: local disclosure regimes or corporate law are only two among a host of factors leading an issuer to choose one or another regulatory home. An issuer's (or an investor's) inability to find a preferred combination of those factors weakens Romano's recourse to those empirical results to support her claims that regulatory competition would not kick off a race to the bottom. But regulatory competition certainly moves firms closer to an optimal set of risks and disclosures in a manner that facilitated capital formation.

Taken together, the cases for regulatory competition, shared standards, and mutual recognition point toward a broader strategy for integration. The practical question, then, is which path offers the most feasible near-term entry point for Israel and its neighbors. While a regime of mutual recognition/substituted compliance in the securities markets has the potential to make capital formation a driving force in international peace where diplomatic efforts have stalled somewhat, a joint regulatory regime in the financial markets would take political will just like other forms of cooperation. Participation by Israeli issuers in AAOIFI and acceptance of AAOFI standards could be an intermediate step driven by more nimble players than national governments, suggesting a shorter timeline. Israel's size relative to Arab countries in the Middle East and North Africa rules out for Israel and its neighbors the sort of agreements the SEC has made with Australia, the EU, and Mexico, for which the SEC has served as a senior partner. The residual competition between regulatory regimes could ultimately be convenient and valuable for investors and issuers alike. This recommended approach turns to third-party approvals, akin to George Akerlof's reliance on third parties to resolve informational asymmetries and market failure in his famous article "The Market for Lemons".[42] (Akerlof, 1970) The attraction of this proposal is that it sidesteps the difficulties of diplomatic negotiations for mutual recognition. The paths to issuance of *sharī a*-compliant securities are at this point well known, even if AAOFI continues to consider modification of its standards. Thus, even if issuance of specific classes of AAOIFI-compliant securities might place a burden on market participants, access to a broader investing public would likely be worth their while. The long-term effects, then, of market cross-pollination from Israel to its neighbors could be, as Klein imagines, "a bridge to commercial growth and peace in the Middle East."

CONCLUSION

There are several ways that financial markets in Abrahamic countries can be integrated. While a mutual recognition regime for securities markets would require the same kind of political will as other forms of cooperation, shared standards offer a path forward that can be driven by institutions and market participants rather than governments. The AAOIFI, for example, has established over 100 standards for *sharī a* compliance that are used by central banks, regulatory authorities, financial institutions, and legal firms in more than 45 countries. The adoption of these standards by Israeli issuers and members of the AAOIFI could allow the Israeli market to participate in the growing Islamic finance market, which is projected to reach $7.7

trillion by 2033. This approach to integration, which relies on third-party approvals and standards, could be a more feasible near-term option than government-led mutual recognition agreements. Such market-driven changes could bring down the cost of capital and create opportunities for cross-border investment throughout the region.

REFERENCES

Accounting and Auditing Organization for Islamic Financial Institutions. (n.d.-a). *About AAOIFI*. https://aaoifi.com/about-aaoifi/?lang=en

Accounting and Auditing Organization for Islamic Financial Institutions. (n.d.-b). *AAOIFI common members*. https://aaoifi.com/aaoifi-common-members/?lang=en

Akerlof, G. A. (1970). The market for "lemons": Quality uncertainty and the market mechanism. *The Quarterly Journal of Economics*, *84*(3), 488–500. DOI: 10.2307/1879431

Akerlof, G. A. (1970). The Market for 'Lemons': Quality Uncertainty and the Market Mechanism. *The Quarterly Journal of Economics*, *84*(3), 488–500. DOI: 10.2307/1879431

Allied Market Research. (n.d.). *Islamic finance market*. https://www.alliedmarketresearch.com/islamic-finance-market-A120276

Allied Market Research. "Islamic Finance Market Size, Share, Competitive Landscape and Trend Analysis Report." Accessed August 31, 2025. https://www.alliedmarketresearch.com/islamic-finance-market-A120276

Andrews, D. M., ... (2005). *The Future of Transatlantic Economic Relations: Continuity amid Discord*. San Domenico di Fiesole: European University Institute.

Australian Securities and Investments Commission. (n.d.). *Consultation paper 98: Cross-border recognition* [PDF]. https://download.asic.gov.au/media/1329068/Consultation_paper_98_Cross_Border_Recognition_v1.pdf

Bateman, M. C., & Beyea, C. R. (2008). Mutual recognition: A step towards greater access to global markets. *The Investment Lawyer*, *15*(5), 3–8.

Bateman, M. C., & Beyea, C. R. (2008). Mutual recognition: A step towards greater access to global markets. *The Investment Lawyer*, *15*(5), 3–8.

Bateman, M. C., & Beyea, C. R. (2008, May). Mutual Recognition: A Step Towards Greater Access to Global Markets. *The Investment Lawyer*, *15*(5), 3–8.

Capital, S. (n.d.). *GCC sukuk: A primer* (3rd ed.)., https://www.saturna.com/insights/thought-leadership/gcc-sukuk-primer-3rd-edition

Cleary Gottlieb Steen & Hamilton LLP. (2021). "Substituted Compliance Application for Mexico Swap Dealers from CEA Sections 4s(e)–(f) and Rules 23.101 and 23.105(d)–(e)." Submitted to CFTC, September 28, 2021. https://www.cftc.gov/media/8111/Mexico_SubstitutedComplianceApplication_20210928/download

Commodity Futures Trading Commission. (2021). *Mexico substituted compliance application* [PDF]. https://www.cftc.gov/media/8111/Mexico_SubstitutedComplianceApplication_20210928/download

Davis, K. (2025, May 29). $1trn sukuk market at risk of unintended disruption. *Financial Times*.

Davis, K. "$1trn Sukuk Market at Risk of Unintended Disruption." *Financial Times*, May 29, 2025.

de Brito, A. C., Kauffmann, C., & Pelkmans, J. (2016). *The contribution of mutual recognition to international regulatory co-operation* (OECD Regulatory Working Paper No. 2). OECD.

de Brito, C., Anabela, C. K., & Pelkmans, J. "The Contribution of Mutual Recognition to International Regulatory Co-Operation." *OECD Regulatory Working Papers*, no. 2 (2016): 1-50.

Dorf, M. C. (2008). Dynamic incorporation of foreign law. *University of Pennsylvania Law Review, 157*, 103–169.

Elmghaamez, I. K., Ntim, C. G., & Yekini, K. C. (2024). Diffusion theory, economic consequences, and adoption of international standards on auditing around the world. *Journal of International Accounting, Auditing & Taxation, 56*, 1–15. DOI: 10.1016/j.intaccaudtax.2024.100641

Federal Register. (2024, July 18). Order granting conditional substituted compliance in connection with certain capital and financial requirements. https://www.federalregister.gov/documents/2024/07/18/2024-15093/order-granting-conditional-substituted-compliance-in-connection-with-certain-capital-and-financial

Federal Reserve Bank of Kansas City. (n.d.). *Bank deposit rates haven't kept pace with yields on other investments, but depositors are staying anyway*. https://www.kansascityfed.org/research/economic-bulletin/bank-deposit-rates-havent-kept-pace-with-yields-on-other-investments-but-depositors-are-staying-anyway/

Hao, J. (2024). Disclosure regulation, cost of capital, and firm values. *Journal of Accounting and Economics, 77*(1), 1–20. DOI: 10.1016/j.jacceco.2023.101605

International Organization of Securities Commissions. "IOSCO: Facilitating Mutual Recognition and Substituted Compliance." Transatlantic Coalition on Financial Regulation, November 2012. https://www.isda.org/a/hdDDE/iosco-paper-final-091112.pdf

Karimov, J., Balli, F., Balli, H. O., & de Bruin, A. (2020). Shariʿah Compliance Requirements and the Cost of Equity Capital. *Pacific-Basin Finance Journal*, *62*, 101353. DOI: 10.1016/j.pacfin.2020.101349

Kerber, W., & Van den Bergh, R. (2008). Mutual recognition revisited: Misunderstandings, inconsistencies, and a suggested reinterpretation. *Kyklos*, *61*(3), 447–465. DOI: 10.1111/j.1467-6435.2008.00412.x

Klein, D. (1995). The Islamic and Jewish laws of usury: A bridge to commercial growth and peace in the Middle East. *Denver Journal of International Law and Policy*, *23*(3), 535–554.

Kopel, C. (2023). Phantom LIBOR Terms and the *Heter Iska*—Part I. *The Banking Law Journal*, *140*(3), 203–217.

Lehmann, M., & Schürger, J. (2021). Multilateralizing deference: A proposal for reforming global financial law. *EBI Working Paper Series, 107*, 1–29.

Marcacci, A. (2023). *Transnational securities regulation: How it works, who shapes it*. Springer. DOI: 10.1007/978-3-031-18063-7

Moloney, N. (2018). *The age of ESMA: Governing EU financial markets*. Hart Publishing.

Nicolaïdis, K., & Steffenson, R. (2005). Managed mutual recognition in the transatlantic marketplace. In Andrews, D. M. (Eds.), *The future of transatlantic economic relations: Continuity amid discord* (pp. 139–163). European University Institute.

Osgoode Hall Law School. (n.d.). *Reports*. https://digitalcommons.osgoode.yorku.ca/cgi/viewcontent.cgi?article=1109&context=reports

Otto, J. M. (Ed.). (2012). *Sharia Incorporated: A Comparative Overview of the Legal Systems of Twelve Muslim Countries in Past and Present*. Leiden University Press. DOI: 10.1515/9789400600171

Romano, R. (2001). The need for competition in international securities regulation. *Theoretical Inquiries in Law*, *2*(2), 387–562. DOI: 10.2202/1565-3404.1029

Securities and Exchange Commission. "Multijurisdictional Disclosure System." Division of Corporation Finance Financial Reporting Manual, Topic 16. Accessed August 31, 2025. https://www.sec.gov/about/divisions-offices/division-corporation-finance/financial-reporting-manual/frm-topic-16

Shahed, W. (2020, June 18). Rise of Islamic law in Turkey. *Michigan State University International Law Review.*

Shahed, W. (2020, June 18). Rise of Islamic Law in Turkey. *Michigan State University International Law Review*, *28*(2), 431–458.

Shetreet, S., & Homolka, W. (2007). *Jewish and Israeli law: An introduction.* De Gruyter.

Stern, Y. (2006). *What is Jewish in Israeli law?* Israel Democracy Institute. • Otto, J. M. (Ed.). (2012). *Sharia incorporated: A comparative overview of the legal systems of twelve Muslim countries in past and present.* Leiden University Press.

Transatlantic Coalition on Financial Regulation. (2012). *IOSCO: Facilitating mutual recognition and substituted compliance.* International Swaps and Derivatives Association. https://www.isda.org/a/hdDDE/iosco-paper-final-091112.pdf

University of Illinois Chicago School of Law. (n.d.). *Global markets law journal.* https://repository.law.uic.edu/cgi/viewcontent.cgi?article=1015&context=globalmarkets

University of Melbourne. (2009). *University of Melbourne Law Review Studies.* https://classic.austlii.edu.au/au/journals/UMelbLRS/2009/11.html

U.S. Securities and Exchange Commission. (n.d.-a). *Financial reporting manual: Topic 16.* https://www.sec.gov/about/divisions-offices/division-corporation-finance/financial-reporting-manual/frm-topic-16

Verdier, P.-H. (n.d.). Mutual recognition in international finance. [Publication details unavailable].

Vremya, R. (n.d.-a). Stock exchange bridges cannot be established without AAOIFI. https://realnoevremya.com/articles/8858-stock-exchange-bridges-cannot-be-established-without-aaoifi

Wiley. (2006). [Abstract]. *Philosophical Forum.* https://onlinelibrary.wiley.com/doi/abs/10.1111/j.1467-646X.2006.121.x

ENDNOTES

1 For the relationship between Jewish law and the law of modern Israel, see Shimon Shetreet and Walter Homolka, *Jewish and Israeli Law: An Introduction* (2007); for the various models for the incorporation into Israeli law of Jewish law, see Yedidia Stern, "What is Jewish in Israeli Law"? (Israel Democracy Institute, 2006).

2 See Jan Michiel Otto (ed.), *Sharia Incorporated: A Comparative Overview of the Legal Systems of Twelve Muslim Countries in Past and Present* (Leiden: Leiden University Press, 2012). For recent developments, see Wesham Shahed's "Rise of Islamic Law in Turkey," *Michigan State University International Law Review* (18 June 2020).

3 Daniel Klein, "The Islamic and Jewish Laws of Usury: A Bridge to Commercial Growth and Peace in the Middle East," *Denver Journal of International Law & Policy* 23.3 (1995): 535-554, 543.

4 See Charles Kopel, "Phantom LIBOR Terms and the *Heter Iska*—Part I," *The Banking Law Journal* (2023): 203-217.

5 Klein, *ibid.*, p.544.

6 Klein, *ibid.*, p.547.

7 https://www.kansascityfed.org/research/economic-bulletin/bank-deposit-rates-havent-kept-pace-with-yields-on-other-investments-but-depositors-are-staying-anyway/

8 Pierre-Hugues Verdier, "Mutual Recognition in International Finance," 56.

9 Verdier, 104-106.

10 Note 113 at https://repository.law.uic.edu/cgi/viewcontent.cgi?article=1015&context=globalmarkets

11 https://www.sec.gov/about/divisions-offices/division-corporation-finance/financial-reporting-manual/frm-topic-16

12 https://onlinelibrary.wiley.com/doi/abs/10.1111/j.1467-646X.2006.121.x

13 https://digitalcommons.osgoode.yorku.ca/cgi/viewcontent.cgi?article=1109&context=reports

14 https://classic.austlii.edu.au/au/journals/UMelbLRS/2009/11.html

15 For this, see p. 17 in https://download.asic.gov.au/media/1329068/Consultation_paper_98_Cross_Border_Recognition_v1.pdf

16 Marguerite C. Bateman and Cynthia R. Beyea, "Mutual Recognition: A Step Towards Greater Access to Global Markets," *The Investment Lawyer* 15.5 (May 2008): 3-8, 5.

17 For this, see Marguerite C. Bateman and Cynthia R. Beyea, *ibid.*, 3-8, 5.

18 https://www.cftc.gov/media/8111/Mexico_SubstitutedComplianceApplication_20210928/download

19 https://www.cftc.gov/LawRegulation/DoddFrankAct/CDSCP/index.htm

20 https://www.federalregister.gov/documents/2024/07/18/2024-15093/order-granting-conditional-substituted-compliance-in-connection-with-certain-capital-and-financial

21 Matthias Lehmann & Jonas Schürger, "Multilateralizing Deference: A Proposal for Reforming Global Financial aw," *EBI Working Paper Series* 107 (2021), 11.

22 For the effects of supremacy on the democratic powers on the members of a legal federation, see Michael C. Dorf, "Dynamic Incorporation of Foreign Law," *University of Pennsylvania Law Review* 157 (2008): 103-169.

23 For this, see Kalypso Nicolaïdis and Rebecca Steffenson, "Managed Mutual Recognition in the Transatlantic Marketplace," in David M. Andrews et al., *The Future of Transatlantic Economic Relations: Continuity amid Discord* (San Domenico di Fiesole: European University Institute, 2005), 139-163, 139-140.

24 *Ibid*, 140.

25 Wolfgang Kerber and Roger Van den Bergh, "Mutual Recognition Revisited: Misunderstandings, Inconsistencies, and a Suggested Reinterpretation," *Kyklos* 61.3 (2008):447-465, 457-459.

26 Anabela Correia de Brito, Celine Kauffmann and Jacques Pelkmans, "The Contribution of Mutual Recognition to International Regulatory Co-Operation," *OECD Regulatory Working Papers*, no. 2 (2016), 23.

27 Niamh Moloney, *The Age of ESMA: Governing EU Financial Markets* (Oxford: Hart Publishing, 2018), 280.

28 https://aaoifi.com/about-aaoifi/?lang=en

[29] Jamshid Karimov, Faruk Balli, Hatice Ozer Balli, and Anne de Bruin, "Shariʿah Compliance Requirements and the Cost of Equity Capital," *Pacific-Basin Finance Journal* 62 (2020).

[30] For the challenges to the current AAOIFI standards regarding *ukūk*, see Kurt Davis, "$1trn Sukuk Market at Risk of Unintended Disruption," *Financial Times*, 29 May 2025. For sovereigns as dominant players in the *ukūk* market, see Saturna Capital, "GCC Sukuk: A Primer, 3rd Edition," https://www.saturna.com/insights/thought-leadership/gcc-sukuk-primer-3rd-edition.

[31] https://realnoevremya.com/articles/8858-stock-exchange-bridges-cannot-be-established-without-aaoifi

[32] https://realnoevremya.com/articles/8858-stock-exchange-bridges-cannot-be-established-without-aaoifi

[33] For a discussion of IOSCO, see Antonio Marcacci, *Transnational Securities Regulation: How it Works, Who Shapes It* (Cham, Switzerland: Springer, 2023).

[34] For the idea that shared international standards can reduce the costs of capital formation, see Ibrahim K. Elmghaamez, Collins G. Ntim, and Kemi C. Yekini, "Diffusion Theory, Economic Consequences, and Adoption of International Standards on Auditing around the World," *Journal of International Accounting, Auditing and Taxation* 56 (2024).

[35] See the Transatlantic Coalition on Financial Regulation, "IOSCO: Facilitating Mutual Recognition and Substituted Compliance," November 2012, https://www.isda.org/a/hdDDE/iosco-paper-final-091112.pdf.

[36] For the list of AAOIFI institutional members, see https://aaoifi.com/aaoifi-common-members/?lang=en.

[37] https://www.alliedmarketresearch.com/islamic-finance-market-A120276.

[38] Roberta Romano, "The Need for Competition in International Securities Regulation," *Theoretical Inquiries in Law* 2 (2001): 387-562.

[39] *Ibid.*, 544.

[40] *Ibid.*, 544.

[41] Jinji Hao, "Disclosure Regulation, Cost of Capital, and Firm Values," *Journal of Accounting and Economics* 77.1 (2024).

[42] George A. Akerlof, "The Market for 'Lemons': Quality Uncertainty and the Market Mechanism," *Quarterly Journal of Economics* 84.3 (1970): 488–500.

Chapter 9
Practice Without Doctrine: Catholic Works of Religion, 1891–1950

Riccardo Semeraro
https://orcid.org/0000-0003-4181-1064
Università Cattolica del Sacro Cuore, Italy

Giovanni Gregorini
https://orcid.org/0000-0003-0652-4852
Università Cattolica del Sacro Cuore, Italy

ABSTRACT

Probing the contradiction between the limited attention to finance within Catholic social teaching and the widespread involvement of the Church in credit operations, this essay explores the economic role of the Catholic Church in the period 1891–1950. Exploring institutional history and unpublished archival sources, the aim is to reconstruct the role of diocesan endowments and the Vatican Administration for the Works of Religion. The study examines asset management models, investment strategies, center-periphery dynamics, and the degree of autonomy exercised by individual dioceses. Particular attention is dedicated to the cases of Milan and Bergamo, analyzed on the basis of quantitative data and evaluated in terms of innovative practices. The paper shows how the Catholic Church functioned as an institutional investor in a "charity market", developing financial practices aligned with religious and social aims, yet lacking a coherent theoretical framework. This research opens up a new area for historiographical inquiry.

DOI: 10.4018/979-8-3373-1887-5.ch009

1. INTRODUCTION

The Catholic Church was deeply engaged, in a variety of sometimes surprisingly innovative ways, in the economic and financial transformations underway in Italy and beyond in the twentieth century. In spite of its active and often well orchestrated participation in these processes, the Church remained substantially unresponsive in embracing and formalizing them into its doctrine, especially as regards finance. This inertia has resulted in a dissonance that has yet to be explored in detail: intensive activity in the realm of modern finance lacking in a coherent, explicit, and common doctrinal framework.

This chapter explores the above incongruity, illustrating a complex network of practices, institutions, and financial strategies developed by the Catholic Church roughly between 1870 and 1950, with particular attention to Italy. Analyzing largely unpublished archival sources, we reconstruct the mechanisms for managing financial resources conferred to the Church for religious and charitable purposes (pious legacies) and the methods and actions adopted by the dioceses and the Holy See to safeguard, valorize, and invest them.

Our approach is two-pronged. We examine the Casse Diocesane (hereinafter "diocesan endowments"), local administrative instruments for managing ecclesiastical assets, prime agents in a novel process of applying financial management principles and methods to charity. We also focus on the Amministrazione per le Opere di Religione (AOR – Administration for the Works of Religion), forerunner of the Istituto per le Opere di Religione (IOR – Institute for the Works of Religion), in its delicate transition toward juridical and operational autonomy in the period immediately prior to Italy's entry into WWII.

These instruments and associated mechanisms, albeit fragmented and at times divergent, embody a stock of administrative competencies caught in a constant tension between central control and centrifugal autonomy. With intelligence and farsightedness—yet without formalized doctrine—, these bodies within the Catholic sphere embarked on innovative paths while exercising prudence, anchoring ecclesiastical finance to principles of social responsibility and sustainability *ante litteram*, well before they became themes in contemporary political debate.

We seek to contribute to the reconstruction of a relatively marginal area in historiography while offering critical grist for rethinking the relationship between economics, ethics, and religious institutions. The history of ecclesiastical finance in the nineteenth and twentieth centuries can be a source of invaluable insights into the crisis in contemporary capitalist models and the renewed impulses within the Church for transparency and ethical investment of assets.

2. LITERATURE

As argued by Cesarini (2004, pp. 309-310):

the social doctrine of the Church appears sketchy and scarcely cogent regarding the issue of credit and finance, whereas it has repeatedly and amply addressed productive factors (especially capital and labor) and has recognized not only the role of the entrepreneur and the enterprise as indispensable instruments in the organization of said factors but also—albeit only recently—the proper function of profit [...]. Contributing to this situation are, on the one hand, the old disputes about the legitimacy of interest on loans, and on the other, an incomplete understanding of the role played by finance in the modern real economy and also a focus on the serious macroeconomic and social consequences of recurring crises [...]. One of the rare explicit references to the question, found in the Quadragesimo anno, written precisely at the beginning of the Great Depression, expresses a very negative vision of credit and a pronounced overestimation of the power of those who exercise it.

In the teachings of the Catholic Church, capital is reduced to a factor of production in the sense of a "collective term representing materials produced not for immediate consumption but for an instrumental use, i.e., to be used in the production process together with labor and natural resources" (Pasinetti, 2004, p. 170), certainly up to the significant critical juncture of the era of globalization.

It is perhaps for reasons such as this that, more generally, "the contribution of the Church's social doctrine has remained substantially in the shadows, almost relegated to the sidelines in mainstream historiography" (Farese, 2019, p. 111), which prevalently references the history of finance in the late modern period. And yet this represents a clear contradiction with the dynamic experience of Catholic Social Teaching in Italy, strongly projected into the realm of finance and especially credit, as witnessed by affairs such as that of Giuseppe Tovini and the Banco Ambrosiano of Milan (Taccolini & Cafaro, 1997; Taccolini & Gregorini, 2019) or the entire cooperative credit movement in the nineteenth and twentieth centuries (Cafaro, 2001), and generally the Church's somewhat fraught relationship with money (via banks) in that period (Pegrari, 2011).

Indeed, on the one hand, organized Catholic groups rejected, both within their own institutional or social role and that of religion as a whole, a role of "festive ornamentation, spiritual additive, [or] ethical reference" (Rumi, 2009, p. 523) and took part in the modernization of the national financial system—albeit at times in a somewhat disorderly manner (Gregorini, 2018). On the other hand, the Church and ecclesiastical organizations were actively engaged in the economy (social market economy), but especially in finance, with dynamics being uncovered by historiographers in reference certainly to the new active religious congregations

(Semeraro, 2017), but also to the Church both centrally and peripherally (Semeraro and Gregorini, 2019; 2021; Semeraro, 2020a; 2020b; 2022).

Looking more closely, the Church—historically engaged in the economy via processes that are at times (apparently) evident but in other cases still (little) explored (Taccolini, 2009)—goes through phases of significant transformation, identifying principles with which to interpret reality and that can inspire its actions (social teaching), but also following concrete practices in the situations in which it operates, situations that are often of significant economic and social import, on the level of both the Holy See and local churches (Rumi, 1986; Gregorini, 2014).

In particular, between the publication of the encyclical *Rerum Novarum*, the first social document of the late-modern papacy, and the celebration of the Second Vatican Council, a twentieth-century turning point in more than doctrinal terms, the Church found itself grappling with an extremely transformative Italian and world context that brought trauma, especially in Italy. It was in this complex phase that the role of finance became decisive in the dynamics of modern economic development, given that it was during the time of the second industrial revolution that investment and risk capital became decisive in the configuration of twentieth-century industrial capitalism (Fornasari, 2017). In this period, the Church operated in the financial realm relatively unfettered by doctrinal constraints or rigorously applicable and applied rules. If anything, it had to reckon with principally international economic circumstances that were anything but favorable in the first half of the twentieth century. It was, thus, finance without rules. Even the most advanced thinking among Catholic spheres on the economic, social, and financial dynamics of the late modern period inevitably had to reckon with the limits of Catholic economic culture at the time, limits exacerbated by the challenge of getting the Church's economic thinking and its social teaching onto the same page.

In this latter respect, the 1930s represent an interesting context for further study. A number of important historiographical studies have been published on the theme in the past twenty-five years. First of all is the work of Ferrari (1995), who researched the origins of the reformative culture that characterized Catholic cultural debate in the post-WWII period and recognized the "constitutive complexity" of Italian social Catholicism, which in one way:

> *prompted a renewed focus on civil society as the preferred setting for a model of development characterized by broad local autonomy, a reaffirmation of associative and mutualistic traditions, extensive reliance on volunteerism, and the defense of rural communities and agricultural economies. However, in its more recent practices, Catholic culture had drawn on other sources and approaches, such as Roosevelt's New Deal. A dominant belief emerged in this context: any appeal, even if limited to economics, to liberal ideas was a step backward in relation to the practical and theoretical advances (Keynesian analysis) achieved by modern*

economics. In short, a remarkably stable synthesis had formed between a certain Thomistic philosophical tradition, an anti-liberal sensibility, and the conviction that Keynesian thought—read and appreciated in Italian universities even before 1940—provided, in analytically grounded and scientifically articulated terms, a systematic expression of what the Church had already been asserting for a century about the fragility of the liberal vision of economy and society (Ferrari, 1995, pp. 20-21).

In many ways, this reasoning does not recognize the critical financial issues associated with the post-1929 Great Depression. In the interpretation of Paolo Pecorari (1997, p. 28):

the most significant attempts to harmonize economic science with the Church's social teachings took place in the academic environment of the Università Cattolica, where Francesco Vito, drawing on the principles of Marshall and assigning to economics a primary role as a guide to action, developed the idea that the economic problem entails a "rational" allocation of "limited means suitable to alternative uses to different ends, which are differently ranked in order of importance" (a marginalist component). He studied "social organicism", particularly with regard to the convergence of individual and social goals (not merely as empirical data), and analyzed non-competitive market forms.

The second theme, social organicism, touched on corporatism, with all its implications in terms of distinction between Catholic thought and the Fascist vulgate. Precisely:

the disparity of these positions did not escape Sergio Paronetto, as evidenced by his contributions in the 1930s to Studium and Illustrazione vaticana, not to mention his role (working for IRI of Beneduce and Menichella) in developing a mixed public-private economic program that would also be implemented during the difficult process of reconstruction after WWII. With Paronetto, we are on the progressive side of the Catholic movement—that of university graduates—where there was a greater effort to break away from (or at least transcend) the logical frameworks of Fascist economics. The goal was to arrive at an economic theory rooted in historical reality and sustained by an openminded and critical analysis of the contemporary world. Paronetto was one of the most original representatives of this new cultural engagement—an approach that no longer saw the teleological interpretation of the "economic principle" as sufficient, that played against the theories of Pigou, Robbins, and Keynes, that was aware of the writings of Spengler and Huizinga, and that reflected deeply on the work of Maritain. And Paronetto was not alone. At his side—and perhaps even ahead of him—was Pasquale Saraceno, especially in terms of rethinking and reconfiguring the relationship between the state and the economy. [...] Economic thought of the 1930s found a kind of Magna Carta in the Code of Camaldoli.

This latter document was drafted between September 1943 and May 1944 (after the organizational failure of July 18-24, 1943 due to the absence of Fanfani, Mazzei, and Vito, then the most eminent Catholic economists), with Paronetto, Saraceno, Vanoni, and Capograssi contributing decisively (Pecorari, 1997, p. 29). Bocci also (1999, p. 208) underscored the importance of Francesco Vito in the 1930s, particularly for his critique of capitalism, which primarily took the form of a forceful denunciation of the "complete separation of economics from ethics" that characterized classical liberal economics. It was partly for this reason that Vito judged Pope Pius XI's Quadragesimo anno as somewhat tepid, condemning capitalism only in its "degenerate effects on social peace and the common good." In his view, something more was needed to pursue the true aim of structural reform of capitalism. But also in this broader analysis, the inquiry into the financial system—its nature and operational mechanisms—was largely set aside.

Writing more specifically on the Church's evolving social thinking, Sorge (2011) identified the novelty of Pius XI's encyclical in its proposal of a "third way":

regarding the ideologies that have now transformed into concrete national models of social and economic organization, the QA addresses—thus broadening the Church's "social discourse"—the question of a third model, which translates the religious and ethical principles of [Church's] social teachings into a Christian form of organization of society. Pope Pius XI proposed "Christian civilization" as a third way, an alternative model both to actually existing socialism and to neoliberalism (Sorge, 2011, pp. 135-136).

However, this is all laid out in a text that never once uses the word "finance" (or its derivatives), uses the word "bank" once (bank internationalization), and the word "money" once (international imperialism of money). However, we find "capital" thirty-three times in reference to a factor of production, or the associated social class (capitalists), or the prevailing system of economic organization in the Western world (capitalism).

Expanding the realm of investigation of the economic and financial debate characterizing the 1930s, Persico (2014) studies the genesis and dissemination of the Code of Camaldoli. In his studies we again find Paronetto figuring prominently, particularly for his growing insistence on the urgent need to revive social and economic studies within the Catholic sphere. In his experience and that of Pasquale Saraceno:

The mixed [public-private] enterprise model embodied by IRI [Institute for Industrial Reconstruction] appeared to the young Catholics at the institute to be the only truly viable means of establishing a genuinely Christian economic and social order. [...] Within the institute, through daily engagement with the reorganization of the vast industrial complex that had come under state control, a new Catholic outlook took shape in the late 1930s. [This was all the more important give that] in the climate of Fascism and in spite of its doctrinal amenability, the Quadragesimo anno had failed to spark truly original thinking on the many issues implicit in the crisis of capitalism (Persico, 2014, pp. 17-18, 21).

Lastly, in his very recent work, Farese argues that there is a particular connection between economic thinking at the Vatican and the Roosevelt doctrine: "There are close ties between the American and Vatican spheres, between the Italian and the German spheres, and among all of them generally" (2019, p. 113). In virtue of these ties, he states that "the now incontestable interdependency among nations is the result of a technical and material process, and not of a simultaneous political and rational process" (2019, p.117).

The theoretical and institutional inquiries outlined in the above studies—and also in Cini (2019)—, while offering an unforgiving critical assessment of the period, systematically overlook the exquisitely financial aspects of late-modern capitalism. The observation of Francesco Cesarini, which opens this essay, is thus in line with what we have documented up to this point, and is not entirely askew if considered in the light of subsequent documents, such as those of the Congregazione per la Dottrina della Fede and Dicastero per il Servizio dello Sviluppo Umano Integrale [CDF & DSSUI] (2018), and of the United States Conference of Catholic Bishops (2021).

Late-modern finance, however, was by no means alien to the operational mechanisms—and especially their distortive aspects—of Western capitalism. And the Church itself, as has been pointed out, made extensive and systematic use of them, applying criteria and structures that are now better documented, though still in need of further investigation, both in reference to the Holy See and to the autonomous operations of ecclesiastical bodies.

In particular, by the mid-nineteenth century, the management of papal finances could only be described as troubled and contested: expenses were out of control, debt was high, no supervisory criteria or policies were applied, and revenue monitoring was ineffective (Crocella, 1982). Historically, the Holy See's borrowing needs were serviced by actors such as the Rothschilds, the Bank of Ireland (which channeled Vatican funds through the London financial market), and Roman bankers such as Alessandro Torlonia. Even after the establishment in 1878 of the Amministrazione dei Beni della Santa Sede [Administration of the Assets of the Holy See], chaired by the Vatican Secretary of State, the management of incoming financial flows (including donations from the faithful, Peter's Pence, and gifts received directly by the Pope) "in the form of equity investments, bonds, and government securities, was typically placed in the hands of trusted European bankers—Swiss, German, French, Dutch, and English—who relied on the Apostolic Nunciatures in those countries. It was a decidedly cumbersome and, in some cases, amateurish system" (Pegrari, 2019, p. 76) that generated serious concerns even within the Catholic Church itself.

Alongside the principles of subsidiarity and canon law (De Franssu & De Salins, 2024, pp. 88-89), these concerns lay at the roots of the historically and progressively consolidated strategy of administrative decentralization of Church assets across dioceses, religious orders and congregations, and a wide range of ecclesiastical entities (Gregorini, 2014). This decentralization invites us to expand our perspective on the financial assessment of Church property beyond the Vatican and recognize a growing trend, emerging in the late nineteenth century, to boost the revenue-generating orientation of these entities, partly as a way of circumventing the confiscatory policies of European governments.

Gradually, starting in the late nineteenth century, ecclesiastical assets dematerialized, taking on a central role in a process of financialization that also involved the increasing resources from various entitles earmarked for "works of religion", to be administered under Church authority. This was the market of charity: the financial management of charity, most often structured in the form of "pious legacies". It is on this component of Church wealth that this essay focuses. This is an item of Christian assets (Nicholls, 2022) that is almost completely unknown in spite of its deeply relational nature (multiple actors linked by specification of donation recipients) and its widespread presence at the local level (diffuse charity).

Recent studies have begun to shed light on the management of this component of Catholic assets in the nineteenth and twentieth centuries. Drawing on unpublished sources they highlight the role of diocesan endowments, analyze the efforts to regulate them and ensure uniform operation, and reconstruct the management of a number of problematic cases (Semeraro, 2020; Semeraro & Gregorini, 2019, 2021; Gregorini & Gregorini, 2022; Gregorini et al., 2022).

Historians have begun to focus attention on the long-term development of the IOR in an attempt to shed light on significant transitions in its long and complex administration (McGoldrick, 2012; Semeraro, 2022; Gregorini, 2024). Often mistakenly referred to as the "Vatican Bank", the IOR, which gained corporate status in 1942, represents a distinct body within the panorama of religious financial institutions. Its history reflects broader socio-political and economic shifts within the context of Catholicism and global finance. The evolution of this institution has entailed the interplay of diverse factors, including organizational structures and management practices, and an entanglement in both ecclesiastical and secular economies.

The establishment of the Institute was primarily intended to safeguard and manage the financial resources of the Catholic Church, distinguishing its mission from that of a typical banking institution, which generally prioritizes profit. This framework aligns well with broader religious objectives regarding charity, support for the needy, and the promotion of Catholic teachings through economic mechanisms. The implications of this alignment are significant within the broader context of the economics of religion, particularly in how financial practices can reflect and reinforce ideological commitments to social welfare and moral responsibility (Rubin, 2020; Iyer, 2016).

Analyzing the operational dynamics of the IOR and its historical context reveals that shifts in governance, including increased scrutiny from international financial regulatory frameworks, have prompted significant reforms. These changes highlight evolving standards of financial transparency and raise critical questions concerning the balance between ecclesiastical autonomy and compliance with global financial regulations (Iannaccone, 2012). Discussions of such issues often draw from broader themes in the economics of religion, particularly how institutional behavior within religious settings reflects larger societal trends regarding finance and ethics (Rubin, 2020).

The interactions between the IOR and global finance can also be understood through the lens of lived religion, which emphasizes the everyday practices and beliefs of individuals. In the case of the Institute, this reflects the tensions between sacred values and secular financial imperatives (Ammerman, 2016). This framework facilitates a deeper understanding of how individuals within the bank reconcile their spiritual commitments with their professional responsibilities in the financial sector.

The socio-political backdrop of global economics during the Institute's formative years, including the rise of secular governance frameworks and market ideologies, further complicates its historical narrative. Researchers suggest that IOR strategies must be examined in conjunction with these shifts. Any comprehensive analysis of such religious financial institutions necessitates a multidimensional approach that integrates historical, sociocultural, and economic perspectives (Coleman, 2015). This approach involves understanding the Institute not as an isolated entity but as part of a larger tapestry of religious and financial interactions that span decades and continents.

Examining the various incomes and expenditures managed by the Institute reveals a complex interplay between religious commitments and pragmatic economic realities. For instance, the financing of charitable works alongside the need for investment returns generates discussions around ethical banking practices that align with the Catholic Church's mission. Scholars have critiqued how such financial management can expose challenges faced by religious institutions in maintaining moral clarity in an increasingly complex economic landscape dominated by profitability and growth objectives (Haddad, 2021).

As research progresses, it is crucial to scrutinize the ethical frameworks that guide the operations of the Institute. Decisions related to investment and asset allocation carry moral weight and necessitate navigating sometimes murky waters of moral theology and capital utilization. The consequences of these decisions reverberate throughout the Catholic community and the global financial community, influencing perceptions of religious institutions' credibility and ethical standing in the eyes of stakeholders (Lei & Traylor, 2023).

Moreover, the context of financial inclusion, especially in light of the Vatican's global influence, raises pertinent questions about the responsibilities of religious organizations in addressing socioeconomic disparities through financial mechanisms. Literature suggests a growing recognition that financial systems must be inclusive and supportive of marginalized populations, aligning religious tenets with modern principles of corporate social responsibility (Attoukou & Nchare, 2022).

Exploring the Institute further through cross-cultural perspectives can yield additional insights into the unique position of religious financial operators within the broader field of financial systems. Comparative investigations into similar entities across different religious traditions could enhance understanding of how various faith-based financial institutions negotiate their faith commitments against global economic pressures (Jensen & Geertz, 2014).

In summary, the history of the Instituto per le Opere di Religione serves as a microcosm of the intersection between financial practice and religious obligation. Emerging scholarly work continues to dissect the implications of its operations within a broader analytical framework that includes religion, economics, social justice, and ethics. As interest in this field increases, ongoing investigations into the Institute's role will yield valuable lessons about the future of religious institutions in an increasingly interconnected world.

3. RESEARCH GAP

In spite of the growing historiographical attention to the economics and finance of the Catholic Church in the late modern period, there are still significant knowledge gaps that this study seeks to fill. In particular, while a number of emblematic cases have been well documented—such as the role of the Banco Ambrosiano or the financial activity of the Holy See in the twentieth century—the operations and institutional status of the diocesan endowments and the administrative practices associated with pious legacies both locally and centrally have been little explored.

Most studies have focused on doctrinal aspects, on the relationship between economy and magisterium, or on individually newsworthy episodes, neglecting a systematic analysis of actual financial dynamics, investment mechanisms, and asset management practiced in Italian dioceses. In other words, what has been lacking is an in-depth understanding of the way in which the Church, via local networks and semi-autonomous structures, has constructed operational models of charitable finance over time, often in the absence of an explicit doctrinal framework.

Furthermore, the tension between practice and doctrine—that is, between the concrete, often innovative and farsighted, action of ecclesiastical institutions and the delay or ambiguity in the development of corresponding magisterial theory—has not been fully affirmed as an area of historiographical study. This void has influenced both how the public perceives Church actions in the financial sphere and also the efficacy of its economic management. This work, unfolding at the intersection of economic history, religious history, and institutional analysis, aims to make inroads into that blind spot, helping to construct a more articulate and complete framework based on the relationship between the Catholic Church and finance during the twentieth century.

4. METHODOLOGY

This study takes a qualitative historical approach in analytically reconstructing the financial practices of the Catholic Church in the period from the late nineteenth century through the first half of the twentieth, with a particular focus on Italy. The study is based principally on primary sources, many of which are hitherto unpublished, found in nationally relevant ecclesiastical and civic archives, particularly the Archivio del Dicastero per il Clero (ADC – Archive of the Dicastery of the Clergy), the Archivio Apostolico Vaticano (AAV – Vatican Apostolic Archive), and the Archivio Storico della Banca d'Italia (ASBI – Historical Archive of the Banca d'Italia). Documents examined include financial statements, administrative reports, correspondence, and charters and regulations of both central structures—such as the AOR—and localized bodies, particularly the diocesan endowments.

The sources were analyzed accounting not only for quantitative aspects (asset value, yield, investment strategy) but also for the institutional and cultural contexts in which the related practices took form. In this sense, the methodology was structured around a continuous comparison between practice and doctrine, examining not only the Church's financial actions, but also what it said—or didn't say—about them in its teachings. This comparison was supported by a critical review of secondary sources, both historical-economic and theological-social, with the objective of shedding light on areas that have been little explored in the relationship between Catholicism and finance.

A central role has been attributed to the comparative analysis of case studies of different natures and scales—such as the dioceses of Milan and Bergamo—, which have made it possible to assess both local variables and the dynamics of interactions with the central Vatican authorities. Work on the micro-institutional scale has proven particularly effective in revealing the inner logic of the asset management choices and the forms of administrative innovation implemented by the ecclesiastical communities.

Recognizing the partial and discontinuous nature of available sources, we have favored a reconstructive and interpretative approach, leveraging the archival information as an indication of broader processes. Our methodology was thus not limited to describing documented facts, but has sought to incorporate them into a broader weave of meanings, highlighting the structural, and not episodic, character of the financial presence of the Church in the late modern period.

5. DIOCESAN ENDOWMENTS AND THE VATICAN ADMINISTRATION FOR THE WORKS OF RELIGION

In the transition from the early to the late modern period—a juncture induced by French domination at the turn of the nineteenth century—the question arose of how to protect and potentially increase the value of assets held by ecclesiastical entities (parishes, religious orders, congregations of nuns) in light of a series of legislative and administrative measures aimed at reducing their holdings through confiscation and appropriation (De Maeyer et al., 2004). Thus began a contentious erosion of the economic space officially accorded to the Church, a space that contemporary historiographers increasingly recognize as supporting local systems of social welfare, both financially and with human resources (Gregorini et al., 2023).

These holdings were substantial, the context favorable, the opportunity ripe, but significant obstacles remained, especially in Italy: predictable conflicts within the Church (from the threat of excommunication to the Lateran Concordat) (Jemolo, 1975); unexpected local administrative and social resistance (nuns ran kindergartens, hospitals, and workers' hostels in cities and towns and enjoyed great local support) (Colombo, 2004; Gregorini, 2008); diversified tax strategies (notably involving newly emerging women's congregations) (Rocca, 2007; Gregorini, 2010); and tacit acceptance (even doctrinal) of the Church's management of financial assets, including both real estate and securities under the rubric of pious legacies (Semeraro, 2020; Gregorini and Gregorini, 2022).

This latter form of asset management, primarily of movable (financial) assets, was especially affected by the disappearance of the informal, historically significant role played by the confraternities prior to the Napoleonic Era (De Luca, 2021; Pegrari, 2014; Vaquero Piñeiro, 2007). Starting in the mid-nineteenth century and developing significantly in the following decades, this led to the establishment at the local level of the diocesan endowments.

Given these dynamics, one of the key issues facing the Church in this period was how to continue its efforts to valorize the many substantial donations received to support the so-called "works of religion" [*opere di religione*]. This issue involved various and complex financial aspects, given that, at the local level, these efforts were in the hands of the diocesan endowments (Semeraro, 2020), whereas at the central level they were overseen by the Amministrazione per le Opere di Religione (AOR – Administration for the Works of Religion), renamed in 1942 Istituto per le Opere di Religione (IOR – Institute for the Works of Religion, often incorrectly referred to as the "Vatican Bank") (Pollard, 2006; Pegrari, 2011; Lai, 2012).

Recent archival findings and updated interpretive models now make it possible to analyze this area of Church economic and financial activity in greater depth, identifying key actors, institutional innovations, and center-periphery dynamics that have thus far remained beyond the scope of even specialized historiography (Semeraro & Gregorini, 2019; Semeraro, 2020; 2022; Pegrari, 2019; 2020).

As recent studies have confirmed, in the period immediately following Italian national unification:

> *institutions of a perpetual nature were also subject to suppression and confiscation. Regardless of designation or title they were generally qualified as foundations or pious legacies dedicated to religious worship. In other words, these measures affected the range of assets that would later be defined in the 1917 Canon Law as "pious foundations" or "ecclesiastical foundations", i.e., "temporal goods given to a collective person within the Church with a perpetual or long-term obligation to promote, and yielding income for, yearly Masses, religious functions, or works of piety or charity" (Semeraro, 2020, p. 41).*

It was therefore necessary to find a way to protect the assets of pious legacies both at the central level and within individual local churches, as had already been done in other cases, such as those concerning religious congregations (Rocca, 2007; Dieguez & Pagano, 2006, pp. 655-656; Gregorini, 2012).

This question is anything but marginal in historiography, even over long time spans. On close examination, the economic and social practices sustained in various ways by the vast array of donations and bequests are relevant not only in early modern Europe, but also in the late modern world. These practices did not decrease in intensity or frequency over the course of the nineteenth and twentieth centuries. On the contrary, their ongoing vitality illustrates the logic of social and economic creativity that underpins the very concept of charity. This holds true in the case of the history of pious legacies—a characteristic of Catholicism and the Catholic Church of bequeathing one's properties to the Church (Colombo and Dotti, 2014; Colombo, 2016)—"whereby the beneficiary assumed an obligation to perform a service in exchange for the income generated by a given asset, with a portion of that income usually not consumed by the required service but retained by the institution for other purposes" (Semeraro & Gregorini, 2019, p. 802).

To manage these resources, beginning in the mid-nineteenth century and with significant developments in the following decades, local diocesan endowments were established, sometimes referred to as "*promotorie*" [charitable trust offices] or ecclesiastical endowments. Their primary purpose was to ensure the effective financial management of these funds, safeguard their autonomy, generate sufficient returns to meet the goals stipulated by the donors (where possible), and also increase overall accumulated capital. These were not episcopal incomes, financial assets administrated by Curia offices of the bishopric for its functions, nor capital received from the bishop to support his personal charitable work. The diocesan endowments often consisted of small—frequently very small—deposits in the form of pious legacies held both at the central facility (the bishop's residence) and by the scattered components (parishes), pooled into a sort of common fund that provided for a more secure—or at least more discreet—and efficient form of centralized management.

For example, in the diocese of Milan in 1906, Cardinal Andrea Carlo Ferrari, then archbishop, documented the operations of the local diocesan endowment as follows:

Assets were divided into 738 accounts, almost all under the names of the diocesan parishes. Each of these 738 accounts has its own distinct funds in the endowment. Each has a separate ledger, separate records for securities subject to drawing, and a special envelope for the biannual coupons that are distributed. This ensures that each party, receiving its own coupons marked with the same numbers, can verify the required drawings of the securities. These 738 accounts are further subdivided to represent the different individuals who established legacies in their respective parishes and reserved the income for their own use during their natural lifetimes. (ADC, M589-D622 Milan, letter from the Archbishop of Milan, Cardinal Andrea Carlo Ferrari, to the president of the Cardinal Commission for the Works of Religion, Cardinal Beniamino Cavicchioni, April 20, 1906).

After several decades of operation (in Mondovì since 1855, Naples since 1867, Milan and Bergamo since 1873, and Brescia since 1874), the diocesan endowments came under centralized regulation in 1904, 1912, and 1935, although not without spirited debate and even conflict between individual dioceses and the Holy See. These debates often led to a substantial degree of local self-management, especially as regards the first set of regulations in the regions of Lombardy and Piedmont (Semeraro, 2020, pp. 42-44). On the other hand, the relevant Vatican body—the Congregation of the Council—sought to standardize procedures across Italy in order to ensure oversight and prevent local financial difficulties, as had occurred in previous decades (Semeraro, 2020, pp. 67-68), and that would have affected the entire system. But this effort provide ineffective, also in the Holy See's management of the AOR (Gregorini, 2024).

To better understand the history of the Vatican AOR, it is helpful to refer to the founding act of the IOR, signed by Pope Pius XII on June 27, 1942:

Our venerated predecessor Leo XIII, in order to safeguard and administer the capital of pious foundations, after careful study entrusted to distinguished Cardinals, established a Cardinal Commission ad pias causas, whose operation was governed by a Regulation approved on February 11, 1887. This Regulation remained in force until August 10, 1904, when Our Predecessor Pius X, of sainted memory, deemed it appropriate to approve a new Regulation. On November 24 of that same year 1904, the Commission ad pias causas took the name of Cardinalitial Commission for the Works of Religion, until 1908, when the Apostolic Constitution Sapienti consilio assigned to the Sacred Congregation of the Council, by authority attributed to it by the same Papal Constitution, a number of responsibilities previously held by the abovementioned Cardinalitial Commission, the Commission itself ceased to be Cardinalitial and became Prelatial. Newly arising administrative needs then prompted the Sacred Congregation of the Council, under a special mandate from the Our Venerated Predecessor Pius XI, to approve on February 10, 1934, on an experimental basis, a new Charter for the Prelatial Commission Administrator of the Works of Religion. Subsequently, on March 17, 1941, the Cardinal Prefect of the same Sacred Congregation of the Council submitted to Us for approval, which We granted, a Charter for the Administration of the Works of Religion, the new name assumed by the abovementioned Commission. With this Charter, the Administration was entrusted to a Commission of Cardinals. A special assembly of Cardinals, held on January 18 of the current year 1942, then expressed its desire that the said Administration of the Works of Religion be established as a juridical person, to give it an organizational structure better suited to the needs of the time and to clarify even more explicitly the separation of responsibilities, which the Holy See has always sought to maintain, between this Administration and the offices of the Holy See (Pius XII, 1942).

The AOR thus functioned as a Vatican-level diocesan endowment, sharing the same goals as its local diocesan counterparts, assuming a role in the financial landscape of the time as the IOR *ante litteram*.

Data has only recently become available on the overall number and distribution of diocesan endowments in Italy (Semeraro, 2020). This section introduces new archival evidence showing the volume and nature of the assets managed by the Vatican AOR compared with those managed at the diocesan level in Italy during a particularly significant period: a few years before the AOR was transformed into the IOR, and a few years after the financial turmoil of the Great Depression in the 1930s.

A number of observations can be made by examining data presented in Tables 1 and 2 (see Appendix), which build on the findings in Riccardo Semeraro's fundamental study of Italian diocesan endowments. In the five-year period under consideration—a time that was far from financially propitious either internationally or domestically—deposits held by the diocesan endowments grew by 25%. This growth reflects increasing trust in this specific form of bequeathal. All ecclesiastical regions reported growth in the assets held by diocesan endowments, with the sole exception of Campania, which declined only slightly (– 6%).

As for the AOR, growth was striking: +67.3%. The combined total assets held by the diocesan endowments and the AOR was rapidly approaching one billion lire.

In detail, aside from the amounts allocated to the reserve fund and the staff pension fund, the majority of deposits fell into three categories: 37.8% was held by various ecclesiastical bodies (chapters, parishes, religious institutes, Benedictine foundations); 32.5% was deposited in the form of pious legacies; and 26.4% were cash deposits in transactional accounts.

There was, thus, a quantitative logic (substantive praxis) underpinning the resources devoted to the "works of religion", by means of which specific objectives were pursued (implicit doctrine). But what, exactly, were these objectives?

6. FINANCIAL CHANGE AND INSTITUTIONAL INNOVATION

To address the above question, it is necessary to go beyond the newly collected, hitherto unpublished but very significant national data. Equally important and of interest are considerations of certain concrete operational aspects of the Italian diocesan endowments within the context of the period of financial transformation in the 1930s.

As an example (but an especially relevant one, i.e., the most highly capitalized diocesan endowment in Italy), we can focus on information regarding the diocese of Milan. This information became available in May of 1936, when the Congregation of the Council (the Vatican dicastery then responsible for oversight) requested a report on the Milanese diocesan endowment for the years 1934 and 1935 according to the model annexed to the new Charter and Regulations. At the same time, the highly eminent bishop was asked to report whether the Cathedral Chapter or other persons, natural or juridical, were in possession of assets allocated to religious or charitable purposes and, if so, whether said assets were properly declared to the diocesan Ordinary (ADC, M589-D622 Milan, letter from the Congregation of the Council to the archbishop of Milan, Cardinal Ildefonso Schuster, May 25, 1936).

In response to this request, the annual report of the diocesan endowment for the year 1934—containing the information presented herein in Table 3 (Appendix)—was dispatched from Milan and registered in Rome on June 1, 1936. Rome responded with comments, particularly regarding the significant decrease in the reserve fund of the diocesan endowment from over 673,000 lire to approximately 347,000 lire. The authorities in Rome wanted a detailed accounting. They also reiterated their request for the submission of the report for the year 1935, with explanations about changes in the fund to support priests in financial difficulty, a question already raised in a previous communication from November 1934. A further request regarded the possible existence of fiduciary assets held by institutions or individuals, a question that had also been raised in a note sent in May of that year (ADC, M589-D622 Milan, letter from the Congregation of the Council to the archbishop of Milan, Cardinal Ildefonso Schuster, September 1, 1936).

On the following November 26, a brief but clear response was received from Milan. It began by explaining that the reduction in the reserve fund had been authorized by a papal concession, granted at the request of the Archbishop of Milan to provide support for the diocesan seminary. It further stated that the report for the year 1935 was still being prepared. As regards support for priests in difficulty, the letter stated that the matter was in the hands of the diocesan pious charity denominated "Ecclesiastical House". Lastly, it stated that no information was available on the existence of fiduciary assets managed by organizations or individuals (ADC, M589-D622 Milan, letter from the Archbishop of Milan, Cardinal Ildefonso Schuster to the prefect of the Congregation of the Council, Cardinal Giulio Serafini, November 26, 1936).

Rome oversaw, Milan invested (growing 3.5% in the period under consideration), guided by the following principles, as evidenced by the balance sheet: the overwhelming majority of capital (59.4 million lire out of 60.2 million) was allocated to support pious legacies, with only a small residual held as simple deposits; a prevalence of capital invested in government securities (77%), with other choices going to municipal and provincial bonds (4.6%), mortgage bonds, especially from Cariplo (8.3%), and miscellaneous bonds (4.6%). Prudence (as dictated by central guidelines, which excluded investments in the stock market) and territoriality (that is, local development, via city and provincial infrastructure) thus represented the fundamental strategies of the Milanese diocesan endowment (Gregorini et al., 2022).

Equally interesting is Bergamo, mainly for the size and composition of its diocesan endowment. In its 1934 balance sheet, accompanied by the customary explanatory note sent to Rome in accordance with the Regulations, several significant changes were reported. As of January 1 of that year, due to financial necessity, the interest rate paid on legacies was reduced from 5.0% to 4.5%. This measure, it was noted, would have a positive effect on the economic outlook for 1935. Additionally, during the course of 1934, all foreign securities previously held in a Swiss bank were repatriated. New government regulations required the transfer of any unsold securities to the local Banca Commerciale, where they were deposited as policies registered in the names of the members of the commission overseeing the pious legacies. To safeguard these assets, each policy was signed in advance by the registered holders, thus ensuring continued access even if one of them should die (Semeraro, 2020, p. 203).

The full data for that year are found in Table 4 (Appendix). Compared to Milan, the overall value of the Bergamo diocesan endowment was naturally lower (just under 37 million lire as opposed to over 60 million), but its yearly growth rate was higher (+7.5%). Some notable differences also emerged as regards investment strategies in Bergamo: 61% of capital was placed in government bonds; only 0.5% went to municipal and provincial bonds; a larger share was in mortgage bonds (11.2%), various bonds (14%), and foreign securities (especially national debt, 13%).

In terms of financial practices, further distinctions came to light between Milan and Bergamo, especially in the latter's more dynamic use of managed resources. The most significant operation by the Bergamo diocese in that period will serve as a concrete illustration of its diversification strategy: the request made by Bishop Luigi Maria Marelli to purchase a high-value property in the city center. The request was addressed to the Congregation of the Council and justified as a need to strengthen the stability of investments linked to perpetually endowed fiduciary legacies, which were steadily increasing (AAV, CC, SA, CD, 2, letter from the Episcopal Curia of Bergamo to the Congregation of the Council, November 18, 1933).

The diocesan commission believed it wise to reduce reliance on government bonds and other fixed-income instruments by supplementing them with real estate holdings, which were seen as offering greater stability and as less vulnerable to financial market fluctuations. A number of such investments had been carried out in the past via ad hoc entities, such as the Società Immobiliare Diocesana (SID – Diocesan Real Estate Company) and the bank known as the Consorzio Economico Diocesano (CED – Diocesan Economic Consortium), with results that were satisfying in terms of both returns and asset security.

The proposed purchase involved a building in the new urban center with a total value of 3,900,000 lire and an anticipated net return of 6%. The operation would result in the investment of roughly one fourth of the diocesan endowment's assets in real estate, which was fully controlled through full ownership of the acquiring companies' shares. These companies would assume no debts or obligations to third parties, thus ensuring the acquisition remained free of external risk.

However, before proceeding, approval by the Holy See was required. The financing plan entailed selling off a portion of industrial and foreign securities—many of which had appreciated in value—for a total of approximately one million lire. They included Swiss federal securities and industrial bonds traded above their purchase price. The remaining amount would be covered by liquid assets typically available at the start of the year, originating from new foundations, drawn bonds, or early repayments of mortgage loans (AAV, CC, SA, CD, 2, letter from the Episcopal Curia of Bergamo to the Congregation of the Council, November 18, 1933).

Several factors thus supported the proposal advanced by the Bergamo diocese: refinement of investment diversification strategies; efficient use of companies associated with the diocesan endowment (Finanziaria Immobiliare Diocesana [FID – Diocesan Real Estate Finance Company] and the CED); enhancement of the endowment's ability to generate income for the aforementioned "perpetually endowed fiduciary legacies, which were steadily increasing"; and further divestiture of industrial stock and foreign securities, deemed less secure than a real estate investment on the scale being proposed.

The documentation sent to the Vatican included a summary balance sheet for the diocesan endowment updated to 1933 and a detailed prospectus of rental income from the property in question, then managed by the Società Immobiliare Centro Bergamo [SICB – Bergamo Center Real Estate Company] (Table 5, Appendix). They were supplemented by a number of technical observations by the episcopal delegate Don Guglielmo Carozzi, who noted that, in addition to legally mandated rent reductions, new leases had been signed at more modest rates. An emblematic example was the Touring Hotel, a rooming house with approximately sixty rooms, whose annual rent had been cut in half with respect to previous years from 80,000 to 40,000 lire. Furthermore, regarding spaces to be used by banks, rental rates were calculated based on offers that had already been received, including one from the Banco Ambrosiano (AAV, CC, SA, CD, 2, annex 2 to the letter from the Episcopal Curia of Bergamo to the Congregation of the Council, November 18, 1933).

A further, highly detailed report described the structural and functional characteristics of the building. Situated strategically in the center of Bergamo, the building gave onto three major traffic routes: Piazza Vittorio Veneto to the east, Piazza Cavour to the south, and Via Francesco Crispi to the west. It bordered to the north on the porticos of the Banca Popolare di Bergamo and with other buildings belonging to that bank. With an overall volume of approximately 39,500 cubic meters, including sublevels, the building encompassed a number of independent spaces: the headquarters of the Banca Bergamasca, five residential apartments, about thirty offices and professional studios, seven commercial establishments, a modern hotel with sixty rooms, and a brewery with a bar and ample sublevel spaces (AAV, CC, SA, CD, 2, annex 3 to the letter from the Episcopal Curia of Bergamo to the Congregation of the Council, November 18, 1933).

The reference to a potential new branch of the Banco Ambrosiano in Bergamo highlighted the emergence of a broader strategy to promote the local presence of a bank that was historically favored in Lombard Catholic social teaching (Taccolini and Cafaro, 1997). Real estate operations funded through the diocesan endowment could thus be undertaken in targeted ways aligning with a broader institutional and financial vision.

In the end, the operation did not go through, in spite of the efforts of Monsignor Giuseppe Rossi of the Apostolic Penitentiary and repeated postponements of the date for signing the sales contract. These delays were attributable to hesitation on the part of the Roman Congregation but could not be continued indefinitely. The Bergamo Curia continued to advocate for the sale, putting forth various arguments in its favor. However, in the end its efforts were fruitless (AAV, CC, SA, CD, 2, letter from the coadjutor bishop of Bergamo, Monsignor Adriano Bernareggi to the prefect of the Congregation of the Council, Cardinal Giulio Serafini, December 5, 1933).

In rejecting the hopes expressed by the leaders of the diocese of Bergamo, the Congregation of the Council sent the following communication to Bernareggi on January 27, 1934:

> *With regard to the purchase of the noted property in your city, I inform Your Most Reverend Excellency that this Sacred Congregation, having examined and fully considered the documentation, and particularly the two appraisals submitted in December, does not deem it appropriate to grant the requested authorization to invest the funds of the diocesan endowment in said property (AAV, CC, SA, CD, 2, letter from the Congregation of the Council to the coadjutor bishop of Bergamo, Monsignor Adriano Bernareggi, January 27, 1934).*

This case illustrates both the complexity and the ambition of the "Bergamo system", which was grounded in the dynamism of an institution that was able to innovate, especially in the financial realm.

Beginning in the 1920s, alongside the diocesan endowment founded in 1873, other bodies were established with complementary purposes to support the economic and social development of the diocese in a more comprehensive and articulate way. Among them was the aforementioned Consorzio Economico Diocesano (CED), instituted in 1921 as a credit institute co-owned by the endowment. The CED sought to incentivize savings and undertake non-speculative banking and credit operations, offering safe, guaranteed investments with an aim to promoting cooperation and ethical, religious, and social works to benefit the people of the Province of Bergamo (Semeraro, 2020, p. 160).

In 1925, the abovementioned Finanziaria Immobiliare Diocesana (FID) was established with capital from the diocesan endowment and the CED, with the aim of managing real estate investments. In parallel, in the same period, a public limited company was set up under the name "Juventus" by direct behest of the bishop to give a legal identity to the Sant'Alessandro religious charity [*opera pia*]. The latter supported various educational and religious entities—including boarding schools, religious houses, vocational schools, kindergartens, and oratories—, whose real estate holdings, previously owned by private individuals, were transferred to Juventus (Semeraro, 2020, p. 163).

The Bergamo strategy sought to optimize diocesan operations both in financial investments (by creating a bank) and in real estate (creating a new real estate company and transforming a religious charity into a legal vehicle for property transfers, including those from religious congregations fearing suppressive measures of which they might be targets [Gregorini, 2010, pp. 134-135]). Importantly, this was done while rigorously avoiding the direct use (and thus the potential misuse) of capital deposited in the diocesan endowment.

The inspection of the Bergamo CED by the Banca d'Italia in 1950, summarized in Table 6 (Appendix), provided a favorable assessment of this approach. After acknowledging the institute's overall soundness and its responsible management, the bank's report noted that its credit activities supported ecclesiastical entities, Catholic associations, and local operators. The use of lines of credit and receivables discounting facilities reflected a management approach oriented toward social proximity and support for cooperation and small-scale entrepreneurship (ASBI, Vigilanza, Pratiche, n. 3481.0, f. 3, letter from the Director General of the Banca d'Italia, Paride Formenti, to the Director of the Bergamo branch, December 3, 1950).

At the Vatican, the reformist thrust followed a distinctly different path. The first step was to revise the organizational structure of the AOR by drawing up a new charter and regulations (1934), then to transform it into a financially operational body with autonomous legal status (1942). Although this structure was suited to the needs of the time and clearly distinguished from other Vatican offices, it was nonetheless destined to operate directly in financial and real estate markets using fiduciary capital, thus running the risk of facilitating the onset of an age of financial adventurism (Galli, 2004; McGoldrick, 2012).

It is worth noting that the Vatican's revision of the charter and regulations generated a series of interesting yet hitherto undiscovered documents that provide a detailed description of the operating structure and purposes of this Vatican administration as it stood in the mid-1930s. For example, the first three articles of Title I (Constitution, Purpose, Responsibilities, and Composition) of the Charter state:

Art. 1 – Within the Vatican City State, a Commission is established for the custody and administration of capital deposited in the form of securities or cash, and destined for works of Christian piety and religion. It shall be called the Commission for the Administration of the Works of Religion and shall be composed of five prelates, including a president.

Art. 2 – The Commission may not accept deposits of capital unless at least part of the funds, presently or in the future, are destined for the purposes stated in the preceding article, with the sole exception of deposits from Cardinals and Bishops residing in the Curia, as well as clerics of the same Curia and of the Vicariate of Rome.

Art. 3 – The Commission bears full responsibility for its management and is subject to the oversight and control of the Sacred Congregation of the Council (ADC, A1-D622 Rome et al., Commissione amministratrice delle opere di religione. Statuto, norme e regolamenti, Tipografia poliglotta vaticana 1934, p. 5).

Now quite distinct from the diocesan endowments, the AOR could accept deposits not strictly destined *ad pias causas*, provided the depositors were clergy in the Vatican Curia or the Roman Vicariate. A further distinction was instituted in 1942 when Pope Pius XII granted it autonomous legal status. In keeping with this, Articles 1 and 2 of Title I of the Commission Rules (Categories of Deposits) specified:

Art. 1 – Deposits referred to in Art. 2 of the Charter are divided into three categories: a) custodial deposits; b) administered deposits; c) current account deposits. Each category shall be managed separately.

Art. 2 – For custodial deposits, the Commission is responsible for safeguarding the assets, collecting interest, and distributing it according to the depositors' instructions. For administrated deposits, the Commission acts in a fiduciary capacity, according to the terms specific to each deposit. Current account deposits consist of all other cash deposits not belonging to the previous two categories (ADC, A1-D622 Rome et al., Commissione amministratrice delle opere di religione. Statuto, norme e regolamenti, Tipografia poliglotta vaticana 1934, p. 10).

Finally, a "Regulation for the Executive Office of the Commission for the Administration of the Works of Religion" and a "Regulation for the Personnel of the Executive Office" were drafted. While a detailed analysis of these regulations is beyond the scope of this paper, the corresponding personnel chart and salaries is presented in Table 7 (Appendix). The pursuit of effective administration functionality—untethered from doctrine—relied on the establishment of stable managerial procedures (praxis), as part of an effort to achieve the difficult goal of operational and legal autonomy (Gregorini & Semeraro, 2025).

7. CONCLUSION AND IMPLICATIONS

The analysis presented here clearly highlights one of the most problematic aspects of twentieth-century Catholic economic culture: the deep disconnect between practice—multiform, historically entrenched, and often innovative—and doctrinal development, which was nearly absent, particularly in the financial realm. This imbalance becomes even more striking when we consider the breadth and significance of the Church's participation in modern financial systems, especially through the management of pious legacies and assets earmarked for works of religion.

In this context, the so-called "Christian patrimony", composed of resources donated by the faithful for charitable, religious, and social purposes, was anything but marginal. It progressively became a concrete grounds for implementing complex financial strategies, particularly those developed in local churches, which claimed—sometimes in conflict with the Holy See—substantial autonomy in how they managed the funds they administrated.

Within this framework, the diocesan endowments became crucial institutions. They were instituted as entities to safeguard charitable capital, investing it prudently but profitably. They were not limited to mere administration, but represented true intermediaries between donors, ecclesiastical entities, and local communities. As documented by Semeraro (2020; 2022) and Semeraro and Gregorini (2019; 2021), the diocesan endowments demonstrated an ability to adapt to changing economic and regulatory circumstances, promoting financial practices grounded in prudence, transparency, and a long-term outlook.

A particularly telling example is the case of Bergamo. In addition to the meticulous management of the pious legacies, it also showed a remarkable capacity for institutional innovation. The creation, as early as the 1920s, of complementary entities such as the Consorzio Economico Diocesano (CED) and the Finanziaria Immobiliare Diocesana (FID) revealed a farsighted strategy: eschew speculation, anchor investments in the local area, and provide direct support for educational, religious, and social works. This approach excluded the direct employment of funds from the diocesan endowments in risky operations, but amplified the effectiveness of investments by leveraging parallel structures (Semeraro, 2020).

And yet, this institutional and financial dynamism stood in sharp contrast to the lack of a coherent and structured social doctrine capable of giving direction and meaning to the adopted practices. The *Quadragesimo anno*, while important, was ambiguous and uncommunicative regarding finance, using terms such as "money" and "bank" only in a general or critical sense (Cesarini, 2004; Sorge, 2011). It was thus ecclesiastical finance "without doctrine", developed out of necessity and fidelity to charitable ends, but lacking an overall guiding framework grounding in theory. This was true at a time not long before the innovation introduced by Pope Paul VI (*Populorum progressio*), which called on Catholicism to engage in a dialogical reflection "along the most perilous fault lines between economic and ethical rationality" (Ferrari, 1995, p. 245). In other words, at a time not far removed from the transition to a cultural attitude that was no longer defensive and substantially tutorial, but wisely inventive and wholly missionary, according to which the true problem was what Paul VI had called "the great misunderstanding between labor and religion", that is, between culture and faith, which had been, and continued to be, too starkly separated (Rumi, 2009, p. 194).

The lag as regards doctrine cannot be overlooked. As stated at the beginning of this paper, the separation between doctrine and financial practices has affected our understanding of the economic role of the Church in the late modern period. And this is true in spite of the growing interest demonstrated in recent years by historiographers in the relationship between the Church and the economy (Friedman, 2021), fueled partly by the deep crisis both are experiencing: on the one hand, the internal fragilities of the Church, as recently acknowledged by Benedict XVI (2023), and on the other, the in-built contradictions of financial capitalism, brought to light by authors such as Piketty (2020; 2021).

Historical researchers have progressively rediscovered the theme of ecclesiastical finance. Studies by Pegrari (2011; 2019; 2020) on the investment policies of the Holy See and by Semeraro (2020a; 2020b; 2022) and Gregorini (2024) on management of charitable funds and research dedicated to women's religious congregations and other ecclesiastical bodies (Chambers & Dimson, 2016; Cavallo, 1995; Gregorini, 2012; 2016; Maffi et al., 2018) are helping to fill a major gap in our understanding of the role played by these particular institutional investors.

Nevertheless, the theme of legacies—drawing in not only the history of charity, but also the structure of relations among the clergy, churchgoers, dioceses, and the Roman core—remains little explored. It represents a locus of study of governance *ante litteram*, exhibiting dynamics of cooperation, oversight, responsibility, and trust that come into play in pursuit of a shared aim. As emphasized by Colombo (2016; 2019), Colombo and Dotti (2014), and Colombo and Semeraro (2022), the practice of "bequeathal for a pious cause" is anything but a premodern remnant: it is an integral part of modern Catholicism. It was certainly active in the early modern period but continued unabated into the late modern period (and on to the present day), very pertinently highlighting the role of the Church in society and its inner mechanisms.

In this light, the Church appears not as an alternative to the market or to capitalism, but as an entity that interacts with them, using them as instruments for higher purposes. As aptly condensed by Fornasari (2020, p. 344), the Church—perhaps mainly the local churches—never rejected the market or capitalism per se, but used them within a logic of giving, reciprocity, and redistribution. In this view, the economy is seen as embedded in society, and a mutualistic relationship between the two is essential to furthering the Church's mission.

Ultimately, this essay contributes to an ongoing and vital pursuit (CDF & DSSUI, 2018; Conferenza Episcopale Italiana, 2020; De Franssu & De Salins, 2024). The study of the diocesan endowments, pious legacies, and charity financing constitutes not only a compelling historiographical field of inquiry, but also an opportunity to ask how today's Catholic Church can align its presence in the world with the integrity of its mission.

The events documented in the years 1870-1950 had significant implications for the following period, and certainly up to 2009. In this period, the finances of the Catholic Church, particularly in Europe and Italy, underwent a phase of great transformation and encountered no few difficulties. This long temporal arc, marked by deep social, economic, and cultural changes, once again highlights the various unresolved issues in the financial management of ecclesiastical institutions.

One of the first problems that emerged was a progressive decline in traditional sources of income. Starting in the 1950s, secularization led to a significant reduction in the participation of the faithful in the life of the Church. One consequence was a decrease in offerings, Sunday collections, and private donations, always one of the principal sources of support for parishes. This difficulty was compounded by a crisis in income from property, due partially to agricultural reforms, urbanization, and changes in the management of ecclesiastical assets. Rural properties, once a stable source of income, lost value or became financially unsustainable. The charity market was thus scaled back (Diotallevi, 2024).

For this reason, starting in the 1980s, the question of public financing for the Church became crucial, especially in Italy. In 1984, the revision of the Concordat between State and Church, dated 1929, introduced the "eight per mille" (0.8%) mechanism, which ensured a constant influx of public funds to recognized religious faiths. This system represented a turning point but it also raised a number of issues. Is it truly ethical for the State to contribute to the Church's finances in an increasingly secular and pluralistic political context? Additionally, there was much discussion about the actual destination of these funds: what portion is effectively used for worship and what portion goes to other purposes, such as charity or cultural works (Consorti, 2009)?

Another delicate question has to do with how ecclesiastical finances are managed internally. Until relatively recently, there had been little development of professional competencies in economics within the Church. Dioceses and parishes were often administrated by non-specialized personnel who lacked adequate training in management or accounting. This situation produced a certain opacity, difficulty in controlling expenses, and even occasional scandals. Examples include the IOR and the collapse of the Banco Ambrosiano in the 1980s, where the intermixing of Vatican finances and political or criminal interests caused a great uproar and loss of credibility. This is clear evidence that practice without doctrine has generated episodes of significant harm (Bellavite Pellegrini, 2001).

In the meantime, the needs of the Church expanded. On the one hand, the cost of maintaining the aging and numerically declining clergy increased. On the other, the Church intensified its social commitment: schools, hospitals, and aid to the poor and migrants began to demand significant resources. This drove many dioceses to seek new sources of funding, resorting to such expedients as public calls for philanthropic/cultural funding proposals, seeking support from private foundations, or establishing partnerships with local organizations. Institutional financial innovation became necessary (Consorti, 2005).

Lastly, on the global scale, imbalances emerged between the "wealthy" churches of the global north and the "poor" churches of the global south. African, Asian, or Latin American churches often depend on funding from Europe or North America, which raises questions as to the sustainability and autonomy of local missions, and also as to the priority of the interests of local identities (Congregazione per gli Istituti di Vita Consacrata e le Società di Vita Apostolica, 2018).

In sum, the period 1950-2009 represented a transition for church financing: from a system based on income from property and offerings to a more complex model, where public financing, social planning, and transparency in accounting acquire critical importance. The ethical challenges are all still there: how to ensure effective financial management that is also consistent with evangelical values?

Some attempt at an answer came in 2009-2010 under Pope Benedict XVI, but the results have yet to be consolidated, partly because it took the form of legislative action and not new doctrinal orientations (Bani & Consorti, 2015).

AUTHOR'S NOTE

All quotations translated by the authors.

ARCHIVES

Rome, Archivio del Dicastero per il Clero (ADC)
Rome, Archivio Storico della Banca d'Italia (ASBI)
Vatican City, Archivio Apostolico Vaticano (AAV)
- Congregazione del Concilio (CC)
- Sezione Amministrativa (SA)
- Casse Diocesane (CD)

REFERENCES

Ammerman, N. (2016). Lived religion as an emerging field: An assessment of its contours and frontiers. *Nordic Journal of Religion and Society*, *29*(2), 83–99. DOI: 10.18261/issn.1890-7008-2016-02-01

Attoukou, M., & Nchare, K. (2022). Financial exclusion and poverty reduction in Benin. *Asian Journal of Economics and Empirical Research*, *9*(2), 121–131. DOI: 10.20448/ajeer.v9i2.4146

Bani, E., & Consorti, P. (Eds.). (2015). *Finanze vaticane e Unione europea. Le riforme di papa Francesco e le sfide della vigilanza internazionale*. Il Mulino.

Bellavite Pellegrini, C. (2001). *Storia del Banco Ambrosiano: Fondazione, ascesa e dissesto 1896–1982*. Laterza.

Benedict, X. V. I. (2023). *Che cos'è il cristianesimo. Quasi un testamento spirituale*. Mondadori.

Bocci, M. (1999). *Oltre lo Stato liberale. Ipotesi su politica e società nel dibattito cattolico tra fascismo e democrazia*. Bulzoni.

Cafaro, P. (2001). *La solidarietà efficiente. Storia e prospettive del credito cooperativo in Italia (1883–2000)*. Laterza.

Cavallo, S. (1995). *Charity and power in early modern Italy: Benefactors and their motives in Turin, 1541–1789*. Cambridge University Press.

Cesarini, F. (2004). Finanza. In Università Cattolica del Sacro Cuore (Ed.), *Dizionario di dottrina sociale della Chiesa. Scienze sociali e magistero* (pp. 309–310). Vita e Pensiero.

Chambers, D., & Dimson, E. (Eds.). (2016). *Financial market history: Reflections on the past for investors today*. The CFA Institute Research Foundation.

Cini, M. (Ed.). (2019). *Alla ricerca della terza via. Politica, economia, istituzioni*. Pisa University Press.

Coleman, H. (2015). Studying Russian religion since the collapse of communism. *Journal of the Canadian Historical Association, 25*(2), 309–318. DOI: 10.7202/1032851ar

Colombo, A. (2004). *Congregazioni religiose e sviluppo in Lombardia tra Otto e Novecento. Il caso delle Suore di Maria Bambina*. Vita e Pensiero.

Colombo, E. C. (2016). Prefazione. In E. Lurgo, *Carità barocca. Opere pie e luoghi pii nello Stato sabaudo fra XVII e XVIII secolo* (pp. IX–XXIV). Fondazione 1563 per l'Arte e la Cultura della Compagnia di San Paolo.

Colombo, E. C. (2019). Premessa. *Quaderni Storici, 54*(3), 601–617.

Colombo, E. C., & Dotti, M. (2014). L'economia rituale. Dalla rendita alle celebrazioni (Lodi, età moderna). *Quaderni Storici, 54*(3), 871–903.

Colombo, E. C., & Semeraro, R. (2022). Introduzione. In Colombo, E. C., & Semeraro, R. (Eds.), *Le ragioni della carità. Economia e funzioni dei legati pii tra età moderna e contemporanea* (pp. 163–189). Il Mulino.

Conferenza Episcopale Italiana. (2020). *La Chiesa cattolica e la gestione delle risorse finanziarie con criteri etici di responsabilità sociale, ambientale e di governance*. Mediagraf.

Congregazione per gli Istituti di Vita Consacrata e le Società di Vita Apostolica (2018). *Economia a servizio del carisma e della missione. Boni dispensatores multiformis gratiae Dei. Orientamenti*. Libreria Editrice Vaticana.

Congregazione per la Dottrina della Fede & Dicastero per il Servizio dello Sviluppo Umano Integrale. (2018). *Oeconomicae et pecuniariae quaestiones: considerazioni per un discernimento etico circa alcuni aspetti dell'attuale sistema economico-finanziario*. Libreria Editrice Vaticana.

Consorti, P. (2005). *Legislazione del terzo settore. Le norme sul "nonprofit", il volontariato, la cooperazione sociale ed internazionale*. Plus.

Consorti, P. (2009). Il prezzo della religione. In Bani, E. (Ed.), *Il "giusto" prezzo tra Stato e mercato. Liber amicorum per Mauro Giusti* (pp. 262–271). Giappichelli.

Crocella, C. (1982). *"Augusta miseria": Aspetti delle finanze pontificie nell'età del capitalismo*. Nuovo Istituto Editoriale Italiano.

De Franssu, J.-B., & De Salins, A. (2024). The Catholic Church and ethical finance: From theory to practice. *Etudes*, *3*, 88–89.

De Luca, G. (2021). Capitali dei privati, notai e modernizzazione economica a Milano tra Sette e Ottocento. In Gregorini, G., & Romani, M. (Eds.), *Borghesie nazionali, borghesie cosmopolite* (pp. 23–34). FrancoAngeli.

De Maeyer, J., Leplae, S., & Schmiedl, J. (Eds.). (2004). *Religious institutes in Western Europe in the 19th and 20th centuries: Historiography, research and legal position*. Leuven University Press.

Dieguez, A. M., & Pagano, S. (2006). *La carte del "sacro tavolo". Aspetti del pontificato di Pio X dai documenti del suo archivio privato* (Vol. II). Archivio Segreto Vaticano.

Diotallevi, L. (2024). *La messa è sbiadita. La partecipazione ai riti religiosi in Italia dal 1993 al 2019*. Rubbettino.

Farese, G. (2019). Un ordine mondiale per lo sviluppo. In R. Mascolo & S. Palermo (Eds.), *Europa domani. Studi in onore di Giuseppe Di Taranto*. Luiss University Press.

Ferrari, A. (1995). *La cultura riformatrice. Uomini, tecniche, filosofie di fronte allo sviluppo (1945–1968)*. Studium.

Fornasari, M. (2017). *La banca, la borsa, lo Stato. Una storia della finanza (secoli XIII–XXI)*. Giappichelli.

Fornasari, M. (2017). Postfazione. In R. Semeraro, *Piccoli IOR* (pp. 331–334). Il Mulino.

Friedman, B. M. (2021). *Religion and the rise of capitalism*. Alfred A. Knopf.

Gregorini, G. (2008). (Ed.). *Religiose, religiosi, economia e società nell'Italia contemporanea*. Vita e Pensiero.

Gregorini, G. (2010). *Un po' di bene. L'Istituto delle Suore Sacramentine di Bergamo dalle origini al secondo dopoguerra (1882–1950)*. Vita e Pensiero.

Gregorini, G. (2012). The organization and economics of religious congregations in North Italy (1861–1929). In Van Dijck, M., De Maeyer, J., Tyssens, J., & Koppen, J. (Eds.), *The economics of providence / L'économie de la providence* (pp. 323–342). Leuven University Press.

Gregorini, G. (2024). Anatomia di un bilancio: Chiesa, finanza, carità nell'Italia della grande depressione. In M. Gregorini & G. Gregorini, *Artificial Intelligence and Economic History. Topics, Tools, Intersections* (pp. 75–134). Vita e Pensiero.

Gregorini, G., Maffi, L., & Rochini, M. (2023). *Social support system in rural Italy: The modern age regional states of the northern peninsula*. Palgrave Macmillan. DOI: 10.1007/978-3-031-24303-5

Gregorini, G., & Semeraro, R. (2025). *La difficile proiezione internazionale della finanza vaticana negli anni del Regno d'Italia (1870–1942)* [Manuscript submitted for publication]. Università Cattolica del Sacro Cuore.

Gregorini, M., & Gregorini, G. (2022). Costruire la comunità. In Colombo, E. C., & Semeraro, R. (Eds.), *Le ragioni della carità* (pp. 123–161). Il Mulino.

Gregorini, M., Semeraro, R., & Gregorini, G. (2022). Le virtù della carità. Patrimonio ecclesiastico, finanza comportamentale e sviluppo territoriale nell'Italia del XX secolo. In Gregorini, G., Semeraro, R., & Taccolini, M. (Eds.), *I volti della povertà. Temi, parole, fonti per la storia dei sistemi di supporto sociale tra modernità e globalizzazione* (pp. 57–79). Vita e Pensiero.

Haddad, A. (2021). Does the country's religion affect the financial performance of conventional and Islamic banks? Comparative study in the international framework. *Journal of Islamic Marketing, 14*(2), 410–434. DOI: 10.1108/JIMA-03-2021-0088

Iannaccone, L. (2012). Extremism and the economics of religion*. *The Economic Record, 88*(s1), 110–115. DOI: 10.1111/j.1475-4932.2012.00803.x

Iyer, S. (2016). The new economics of religion. *Journal of Economic Literature, 54*(2), 395–441. DOI: 10.1257/jel.54.2.395

Jemolo, A. C. (1975). *Chiesa e Stato in Italia negli ultimi cento anni*. Einaudi.

Jensen, T., & Geertz, A. (2014). From the history of religions to the study of religion in Denmark: An essay on the subject, organizational history and research themes. *Temenos - Nordic Journal for the Study of Religion, 50*(1), 79–114. https://doi.org/ DOI: 10.33356/temenos.46252

Lai, B. (2012). *Finanze vaticane. Da Pio XI a Benedetto XVI*. Rubbettino.

Lei, L., & Traylor, F. (2023). How does religion influence parental support of young adult children? *Journal of Family Issues*, *45*(9), 2135–2157. DOI: 10.1177/0192513X231195653

Maffi, L., Rochini, M., & Gregorini, G. (Eds.). (2018). *I sistemi del dare nell'Italia rurale del XVIII secolo*. FrancoAngeli.

McGoldrick, P. M. (2012). New perspectives on Pius XII and Vatican financial transactions during the Second World War. *Historical Journal (Cambridge, England)*, *55*(4), 1029–1048. DOI: 10.1017/S0018246X12000416

Nicholls, A. (2022). *Oxford Faith-Aligned Impact Finance Project Phase 1 Report*. Saïd Business School – University of Oxford.

Pasinetti, L. (2004). Capitale. In Università Cattolica del Sacro Cuore (Ed.), *Dizionario di dottrina sociale della Chiesa* (p. 170). Vita e Pensiero.

Pecorari, P. (1997). La cultura economico-sociale del movimento cattolico (1861–1995). In Traniello, F., & Campanini, G. (Eds.), *Dizionario storico del movimento cattolico. Aggiornamento 1980–1995* (pp. 25–34). Marietti.

Pegrari, M. (2011). De pecunia. Chiesa, cattolici e finanza nello Stato unitario. In *Cristiani d'Italia. Chiese, società, Stato, 1861–2011* (pp. 1053–1079). [Editore non specificato].

Pegrari, M. (2014). La città e il credito. In Carboni, M., & Muzzarelli, M. G. (Eds.), *Reti di credito. Circuiti informali, impropri, nascosti (secoli XIII–XIX)* (pp. 195–220). Il Mulino.

Pegrari, M. (2019). Le finanze della Santa Sede e il Terzo Reich. *Studi storici Luigi Simeoni*, 69, 75–86.

Pegrari, M. (2020). Le finanze della Santa Sede e la black list: la questione Sudameris (1910–1948). *Studi storici Luigi Simeoni*, 70, 97–106.

Persico, A. A. (2014). *Il Codice di Camaldoli. La DC e la ricerca della «terza via» tra Stato e mercato (1943–1993)*. Guerini.

Piketty, T. (2020). *Capitale e ideologia*. La nave di Teseo.

Piketty, T. (2021). *Una breve storia dell'uguaglianza*. La nave di Teseo.

Pius, X. I. I. (1942, 27 June). *Chirografo di papa Pio XII con il quale il pontefice erige l'Istituto per le opere di religione*. https://www.vatican.va/content/pius-xii/it/letters/documents/hf_p-xii_lett_19420627_chirografo-ior.html

Pollard, J. F. (2006). *L'obolo di Pietro. Le finanze del Papato moderno: 1850–1950*. Corbaccio.

Rocca, G. (2007). Le strategie anticonfisca degli istituti religiosi in Italia dall'Unità al Concordato del 1929. In R. Di Pietra & F. Landi (Eds.), *Clero, economia e contabilità in Europa. Tra medioevo ed età contemporanea* (pp. 226–247). Carocci.

Rubin, J. (2020). Introduction to the special issue on the economics of religion. *Journal of Demographic Economics*, *86*(3), 207–211. DOI: 10.1017/dem.2020.20

Rumi, G. (1986). Introduzione al problema storiografico della "storia diocesana". In Caprioli, A., Rimoldi, A., & Vaccaro, L. (Eds.), *Chiesa e società. Appunti per una storia delle diocesi lombarde* (pp. 29–38). La Scuola.

Rumi, G. (2009a). La cultura cattolica italiana nel '900. In E. Bressan & D. Saresella (Eds.), *Perché la storia. Itinerari di ricerca (1963–2006)* (Vol. I, pp. 193–201). Led.

Rumi, G. (2009b). Una cattedra tra Milano e Roma. In E. Bressan & D. Saresella (Eds.), *Perché la storia. Itinerari di ricerca (1963–2006)* (Vol. II, pp. 511–532). Led.

Semeraro, R. (2017). Economic and Financial Management of Religious Congregations in Late Modern Italy. In Gregorini, G. (Ed.), *For the needy youth that we care* (pp. 57–87). Vita e Pensiero.

Semeraro, R. (2020a). *Piccoli IOR. Le Casse Diocesane da Porta Pia alla Seconda guerra mondiale*. Il Mulino.

Semeraro, R. (2020b). "Non essendo cosa di sua competenza". *Studi storici Luigi Simeoni*, 70, 73–84.

Semeraro, R. (2022). «Per il rispetto alle somme chiavi»: storia dello IOR prima dello IOR. In Colombo, E. C., & Semeraro, R. (Eds.), *Le ragioni della carità* (pp. 163–189). Il Mulino.

Semeraro, R., & Gregorini, G. (2019). Destini legati. *Quaderni Storici*, *3*, 801–829.

Semeraro, R., & Gregorini, G. (2021). Il vanto di Napoli. In Gregorini, G., & Romani, M. (Eds.), *Borghesie nazionali, borghesie cosmopolite* (pp. 82–105). FrancoAngeli.

Sorge, B. (2011). *Introduzione alla dottrina sociale della Chiesa*. Queriniana.

Taccolini, M. (2009). Chiesa ed economia. In M. Taccolini (Ed.), *Nuovi percorsi della storia economica* (pp. 133–147). Vita e Pensiero.

Taccolini, M., & Cafaro, P. (1997). *Il Banco Ambrosiano. Una banca cattolica negli anni dell'ascesa economica lombarda*. Laterza.

Taccolini, M., & Gregorini, G. (2019). *Banco di Brescia, vent'anni nel futuro*. Morcelliana.

United States Conference of Catholic Bishops. (2021). Socially Responsible Investment Guidelines for the United States Conference of Catholic Bishops. https://www.usccb.org/resources/Socially%20Responsible%20Investment%20Guidelines%202021%20(003).pdf

Vaquero Piñeiro, M. (2007). I censi consegnativi. *Rivista di storia dell'agricoltura*, 47(1), 57–94.

KEY TERMS AND DEFINITIONS

Catholic Social Teaching: The teachings of the Catholic Church regarding ethical and moral principles applicable to social, economic, and political life. They are rooted in the Gospels, the Christian tradition, and the theology and philosophy that has developed over the centuries. They champion values such as human dignity, the common good, solidarity, and subsidiarity. Catholic Social Doctrine offers guidelines for building a more just, fraternal society, inspiring the actions of the faithful, and forging dialogue with all persons of good will.

Diocesan endowment [Cassa Diocesana]: an institutional instrument established in Italian dioceses starting in the second half of the nineteenth century to centrally administrate funds destined for works of Christian piety and charity in the form of pious legacies.

Encyclical: pastoral document issued by the Pope within the ordinary magisterium, addressed to bishops and to the faithful as an authoritative teaching on doctrinal, moral, spiritual, or social questions.

Pious legacy: an arrangement by which a member of the church destines assets or incomes for religious or charitable purposes in line with the mission of the Catholic Church, either while living or by testament, according to Can. 1299 of the Code of Canon Law.

Populorum Progressio: social encyclical issued by Pope Paul VI, published on March 26, 1967, dedicated to the theme of the universal development of peoples.

Quadregesimo Anno: social encyclical issued by Pope Pius XI, published on May 15, 1931, on the occasion of the 40th anniversary of the *Rerum Novarum* of Pope Leo XIII.

Rerum Novarum: social encyclical issued by Pope Leo XIII on May 15, 1891, considered to be the founding document of Catholic Social Doctrine.

Works of religion: activities, institutions, or initiatives whose main purpose is the promotion of the faith, evangelization, Christian education and training, and charity according to the principles of the Catholic Church.

APPENDIX

Table 1. Value of diocesan endowments in Italy and of the Vatican AOR, 1930 and 1935 (lire)

	1930	**1935**
Piedmont	95,553,484.28	125,852,464.79
Liguria	40,892,588.00	47,500,955.00
Lombardy	117,869,919.65	156,138,869.48
Veneto	34,071,432.73	42,948,184.22
Emilia	14,340,073.59	18,544,362.01
Romagna	22,184,938.44	24,845,702.95
Lazio	7,664,724.03	10,955,385.61
Tuscany	27,339,890.91	33,956,484.59
Umbria	7,339,807.16	9,903,185.71
Marche	13,853,705.78	15,889,822.88
Abruzzi and Molise	4,149,161.99	5,872,973.61
Beneventano	5,386,267.00	7,352,594.61
Campania	49,867,505.91	46,744,184.48
Salernitano	10,217,393.59	13,178,429.67
Apulia	16,815,095.62	23,817,158.72
Calabria	4,191,044.50	4,518,225.99
Sicily Sardinia	31,245,898.17	42,534,540.93
Total	**506,990,362.59**	**635,485,876.68**
AOR – Vatican	143,902,856.33	240,718,458.08
Total	**650,893,218.92**	**876,204,334.76**

Source: AAV, CC, SA, CD, 20.

Table 2. AOR deposits, Vatican City, 1935 (lire)

Diocesan endowments	91,383,707.71	
Chapters, parishes, etc. in Rome		31,412,629.17
Legacies, s. congregations, eccl. colleges in Rome		44,667,854.01
Legacies, religious charities outside Rome		33,730,746.00

continued on following page

Table 2. Continued

Religious institutes		31,261,784.39
Shared endowment accounts		3,653,991.29
Holy masses		884,451.00
Benedictine and Pian foundations		28,272,580.00
Cash deposits		63,474,060.42
General reserve fund		1,019,158.30
Staff pension fund		2,341,203.50
Total		**240,718,458.08**

Source: AAV, CC, SA, CD, 20.

Table 3. Balance for endowment of diocese of Milan, March 31, 1935 (lire)

1) Capital movements		
Total capital on April 1, 1934		58,223,976.10
Capital inflow during year	2,666,915.85	
Capital outflow during year	645,681.75	
Difference		2,021,234.10
Total capital on March 31, 1935		60,245,210.20
2) Capital breakdown		
Pious legacies		59,409,934.60
Cash deposits		488,100.30
Reserve fund		347,175.30
Total capital on March 31, 1935		60,245,210.20
3) Capital inventory on March 31, 1935		
1) Government securities		
Registered 3.5% government domestic bonds	176,800.00	
Bearer 3.5% government domestic bonds	35,256,900.00	
Redeemable 3.5% government domestic bonds	9,888,000.00	
5% treasury bonds	838,500.00	
4% treasury bonds	128,000.00	
3% government domestic bonds	36,100.00	
5% national loan	4,300.00	
4% post office certificates	71,000.00	
		46,399,600.00

continued on following page

Table 3. Continued

2) State-backed securities		
200 bonds, Consorzio di credito per le opere pubbliche	100,000.00	
70 bonds, IRI	35,000.00	
150 bonds, Elettrificazione ferr. dello Stato	75,000.00	
494 bonds, Ferrovie Danubio Sava Adriatico	99,800.00	
5% unified Naples loan (gross)	13,600.00	
		323,400.00
3) Provincial and municipal loans		
500 bonds, Consiglio Econ. Prov. Milano, 4.50%	250,000.00	
City of Milan, 4%	1,836,600.00	
1086 bonds, City of Turin, 5%	543,000.00	
City of Genoa 1919, 5.50%	100,000.00	
25 bonds, City of Genoa, 5%	12,500.00	
51 bonds, City of Monza, 4%	25,500.00	
5 bonds, City of Ancona	2,543.00	
2 bonds, City of Chieti	1,000.00	
		2,771,134.00
4) Mortgage bonds		
2,471 bonds, Cassa risp. Milano, 4%	1235,500.00	
230 bonds, Cassa risp. Milano, 3.50%	115,000.00	
3,575 bonds, Istituto cr. Fondiario Venezia, 4%	1,787,500.00	
245 bonds, Cred. Fond. Monte de' Paschi, 4%	122,500.00	
380 bonds, Ist. It. Cred. Fond. Roma, 4%	190,000.00	
802 bonds, Cred. Fond. Sardo, 4%	401,000.00	
160 bonds, Banca lav. e cooperaz., 4%	80,000.00	
4 bonds, Banca d'Italia (formerly Banca nazionale)	2,000.00	
50 bonds, Cassa di risp. Bologna, 4%	25,000.00	
150 bonds, Ist. Opere pie S.Paolo, 4%	75,000.00	
1,040 bonds, Cred. Im. Pubbl. util., 6%	520,000.00	
206 bonds, Istit. Naz. cred. Edilizio, 6%	103,000.00	
328 bonds, Ist. Mobiliare ital., 5%	328,000.00	
18 bonds, Cred. Fond. Banco di Napoli, 3.50%	9,000.00	
Total mortgage bonds		4,993,500.00
5) Miscellaneous bonds		
384 bonds, Società immobiliare, 4%	96,000.00	

continued on following page

Table 3. Continued

1226 bonds, Ferr. Meridionali, 3.50%	613,000.00	
80 bonds, Ferr. Meridionali secondarie, 4%	40,000.00	
101 bonds, Ferr. Marsala Trapani, 5%	30,300.00	
404 bonds, Ferr. Sarde, 3%	220,000.00	
76 bonds, Ferr. Sarde secondarie, 4%	38,000.00	
125 bonds, Ferr. Mediterranee, 4%	62,500.00	
375 bonds, Ferr. Mediterranee, 6%	187,500.00	
456 bonds, Ferr. Tirrene, 4%	228,000.00	
138 bonds, Ferr. Società Italiana, 3%	69,000.00	
1 bond, Ferr. Adriatica Appennino, 5%	600.00	
9 bonds, Ferr. Padane	4,500.00	
38 bonds, Ferr. Verona Caprino	19,000.00	
36 bonds, ferr. Alta Valtellina, 4%	9,000.00	
1 bond, Ferr. Sassuolo Modena, 5%	300.00	
206 bonds, Adriatica di elettricità, 6%	103,000.00	
50 bonds, S.a. Forze idr. Trezzo d'Adda	25,000.00	
435 bonds, S.tel. piemontese e lombarda, 6%	217,500.00	
416 bonds, Soc. tranvie e ferr. el. Roma	208,000.00	
189 bonds, Soc. an. "La Lariana", 5.50%	94,500.00	
440 bonds, Gen.It. Edison di elettricità, 6%	220,000.00	
10 bonds, Soc. veneta costr. Eserc. FS	5,000.00	
100 bonds, Soc. Forze idr. Liguria, 6%	50,000.00	
340 bonds, Soc. elettr. Sicilia orient.	170,000.00	
125 bonds, Soc. "La centrale", 5%	62,500.00	
Total miscellaneous bonds		2,773,200.00
6) Mortgages		
Dioccsan scminary, Italian nat. dcbt, 3.50%	1,213,900.00	
Lombardy-Rome seminary, cash	382,571.80	
7) Bank deposits		
Banco Ambrosiano	1,000,679.40	
Banca lombarda	73,025.00	
8) Foreign securities		
Hungarian 4% gold bond	23,200.00	
Uruguayan 3.50% bond	1,000.00	
Rep. Czechoslovakia 5% bond (25/1000)	25,000.00	

continued on following page

Table 3. Continued

French 7% treasury bond (1926)	10,000.00	
French 5% treasury bond (1934)	150,000.00	
French 4.5% treasury bond (1933)	10,000.00	
French 4% treasury bond (1933)	28,000.00	
French 5% bond (1920)	5,000.00	
Ferrovie Marocco 6% bond, (60/500)	30,000.00	
French municipal Credito Foncier 4.5% bond (30/1000)	30,000.00	
9) Other investments		
20 Banco Ambrosiano nominal shares	2,000.00	
Total items 6 - 9		2,984,376.20
Total		60,245,210.20
4) Cash flow		
Cash on hand on April 1, 1934		297,364.50
Inflow:		
Deposited cash for investment	917,109.25	
Drawn securities	2,161,901.20	
Coupon bonds and interest	2,578,223.95	
Interest fees, reserve fund	178,098.05	5,835,332.45
Total inflow		6,132,696.95
Outflow:		
Investments and reinvestments	3,104,494.65	
Execution of pious legacies	2,343,793.90	
Administration expenses	44,417.95	
Total outflow		5,492,706.50
Cash on hand on April 1, 1935		639,990.45

Source: ADC, M589-D622 Milan, annual report for 1934: situation on March 31, 1935.

Table 4. Balance for endowment of diocese of Bergamo, 1934 (lire)

I – Capital movements		
Total capital at beginning of year		29,697,231.30
Capital inflow during year	3,378,651.00	
Capital outflow during year	1,145,841.50	
Difference	2,232,809.50	2,232,809.50

continued on following page

Table 4. Continued

Total capital at year end		31,930,040.80
II – Capital breakdown		
Pious legacies		28,569,427.50
Cash deposits		2,522,550.00
Fund for needy priests		
Reserve fund		838,063.30
Total capital at year end		31,930,040.80
III – Capital inventory at year end		
1) Government securities		
In pious legacies and reserve fund		17,079,765.00
In deposits		2,007,100.00
2) State-backed securities		
In pious legacies		3,352,800.00
In deposits		19,200.00
3). Provincial and municipal loans		
In pious legacies		184,800.00
In deposits		13,500.00
4) Mortgage bonds		
In pious legacies		3,914,000.00
In deposits		212,500.00
5) Miscellaneous stocks and bonds		
In pious legacies: bonds		3,459,162.00
In legacies: stocks		1,523,200.00
In deposits		219,000.00
6) Mortgages		
7) Credit		
8) Bank deposits		
Consorzio Economico Diocesano – Bergamo		39,744.05
Banque Suisse Zurich		1,333.80
9) Foreign securities		
In pious legacies		4,736,030.00
In deposits		51,250.00
Total capital at year end		36,813,384.85
IV – Cash flow		
Cash on hand at beginning of year including bank deposits		384,028.20

continued on following page

Table 4. Continued

Inflow:		
Deposited cash for investment	2,373,581.15	
Drawn, redeemed, and disposed securities	7,115,519.35	
Coupon bonds and interest	1,555,562.85	
Total inflow		11,044,753.35
		11,428,781.55
Outflow:		
Investments and reinvestments	9,834,141.45	
Execution of pious legacies	1,365,589.75	
Interest on capital in simple deposits	129,774.95	
General administration expenses	46,288.55	
Total outflow		11,375,794.70
Cash on hand at year end		52,986.85

Source: ADC, B452-D622 Bergamo, annual report for 1934, June 22, 1935

Table 5. Società Immobiliare Centro Bergamo rents, 1933 (lire)

Leased apartments		
Ing. A.Crovetto	9,500.00	
Prof. Franco d'Alessandro	8,000.00	
Ing. Guido Romiti	9,500.00	
Ing. Vincenzo Indaco	6,500.00	
G. Casari	8,000.00	41,500.00
Leased offices		
Avv. Mazzi and notary Messa	2,700.00	
Avv. Domenico Gennati	10,000.00	
Dott. V. Dal Lago	9,000.00	
Istituto Case Popolari	3,300.00	
Compagnia Assicurazioni Milano	4,200.00	29,200.00
Leased commercial spaces		
Dante Oliva	6,000.00	
Levi and priest	41,000.00	
Ginevra Pallotta Boerio Company	5,400.00	
Rosa Boerio	9,000.00	

continued on following page

Table 5. Continued

Luigi Tarantola	4,500.00	
Giuseppe Casari	11,000.00	76,900.00
Apartments for rent		
1st floor, 12 rooms plus bathrooms		12,000.00
Commercial spaces for rent		
6 storefronts		37,000.00
Touring Hotel		40,000.00
Spaces for bank use		70,000.00
Subtotal		306,600.00
Annual expenses		25,000.00
Net total		281,600.00

Source: AAV, CC, SA, CD, 2, annex 2 to the letter from the Episcopal Curia of Bergamo to the Congregation of the Council, November 18, 1933.

Table 6. Exposure of the Banca Cooperativa Diocesana on September 12, 1950: selection from the list of non-religious borrowers, letters A-B (lire)

Name	Description	Amount
ARC Aziende riunite confezioni	An active, well organized company with estimated asset value of 20,000,000. It employs 100 women. Good discounted commercial paper except for a few returns regularly collected by the presenter.	1,000,000
Bagini, Attilio	Representative for confectionary products	35,000
Bagnulo, dott. Luigi	Consultant to Ansaldo and the Gaslini hospital in Genoa	200,000
Baldoni, Domenico	Trucker. Long-term bank customer. He owns a house and two trucks with trailers, free of encumbrances. The bank did not require a mortgage on the truck purchased with the loan in order to avoid imposing costs on a reliable borrower.	600,000
Balduzzi, Carlo	Tailor. Guaranteed by Cesare Balduzzi, landowner	400,000
Bassanelli, Alessandro	Dealer in construction materials. Receivables discounting facility. Good, long-term customer. He owns a building, two trucks, and goods worth 5,000,000	1,200,000
Benedetti, Alfredo	Mechanic	

continued on following page

Table 6. Continued

Name	Description	Amount
Bettineschi, Giovanni Maria	Trucker. Overdraft facility. The debtor is an upstanding individual. He owns a house and a truck with trailer. Guaranteed by the Lanfranchi Company, which sold him the truck.	430,000
Biava, Giuseppe	Farmer. Mr. Biava is an honest farmer with substantial land holdings, but his assets are tied up due to heavy expenses for speculative geological surveys (quartzite mine). Once a deposit is found, he puts the mine into operation and then sells it. His account shows limited activity and occasional overdrafts sometimes exceeding his credit limit. As a result, the bank has demanded repayment of the debt, threatening to call in the promissory note. Nevertheless, there are no doubts about recovery of funds.	450,238

Source: ASBI, Vigilanza, Pratiche, n. 3481.0, f. 3

Table 7. AOR monthly staff salaries, 1934 (lire)

President	3,400, no 5-year raise
Secretary	2,600, no 5-year raise
Substitute	1,600 with three 5-year raises of 200 lire each
Archivist-writer (also assistant treasurer)	1,200 with three 5-year raises of 200 lire each
Accountant	1,600 with three 5-year raises of 200 lire each
First bookkeeper	1,400 with three 5-year raises of 200 lire each
Bookkeeper 4	1,200 with three 5-year raises of 200 lire each
Treasurer	1,400 with three 5-year raises of 200 lire each
Clerk 2	900 with three 5-year raises of 100 lire each
NB	All staff receive a monthly bonus of 50 lire. Those hired prior to 1927 receive an additional 440 lire per month.

Source: ADC, A1-D622 Rome et al., *Commissione amministratrice delle opere di religione. Statuto, norme e regolamenti*, Tipografia poliglotta vaticana, 1934, p. 25.

Compilation of References

Abbasi, M. Z. (2012). The Classical Islamic Law of Waqf: A Concise Introduction. *Arab Law Quarterly*, *26*(2), 121–153. https://www.jstor.org/stable/23234650. DOI: 10.1163/157302512X629124

Abdul Razak, L., & Saupi, M. N. (2017). The concept and application of amān al-milkiyyah (ownership risk): Islamic law of contract perspective. *ISRA International Journal of Islamic Finance*, *9*(2), 148–163. DOI: 10.1108/IJIF-06-2017-0002

AbdulKareem, I. A., & Mahmud, M. S. B. (2019). Infrastructure project financing through sukuk as an alternative to conventional bond financing. *Journal of management and operation research, 1*(19), 1-11.

Abdullah, S. F. S., Muhamad, M. D., Ishak, A. H., Rani, M. A. M., Jaapar, N., Daud, M. Z., & Bhari, A. (2022). Waqf-Based Infrastructure; Lessons Learnt from Traditional Islamic Neighborhood Practices. *Journal of Pharmaceutical Negative Results*, *13*(9), 5826–5832. DOI: 10.47750/pnr.2022.13.S09.702

Abdul-Wahab, A., & Abdul-Razak, D. (2019). Islamic banking adoption in Ghana. *International Journal of Business, Economics and Law, 19*(2), 14-21. https://www.ijbel.com/wp-content/uploads/2019/09/BUS_66.pdf

Abiola-Adams, O., Azubuike, C., Sule, A. K., & Okon, R. (2025). Integrating asset and liability management with Islamic finance: A strategic framework for global financial institutions. *Gulf Journal of Advance Business Research*, *3*(1), 128–142. Advance online publication. DOI: 10.51594/gjabr.v3i1.70

Abubakar, A. M., & Baba, I. M. (2020). *Sukuk and nation-building: A theoretical analysis of sukuk financing in Nigeria*. Ikonomika, 5(1), 76–87. https://ejournal.radenintan.ac.id/index.php/ikonomika

Accounting and Auditing Organization for Islamic Financial Institutions. (n.d.-a). *About AAOIFI*. https://aaoifi.com/about-aaoifi/?lang=en

Accounting and Auditing Organization for Islamic Financial Institutions. (n.d.-b). *AAOIFI common members*. https://aaoifi.com/aaoifi-common-members/?lang=en

Acemoglu, D. (2024, November 29). The world needs a pro-human AI agenda. *Project Syndicate*. Retrieved from: https://www.project-syndicate.org/onpoint/ai-and-agi-designed-to-replace-workers-worst-of-all-possible-worlds-by-daron-acemoglu-2024-11

Acemoglu, D., & Robinson, J. A. (2013). *Why nations fail: The origins of power, prosperity, and poverty*. Profile Books. [does not have a DOI registered in Crossref or other major databases]

Admati, A., & Hellwig, M. (2013). *The bankers' new clothes: What's wrong with banking and what to do about it*. Princeton University Press. DOI: 10.1515/9780691251714

Ahmed, J. (2020). Promoting financial stability: issues and challenges in Islamic finance. *Law & Financial Stability, 193*. https://www.elibrary.imf.org/display/book/9781513523002/ch012.xml

Ahmed, R. (2024). Waqf; an instrument of poverty elimination and development. *Maktoob Media*. https://maktoobmedia.com/opinion/Waqf-instrument-of-poverty-elimination-and-development/

Akbar, J. (2023, November). *Property rights (uquq) and civilizations* [Keynote speech]. "City and Civilization Congress" Ankara, Turkey. Retrieved from https://www.researchgate.net/publication/367052857_Property_Rights_Huquq_and_Civilizations

Akerlof, G. A. (1970). The market for "lemons": Quality uncertainty and the market mechanism. *The Quarterly Journal of Economics*, *84*(3), 488–500. DOI: 10.2307/1879431

Alam Choudhury, M., & Nurul Alam, M. (2013). Corporate governance in Islamic perspective. *International journal of Islamic and Middle Eastern finance and management, 6*(3), 180-199.

Albeck, S. (1976). *Dinei HaMamomnot BaTalmud* [Hebrew]. Dvir.

Aldhaheri, W. (2025). Islamic Green Finance: Shariah-Compliant Pathways towards Sustainable Development Goals (SDGs). *Open Journal of Applied Sciences*, *15*(5), 1294–1309. DOI: 10.4236/ojapps.2025.155090

Alexakis, C., & Tsikouras, A. (2009). Islamic finance: Regulatory framework–challenges lying ahead. *International Journal of Islamic and Middle Eastern Finance and Management*, *2*(2), 90–104. DOI: 10.1108/17538390910965121

Allied Market Research. (n.d.). *Islamic finance market.* https://www.alliedmarketresearch.com/islamic-finance-market-A120276

Allied Market Research. "Islamic Finance Market Size, Share, Competitive Landscape and Trend Analysis Report." Accessed August 31, 2025. https://www.alliedmarketresearch.com/islamic-finance-market-A120276

Al-Zaabi, O. S. (2010). Salam contract in Islamic law: A survey. *Review of Islamic Economics, 14*(2), 91–122. https://www.iefpedia.com/english/wp-content/uploads/2011/11/rie-2010-14-2-al-zaabi-salam-contract-in-islamic-law.pdf

Ammerman, N. (2016). Lived religion as an emerging field: An assessment of its contours and frontiers. *Nordic Journal of Religion and Society*, *29*(2), 83–99. DOI: 10.18261/issn.1890-7008-2016-02-01

Andrews, D. M., ... (2005). *The Future of Transatlantic Economic Relations: Continuity amid Discord*. San Domenico di Fiesole: European University Institute.

Annett, A. (2018, March). Restoring ethics to economics: Modern economics should return to its roots. Finance & Development, 55(1). IMF, https://www.elibrary.imf.org/view/journals/022/0055/001/article-A016-en.xmlDOI: 10.5089/9781484343418.022

Aquinas, T. (n.d.). *Summa Theologica*, Secunda Secundae, Question 78, Article 1. [written in the 13th century] Christian Classics Ethereal Library; Retrieved May 11, 2025, from https://www.newadvent.org/summa/3078.htm

Ari, I., & Koc, M. (2021). Towards sustainable financing models: A proof-of-concept for a Waqf-based alternative financing model for renewable energy investments. *Borsa Istanbul Review*, *21*, S46–S56. DOI: 10.1016/j.bir.2021.03.007

Aristotle. (1946). *The politics of Aristotle* (E. Barker, Trans., Book I, Ch. 10, 1258b4–8). Oxford University Press. (Original work published ca. 350 B.C.E.) https://archive.org/details/in.ernet.dli.2015.50166

Askari, H., Iqbal, Z., & Mirakhor, A. (2010). *Globalization and Islamic finance: Convergence, prospects and challenges*. John Wiley Sons.

Asutay, M. (2012). Conceptualising and Locating the Social Failure of Islamic Finance: Aspirations of Islamic Moral Economy vs the Realities of Islamic Finance. *Asian and African Area Studies*, *11*(2), 93–113. DOI: 10.14956/asafas.11.93

Asutay, M. (2013). Islamic moral economy as the foundation of Islamic finance. In Cattelan, V. (Ed.), *Islamic Finance in Europe*. Edward Elgar., DOI: 10.4337/9781781002513.00014

Attoukou, M., & Nchare, K. (2022). Financial exclusion and poverty reduction in Benin. *Asian Journal of Economics and Empirical Research*, *9*(2), 121–131. DOI: 10.20448/ajeer.v9i2.4146

Australian Securities and Investments Commission. (n.d.). *Consultation paper 98: Cross-border recognition* [PDF]. https://download.asic.gov.au/media/1329068/Consultation_paper_98_Cross_Border_Recognition_v1.pdf

Avraham Yeshayau. (n.d.). *Chazon Ish*, Yoreh De'ah §272:2; Choshen Mishpat §16:26. *Choshen Mishpat*, *16*, 24.

Ayub, M. (2021), "The Corporate Governance for Islamic Financial Institutions in Pakistan: Need for Dynamic Regulatory Policies", Azid, T., Mukhlisin, M., Akbar, N. and Tahir, M. (Ed.) *Monetary Policy, Islamic Finance, and Islamic Corporate Governance: An International Overview*, Emerald Publishing Limited, Leeds, pp. 37-60. DOI: 10.1108/978-1-80043-786-920211003

Ayub, M. (2007). *Understanding Islamic finance*. John Wiley & Sons.

Ayub, M. (Ed.). (2022). *Economics and economic policy: Islamic perspective*. IPS.

Ayub, M., Fahim, K., & Rashid, A. (2022). Forward trading and futures markets in Islamic perspective. *Journal of Islamic Finance Accountancy*, *6*(1), 21–34. https://aaoifi.com/joifa/?lang=en

Azeem, M. M., Marsap, A., & Özari, C. (2015). Impact of Basel Accord on Banking System (Evidence from Islamic Banks of Pakistan). *Applied Finance and Accounting*, *1*(2), 1–9. DOI: 10.11114/afa.v1i2.724

Aziz, Z. A. (2014). Sukuk development and financial stability. 10th World Islamic Economic Forum. *Dubai (October)*, 1-3. https://www.bis.org/review/r141029c.htm

Azmat, S., Bhatti, A., & Hassan, M. K. (2021). Understanding "Riba" (interest): The religious and the rational. *Emerald Emerging Markets Case Studies.*, *11*(3), 1–11. Advance online publication. DOI: 10.1108/EEMCS-08-2020-0288

Azmi, K., & Akmal, K. M. (2024). Unlocking Growth Potential: How to Increase Market Depth and Liquidity in Islamic Bonds. *SSRN*, *4846112*, •••. https://www.researchgate.net/publication/380930325_Unlocking_Growth_Potential_How_to_Increase_Market_Depth_and_Liquidity_in_Islamic_Bonds

Bakhos, C., & Shayegan, R. (Eds.). (2010). *The Talmud and its Iranian Context*. Mohr Siebeck. DOI: 10.1628/978-3-16-151468-5

Balibek, E. (2017). *Establishing a legal framework for sovereign sukuk issuance: A public debt management perspective* (No. 116308, pp. 1-33). The World Bank. https://documents1.worldbank.org/curated/en/907001497472893193/pdf/P161573-06-14-2017-1497472889089.pdf

Bani, E., & Consorti, P. (Eds.). (2015). *Finanze vaticane e Unione europea. Le riforme di papa Francesco e le sfide della vigilanza internazionale.* Il Mulino.

Bank Negara Malaysia. (2007). Development of the Financial Sector. Financial Stability and Payment Systems Report 2007. Bank Negara Malaysia. https://www.bnm.gov.my/documents/20124/856398/cp02_001_whitebox.pdf

Bateman, M. C., & Beyea, C. R. (2008). Mutual recognition: A step towards greater access to global markets. *The Investment Lawyer, 15*(5), 3–8.

Bateman, M. C., & Beyea, C. R. (2008, May). Mutual Recognition: A Step Towards Greater Access to Global Markets. *The Investment Lawyer, 15*(5), 3–8.

Beed, C., & Beed, C. (1996). A Christian perspective on economics. *Journal of Economic Methodology, 3*(1), 91–112. https://doi.org/ C (1996). From total war to local war: it's a revolution; The Independent, 22 July; https://www.the-independent.com/voices/from-total-war-to-local-war-it-s-a-revolution-1330045.html?utm_source=chatgpt.comDOI: 10.1080/13501789600000006Bellamy

Beer, M. (1976). *Rashut ha-golah bi-yemei ha-mishnah ve-ha-talmud* [The Babylonian exilarchate in the Mishnaic and Talmudic era]. 2nd ed.). Bar-Ilan University Press.

Bellavite Pellegrini, C. (2001). *Storia del Banco Ambrosiano: Fondazione, ascesa e dissesto 1896–1982.* Laterza.

Benedict, X. V. I. (2023). *Che cos'è il cristianesimo. Quasi un testamento spirituale.* Mondadori.

Bennett, M., & Coyle, H. (2025). *State of the Sukuk Market and Prospects for Growth.* World Bank Group. All About Finance (Blog). https://blogs.worldbank.org/en/allaboutfinance/state-of-the-sukuk-market-and-prospects-for-growth

Ben-Shlomo, E. (1998). The Obligation to Save Life. *Assia* 3 (2), accessible online: https://www.daat.ac.il/daat/kitveyet/assia_english/benshlomo.htm

Beverley, E. L. (2011). Property, authority and personal law: Waqf in colonial South Asia. *South Asia Research, 31*(2), 155–182. DOI: 10.1177/026272801103100204

Bocci, M. (1999). *Oltre lo Stato liberale. Ipotesi su politica e società nel dibattito cattolico tra fascismo e democrazia.* Bulzoni.

Cafaro, P. (2001). *La solidarietà efficiente. Storia e prospettive del credito cooperativo in Italia (1883–2000)*. Laterza.

Cakir, S., & Raei, F. (2007). Sukuk vs. Eurobonds: is there a difference in value-at-risk? *IMF Working Paper No. 07/237*. https://papers.ssrn.com/sol3/papers.cfm?abstract_id=1087156

Capital, S. (2023). *Amana Mutual Funds Trust overview*. Retrieved from https://www.saturna.com/amana

Capital, S. (n.d.). *GCC sukuk: A primer* (3rd ed.)., https://www.saturna.com/insights/thought-leadership/gcc-sukuk-primer-3rd-edition

Cattelan, V. (2016, January). Islamic finance as Islamic justice. *Islamic Finance Today*. https://www.scribd.com/document/818856658/Islamic-Finance-as-Islamic-Justice

Cavallo, S. (1995). *Charity and power in early modern Italy: Benefactors and their motives in Turin, 1541–1789*. Cambridge University Press.

Cesarini, F. (2004). Finanza. In Università Cattolica del Sacro Cuore (Ed.), *Dizionario di dottrina sociale della Chiesa. Scienze sociali e magistero* (pp. 309–310). Vita e Pensiero.

Chambers, D., & Dimson, E. (Eds.). (2016). *Financial market history: Reflections on the past for investors today*. The CFA Institute Research Foundation.

Chapra, M. U., Khan, S., & Al Shaikh-Ali, A. (2008). *The Islamic Vision of Development in the Light of Maqasid Al-Shariah (Occasional Paper)*. International Institute of Islamic Thought (IIIT).

Chaudhary, Y. (2024). Islam and artificial intelligence. In Singler, B., & Watts, F. (Eds.), *The Cambridge Companion to Religion and Artificial Intelligence* (pp. 109–128). Cambridge University Press., DOI: 10.1017/9781009031721.008

Chomsky, N., Roberts, I., & Watumull, J. (2023, March 8). The false promise of ChatGPT. *The New York Times*. https://www.nytimes.com/2023/03/08/opinion/noam-chomsky-chatgpt-ai.html

Cini, M. (Ed.). (2019). *Alla ricerca della terza via. Politica, economia, istituzioni*. Pisa University Press.

Citron, D. K., & Chesney, B. (2019). Deep fakes: A looming challenge for privacy, democracy, and national security. *California Law Review, 107*(5), 1753–1819. DOI: 10.15779/Z38RV0D15J

Cleary Gottlieb Steen & Hamilton LLP. (2021). "Substituted Compliance Application for Mexico Swap Dealers from CEA Sections 4s(e)–(f) and Rules 23.101 and 23.105(d)–(e)." Submitted to CFTC, September 28, 2021. https://www.cftc.gov/media/8111/Mexico_SubstitutedComplianceApplication_20210928/download

Cohen, S. (2013). Rural Trade and Economy in Hellenistic and Roman Palestine. A Case Study from Tel Zahara. *Res Antiquae*, *10*, 85–100.

Coleman, H. (2015). Studying Russian religion since the collapse of communism. *Journal of the Canadian Historical Association*, *25*(2), 309–318. DOI: 10.7202/1032851ar

Colombo, E. C. (2016). Prefazione. In E. Lurgo, *Carità barocca. Opere pie e luoghi pii nello Stato sabaudo fra XVII e XVIII secolo* (pp. IX–XXIV). Fondazione 1563 per l'Arte e la Cultura della Compagnia di San Paolo.

Colombo, A. (2004). *Congregazioni religiose e sviluppo in Lombardia tra Otto e Novecento. Il caso delle Suore di Maria Bambina*. Vita e Pensiero.

Colombo, E. C. (2019). Premessa. *Quaderni Storici*, *54*(3), 601–617.

Colombo, E. C., & Dotti, M. (2014). L'economia rituale. Dalla rendita alle celebrazioni (Lodi, età moderna). *Quaderni Storici*, *54*(3), 871–903.

Colombo, E. C., & Semeraro, R. (2022). Introduzione. In Colombo, E. C., & Semeraro, R. (Eds.), *Le ragioni della carità. Economia e funzioni dei legati pii tra età moderna e contemporanea* (pp. 163–189). Il Mulino.

Commodity Futures Trading Commission. (2021). *Mexico substituted compliance application* [PDF]. https://www.cftc.gov/media/8111/Mexico_SubstitutedComplianceApplication_20210928/download

Conferenza Episcopale Italiana. (2020). *La Chiesa cattolica e la gestione delle risorse finanziarie con criteri etici di responsabilità sociale, ambientale e di governance*. Mediagraf.

Congregazione per gli Istituti di Vita Consacrata e le Società di Vita Apostolica (2018). *Economia a servizio del carisma e della missione. Boni dispensatores multiformis gratiae Dei. Orientamenti*. Libreria Editrice Vaticana.

Congregazione per la Dottrina della Fede & Dicastero per il Servizio dello Sviluppo Umano Integrale. (2018). *Oeconomicae et pecuniariae quaestiones: considerazioni per un discernimento etico circa alcuni aspetti dell'attuale sistema economico-finanziario*. Libreria Editrice Vaticana.

Consorti, P. (2005). *Legislazione del terzo settore. Le norme sul "nonprofit", il volontariato, la cooperazione sociale ed internazionale*. Plus.

Consorti, P. (2009). Il prezzo della religione. In Bani, E. (Ed.), *Il "giusto" prezzo tra Stato e mercato. Liber amicorum per Mauro Giusti* (pp. 262–271). Giappichelli.

Crocella, C. (1982). *"Augusta miseria": Aspetti delle finanze pontificie nell'età del capitalismo*. Nuovo Istituto Editoriale Italiano.

Cross, M. S. (2021, January 27). Reincarnating the East India Company. *The Juggernaut*. https://www.thejuggernaut.com/reincarnating-east-india-company

Dal Bo, F. (2018). "Economic speculation and the sacred," "Market prices," "Market intervention and the common good," and "Market intervention and the common good," in M. Satlow (Ed.), *Judaism and the Economy. A Sourcebook*, London, Routledge, 2018, 46-47, 48, 53-54, 69-70.

Dal Bo, F. (2013). *Massekhet Keritot. Text, Translation, and Commentary*. Mohr Siebeck.

Dallh, M. (2023). Accumulate but distribute: Islamic emphasis on the establishment of Waqf (pious endowment). *Religion and Development*, *2*(1), 21–40. DOI: 10.30965/27507955-20230014

Dar, Z. A. (2020). Islamic Concept of Waqf: Challenges and Prospects with Reference to the Jammu and Kashmir Muslim Waqf Board. *Airlangga International Journal of Islamic Economics and Finance*, *3*(2), 89. DOI: 10.20473/aijief.v3i2.23880

Davis, K. (2025, May 29). $1trn sukuk market at risk of unintended disruption. *Financial Times*.

Davis, K. "$1trn Sukuk Market at Risk of Unintended Disruption." *Financial Times*, May 29, 2025.

DDCAP. (2023). Sovereign Sukuk – South Africa ZAR20.4bn Sukuk Ijarahh. DDCAP Group. https://www.ddcap.com/sovereign-sukuk-south-africa-zar20-4bn-sukuk-Ijarahh/

de Brito, A. C., Kauffmann, C., & Pelkmans, J. (2016). *The contribution of mutual recognition to international regulatory co-operation* (OECD Regulatory Working Paper No. 2). OECD.

de Brito, C., Anabela, C. K., & Pelkmans, J. "The Contribution of Mutual Recognition to International Regulatory Co-Operation." *OECD Regulatory Working Papers*, no. 2 (2016): 1-50.

De Franssu, J.-B., & De Salins, A. (2024). The Catholic Church and ethical finance: From theory to practice. *Etudes*, *3*, 88–89.

De Luca, G. (2021). Capitali dei privati, notai e modernizzazione economica a Milano tra Sette e Ottocento. In Gregorini, G., & Romani, M. (Eds.), *Borghesie nazionali, borghesie cosmopolite* (pp. 23–34). FrancoAngeli.

De Maeyer, J., Leplae, S., & Schmiedl, J. (Eds.). (2004). *Religious institutes in Western Europe in the 19th and 20th centuries: Historiography, research and legal position*. Leuven University Press.

Deaton, A. (2024, March). *Rethinking my economics. Finance & Development*. International Monetary Fund. https://www.imf.org/en/Publications/fandd/issues/2024/03/Symposium-Rethinking-Economics-Angus-Deaton

Debt Management Office. (2017). *Nigeria Offers its First Sovereign Sukuk*. Central Bank of Nigeria (CBN). https://www.dmo.gov.ng/fgn-bonds/sovereign-sukuk/2095-new-advert-on-sukuk/file

Demir, H. (2024). Story of Humanitarian Efforts from USA to the World. Executive Interview with ISFIRE; ISFIRE COVER STORY, *ISFIRE*, London; 14(6), 12–21. Retrieved from https://www.isfire.net:contentReference[oaicite:15]{index=15}

Dey, D., & Jin, X. (2018). Islamic Finance in Africa: Opportunities and Challenges. *White and Case*. https://www.lexology.com/library/detail.aspx?g=a894d8a4-f5e7-45bc-9b6a-05ac657e8984

Dhahri, S., Slimani, S., & Omri, A. (2021). Behavioral entrepreneurship for achieving the sustainable development goals. *Technological Forecasting and Social Change, 165*, 120561. DOI: 10.1016/j.techfore.2020.120561

Diala, A. C. (2021). Legal Pluralism and the Future of Personal Family Laws in Africa. *International Journal of Law, Policy and the Family, 35*(1), ebab023. DOI: 10.1093/lawfam/ebab023

Diatmoko, T., Absori, A., Wardiono, K., Nashirudin, M., & Budiono, A. (2025). Islamic legal policy on ultra-micro enterprise financing and its implementation from the perspective of Maqā id al-Sharī'a. *Al-Ahkam, 35*(1), 87–116. DOI: 10.21580/ahkam.2025.35.1.25207

Dieguez, A. M., & Pagano, S. (2006). *La carte del "sacro tavolo". Aspetti del pontificato di Pio X dai documenti del suo archivio privato* (Vol. II). Archivio Segreto Vaticano.

Diotallevi, L. (2024). *La messa è sbiadita. La partecipazione ai riti religiosi in Italia dal 1993 al 2019*. Rubbettino.

Dorf, M. C. (2008). Dynamic incorporation of foreign law. *University of Pennsylvania Law Review*, *157*, 103–169.

Dorobantu, M. (2024). Artificial intelligence and Christianity: Friends or foes? In Singler, B., & Watts, F. (Eds.), *The Cambridge companion to religion and artificial intelligence*. Cambridge University Press., DOI: 10.1017/9781009031721.007

Dusuki, A. W. (2010). Do equity-based Sukuk structures in Islamic capital markets manifest the objectives of Shariah? *Journal of Financial Services Marketing*, *15*(3), 203–214. https://jibm.org/wp-content/uploads/2018/05/10-Asyraf-Wajdi-Dusuki1.pdf. DOI: 10.1057/fsm.2010.17

El Aynaoui, K., & Dinh, H. T. (2025, January 28). *Economic development after the Washington Consensus*. Project Syndicate. https://www.project-syndicate.org/commentary/new-development-policy-framework-to-replace-washington-consensus-by-karim-el-aynaoui-and-hinh-t-dinh-2025-01

El-Gamal, M. A. (2006). *Islamic finance: Law, economics, and practice*. Cambridge University Press. ISBN-13 978-0-511-22021-0 DOI: 10.1017/CBO9780511753756

Elmahgop, F., Alsulami, F., Mohammed, M. G. A., Abdel-Gadir, S., & Elhassan, T. (2025). The Socio-Economic Impacts of Waqf Investment Funds as a Model for Sustainable Financing in Saudi Arabia. *Sustainability (Basel)*, *17*(9), 3805. DOI: 10.3390/su17093805

Elman, Y. (1994). *Authority and Tradition: Toseftan Baraitot in Talmudic Babylonia*. KTAV Hokoken.

Elmghaamez, I. K., Ntim, C. G., & Yekini, K. C. (2024). Diffusion theory, economic consequences, and adoption of international standards on auditing around the world. *Journal of International Accounting, Auditing & Taxation*, *56*, 1–15. DOI: 10.1016/j.intaccaudtax.2024.100641

Epstein, G. A. (Ed.). (2005). *Financialization and the World Economy*. Edward Elgar Publishing. ISBN: 978 1 84376 874 6 DOI: 10.4337/9781781008263

Farese, G. (2019). Un ordine mondiale per lo sviluppo. In R. Mascolo & S. Palermo (Eds.), *Europa domani. Studi in onore di Giuseppe Di Taranto*. Luiss University Press.

Faruki, A. (2024). The Concept of Waqf in Islam: A Textual Study of Hanafi Jurisprudential Thoughts. *Islamonweb*. https://en.islamonweb.net/the-concept-of-Waqf-in-islam-a-textual-study-of-hanafi-jurisprudential-thoughts#:~:text=In%20Islamic%20jurisprudence%2C%20particularly%20within,benefits%20solely%20to%20charitable%20causes

Fauzi, M., Haji-Othman, Y., & Pakkanna, M. (2023). The strategy of micro Waqf banks for job creation on micro-scale enterprises in Indonesia. *International Journal of Academic Research in Business & Social Sciences, 13*(6). Advance online publication. DOI: 10.6007/IJARBSS/v13-i6/17407

Federal Register. (2024, July 18). Order granting conditional substituted compliance in connection with certain capital and financial requirements. https://www.federalregister.gov/documents/2024/07/18/2024-15093/order-granting-conditional-substituted-compliance-in-connection-with-certain-capital-and-financial

Federal Reserve Bank of Kansas City. (n.d.). *Bank deposit rates haven't kept pace with yields on other investments, but depositors are staying anyway.* https://www.kansascityfed.org/research/economic-bulletin/bank-deposit-rates-havent-kept-pace-with-yields-on-other-investments-but-depositors-are-staying-anyway/

Ferrari, A. (1995). *La cultura riformatrice. Uomini, tecniche, filosofie di fronte allo sviluppo (1945–1968).* Studium.

Fikra, A. (2025). An Islamic law perspective on online buying and selling without direct inspection of goods (Bay' al-ghaib) in e-commerce practices. *SYARIAT: Akhwal Syaksiyah, Jinayah. Siyasah and Muamala, 1*(4), 206–214. DOI: 10.35335/ha7pps79

Fitch Ratings. (2024). Pakistan's Islamic Finance Prospects Positive on Government Push. Fitch Ratings. https://www.fitchratings.com/research/non-bank-financial-institutions/pakistans-islamic-finance-prospects-positive-on-government-push-30-01-2024

Fitch Ratings. (2025). Nigeria's Islamic Finance Industry to Benefit from Sovereign Sukuk; New Liquidity Tools. Fitch Ratings. https://www.fitchratings.com/research/islamic-finance/nigerias-islamic-finance-industry-to-benefit-from-sovereign-sukuk-new-liquidity-tools-03-06-2025

Floor, W. (1979). Das Amt des Muhtasib im Iran—Zur Kontrolle der "öffentlichen Moral" in der iranischen Geschichte. In Greussing, K., & Grevemeyer, J. H. (Eds.), *Revolution in Iran und Afghanistan* (pp. 122–139). Syndakat.

Fornasari, M. (2017). Postfazione. In R. Semeraro, *Piccoli IOR* (pp. 331–334). Il Mulino.

Fornasari, M. (2017). *La banca, la borsa, lo Stato. Una storia della finanza (secoli XIII–XXI).* Giappichelli.

Fraade, S. D. (2012). Concepts of Scripture in Rabbinic Judaism: Oral Torah and Written Torah. In Sommer, B. D. (Ed.), *Jewish concepts of scripture: A comparative introduction* (pp. 31–46). New York University Press., DOI: 10.18574/nyu/9780814740620.003.0003

Friedman, B. M. (2021). *Religion and the rise of capitalism.* Alfred A. Knopf.

Friedman, H. H. (1980). Talmudic business ethics: A historical perspective. *Akron Business and Economic Review, 11*, 45–49.

Friedman, H. H. (1984). Ancient marketing practices: The view from Talmudic times. *Journal of Public Policy & Marketing, 3*(1), 194–204. DOI: 10.1177/074391568400300114

Friedman, H. H. (1985). Ethical behavior in business: A hierarchical approach from the Talmud. *Journal of Business Ethics, 4*(2), 117–129. DOI: 10.1007/BF00383564

Friedman, H. H. (2000). Biblical foundations of business ethics. *Journal of Markets & Morality, 3*(1), 43–57.

Friedman, H. H. (2004). Talmudic business ethics: A historical perspective. *Business and Society Review, 10*(2), 23–47.

Friedman, H. H. (2012). The Talmud as a business guide. *MJAE, 1*(1), 38–48.

Friedman, H. H., & Adler, W. D. (2011). Moral capitalism: A biblical perspective. *American Journal of Economics and Sociology, 70*(4), 1014–1028. DOI: 10.1111/j.1536-7150.2011.00800.x

Friedman, H. H., & Klein, Y. (2010). Respect for God's world: The biblical and rabbinic foundations of environmentalism. *International Journal of Business and Globalisation, 4*(2), 129–200. DOI: 10.1504/IJBG.2010.030668

Frierson, J. G. (1969). Changing concepts on usury: Ancient times through the time of John Calvin. *American Business Law Journal, 7*(2), 115–130. DOI: 10.1111/j.1744-1714.1969.tb01330.x

Garnsey, P. (1988). *Famine and food supply in the Graeco-Roman world: Responses to risk and crisis.* Cambridge University Press. DOI: 10.1017/CBO9780511583827

Gellis, H., Giladi, K., & Friedman, H. H. (2002). Biblical and Talmudic basis of accounting ethics. *The CPA Journal*, (September), 11–13.

Georgiou, M. A. (2009). *Excessive Lending, Leverage, and Risk-Taking in the Presence of Bailout Expectations.* IMF Working Paper No. 2009/233. https://www.elibrary.imf.org/view/journals/001/2009/233/article-A001-en.xml

Ghaffour, A. R. (2025). The significance of Malaysian government bond market – resilience against global backdrop. Bank for International Settlements. The International Monetary Fund's 20th Public Debt Management Forum, Kuala Lumpur, 28 May 2025. https://www.bis.org/review/r250528p.htm

Goldin, I. (2025, January 10). *The truth about migration. Project Syndicate.* https://www.project-syndicate.org/onpoint/migration-facts-versus-myths-by-ian-goldin-2025-01

Golinkin, D. (2003). The basic principles of Jewish business ethics. *Insight Israel, 3*(1), 1–7.

Gregorini, G. (2008). (Ed.). *Religiose, religiosi, economia e società nell'Italia contemporanea.* Vita e Pensiero.

Gregorini, G. (2024). Anatomia di un bilancio: Chiesa, finanza, carità nell'Italia della grande depressione. In M. Gregorini & G. Gregorini, *Artificial Intelligence and Economic History. Topics, Tools, Intersections* (pp. 75–134). Vita e Pensiero.

Gregorini, G. (2010). *Un po' di bene. L'Istituto delle Suore Sacramentine di Bergamo dalle origini al secondo dopoguerra (1882–1950).* Vita e Pensiero.

Gregorini, G. (2012). The organization and economics of religious congregations in North Italy (1861–1929). In Van Dijck, M., De Maeyer, J., Tyssens, J., & Koppen, J. (Eds.), *The economics of providence / L'économie de la providence* (pp. 323–342). Leuven University Press.

Gregorini, G., Maffi, L., & Rochini, M. (2023). *Social support system in rural Italy: The modern age regional states of the northern peninsula.* Palgrave Macmillan. DOI: 10.1007/978-3-031-24303-5

Gregorini, G., & Semeraro, R. (2025). *La difficile proiezione internazionale della finanza vaticana negli anni del Regno d'Italia (1870–1942)* [Manuscript submitted for publication]. Università Cattolica del Sacro Cuore.

Gregorini, M., & Gregorini, G. (2022). Costruire la comunità. In Colombo, E. C., & Semeraro, R. (Eds.), *Le ragioni della carità* (pp. 123–161). Il Mulino.

Gregorini, M., Semeraro, R., & Gregorini, G. (2022). Le virtù della carità. Patrimonio ecclesiastico, finanza comportamentale e sviluppo territoriale nell'Italia del XX secolo. In Gregorini, G., Semeraro, R., & Taccolini, M. (Eds.), *I volti della povertà. Temi, parole, fonti per la storia dei sistemi di supporto sociale tra modernità e globalizzazione* (pp. 57–79). Vita e Pensiero.

Griffin, D. R., & Scott, P. D. (Eds.). (2006). *9/11 and American Empire: Intellectuals Speak Out* (Vol. 1). Olive Branch Press., Retrieved from https://books.google.com/books?id=Uvm66cPtb3cC

Gross, S. (2024). *Babylonian Jews and Sasanian Imperialism in Late Antiquity.* Cambridge Press. DOI: 10.1017/9781009280549

Gurumurthy, S. (2002, June 26). Neo-economics: Saving is a sin, spending is a virtue. https://gurumurthy.net/neo-economics-saving-is-sin-spending-is-virtue/

Habisch, A. (2023). The concept of economy in Christianity. In Böttigheimer, C., & Widenka, W. M. (Eds.), *The concept of economy in Judaism, Christianity, and Islam* (pp. 43–70). LSC Communications / De Gruyter., DOI: 10.1515/9783110782486-004

Haddad, A. (2021). Does the country's religion affect the financial performance of conventional and Islamic banks? Comparative study in the international framework. *Journal of Islamic Marketing, 14*(2), 410–434. DOI: 10.1108/JIMA-03-2021-0088

Hadi, M., Rum, J., Maguni, W., & Radiamoda, A. M. (2025). Toward a holistic legal framework for effective Waqf implementation: Integrating Islamic socio-economic models. *Volksgeist: Jurnal Ilmu Hukum Dan Konstitusi*, 15–42. https://doi.org/DOI: 10.24090/volksgeist.v8i1.12590

Hafid, A., Bahri, S., Marzuki, S. N., Muis, M., & Idayanti, R. (2024). The application of khiyar principles to e-commerce transaction: The Islamic economy perspective. *Samarah: Jurnal Hukum Keluarga Dan Hukum Islam, 8*(1), 403–420. DOI: 10.22373/sjhk.v8i1.20890

Hai Gaon. (n.d.). *Sefer HaMekach ve-haMimkar*, Sha'ar 41.

Halima, A., Betul, D., & Anitë, S. (2024). Islamic Finance as a Crisis-Resilient Framework. *Journal of Economics, Law, and Society, 1*(2), 3. DOI: 10.70009/jels.2024.1.2.3

Halkjaer Pedersen, N. (2024). The defence sector in focus: Common ESG risks. *Principles for Responsible Investment.* Accessed February 19, 2025, https://www.unpri.org/pri-blog/the-defence-sector-in-focus-common-esg-risks/12689.article

Hanif, M. (2017). Anatomy of Islamic Finance. *Management Accountant (Official Journal of ICMA-Pakistan) Vol, 26*, 15-21. https://papers.ssrn.com/sol3/papers.cfm?abstract_id=2921821

Hao, J. (2024). Disclosure regulation, cost of capital, and firm values. *Journal of Accounting and Economics, 77*(1), 1–20. DOI: 10.1016/j.jacceco.2023.101605

Hardin, G. (1968). The tragedy of the commons. *Science*, *162*(3859), 1243–1248. DOI: 10.1126/science.162.3859.1243 PMID: 5699198

Harper, K., & Smirl, L. (2014). Usury and Religion: Historical Perspectives on Jewish and Christian Views. *BMC Public Health*, *14*, 566. DOI: 10.1186/1471-2458-14-566

Hasan, R., Ahmad, A. U. F., & Bt. Siraj, S. A. (2020). Building Trust in Waqf Management - Implications of Good Governance and Transparent Reporting. *The Singapore Economic Review*, *67*(01), 459–475. DOI: 10.1142/S0217590820420059

Hassan, K., Tarazi, A., & Echchabi, A. (2023). The Impact of Basel III on Islamic Banks: Ethical Finance and Regulatory Challenges. *Journal of Banking Regulation*, *24*(3), 345–362. DOI: 10.1057/s41261-023-00210-1

Hassan, M. K., Kayed, R. N., & Oseni, U. A. (2013). *Introduction to Islamic Banking and Finance: Principles and Practice*. Pearson Education Limited.

Helvacıoğlu, M. (2022). Islamic finance: What is it? In Kahf, M. (Ed.), *Towards a new theory of finance: Can Islamic finance be it?* (pp. 321–360). İstanbul Zaim University., DOI: 10.12816/0036633

Herman, G. (2021), In Search of Non-Rabbinic Judaism in Sasanian Babylonia. In G. McDowell (ed.), *Diversity and Rabbinization*, Open Book Publishers, 121-137, accessible online: https://books.openedition.org/obp/19940

Herman, G. (2012). *A prince without a kingdom: The exilarch in the Sasanian era*. Mohr Siebeck. DOI: 10.1628/978-3-16-152138-6

Honarchiansaky, A. (2018). Connected Histories in Late Antiquity. Study of a Peace between the Roman and Sasanian Empires and Its Diverging Impacts on Christianity in Greater Armenia and Iran. Unpublished PhD Thesis, UCLA, accessible online: https://escholarship.org/uc/item/1r46d0h3

Hong Kong Monetary Authority. (2014). HKSAR Government's Inaugural Sukuk Offering. Hong Kong Monetary Authority. https://www.hkma.gov.hk/eng/news-and-media/press-releases/2014/09/20140911-3/#:~:text=The%20Sukuk%20is%20issued%20by,Exempt%20Regime)%20and%20NASDAQ%20Dubai.

Humanistic Management Network. (2005). *About us*. Retrieved from https://humanisticmanagement.network/about-us/

Hunjra, A. I., Islam, F., Verhoeven, P., & Hassan, M. K. (2022). The impact of a dual banking system on macroeconomic efficiency. *Research in International Business and Finance*, *61*, 101647. DOI: 10.1016/j.ribaf.2022.101647

Hussain, M. M., Shahmoradi, A., & Turk, R. (2015). An overview of Islamic finance. IMF Working Paper (WP/15/120). https://www.imf.org/external/pubs/ft/wp/2015/wp15120.pdf

Iannaccone, L. (2012). Extremism and the economics of religion*. *The Economic Record*, *88*(s1), 110–115. DOI: 10.1111/j.1475-4932.2012.00803.x

Ibrahim, A. A., Hussein, J. M., & Kulmie, D. A. (2024). Islamic Banking in Africa: A Booming Market with Growing Pains. *International Journal of Religion*, *5*(9), 318–333. DOI: 10.61707/3dg7rh70

IFN. (2016). Ivory Coast's maiden Sukuk: A landmark deal for the West African nation. Islamic Finance News (IFN). https://www.islamicfinancenews.com/ivory-coasts-maiden-sukuk-a-landmark-deal-for-the-west-african-nation-2.html

IFN. (2022). Islamic finance in the Ivory Coast: Timid enthusiasm. Islamic Finance News (IFN). https://www.islamicfinancenews.com/islamic-finance-in-the-ivory-coast-timid-enthusiasm.html

IFN. (2025). Pakistan marks milestone in sustainable Islamic finance with debut sovereign green Sukuk. Islamic Finance News (IFN). https://www.islamicfinancenews.com/pakistan-marks-milestone-in-sustainable-islamic-finance-with-debut-sovereign-green-sukuk.html

Ikhyanuddin, I. (2022). Waqf Accountability Around the World: A Mini-Review. *International Journal of Islamic Business Ethics*, *7*(2), 100. DOI: 10.30659/ijibe.7.2.100-107

IMF. (2017a). Togo Context and Recent Developments. IMF eLibrary. https://www.elibrary.imf.org/view/journals/002/2017/127/article-A001-en.xml?ArticleTabs=fulltext

IMF. (2017b). *Ensuring financial stability in countries with Islamic banking: Selected issues*. International Monetary Fund (IMF) Policy Paper. https://www.elibrary.imf.org/view/journals/007/2017/007/article-A001-en.xml

Inner Peace Fellowship. (n.d.). *Why we should do the right thing even when others don't*. Retrieved June 12, 2025, from https://www.innerpeacefellowship.org/do-the-right-thing

Institute of International Finance. (2024, May 7). *Global debt monitor: Navigating the new normal*. https://www.iif.com/Products/Global-Debt-Monitor

International Finance Corporation. (2017). Islamic Banking Opportunities Across Small and Medium Enterprises: Pakistan. International Finance Corporation. http://hdl.handle.net/10986/26098

International Labour Organization. (ILO, 2024). *World employment and social outlook: September 2024 update* [Brief]. https://researchrepository.ilo.org/esploro/outputs/encyclopediaEntry/World-employment-and-social-outlook-September/995381680802676DOI: 10.54394/OPQH3749

International Monetary Fund. (2024). IMF members' quotas and voting power, Retrieved from https://www.imf.org

International Monetary Fund. (n.d.). *Articles of agreement of the International Monetary Fund.* https://www.imf.org/external/pubs/ft/aa/index.htm

International Organization of Securities Commissions. "IOSCO: Facilitating Mutual Recognition and Substituted Compliance." Transatlantic Coalition on Financial Regulation, November 2012. https://www.isda.org/a/hdDDE/iosco-paper-final-091112.pdf

Iqbal, Z., & Mirakhor, A. (2011). An introduction to Islamic finance [). John Wiley & Sons.]. *Theory into Practice, 687.*

Iqbal, Z., & Mirakhor, A. (2011). *An introduction to Islamic finance: Theory and practice* (Vol. 687). John Wiley & Sons. DOI: 10.1002/9781118390474

Iqbal, Z., & Mirakhor, A. (2017). *Ethical dimensions of Islamic finance: Theory and practice*. Springer. DOI: 10.1007/978-3-319-66390-6

IsDB. (2020). The Covid-19 Crisis and Islamic Finance Response of the Islamic Development Bank Group. Islamic Development Bank (IsDB). https://www.isdb.org/sites/default/files/media/documents/2020-10/1.%20IsDB%20Group%20Report%20on%20Covid-19%20and%20Islamic%20Finance__FINAL.pdf

Ishak, A. H., Amira Mohamad, S. N., Ab Manan, S. K., Yahaya, M. H., Wan Daud, W. N., & Sharif, D. (2025). The critical success factors of Waqf land development for sustainable agriculture. *Social Sciences & Humanities Open*, *11*, 101244. DOI: 10.1016/j.ssaho.2024.101244

Iskandar, I., & Sofuoğlu, H. (2023). Exploring the evolution of Waqf laws and contemporary practices in Muslim countries. *Islam Realitas: Journal of Islamic and Social Studies*, *9*(1), 57. DOI: 10.30983/islam_realitas.v9i1.6229

Islamic Development Bank (IsDB). (2022). *Annual development effectiveness report.* https://www.isdb.org

Islamic Financial Services Board (IFSB). (2015). *Islamic financial services industry stability report*. https://www.ifsb.org

ISRA. (2012). *Islamic Financial System: Principles and Operations. International Shari'ah Research Academy for Islamic Finance*. ISRA.

Iyer, S. (2016). The new economics of religion. *Journal of Economic Literature, 54*(2), 395–441. DOI: 10.1257/jel.54.2.395

Jacobs, L. (1957). The economic conditions of the Jews in Babylon in Talmudic times compared with Palestine. *Journal of Semitic Studies, 2*(4), 349–359. DOI: 10.1093/jss/2.4.349

Jalil, A., & Rahman, M. K. (2010). Islamic law of contract is getting momentum. *International Journal of Business and Social Science, 1*(2), 175–192. https://ijbssnet.com/journals/Vol._1_No._2_November_2010/14.pdf

Jemolo, A. C. (1975). *Chiesa e Stato in Italia negli ultimi cento anni*. Einaudi.

Jensen, T., & Geertz, A. (2014). From the history of religions to the study of religion in Denmark: An essay on the subject, organizational history and research themes. *Temenos - Nordic Journal for the Study of Religion, 50*(1), 79–114. https://doi.org/ DOI: 10.33356/temenos.46252

JLens. (2022). *Faith-based ESG investing framework*. https://jlensnetwork.org

Jobst, A. A. (2007). *The economics of Islamic finance and securitization* (IMF Working Paper No. 07/117). International Monetary Fund. https://www.elibrary.imf.org/view/journals/001/2007/117/article-A001-en.xml

Jobst, A., Kunzel, P., Mills, P., & Sy, A. (2008). Islamic bond issuance: What sovereign debt managers need to know. *International Journal of Islamic and Middle Eastern Finance and Management, 1*(4), 330–344. DOI: 10.1108/17538390810919637

Jr, B., & Wade, R. H. (2024). Will the IMF Survive to 100? Project Syndicate. https://www.project-syndicate.org/onpoint/imf-necessary-reforms-greater-influence-for-emerging-developing-economies-by-paulo-nogueira-batista-and-robert-h-wade-2024-10

Jung, A., Romelli, D., & Farvaque, E. (2025). Do central bank reforms lead to more monetary discipline? European Central Bank (Working Paper Series No 3049). https://www.ecb.europa.eu/pub/pdf/scpwps/ecb.wp3049~bca750cd0a.en.pdf

Kahaner, L. (2003). *Values, prosperity and the Talmud*. Wiley.

Kahf, M. (2004). Shariah and historical aspects of Zakah and Awqaf. *Background paper prepared for Islamic Research and Training Institute, Islamic Development Bank.*

Kamali, M. H. (2018). Shari'ah and the ethical tradition: Ethics and morality in Islamic thought. *Islam and Civilisational Renewal*, *9*(1), 11–32. DOI: 10.12816/0043453

Kamaruddin, M. I. H., Hanefah, M. M., & Masruki, R. (2022). Challenges and prospects in Waqf reporting practices in Malaysia. *Journal of Financial Reporting and Accounting*, *22*(3), 752–765. DOI: 10.1108/JFRA-01-2022-0018

Kammer, M. A., Norat, M. M., Pinon, M. M., Prasad, A., Towe, M. C. M., & Zeidane, M. Z. (2015). *Islamic finance: Opportunities, challenges, and policy options. International Monetary Fund (Discussion note SDN/15/05).* International Monetary Fund., DOI: 10.5089/9781498325035.006

Karimah, D. A., Pamuncak, M. B., & Mubin, M. K. (2023). The Role of Waqf in Supporting Sustainable Development Goals: Linking theory and its practices. *SUHUF*, *35*(2), 31–38. DOI: 10.23917/suhuf.v35i2.23018

Karimov, J., Balli, F., Balli, H. O., & de Bruin, A. (2020). Shariʿah Compliance Requirements and the Cost of Equity Capital. *Pacific-Basin Finance Journal*, *62*, 101353. DOI: 10.1016/j.pacfin.2020.101349

Keir, J. (2016). Two hearts believing in just one mind? The Humanistic Management Network and the Global Ethic Project. *Humanistic Management Journal*, *1*(1), 139–147. https://link.springer.com/article/10.1007/s41463-016-0008-0?fromPaywallRec=true. DOI: 10.1007/s41463-016-0008-0

Kerber, W., & Van den Bergh, R. (2008). Mutual recognition revisited: Misunderstandings, inconsistencies, and a suggested reinterpretation. *Kyklos*, *61*(3), 447–465. DOI: 10.1111/j.1467-6435.2008.00412.x

Keynes, J. M. (1936). *The general theory of employment, interest, and money.* Retrieved from https://www.files.ethz.ch/isn/125515/1366_KeynesTheoryofEmployment.pdf

Khan, F. (2010). How "Islamic" is Islamic banking? *Journal of Economic Behavior & Organization*, *76*(3), 805–820. DOI: 10.1016/j.jebo.2010.09.015

Khan, M. A. (2011). Consumer protection and the Islamic law of contract. *Islamabad Law Review*, *2*(2), 20–37.

Khan, M. T., Khan, S., & Khan, M. H. (2018). Historical contribution of Islamic Waqf in human capital development through funding education. *Journal of Islamic and Religious Studies*, *3*(2), 57–74. DOI: 10.36476/JIRS.3:2.12.2018.12

Kim, U. Y. (2025). The Role of Islamic Finance in Advancing the United Nations Sustainable Development Goals (SDGs): Case Studies and critical gap. Intergovernmental Research and Policy Journal. https://irpj.euclid.int/articles/the-role-of-islamic-finance-in-advancing-the-united-nations-sustainable-development-goals-sdgs-case-studies-and-critical-gaps-in-the-banking-sector-in-asean-countries/

Klein, D. (1995). The Islamic and Jewish laws of usury: A bridge to commercial growth and peace in the Middle East. *Denver Journal of International Law and Policy*, *23*(3), 535–554.

Kopel, C. (2023). Phantom LIBOR Terms and the *Heter Iska*—Part I. *The Banking Law Journal*, *140*(3), 203–217.

Krippner, G. R. (2005). The financialization of the American economy. *Socio-economic Review*, *3*(2), 173–208. DOI: 10.1093/SER/mwi008

Krugman, P. (1998). *The return of depression economics*. W. W. Norton & Company.

Küng, H. (2004). *Global responsibility: In search of a new world ethic*. Imprint: Wipf and Stock. DOI: 10.1111/j.1741-2005.1991.tb03744.x

Kunhibava, S., Muneeza, A., Khalid, M. B., Mustapha, Z., & Sen, T. M. (2024). Social Sukuk. In *Islamic Social Finance: Law and Practice in Malaysia* (pp. 105-128). Singapore: Springer Nature Singapore. https://doi.org/DOI: 10.1007/978-981-97-1410-0_6

Kushnir-Stein, A. & Holland, L. (2008). New Inscribed Lead Weights from Cesarea. In K.G. Holum – J.A. Stabler – E.G. Reinhardt. *Cesarea Report and Studies. Excavations 1995-2007 within the Old City and the Ancient Harbor.* British Archeological Reports, 209-211.

Kusuma, K. A., & Silva, A. C. (2014). Sukuk markets: a proposed approach for development. *World Bank Policy Research Working Paper*, (7133). https://documents1.worldbank.org/curated/en/637041468320946094/pdf/WPS7133.pdf

Lai, B. (2012). *Finanze vaticane. Da Pio XI a Benedetto XVI.* Rubbettino.

Laldin, M. A., & Furqani, H. (2013). *The foundations of Islamic finance and the Maqā id al-Sharī ah requirements*. Journal of Islamic Finance, 2(1), 31–37. IIUM Institute of Islamic Banking and Finance. DOI: https://doi.org/DOI: 10.31436/jif.v2i1.9

Lapin, D. (2007). *Jewish theology and economic theory*. Acton Institute. Retrieved from https://www.acton.org/pub/religion-liberty/volume-17-number-1/jewish-theology-and-economic-theory

Lauffer, S. (1971). *Diokletians Preisedikt*. DeGruyter. DOI: 10.1515/9783110825398

Lee, M. J. (2022). Islamic Finance Provides Better Solutions in Overcoming the Financial Distress Ascribable to COVID-19: Evidence from Malaysia. In *Towards a Post-Covid Global Financial System* (pp. 261-269). Emerald Publishing Limited. https://doi.org/DOI: 10.1108/978-1-80071-625-420210014

Leff, B. (2025). Ethical Investing: Praiseworthy, or Obligatory? *Rabbinic Assembly*, published online April 1, 2025: https://www.rabbinicalassembly.org/sites/default/files/2025-04/ethical-investing-final.pdf

Lehmann, M., & Schürger, J. (2021). Multilateralizing deference: A proposal for reforming global financial law. *EBI Working Paper Series, 107*, 1–29.

Lei, L., & Traylor, F. (2023). How does religion influence parental support of young adult children? *Journal of Family Issues*, *45*(9), 2135–2157. DOI: 10.1177/0192513X231195653

Leo, X. I. I. I. (1891). Rerum Novarum [Encyclical letter on capital and labor]. Vatican. https://www.vatican.va/content/leo-xiii/en/encyclicals/documents/hf_l-xiii_enc_15051891_rerum-novarum.html

Levine, A. (1987). *Economics & Jewish law*. Ktav Publishing.

Levine, A. (2005). *Moral issues in the marketplace in Jewish law*. Yashar Books.

Loberbaum, M. (2019). The necessity of exile in Jewish political thought. *Jewish Studies Quarterly*, *26*(4), 382–401.

Lopes, C. (2012). Economic growth and inequality: The new post-Washington consensus. *RCCS Annual Review*, *4*(4), 69–85. DOI: 10.4000/rccsar.426

Luther, M. (2003). *Commentary on Romans* (J. T. Mueller, Trans.). Kregel Publications. (Original work published 1522). https://www.kregel.com/bible-commentaries/commentary-on-romans/

Macsudov, V. G., Amsalu, A., Souza-Junior, J., & Tattaqillah, N. (2024). Implementation of salam contracts in the Sharia principles framework: Surveys and prospects in the field. *Demak Universal Journal of Islam and Sharia*, *2*(02), 111–132. DOI: 10.61455/deujis.v2i02.106

Maffi, L., Rochini, M., & Gregorini, G. (Eds.). (2018). *I sistemi del dare nell'Italia rurale del XVIII secolo*. FrancoAngeli.

Magid, S. (2018). The necessity of exile: A post-Zionist theology. *Tikkun*, *33*(4), 30–35.

Maimonides. (n.d.). *Mishne Torah, Neighbors*, 2:11.

Maimonides. (n.d.). *Mishne Torah, Ownerless Property and Gifts*, 6:17.

Maimonides. (n.d.). *Mishne Torah, Sales*, 22:1.

Maimonides. (n.d.). *Mishne Torah, Sales*, 22:3.

Maimonides. (n.d.). *Mishne Torah, Sales*, 6:7.

Manaf, A. W. B. A., Siong, W. H., & Razak, H. B. A. (2025). Modernizing Waqf: Navigating Legal and Digital Frontiers in the 21st Century. *Azka International Journal of Zakat & Social Science*, *6*(1), 117–135. DOI: 10.51377/azjaf.vol6no1.201

Mapenzauswa, S. (2015). Ivory Coast to issue 150 billion CFA francs worth of 5-year sukuk. Reuters. https://www.reuters.com/article/ivorycoast-sukuk-idAFJ8N12101Y20151120/

Marcacci, A. (2023). *Transnational securities regulation: How it works, who shapes it*. Springer. DOI: 10.1007/978-3-031-18063-7

Maududi, S. A. A. (1977). *Islamic Riyasat*. Islamic Publications. https://faakhirislamic.wordpress.com/2015/08/04/islami-riyasat-by-syed-abul-aala-maududi/

Maulina, R., Dhewanto, W., & Faturohman, T. (2023). Waqf-Based entrepreneurship direct financing model: Potential and challenges. *International Journal of Emerging Issues in Islamic Studies*, *3*(1), 70–91. DOI: 10.31098/ijeiis.v3i1.1398

McGoldrick, P. M. (2012). New perspectives on Pius XII and Vatican financial transactions during the Second World War. *Historical Journal (Cambridge, England)*, *55*(4), 1029–1048. DOI: 10.1017/S0018246X12000416

McRorie, C. G. (2018). Religion and globalization: *Riba*, usury, and the evolution of moral finance: A comparison of two arguments. *Journal of Religion & Society*, Supplement Series 16, 109–124. https://cdr.creighton.edu/server/api/core/bitstreams/1af6d44c-7f40-4c3c-87b9-47f46596b654/content

Mearsheimer, J. J. (2019). Bound to fail: The rise and fall of the liberal international order. *International Security*, *43*(4), 7–50. DOI: 10.1162/isec_a_00342

Meeks, D. M. (2014). Economics in the Christian Scriptures. In Oslington, P. (Ed.), *The Oxford handbook of Christianity and economics* (pp. 3–21). Oxford University Press., DOI: 10.1093/oxfordhb/9780199729715.013.001

Ministry of Finance Malaysia. (2020). Sukuk Prihatin: From RM500 Million to More Than RM666 Million; Proof of Malaysians' Solidarity in Supporting Economic Recovery Efforts. Official Portal of Ministry of Finance Malaysia. https://www.mof.gov.my/portal/en/news/press-release/sukuk-prihatin-from-rm500-million-to-more-than-rm666-million-proof-of-malaysians-solidarity-in-supporting-economic-recovery-efforts

Ministry of Finance Pakistan. (2025). Semi-Annual Public Debt Bulletin (July – December 2024). Debt Management Office, Ministry of Finance – Government of Pakistan. https://www.finance.gov.pk/dpco/semi_annual_debt_bulletin_1H_28032025.pdf

Mirakhor, A., & Krichene, N. (2009). The recent crisis: Lessons for Islamic Finance. Published in: IFSB 2nd Public Lecture on Financial Policy and Stability (2009): pp. 1-92. https://mpra.ub.uni-muenchen.de/56022/

Mishna. (n.d.). *Baba Mezia*, 4:1.

Mohaiyadin, N. M., Aman, A., Palil, M. R., & Muhamad Said, S. (2022). Addressing Accountability and Transparency Challenges in Waqf Management Using Blockchain Technology. *Journal of Islamic Monetary Economics and Finance*, *8*, 53–80. DOI: 10.21098/jimf.v8i0.1413

Mohd Zameri, S. N., Syed Alwi, S. F., Mohammad Hatta, M. F., & Saiful Fikri, A. A. H. (2024). Maslahah and its Application in Islamic Finance. [IJIB]. *International Journal of Islamic Business*, *9*(1), 82–94.

Mohieldin, M., Iqbal, Z., Rostom, A., & Fu, X. (2015). The role of Islamic finance in enhancing financial inclusion in Organization of Islamic Cooperation (OIC) countries. *Islamic Economic Studies*, *20*(2). https://ssrn.com/abstract=3158639

Mohsin, M. I. A., Khattab, I., & Alchaar, M. O. (2020). Economic and Social Impacts of Sovereign Sukuk. In *Handbook of Research on Theory and Practice of Global Islamic Finance* (pp. 732–751). IGI Global Scientific Publishing., https://www.igi-global.com/gateway/chapter/247234#pnlRecommendationForm

Mokhtarian, J. S. (2015). *Rabbis, Sorcerers, Kings, and Priests: The Culture of the Talmud in Ancient Iran*. University of California Press. DOI: 10.1525/california/9780520286207.001.0001

Moloney, N. (2018). *The age of ESMA: Governing EU financial markets*. Hart Publishing.

Muhit, M., & Al-Hakim, UIN, S., & Setiawan, I. (2024). Flexibility of al-ijarah contract perspective of Islamic economic law. *al-Afkar. Journal of Islamic Studies*, *7*(1), 762–787. DOI: 10.31943/afkarjournal.v7i1.888

Muhmad, S. N., Muhamad, R., & Sulong, F. (2021). Sustainable development goals and Islamic finance: An integrated approach for Islamic financial institutions. *Indonesian Journal of Sustainability Accounting and Management*, *5*(1). Advance online publication. DOI: 10.28992/ijsam.v5i1.286

Nabiyeva, G. N., Wheeler, S. M., London, J. K., & Brazil, N. (2023). Implementation of sustainable development goal 11 (sustainable cities and communities): Initial good practices data. *Sustainability (Basel)*, *15*(20), 14810. DOI: 10.3390/su152014810

Nafar, N. (2019). The investment of Waqf properties and infrastructure development. *Springer International Publishing*, *1*, 285–308. DOI: 10.1007/978-3-030-18445-2_14

Naqvi, S. N. H. (1981). *Ethics and economics: An Islamic synthesis*. The Islamic Foundation. ISBN: 0-86037-079-8 (hardback) / 0-86037-080-1 (paperback)

Nasrullah, N., & Muthoifin, N. (2024). Implementation of fiqh rules in economic transactions in Islamic financial institutions: A literature review study. *Demak Universal Journal of Islam and Sharia*, *2*(3), 347–360. DOI: 10.61455/deujis.v2i03.194

National Treasury. (2014). South Africa concludes debut sukuk bond. National Treasury, Republic of South Africa. https://www.treasury.gov.za/comm_media/press/2014/2014091701%20-%20Sukuk%20Statement.pdf

Naz, A., Ali, M., & Barut, A. K. (2025). Sukuk and Corporate Governance: Ethical Foundations, Economic Impact, and Global Relevance in Islamic Finance. In *Islamic Finance and Corporate Governance: Synergies for Sustainable Growth* (pp. 147-173). Emerald Publishing Limited. https://doi.org/DOI: 10.1108/978-1-83662-346-520251022

Neusner, J. (1969). Israel's politics in Sasanian Iran. *Jewish Quarterly Review (Philadelphia, Pa.)*, *60*(1), 80–90.

Nicholls, A. (2022). *Oxford Faith-Aligned Impact Finance Project Phase 1 Report*. Saïd Business School – University of Oxford.

Nicolaïdis, K., & Steffenson, R. (2005). Managed mutual recognition in the transatlantic marketplace. In Andrews, D. M. (Eds.), *The future of transatlantic economic relations: Continuity amid discord* (pp. 139–163). European University Institute.

Norchaevna, N. S. (2024). Islamic Finance: Principles, Governance, Sustainability and Investment Insights. *European Journal of Management. Economics and Business*, *1*(3), 206–216. DOI: 10.59324/ejmeb.2024.1(3).17

Nouman, M., & Ullah, K. (2023). *Participatory islamic finance: Ideals, contemporary practices, and innovations*. Springer Nature., DOI: 10.1007/978-981-19-9555-2

Osgoode Hall Law School. (n.d.). *Reports*. https://digitalcommons.osgoode.yorku.ca/cgi/viewcontent.cgi?article=1109&context=reports

Osun State Government. (2013, October 11). *Osun successfully completes N11.4 billion sukuk bond, Aregbesola commended for exploring new development options*. Osun State Government. https://www.osunstate.gov.ng/2013/10/osun-successfully-completes-n11-4-billion-sukuk-bond-aregbesola-commended-for-exploring-new-development-options/

Otto, J. M. (Ed.). (2012). *Sharia Incorporated: A Comparative Overview of the Legal Systems of Twelve Muslim Countries in Past and Present*. Leiden University Press. DOI: 10.1515/9789400600171

Owais, M., & Manaf, Z. I. A. (2023). Comparative Analysis of Waqf Institutions Governance in India and Singapore. *Journal of Islamic Economics and Business*, *6*(2), 257–282. DOI: 10.21154/elbarka.v6i2.5321

Oxfam International. (2024, January 15). *Wealth of five richest men doubles since 2020 as five billion people made poorer in "decade of division," says Oxfam* [Press release]. https://www.oxfam.org/en/press-releases/wealth-five-richest-men-doubles-2020-five-billion-people-made-poorer-decade-division

Oxfam. (2025, January 20). *Takers not makers*. https://www.oxfam.org.hk/en/news-and-publication/davos-2025

Paldi, C. (2016, January 8). *Financial principles found in Judaism* [Video]. YouTube. https://www.youtube.com/watch?v=2U7NzbaTeqo

Paldi, C. (2024). Abrahamic finance: The path forward? *ISFIRE*, 14(6), 34–41. Retrieved from https://www.isfire.net:contentReference[oaicite:15]{index=15}

Pasinetti, L. (2004). Capitale. In Università Cattolica del Sacro Cuore (Ed.), *Dizionario di dottrina sociale della Chiesa* (p. 170). Vita e Pensiero.

Pecorari, P. (1997). La cultura economico-sociale del movimento cattolico (1861–1995). In Traniello, F., & Campanini, G. (Eds.), *Dizionario storico del movimento cattolico. Aggiornamento 1980–1995* (pp. 25–34). Marietti.

Pegrari, M. (2011). De pecunia. Chiesa, cattolici e finanza nello Stato unitario. In *Cristiani d'Italia. Chiese, società, Stato, 1861–2011* (pp. 1053–1079). [Editore non specificato].

Pegrari, M. (2019). Le finanze della Santa Sede e il Terzo Reich. *Studi storici Luigi Simeoni*, 69, 75–86.

Pegrari, M. (2020). Le finanze della Santa Sede e la black list: la questione Sudameris (1910–1948). *Studi storici Luigi Simeoni*, 70, 97–106.

Pegrari, M. (2014). La città e il credito. In Carboni, M., & Muzzarelli, M. G. (Eds.), *Reti di credito. Circuiti informali, impropri, nascosti (secoli XIII–XIX)* (pp. 195–220). Il Mulino.

Perry, J. H. (2018). *Gay Girl, Good God: The story of who I was, and who God has always been* (Vol. 1). B&H Publishing Group. Retrieved from https://www.bhpublishinggroup.com/products/gay-girl/

Persico, A. A. (2014). *Il Codice di Camaldoli. La DC e la ricerca della «terza via» tra Stato e mercato (1943–1993)*. Guerini.

Peyton, N., & King, L. (2016). Togo issues first $251 mln, 10-yr sukuk bond with 6.5 pct yield. Reuters. https://www.reuters.com/article/business/finance/togo-issues-first-251-mln-10-yr-sukuk-bond-with-65-pct-yield-idUSKCN1071OC/

Phougat, A., Mishra, A., & Oinam, R. (2025). Waqf Law In India: A Critical Analysis of Estate Management, Powers and Socio-Legal Impact. *International Journal of Legal Studies and Social Sciences*, *3*(2), 86–102. https://ijlsss.com/wp-content/uploads/2025/04/09.-Ashima-Phougat-Arkaja-Mishra-Rameshwori-Oinam.pdf

Piketty, T. (2020). *Capitale e ideologia*. La nave di Teseo.

Piketty, T. (2021). *Una breve storia dell'uguaglianza*. La nave di Teseo.

Piketty, T. (2014). *Capital in the twenty-first century*. Harvard University Press., DOI: 10.4159/9780674369542

Piketty, T. (2020). *Capital and ideology*. Belknap Press of Harvard University Press., DOI: 10.4159/9780674245075

Pistor, K. (2024, January 28). The social costs of price. *Finance & Development*, *61*(1). https://www.elibrary.imf.org/view/journals/022/0061/001/article-A004-en.xml

Pius, X. I. I. (1942, 27 June). *Chirografo di papa Pio XII con il quale il pontefice erige l'Istituto per le opere di religione*. https://www.vatican.va/content/pius-xii/it/letters/documents/hf_p-xii_lett_19420627_chirografo-ior.html

Pollard, J. F. (2006). *L'obolo di Pietro. Le finanze del Papato moderno: 1850–1950*. Corbaccio.

Pope Leo, X. I. I. I. (1891). *Rerum novarum: On capital and labor*. Vatican. https://www.vatican.va/content/leo-xiii/en/encyclicals/documents/hf_l-xiii_enc_15051891_rerum-novarum.html

Rahmalan, M. T., & Abu-Hussin, M. F. (2021). A Systematic Review of Contemporary and Innovative Waqf Sources: Cash and Service Waqf. *Jurnal Syariah, 29*(2), 257–284. DOI: 10.22452/js.vol29no2.5

Ramli, N. M., Mohd Salleh, N. H., & Muhamed, N. A. (2015). Discharging Accountability Through Governance: Cases from Waqf Institutions in Indonesia. *Online Journal of Research in Islamic Studies, 2*(1). https://mojem.um.edu.my/index.php/RIS/article/view/9892

Ramli, N. M., & Muhamed, N. A. (2014). Good governance framework for corporate Waqf: Towards accountability enhancement. *SSRN*. https://ssrn.com/abstract=2437260

Rasool, T. (2024). Waqf - The Muslim endowments in India: Ideological and legal intricacies. *Trusts & Trustees, 30*(5), 258–266. DOI: 10.1093/tandt/ttae012

Razak, S. S., Saiti, B., & Dinç, Y. (2019). The contracts, structures and pricing mechanisms of sukuk: A critical assessment. *Borsa Istanbul review, 19*, S21-S33. https://doi.org/DOI: 10.1016/j.bir.2018.10.001

Republic of Indonesia, Ministry of Finance. (2020). *Green Sukuk report 2020*. https://www.djppr.kemenkeu.go.id/page/load/2790

Reuters. (2025, February 28). What happens if the US pulls out from IMF, World Bank? *Dawn*. https://www.dawn.com/news/1894790

Riani, R., & Fatoni, A. (2022). Waqf on Infrastructure: How Far has been Researched? *International Journal of Waqf, 2*(2). Advance online publication. DOI: 10.58968/ijf.v2i2.167

Riaz, U., Burton, B., & Monk, E. (2017). Perceptions on the accessibility of Islamic banking in the UK—Challenges, opportunities and divergence in opinion. *Accounting Forum, 41*(4), 353–374. DOI: 10.1016/j.accfor.2017.10.002

Richman, S. (2007). *Christianity's free-market tradition.* Mises Institute. [Page-printed not available] Retrieved from https://mises.org/mises-daily/christianitys-free-market-tradition

Rizwan, S., & Khan, N. (2015). Basel III liquidity requirement ratios and Islamic banking. *Journal of Banking Regulation, 16*(3), 251–264. DOI: 10.1057/jbr.2014.20

Roberts, J. (2024). Worlds apart: The global financial system is in danger of fragmenting; The Economist, May 11, https://www.economist.com/special-report/2024-05-11?utm_source=chatgpt.com

Rocca, G. (2007). Le strategie anticonfisca degli istituti religiosi in Italia dall'Unità al Concordato del 1929. In R. Di Pietra & F. Landi (Eds.), *Clero, economia e contabilità in Europa. Tra medioevo ed età contemporanea* (pp. 226–247). Carocci.

Romano, R. (2001). The need for competition in international securities regulation. *Theoretical Inquiries in Law, 2*(2), 387–562. DOI: 10.2202/1565-3404.1029

Romer, P. M. (2016). The trouble with macroeconomics. *The American Economist, 61*(1), 1–20. DOI: 10.1177/0569434516652456

Rosenfeld, B. Z & Menirav, J. (2005). *Markets and Marketing in Roman Palestine.* Brill.

Rosenfeld, B. Z. (2010). *Torah Centers and Rabbinic Activity in Palestine, 70-400 CE. History and Geographic Distribution.* Brill. DOI: 10.1163/ej.9789004178380.i-322

Rubin, J. (2020). Introduction to the special issue on the economics of religion. *Journal of Demographic Economics, 86*(3), 207–211. DOI: 10.1017/dem.2020.20

Rulings of the Rabbinical Court of Jerusalem. (n.d.). Monetary law ruling: "…and with this the sale is concluded." See also Feinstein, M. (n.d.). *Responsa Igrot Moshe*, Choshen Mishpat Part 1 §52.

Rumi, G. (2009a). La cultura cattolica italiana nel '900. In E. Bressan & D. Saresella (Eds.), *Perché la storia. Itinerari di ricerca (1963–2006)* (Vol. I, pp. 193–201). Led.

Rumi, G. (2009b). Una cattedra tra Milano e Roma. In E. Bressan & D. Saresella (Eds.), *Perché la storia. Itinerari di ricerca (1963–2006)* (Vol. II, pp. 511–532). Led.

Rumi, G. (1986). Introduzione al problema storiografico della "storia diocesana". In Caprioli, A., Rimoldi, A., & Vaccaro, L. (Eds.), *Chiesa e società. Appunti per una storia delle diocesi lombarde* (pp. 29–38). La Scuola.

Sa'ad, A. A., Muneeza, A., Haron, R., & Othman, A. H. A. (2022). ukūk structure for deficit financing during COVID-19 crisis. *Islamic Economic Studies*, *30*(1), 23–41. DOI: 10.1108/IES-01-2021-0007

Samad, A., Gardner, N. D., & Cook, B. J. (2005). Islamic Banking and Finance in Theory and Practice: The Experience of Malaysia and Bahrain. *American Journal of Islam and Society*, *22*(2), 69–86. DOI: 10.35632/ajis.v22i2.458

Sano, M. A., & Kassim, S. (2021). Waqf governance in the Republic of Guinea: Legal framework, issues, challenges and way forward. *ISRA International Journal of Islamic Finance*, *13*(2), 194–210. DOI: 10.1108/IJIF-03-2020-0064

Sarac, M., & Hassan, M. K. (2023). *Islamic Perspective for a Sustainable Financial System*. Istanbul University Press., DOI: 10.26650/B/SS10.2020.017

Schwartz, M. S. (2012). A Jewish approach to business ethics. *Philosophical Studies*, *2*(10), 754–766.

Seater, J. J. (1993). Ricardian equivalence. *Journal of Economic Literature*, *31*(1), 142–190. https://www.jstor.org/stable/2728152

Secunda, S. (2013). *The Iranian Talmud: Reading the Bavli in Its Sasanian Context*. University of Pennsylvenia Press.

Securities and Exchange Commission. "Multijurisdictional Disclosure System." Division of Corporation Finance Financial Reporting Manual, Topic 16. Accessed August 31, 2025. https://www.sec.gov/about/divisions-offices/division-corporation-finance/financial-reporting-manual/frm-topic-16

Securities Commission Malaysia & World Bank. (2019). Islamic green finance: development, ecosystem and prospects. Securities Commission Malaysia & World Bank. https://documents1.worldbank.org/curated/en/591721554824346344/pdf/Islamic-Green-Finance-Development-Ecosystem-and-Prospects.pdf

Semeraro, R. (2020b). "Non essendo cosa di sua competenza". *Studi storici Luigi Simeoni*, 70, 73–84.

Semeraro, R. (2017). Economic and Financial Management of Religious Congregations in Late Modern Italy. In Gregorini, G. (Ed.), *For the needy youth that we care* (pp. 57–87). Vita e Pensiero.

Semeraro, R. (2020a). *Piccoli IOR. Le Casse Diocesane da Porta Pia alla Seconda guerra mondiale*. Il Mulino.

Semeraro, R., & Gregorini, G. (2019). Destini legati. *Quaderni Storici*, *3*, 801–829.

Shabbir, M. S. (2022). Regulatory and Supervisory Regime of Islamic Banking System in Nigeria: Challenges, Constraints and Way Forward. *Journal of Islamic Banking & Finance*, *39*(2).

Shahed, W. (2020, June 18). Rise of Islamic law in Turkey. *Michigan State University International Law Review*.

Shahed, W. (2020, June 18). Rise of Islamic Law in Turkey. *Michigan State University International Law Review*, *28*(2), 431–458.

Shahid, A. (2025). Pakistan Signs $4.5 billion Loans with Local Banks to Ease Power Sector Debt. Reuters. https://www.reuters.com/sustainability/boards-policy-regulation/pakistan-signs-45-billion-loans-with-local-banks-ease-power-sector-debt-2025-06-20/?utm_source=chatgpt.com

Shaikh, S. A. (2014). Analysis of challenges and opportunities in Islamic banking. *International Journal of Financial Services Management*, *7*(3-4), 286–300. DOI: 10.1504/IJFSM.2014.065581

Shamsuddeen, M. (2016). *Islam is compatible with a free economy, argue Muslim scholars*. Institute of Economic Affairs. Retrieved from https://iea.org.uk/blog/islam-is-compatible-with-a-free-economy-argue-muslim-scholars

Shanafelt, C. D. (2021). "A world of debt": Quobna Ottobah Cugoano, *The Wealth Of Nations*, and the end of finance. *Eighteenth-Century Studies*, *55*(1), 21–43. DOI: 10.1353/ecs.2021.0106

Shebaita, M. (2025). The general principles of law recognised by civilised nations in Islamic law. *The Liverpool Law Review*, *46*(2), 219–243. Advance online publication. DOI: 10.1007/s10991-025-09384-2

Shetreet, S., & Homolka, W. (2007). *Jewish and Israeli law: An introduction*. De Gruyter.

Siddiqi, M. N. (2006). Islamic banking and finance in theory and practice: A survey of state of the art. *Islamic Economic Studies*, *13*(2), 1–48. https://ssrn.com/abstract=3161388

Siddiqi, M. N. (2010). *Islamic banking and finance: What it is and what it could be*. The Islamic Foundation. [DOI not available]

Sivanandan, P., & Ahmad, R. (2025). Ethical Investment in Islamic Finance: The Role of ESG Toward Sustainable Growth. In *Islamic Finance and Corporate Governance: Synergies for Sustainable Growth* (pp. 43-56). Emerald Publishing Limited.

Smith, A. (1759/2002). *The Theory of Moral Sentiments* (D. D. Raphael & A. L. Macfie, Eds.; Glasgow Edition, Vol. I). Indianapolis: Liberty Fund (online at Online Library of Liberty). ISBN 9780521591508

Smith, Q. (2018). *The Geonim of Babylonia and the shaping of medieval Jewish culture*. Yale University Press.

Smolo, E., & Habibovic, E. (2012). Barriers to growth of Islamic finance: Issue of standardization. *Islamic Banking and Finance: Principles, Instruments and Operations, 1st ed. Ampang: The Malaysian Current Law Journal in Malaysia, chp, 29*, 715-37. https://www.researchgate.net/profile/Edib-Smolo/publication/317063250_Barriers_to_Growth_of_Islamic_Finance_Issue_of_Standardization/links/5923e4a3a6fdcc4443fa3bca/Barriers-to-Growth-of-Islamic-Finance-Issue-of-Standardization.pdf

Sofer, M. (n.d.). *Responsa Chatam Sofer*, Part 2 (Yoreh De'ah) §141; *Responsa Choshen Mishpat*, siman 200:1.

Sofer, M. (n.d.). *Responsa Chatam Sofer*, Part 2 (Yoreh De'ah) §144.

Sorge, B. (2011). *Introduzione alla dottrina sociale della Chiesa*. Queriniana.

Sperber, D. (1977). On the office of the Agoranomos in Roman Palestine. *ZDMG, 127*, 227–243.

Stern, Y. (2006). *What is Jewish in Israeli law?* Israel Democracy Institute. • Otto, J. M. (Ed.). (2012). *Sharia incorporated: A comparative overview of the legal systems of twelve Muslim countries in past and present*. Leiden University Press.

Stiglitz, J. E. (2002). *Globalization and Its Discontents*. W. W. Norton & Company. https://wwnorton.com/books/9780393324396

Stiglitz, J. E. (2024). *The road to freedom: Economics and the good society*. W. W. Norton & Company. https://wwnorton.com/books/The-Road-to-Freedom

Stiglitz, J. E., Gallagher, K. P., Guzmán, M., & Uy, M. (2024). The IMF must end its destructive surcharges. *Project Syndicate*. Retrieved from: https://www.project-syndicate.org/commentary/imf-must-end-surcharge-policy-by-joseph-e-stiglitz-et-al-2024-09

Sukmana, R. (2020). Critical assessment of Islamic endowment funds (Waqf) literature: Lesson for government and future directions. *Heliyon, 6*(10), e05074. DOI: 10.1016/j.heliyon.2020.e05074 PMID: 33088936

Svoboda, A. (2024). Investing in the Islamic World: Opportunities, Challenges, and Implications. Economics and Finance, 12(1), 13-21. https://economics-and-finance.com/archive/EF_2024_1.pdf#page=13

Taccolini, M. (2009). Chiesa ed economia. In M. Taccolini (Ed.), *Nuovi percorsi della storia economica* (pp. 133–147). Vita e Pensiero.

Taccolini, M., & Cafaro, P. (1997). *Il Banco Ambrosiano. Una banca cattolica negli anni dell'ascesa economica lombarda.* Laterza.

Taccolini, M., & Gregorini, G. (2019). *Banco di Brescia, vent'anni nel futuro.* Morcelliana.

Talmud Bavli. (n.d.). *Baba Batra*, 106b.

Talmud Bavli. (n.d.). *Baba Mezia*, 44a–44b.

Tamari, M. (1987). *With all your possessions: Jewish ethics and economic life.* The Free Press.

Tamari, M. (1991). *In the marketplace: Jewish business ethics.* Targum.

Tamari, M. (1995). *The challenge of wealth.* Jason Aronson Inc.

The Economist. (2023, January 26)Christians fight about how to serve God and mammon: Is ESG simply a social-Marxist agenda? Retrieved from: https://www.economist.com/finance-and-economics/2023/01/26/christians-fight-about-how-to-serve-god-and-mammon

The Economist. (2023, June 24). The trouble with sticky inflation. *The Economist.* https://www.economist.com/finance-and-economics/2023/06/24/the-trouble-with-sticky-inflation

The Jakarta Post. (2024). Sovereign sukuk plays major role in decade of Indonesian development. *The Jakarta Post.* https://www.thejakartapost.com/business/2024/10/16/sovereign-sukuk-plays-major-role-in-decade-of-indonesian-development.html

The World Bank. (2024). Voting powers of member countries. Retrieved from https://www.worldbank.org](https://www.worldbank.org

Togo First. (2025). *Togo prepares to repay CFA12.1 billion on Islamic Sukuk loan by August 2025.* Togo First. https://www.togofirst.com/en/economic-governance/2307-16815-togo-prepares-to-repay-cfa12-1-billion-on-islamic-sukuk-loan-by-august-2025

Tohidi, M., Freydooni, M. M., & Easaei, M. (2024). Designing an innovative way for financing SMEs through Sukuk issuance. *Iranian Journal of Finance, 8*(4), 113–135. DOI: 10.61186/ijf.2024.474814.1485

Transatlantic Coalition on Financial Regulation. (2012). *IOSCO: Facilitating mutual recognition and substituted compliance*. International Swaps and Derivatives Association. https://www.isda.org/a/hdDDE/iosco-paper-final-091112.pdf

Treasury, H. M. (2021, March 31). UK Sovereign Sukuk PLC's Offering Circular. Retrieved from https://www.gov.uk/government/publications/uk-sovereign-sukuk-plcs-offering-circular--2

Triodos Bank. (2023). *Annual impact report 2023*. https://www.triodos.com/annual-report

U.S. Securities and Exchange Commission. (n.d.-a). *Financial reporting manual: Topic 16*. https://www.sec.gov/about/divisions-offices/division-corporation-finance/financial-reporting-manual/frm-topic-16

UK Government. (2014). Government issues first Islamic bond. The UK Government. https://www.gov.uk/government/news/government-issues-first-islamic-bond

UK Government. (2021). UK bolsters Islamic finance offering with second Sukuk. The UK Government. https://www.gov.uk/government/news/uk-bolsters-islamic-finance-offering-with-second-sukuk#:~:text=The%20UK%20has%20bolstered%20its,financial%20centre%20in%20the%20world

Ulusoy, A., & Ela, M. (2017). Lack of standardization in Sukuk market. *Journal of Islamic Economics, Banking and Finance, 13*(1), 147-169. https://www.researchgate.net/profile/Mehmet-Ela/publication/318787697_Lack_of_Standardization_in_Sukuk_Market/links/5a142c7eaca27240e3086299/Lack-of-Standardization-in-Sukuk-Market.pdf

UNCTAD. (2023). *Trade and development report 2023: Growth, debt and climate - Realigning the global financial architecture*. United Nations Publications. https://unctad.org/system/files/official-document/tdr2023_en.pdf

UNDP. (2018). Indonesia's green bonds & sukuk initiative. *UNDP Climate Promise*. https://climatepromise.undp.org/research-and-reports/indonesias-green-bond-sukuk-initiative

UNDP. (2024). The Potential Growth and Future Trends of Green Sukuk as a Tool for Sustainable Financing. United Nations Development Programme (UNDP). https://www.undp.org/sites/g/files/zskgke326/files/2025-05/undp-kfh-green-sukuk-tool-for-sustainable-financing.pdf

United States Conference of Catholic Bishops. (2021). Socially Responsible Investment Guidelines for the United States Conference of Catholic Bishops. https://www.usccb.org/resources/Socially%20Responsible%20Investment%20Guidelines%20 2021%20(003).pdf

University of Illinois Chicago School of Law. (n.d.). *Global markets law journal.* https://repository.law.uic.edu/cgi/viewcontent.cgi?article=1015&context=global-markets

University of Melbourne. (2009). *University of Melbourne Law Review Studies.* https://classic.austlii.edu.au/au/journals/UMelbLRS/2009/11.html

Usmani, M. T. (2002). *An introduction to Islamic finance* (Vol. 20). Kluwer Law International.

Vaquero Piñeiro, M. (2007). I censi consegnativi. *Rivista di storia dell'agricoltura,* 47(1), 57–94.

Verdier, P.-H. (n.d.). Mutual recognition in international finance. [Publication details unavailable].

Vizcaino, B. (2014). Luxembourg's debut sukuk sees strong demand from government accounts. Reuters. https://www.reuters.com/article/markets/luxembourgs-debut-sukuk-sees-strong-demand-from-government-accounts-idUSL6N0RW0DY/

Vogel, E. F., & Hayes, S. L. (1998). *Islamic law and finance: Religion, risk and return.* Kluwer Law International. DOI: 10.1163/9789004634916

Vremya, R. (n.d.-a). Stock exchange bridges cannot be established without AAOIFI. https://realnoevremya.com/articles/8858-stock-exchange-bridges-cannot-be-established-without-aaoifi

Wan Ismail, W. M., Misba, N. T., & Mat Isa, N. A. (2025). Reimagining Waqf in the digital age: A framework for smart Waqf governance through emerging technologies. *International Journal of Research and Innovation in Social Science, 9*(5), 4704–4714. DOI: 10.47772/IJRISS.2025.905000361

Wasim, M. H., & Zafar, M. B. (2024). Shariah governance and Islamic banks: A systematic literature review. *Journal of Islamic Accounting and Business Research.* Advance online publication. DOI: 10.1108/JIABR-11-2023-0386

Webster, C. (2023). *Conclusion: 'There's One Law for the Rich and Another for the Poor'.* In *Rich Crime, Poor Crime: Inequality and the Rule of Law* (pp. 217–222). Emerald Publishing Limited. https://doi.org/DOI: 10.1108/978-1-83909-822-2 00230011

Wellness, W. (2025). *The Economics of Enough.* Wellness Warehouse. https://www.wellnesswarehouse.com/catalog/product/view/id/22983/terms-and-conditions?utm_source=chatgpt.com

Wespath. (2024, February 7). Wespath CIO Dave Zellner announces retirement [Press release]. https://www.wespath.org/News/Zellner-Retirement#!/page:1

Wiley. (2006). [Abstract]. *Philosophical Forum.* https://onlinelibrary.wiley.com/doi/abs/10.1111/j.1467-646X.2006.121.x

Wilson, R. (1997). Economics, ethics and religion: Jewish, Christian and Muslim economic thought, New York: New York University Press; ISBN 0-8147-9313-4 DOI for Chapter 1 (pp. 1–21); Palgrave Macmillan. DOI: 10.1057/9780230374720

Wilson, A. (2000). The new rules: Ethics, social responsibility and strategy. *Strategy and Leadership*, *28*(3), 12–16. DOI: 10.1108/10878570010348549

World Bank. (2017). Mobilizing Islamic Finance for Infrastructure Public-Private Partnerships. International Bank for Reconstruction and Development / The World Bank. https://ppp.worldbank.org/sites/default/files/2024-08/Mobilizing_Islamic_Finance_for_Infrastructure_PPPs_FINAL.pdf

World Bank. (2018). *Turkey public-private partnership (PPP) healthcare projects: Case study.* https://documents.worldbank.org

World Bank. (2019). Reference Guide: Islamic Finance for Infrastructure PPP Projects. International Bank for Reconstruction and Development / The World Bank. https://ppp.worldbank.org/public-private-partnership/sites/ppp.worldbank.org/files/2022-02/REFERENCE_GUIDE_ISLAMIC_FINANCE_FOR_INFRASTRUCTURE_PPP_PROJECTS.pdf

World Bank. (2022). *Case study: Malaysia—Green sukuk market development.* The World Bank. https://thedocs.worldbank.org/en/doc/21c2fb7dfb-189f10a0503004757b03f4-0340012022/original/Case-Study-Malaysia-Green-Sukuk-Market-Development.pdf

Zaher, T. S., & Hassan, M. K. (2002). A comparative literature survey of Islamic finance and banking. *Financial Markets, Institutions and Instruments, 10*(4), 155–199. DOI: 10.1111/1468-0416.00044

Zain, S., & Muhamad Sobri, Z. (2017). Musharakah SRI Sukuk & Development of Waqf Properties/Assets in Malaysia. *ResearchGate.* https://www.researchgate.net/publication/320540872_MUSHARAKAH_SRI_SUKUK_DEVELOPMENT_OF_WAQF_PROPERTIESASSETS_IN_MALAYSIA

Zanev, V., & Barchman, A. (2014). Luxembourg: all sukuk welcome. IFLR. https://www.iflr.com/article/2a63733ixysbvckz8y4s0/luxembourg-all-sukuk-welcome?utm_source=chatgpt.com

ZAWYA. (2024). Islamic finance. https://www.zawya.com/en/economy/islamic-economy/saudi-arabia-leads-gcc-in-sustainable-sukuk-issuances-smnx5ezs?utm_source=chatgpt.com

Zhang, S. (2024, January 15). World's richest men have added $14M to their wealth every hour since 2020. *Truthout.* https://truthout.org/articles/in-past-3-years-worlds-5-richest-men-have-doubled-their-wealth-to-870-billion/

Zolotova, E. A., Aphudova, A. T., Klochkova, E. V., & Sidakova, D. I. (2024). *Fundamentals of Islamic Finance and Banking: Principles and Practice. EKONOMIKA I UPRAVLENIE: PROBLEMY.* RESHENIYA., DOI: 10.36871/ek.up.p.r.2024.04.05.015

Zulkhibri, M. (2015). A synthesis of theoretical and empirical research on sukuk. *Borsa Istanbul Review*, *15*(4), 237–248. DOI: 10.1016/j.bir.2015.10.001

About the Contributors

Camille Silla Paldi has a BA in East Asian Studies (Honors) from Colgate University, Graduate Diploma in World Politics from the London School of Economics, Juris Doctor in Law from the University of Melbourne, Master of International Law from the University of Sydney, LL.M from the University of Hawaii William S. Richardson School of Law School, MA in Islamic Finance from Durham University, and a Certificate in Inter-Religious Studies from the Graduate Theological Union. Paldi has previously qualified as a lawyer in Australia and New Zealand and successfully completed the UK Qualified Lawyers Transfer Test in June 2013 in London, United Kingdom. Paldi has widely published on Islamic Finance, Holy Book Finance, and Abrahamic Finance in books, journals, and magazines across the world. Paldi is currently a student of Medicinal Plants and Nutrition at Cornell University. She is also an avid learner of foreign languages.

Phil Lieberman is Professor of Jewish Studies, Professor and Chair of Classical and Mediterranean Studies, and Professor of Law, at Vanderbilt University. He is currently on military leave serving the Department of History at the United States Naval Academy. Phil is an economic, social, and legal historian of the Jews of the medieval Islamic world. His *Business of Identity: Jews, Muslims and Economic Life in Medieval Egypt* (Stanford University Press, 2014) was a finalist for the National Jewish Book Award. His most recent monograph is *The Fate of the Jews in the Early Islamic Near East: Tracing the Demographic Shift from East to West* (Cambridge University Press, 2022). He served as a section editor for the award-winning *Encyclopedia of Jews in the Islamic World* (Brill, 2010) and *The Cambridge History of Judaism, Volume 5: Jews in the Medieval Islamic World* (Cambridge University Press, 2021). His translation with Lenn Goodman of Vanderbilt University's Philosophy Department of Moses Maimonides' philosophical classic *The Guide to the Perplexed* was published by Stanford University Press in 2024. He is currently working on a monograph about commercial manuals. Phil holds a PhD from Princeton University, a LLM in US Law from George Mason University, a MSc in Economics from the London School of Economics, a MA in Talmud and Rabbinics from the Jewish Theological Seminary, and a BA with distinction in Economics from the University of Washington.

Mohammad Kabir Hassan is Professor of Finance in the Department of Economics and Finance in the University of New Orleans. He currently holds three endowed Chairs-Hibernia Professor of Economics and Finance, Hancock Whitney Chair Professor in Business, and Bank One Professor in Business- in the University of New Orleans. Professor Hassan is the winner of the 2016 Islamic Development Bank (IDB) Prize in Islamic Banking and Finance. Professor Hassan received his BA in Economics and Mathematics from Gustavus Adolphus College, Minnesota, USA, and M.A. in Economics and Ph.D. in Finance from the University of Nebraska-Lincoln, USA respectively. Professor Hassan is a financial economist with consulting, research and teaching experiences in development finance, money and capital markets, Islamic finance, corporate finance, investments, monetary economics, macroeconomics, Islamic banking and finance, and international trade and finance. Professor Hassan has done consulting work for the World Bank, International Monetary Fund, African Development Bank, Transparency International-Bangladesh (TIB), Islamic Development Bank, United Nations Development Program (UNDP), Government of Turkey and many private organizations. Professor Hassan has been elected a Board Member of Ethics and Governance Committee and Education Board of the Accounting and Auditing Organization for the Islamic Financial Institutions (AAOIFI).

Isaac Lifshitz is an expert on Jewish philosophy and history, with an emphasis on the philosophy of Ashkenaz in the high Middle Ages. He received his rabbinical ordination from Rabbis Yitzhak Kulitz and David Nesher. He earned his Ph.D. in Jewish Thought from Tel Aviv University, and holds an M.A. in Jewish history from Touro College. Author of numerous books, most recently Judaism, Law & The Free Market (Acton, 2012), Dr. Lifshitz has written both scholarly and popular articles on subjects related to Judaism and economics.

***

Abdul-Hamid Abdul-Wahab is an academic and researcher specializing in finance, Islamic banking and finance, and sustainable development goals (SDGs). He earned his bachelor's, master's, and PhD degrees from the International Islamic University Malaysia (IIUM). His industry experience includes roles at the Islamic Financial Services Board (IFSB) and SWIFT Support Services Malaysia. Currently a lecturer and Head of the Business Analytics Department at the University for Development Studies (UDS), Ghana, he teaches business finance, corporate finance, investment and portfolio management, among others. His research interests include Islamic finance, banking efficiency, sustainability, and financial inclusion. He has a number of publications in reputable academic journals.

Md. Kashif Ansari is an assistant professor of finance at O P Jindal Global University. He has been imparting knowledge to undergraduate and graduate on personal finance for the last 8 years with special focus on credit cards and taxation. His research focuses on optimization of banking products, business models of fintech and taxation policies. He has published several articles in leading business newspapers and portals. He has shared his views on personal finance in many podcasts and interviews by reputed media houses including Mint, Moneycontrol, Kotak Bank and The Ken.

Sanaullah Ansari has 32 years of experience in academics, training, consultancy and research. Currently, he is working as Assistant Professor with SZABIST University, Islamabad, Pakistan. With an extensive academic background, including PhD in Islamic Finance from University Sains Malaysia (USM), and over three decades of experience in both the financial and academic sectors, Dr. Ansari is a recognized authority in his area of specialization. His deep understanding of Islamic financial principles, combined with his expertise in international finance, has enabled him providing innovative, Sharia'h-compliant solutions that meet the evolving needs of the global market. Dr. Ansari is an active contributor to the advancement of Islamic Finance education, having authored several research papers, articles, book chapters, and thought leadership pieces. His passion for nurturing the next generation of finance professionals and his commitment to the development of the Islamic financial sector continues to influence and inspire. Till today, he has provided his exceptional services in world renowned universities and financial institutions in USA, Malaysia, Turkey, Jordan, UAE, Qatar, Poland, Algeria, Saudi Arabia, Germany, Thailand, China, France, Azerbaijan, Bosnia, Austria and Greek Cyprus.

Muhammad Ayub is Professor of Islamic Economics and Finance and the founding Editor of the *Journal of Islamic Business and Management (JIBM)* at Riphah International University, Islamabad. He also serves as the non-resident Editor of the *Journal of Islamic Finance Accountancy (JOIFA)* published by AAOIFI, Bahrain, and was a Juris-consult for the rehearing of the Ribā Case at the Federal Shariat Court of Pakistan. Over a career spanning 28 years at the State Bank of Pakistan, he contributed significantly through the Research Department, the Islamic Banking Department, and the National Institute of Banking and Finance (NIBAF), the Bank's training arm. Recognized as a master trainer in Islamic finance and a leading educationist, Dr. Ayub is a member of AAOIFI's Education Board in Bahrain and currently chairs its Curriculum Review Committee. He also served on the Shariah Board of the Bank of Khyber from 2010 to 2018. His contributions to the discipline include designing the Islamic Banking Certificate Course offered by SBP/NIBAF since 2005, authoring the widely used textbook *Understanding Islamic Finance* (John Wiley & Sons, London, 2007)—translated into Arabic, Turkish, Malay, Urdu, and other languages—and writing *Economics and Economic Policy: Islamic Perspective* (Riphah International University and IIIT, 2022).

Federico Dal Bo is a senior lecturer in Jewish studies at the University of Modena and Reggio Emilia (Italy). He previously worked at the Universities of Bologna, Berlin, Barcelona, Lucerne, and Heidelberg. Among his publication on the Talmud are *Massekhet Keritot: Text, Translation, and Commentary. A Feminist Commentary on the Babylonian Talmud* (2013); *Deconstructing the Talmud: The Absolute Book* (2019); and *Jesus in the Latin Talmud. Judaism and Christianity during the Disputation of Paris in 1240 and Other Transcultural Issues* (2024).

Giovanni Gregorini is Full Professor of Economic History and Head of the Department of Historical, Philological and Social Sciences at the Università Cattolica del Sacro Cuore (Milan, Italy). His research interests focus on public finance in the 17th-century State of Milan; the history of the Lombard banking and finance sector between the 19th and 20th centuries; and Italian and European economic history in the second half of the 20th century. He has edited the proceedings of several national and international conferences, as well as numerous publications on the development of local economic systems, particularly in the areas of Brescia and Bergamo. In recent years, his work has also explored the economic and financial history of Italian charities and religious congregations.

Pranjal Khare is a distinguished corporate lawyer and is currently working as a law faculty at O.P. Jindal Global University, India. He specializes in Property Law, Corporate laws, Intellectual Property Rights, and International law. Mr. Pranjal is a highly regarded scholar and has published on numerous issues related to international affairs, economy, politics, data & privacy, artificial intelligence and IP disputes. He is also a frequent speaker at legal conferences and has served as a consultant to numerous law firms and corporations.

Aishatu Usman Muhammad holds a PhD in Islamic Finance from Universiti Sains Malaysia, an MSc and BSc in Accounting from the University of Maiduguri. She is a Lecturer in the Department of Accounting at Gombe State University,

Nigeria. Her teaching and research interests include Islamic finance, corporate governance, ethics, and entrepreneurship. Dr. Muhammad has authored and co-authored several academic papers in peer-reviewed journals and has presented at international conferences on Islamic banking and finance. She has also served in professional and community development roles, including as Coordinator of the Halal Business Transformation Program at the Africa Islamic Economic Foundation and Editor of *WiMAG Magazine*. Beyond academia, she is actively involved in cooperative societies, zakah and waqf administration, and professional associations. Her work reflects a strong commitment to advancing Islamic finance and entrepreneurship as tools for ethical financial inclusion and sustainable development in Africa.

Sirajo Murtala is an academic and researcher with expertise in financial reporting, Islamic finance, and taxation. He obtained his National Certificate in Education (NCE) from the Federal College of Education (Technical), Gombe, before pursuing a Bachelor's degree at Abubakar Tafawa Balewa University (ATBU). He later earned a Master's degree from Bayero University, Kano (BUK), and completed his PhD jointly at Universiti Utara Malaysia (UUM) and Modibbo Adama University of Technology (MAUTECH), Yola. Dr. Sirajo has supervised numerous undergraduate and postgraduate students and has published widely in both local and international journals. He has also presented his research at several academic conferences. His scholarly contributions continue to advance the fields of accounting and Islamic finance in Nigeria and beyond.

Riccardo Semeraro holds a Ph.D. in Economics and Management from the University of Verona, Italy, and is currently a Research Fellow in Economic History at the Università Cattolica del Sacro Cuore (Brescia, Italy). In 2015–2016, he was a visiting researcher at the Department of Applied Economic Analysis at the University of Alicante, Spain, and continues to collaborate with its scholars on comparative studies of Italy and Spain in a broader European and global framework. His research spans business, financial, and tourism history, focusing on socioeconomic resilience, the role of the Catholic Church in Italian economic development, and the evolution of mass tourism.

Paridhi Sharma is currently working as a faculty of law at Jindal Global Law School, O.P. Jindal Global University, Sonipat. She completed her bachelor's degree in law from KIIT University, Bhubaneshwar with a specialization in Business Law. Her keen interest in academia made her pursue her master's degree which she obtained from National Law Institute University, Bhopal with a specialization in Constitutional and Administrative Law. She has researched and published earnestly on Delay of Justice and Decoding the flawed justice delivery system in India, Analyzing the barriers preventing the effective protection of refugee women, The challenges of cyber security and impact on latest technologies, etc.

Ibrahim Nandom holds a PhD in Banking and Finance. His research focuses on banking, corporate finance, and energy finance. His research works have appeared in various internationally ranked journals and he has presented his research findings in international and national conferences. Ibrahim also serves as an ad hoc reviewer for a number of journals published by Emerald, Taylor & Francis, SAGE and Springer.

Abubakar Yusuf is a Senior Lecturer in the Department of Accounting at Gombe State University, Nigeria. He obtained his BSc in Accounting from Gombe State University and completed his MSc and PhD in Accounting at Bayero University, Kano. Before joining academia, he worked with Gombe State Transport Service (Gombe Line), rising to the position of Assistant Commercial Manager. In 2011, he began his academic career as a Graduate Assistant at Gombe State University, where he has since advanced through the ranks to become a Senior Lecturer. He teaches Financial Accounting, International Accounting, Intermediate Accounting, and Entrepreneurial Accounting. Dr. Yusuf has held leadership roles within the GSU Alumni Association, ASUU (GSU Branch), and as Staff Adviser of the Faculty of Arts and Social Science Students Association. His teaching, research, and community service reflect a strong commitment to advancing accounting education and scholarship in Nigeria.

Index

A

C

D

E

F

G

I

www.ingramcontent.com/pod-product-compliance
Lightning Source LLC
LaVergne TN
LVHW081341300926
849161LV00008B/2036
* 9 7 9 8 3 3 7 3 1 8 8 7 5 *